MW01618048

DEBUNKED

UNCOVERING HARD TRUTHS ABOUT EDSA, MARTIAL LAW, MARCOS, AQUINO, WITH A SPECIAL SECTION ON THE DUTERTE PRESIDENCY

Selected Essays by

RIGOBERTO D. TIGLAO

Columnist

The Manila Times

DEBUNKED
Uncovering hard truths about EDSA, Martial Law, Marcos, Aquino, with a special section on the Duterte Presidency
Selected Essays by Rigoberto D. Tiglao

Published by Akropolis Publishing
Book Design by TVC
Printed in the Republic of the Philippines

ISBN: 978-621-96047-0-3

Also by Rigoberto D. Tiglao

COLOSSAL DECEPTION:
How Foreigners Control Our Telecom Sector

CONTENTS

THE COMMUNIST INSURGENCY

GLORIA MACAPAGAL ARROYO

THE CORONA IMPEACHMENT

BENIGNO SIMEON COJUANGCO AQUINO

THE MAMASAPANO MASSACRE

TERRITORIAL DISPUTE

NATIONALISM

RODRIGO ROA DUTERTE

STRONG REPUBLIC

MEDIA

HARSH REALITIES

PREFACE

The 92 articles in this book were among 872 columns published in the *Philippine Daily Inquirer* (March 2010 to January 2013) and *The Manila Times* starting January 2013, except for the essay "The Strong Republic" which I wrote in 2002 when I was a research fellow at the Kyoto University's Center for Southeast Asian Studies.

The columns have been edited and revised for this collection, but some were kept in their original form. Most titles were changed for brevity. I have resisted the temptation to update the articles to reflect current events as I believe the analyses and data I have presented have withstood the test of time.

The dates at the end of each article refer to when it was published. I am proud to say that I was during the past regime among the very few columnists who were not bewitched by the Yellow Cult and were critical of Benigno Aquino III's presidency. Subsequent events have proven such views to be correct.

This book would not have been possible without the editorial guidance, editing, and moral support of my dear wife, Getsy, an accomplished journalist herself and currently a Wednesday columnist at the *Manila Bulletin.*

I am deeply grateful to Dr. Dante Ang, owner and publisher emeritus of *The Manila Times* and to the *Inquirer's* late Letty Jimenez-Magsanoc for inviting me to write these columns in their newspapers, which have been reincarnated as essays in this collection.

This book is dedicated to my inspiration, my children Ria, Xandro, and Dart — and my grandson Ocean.

INTRODUCTION

Journalism, it is said, is history in a hurry. Reporters write, as an American editor popularized the phrase in the 1960s, "the first rough drafts" of history, documenting important events in a nation's life, narrating the concerns of its people.

Columnists or opinion writers, however, are a specialized breed of journalists. They also tackle the news but they do one better: they analyze, probe, criticize, berate or praise, harangue when needed, with the intent of helping readers know the meaning and significance of the "straight news."

The best columnists in general are former reporters, because of their profession trained to gather facts and glean their meanings. But columnists are not bound by the same convention as reporters. Almost by definition, opinion columnists expound their analyses, their take, their reasoned but personal view on mostly current news developments. They explain what they think a particular issue means for their readers' lives, or for the future of their nation.

They have, by nature of their job, a bias for their own perspective and judgment of news events and more so, of the people that are in the public eye.

This is not to say however that columnists can just run roughshod over the facts. Columnists still need to stick to standards of factual accuracy, even as they interpret these events through the prism of their minds formed by their varying education, pursuits, passions, and other life experiences.

I have been lucky to have lived, as they say, a life path less-travelled, from which I have drawn many elements and inspiration for my column writing. My opinion pieces published in the *Philippine Daily Inquirer* and *The Manila Times* of which this book contains a sample of, aren't in the mold of traditional columns though.

Many are investigative pieces that unearthed information that were unknown to the public before, such as the Indonesian control of our major public utility firms, a subject most in mainstream media wouldn't touch with a ten-foot pole. These columns were the material for my earlier book **Colossal Deception**.

I have also uncovered through the research for my columns a view of the Marcos era radically different from that I myself had embraced in my younger years and disseminated by the Aquino clan's "Yellow" political cult.

Several of my columns also debunked what have been practically myths of our time, such as the so-called Jabidah Massacre that didn't occur, but served as propaganda weapon for the Liberal Party bent on stopping Marcos from winning a second term in 1969. Another modern-day myth being fostered is that one stormy day, China simply grabbed Panatag Shoal from us, when the fact is that it was Benigno S. Aquino III and his officials who lost it due to their bungling.

I have strived to back up the opinions I have expressed with as much data as I could muster. This empirical bent springs from my early dream to be an astrophysicist: I had entered Ateneo de Manila's honors course as a B.S. Physics major in 1970.

I had thought I could just tinker with the huge telescopes and the devices at the physics laboratory at the Jesuits' renowned Manila Observatory. Instead, I found myself struggling in mind-numbing courses such as Multivariable Calculus and Mathematical Logic, which made me conclude that I'd never be a physicist.

I had my first dip into the waters of journalism when I wrote several articles in the Ateneo's student newspapers. One of my accomplishments when I became a radical (read: communist) activist was getting together with Perfecto Martin Jr. for the literary magazine Heights to be published in Pilipino and renamed *Panday*. To the horror of our Jesuit overseers, one issue had as its cover — in a shade of commie red — Nilo Tayag, the chairman of the *Kabataang Makabayan*, the youth front of the Communist Party, who had just been captured at that time.

I was drawn to the communist movement in 1969, together with my late wife Raquel, a heroine of activists and feminists in that era. After heading its regional Youth and Students Bureau in the early 1970s, I became in 1972 the head of the Communist Party's Manila-Rizal Regional Committee, which post would have made me a member of the Party's purported policy-making body, the Central Committee.

As much as to my background in humanities and science, I owed my initial training and work in journalism to my involvement in the Party, particularly to the ideas of Russian revolutionary Vladimir Ilyich Lenin, founder of the first communist-controlled state on the planet.

Lenin saw newspapers as having a crucial role in the task of fomenting revolution. In a 1901 article, he pointed out: "The role of a newspaper is not limited merely to the spreading of ideas, merely to political education and attracting political allies. A newspaper is not only a collective propagandist and collective agitator, but also a collective organizer." Indeed, much of the Bolsheviks' success in fomenting revolution and capturing power was through its newspaper founded in 1901, *Iskra*.

Little appreciated because of the prevailing Western notion of the Press as a check on government and the powerful, is the expansion of Lenin's idea on a nationwide scale: A national newspaper helps people living in a particular territory to realize they are members of a nation.

Nine decades later, the renowned scholar of nationalism, Benedict Anderson (in his book **Imagined Communities**, a best seller among Philippine academics) argued that "print capitalism" the bigger class of which newspapers are members of, has been essential in the development of nationalism, in making residents of a particular territory imagine themselves as a nation.

In roughly the way Catholics experience their Church as a community almost only on Sunday masses, citizens of a nation experience their membership in the nation when they read a national newspaper over breakfast. An American could never really relate to *The Manila Times*, just as a Filipino (one living here, not the Fil-Americans, who are, let's be frank, just Americans) would never be absorbed in reading *The New York Times*.

As a petty-bourgeoisie who had little experience or skill in organizing the masses, I took to heart Lenin's notion of the role of a newspaper in the revolution, and devoted much of my time and efforts in the Party to publishing newsletters.

When I was the head of the regional Youth and Students Bureau, we published *Ang Aktibista* edited by Ricardo Nolasco, now one of the country's few PhDs in linguistics. After recruiting fellow Atenean and renowned student leader Edgar Jopson into the Party in 1973, and assigning him the task of transforming the Associated Labor Union where he was an organizer and lawyer of, into a Red workers' organization, we published *Anak-Pawis*.

After my two-year incarceration after my arrest in 1973, together with my wife Raquel and my almost 2-year old daughter Andrea, in 1973 for my communist activities (see my column, "Inside the Marcos prisons"), it still hadn't crossed my mind to be a journalist. I thought my contribution to the Revolution would be à la Marx, that is, doing deep research on the actual conditions of class exploitation in the Philippines. With a P5,000 budget given to me by the fledgling Third World Studies Center at the University of the Philippines, I researched on the coconut industry, travelled all over Mindanao to gather facts, and wrote in 1984 a monograph, **The Philippine Coconut Industry: Export-Oriented Agricultural Growth.**

The real intent of the book was to debunk the communist party's view, plagiarized from Mao Zedong's and Indonesian communist chief Dipa Nusantara Aidit's works, that the Philippines was a semi-feudal, semi-capitalist society, which was a raging issue at that time among the communist movement. Despite the mountain of evidence that shows that Maoist analysis is so ridiculous if applied to the Philippines in this era, it remains as the framework of the Communist Party.

But it was my deep involvement in the communist movement that gave me a unique perspective to criticize it, as shown in the essays in this book.

My first newspaper job was as a reporter with the business newspaper *Business Day*. To their credit, the paper's owner-editors Raul Locsin and his wife Leticia had no qualms over recruiting ex-activists, and even appreciated their competence and extraordinary interest in the life of the nation. Thus, other than myself, other ex-detainees at Business Day were Sison's former aide-de-camp of sorts Ramon Isberto, Abrino Aydinan- the pioneer in the Mountain Province insurgency, and two other activists.

I was at *Business Day* from 1981 to 1986 and starting 1983, covered the financial system and the central bank. Normally as bland as bank reports, that area of reportage turned out to be an extraordinarily eventful beat because of the unravelling of the Philippine debt crisis in 1983. For my exclusive and investigative articles on the financial and economic crisis at that period — one was my exposé on the central bank's doctoring of the country's international reserve data — I won the 1983 Catholic Mass Media Best Reporter award. It was an especially distinct honor as one would have expected the awardee for that politically volatile year to be a reporter on politics, rather than an economic journalist.

My years as a business reporter further strengthened my predilection for seeking and establishing facts in my journalism work. Unlike other fields of journalism, business and economic reporting requires more respect for facts and figures.

After EDSA 1, Amando Doronila, an editor of the pre-martial law *Manila Chronicle*, recruited me as the business editor of the resurrected paper, owned again by the Eugenio Lopez clan, where I also had a regular business column.

It's a bit ironic that an ex-communist like me got to spend a year in the bosom of imperialism, the United States, as a Fellow at Harvard's Neiman Foundation for Journalism, which enriched my understanding of mass media. I spent my last months at Harvard researching on American institutes devoted to investigative journalism. My report on this became the concept paper for the establishment in 1989, with several other reporters, of the Philippine Center for Investigative Journalism.

I left the *Manila Chronicle* that year to join the renowned Hong Kong-based *Far Eastern Economic Review (FEER)*, a weekly that covered Asia. That liberated me not just from the usual penury of Philippine journalists, but from most of local media's parochial worldview.

The *FEER* was at that era a must-read for Westerners and the Asian elite to know what's really happening in Asia, since the press in this continent were tightly controlled by their governments (as in China and Singapore) or run by very nationalistic businessmen (as in Japan and Korea) who don't tolerate criticism of their states. Famous spy novelist John le Carré, in one of his books had been profuse in thanking Review correspondents for companionship when he spent time in Hong Kong — which bolstered the rumors that the magazine had been a front for the British intelligence operatives in Asia.

The FEER, at that time run mostly by British editors, enhanced my journalistic skills not just because of the editors' being sticklers for accuracy. They were devotees of the English language, who constantly reminded me that good journalists employ its richness and precision.

Space in the magazine was also very limited, so I had to learn to be concise and to take to heart that dictum of great writers, of which novelist Stephen King's version reads: *"Kill your darlings, even when it breaks your egocentric little scribbler's heart."*

However, even as they prided themselves on being objective, Western media I realized had deep biases, almost impossible to change except through a change of the paper's ownership and editors. A reporter in most Western media will see his career flounder, if he doesn't toe the usual neoliberal ideological line the editors and company owners expect their staff to believe in.

Working for the magazine also helped me realize how parochial and so US-oriented we Filipinos are. Most of our local media know more about what's happening in America than in Asia, where our country is. A valuable lesson from my stint at the Review was an understanding of how the Asian Tiger Economics developed into first-world nations under the rule of strongmen — whom the magazine's Western editors detested. This freed me from the US and Philippine mystification of the value of electoral democracies.

The *Philippine Daily Inquirer's* editor-in-chief, the late Letty Jimenez-Magsanoc, invited me in 2000 to be editor-in-chief and senior vice president of the news website that was at that time a joint venture between the newspaper and GMA Network, which was then called Inq7.net. That job opened to me the new, rapidly expanding world of worldwide-web and social media. Letty also asked me to write once a week for the *Inquirer's* opinion page, a column that I called "Outlook".

After President Joseph Estrada was forced to abandon his post in 2001, I joined the government of his successor Gloria Macapagal-Arroyo as her spokesman and later as her Presidential Chief of Staff, a position I convinced her to create and even drafted the executive order for the post.

Arroyo's administration was besieged by different factions of the elite at various times, by the Left and by radical Muslim extremists. My five years at the center of state power that was the epicenter of political turmoil at that era, was the most exciting yet challenging period of my life, on par with my four years in the core of the communist revolutionary movement. I had insights on Philippine society and its harsh realities I would never have learned from books.

After nearly five years as ambassador to Greece and Cyprus, Letty welcomed me back as a once-a-week columnist at the *Inquirer* in 2010. The political waters had changed drastically in the five years I was away from the country. The election of Benigno Aquino III ushered in a vindictive kind of politics not seen since 1986. With my hard-hitting columns I became a huge headache for Letty (a self-confessed "Coryista") as I had been practically the sole critic — a vociferous one at that — of Aquino III's administration.

An old friend and colleague in the Arroyo administration, Dante

Ang in 2013 invited me as a thrice-weekly columnist in *The Manila Times*. Most of the articles in this book were published in this newspaper. Dante started the trend of featuring on the front pages of the newspaper the top columns of the day, which highlighted the importance of columnists in molding public opinion.

My work and life experiences have informed my writing.

Science and my interest in it gave me the discipline of supporting my opinion pieces ("thesis") with research ("data"). On the other hand, Marxist theory and my involvement in the communist movement in the 1970s are reflected in my many critiques of the elites as well as the big foreign capitalists.

Despite its failure as an ideology, Marxism actually has two powerful insights in understanding society that journalists should embrace. First is its analysis that the ideas of the ruling class prevail in society, and that of a faction of that class when it is in power; thus, it is the journalist's duty to expose these and to critique it. Second is the Marxist insight that the economy is the base of politics and almost everything else in society.

Science and Marxism, as well as modern Philosophy, have a common mental attitude that make up my intellectual framework: That there is a reality beneath what immediately appears before us, what most people believe in, which can be uncovered through reason and empirical investigation.

I am also fortunate to have been in both sides of political fences, which has helped me to be faithful to that journalism dictum — to see both sides of any issue.

I was a "grim and determined" revolutionary communist cadre in my youth, and then years later one who abhors the Communist Party for its killing of thousands of innocent Filipinos in its lust to capture political power, and its stupid insistence that a Mao-style revolution that occurred seven decades ago can be replicated in this day and age.

Later I was an activist-journalist who viewed journalism primarily as a check on government. And then I would become Presidential Spokesman and Presidential Chief of Staff, and in so many instances I would be shocked at how media could be so biased, often abandoning journalism's cardinal rules of fact-checking and fair play in order to protect their newspaper owners' political interests.

My experience in government was crucial in my work as an opinion columnist. My nine years in government, mostly at its very command center, gave me a whole lot of real-world perspective, that made me realize the enormous problems the country faces that can't be solved with simplistic solutions intended for one-day news stories.

In my youth, I viewed journalism primarily as adversarial towards government — the "The Fourth Estate" notion — an American viewpoint handed down to us by our colonizer.

I now believe that as important is newspapers' role in strengthening a people's nationalism — the dominant view actually in Asian countries — or the realization that in this era of humanity's evolution, the nation is the most important organization for a human being to be a member of, which he has a moral imperative to help develop.

— Rigoberto D. Tiglao, August 27, 2018

The EDSA Revolt

Was it Mama Mary or US President Reagan? Statue of the Virgin Mary onstage with Enrile and Ramos during EDSA 1.
(Photo by Sonny Camarillo published in ***People Power, An Eyewitness History: The Philippine Revolution of 1986,*** *From officialgazette.gov.ph)*

HOW THE US MANEUVERED TO PUT CORY IN POWER

WHAT WAS AMAZING in the assassination of Ninoy Aquino on August 21, 1983 was its precision. Just five seconds after he stepped off the plane, the gunman fired a single bullet to his head that killed him even before he touched ground.

Can any Filipino hitman execute such a perfect assassination? I have never heard of any other killing of a public figure done with such precision, one that circumvented what Aquino thought would be his human shields and witnesses.

Aquino's murder in 1983 did fire up outrage against the Marcos dictatorship, with his funeral procession estimated to have been attended by at least a million people. However, it didn't actually trigger the events that led to EDSA 1 in 1986. That it did is a myth.

It was the brilliant maneuverings by the US that toppled Marcos, which the Yellow Narrative, propagated by the two Aquino presidents and President Fidel V. Ramos, had cloaked.

Perhaps, if anything else, President Rodrigo Duterte's anti-US stance would bring to light America's role in bringing the Yellow Cult to power while we remained a nation without control of our destiny.

Marcos weathered the political storm of the Aquino assassination. The findings of the "Agrava Commission," the independent body that was created to investigate it, cleared Armed Forces Chief of Staff General Fabian Ver of complicity in the assassination. With Ver portrayed as the villain, the elite had an excuse to continue its support for Marcos, and "move on."

More importantly, Marcos bought the Philippine elite's support at that time by giving them the means not only to survive the severe 1984-1985 economic crisis, but also to grow richer.

But that economic conflagration was the worst ever in our history, in part due to the global debt crisis triggered by the Mexican default on its foreign loans on March 1982. With the ensuing rise of global interest rates, the Philippines defaulted on its own loans on October 1983. This in effect barred the country from receiving any foreign exchange for its exports of goods and services.

The Philippines was effectively isolated from the world business economy. As a result, the economy shrank by 20 percent from 1983 to 1985 percent, the deepest such contraction in the post-war period.

Elite richer

The Philippine elite though was protected from the economic meltdown, to a great extent through the Marcos' regime's so-called "Jobo bills," named after the banker Jose B. Fernandez, Jr., who replaced Jaime Laya as central bank governor in 1983. "Jobo" broke all monetary policy precedents and had the central bank and the National Treasury issue these bills, which had unheard of interest rates that steadily went up to as high as 60 percent in mid-1985.

The economic crisis from 1983 to 1985 reduced average Filipinos' income (measured as per capita GNP) by a staggering 20 percent — which meant that it was only 21 years later, in 2003, that GDP per capita exceeded that of 1983.

In contrast, the Filipino elite in effect saw their funds grow 40 percent bigger through the Jobo bills they invested in. The central bank economists justified the bills as necessary to contain inflation.

Which in fact it did. Reaching a high of, believe it or not, 80 percent in mid-1984, inflation fast receded, to end up only 10 percent by the end of 1985. The rich were happy as they were much richer, ordinary Filipinos even became relieved that prices of commodities that had rocketed in 1984 returned nearly back to normal.

Marcos seemed to have recovered from his kidney transplant by 1984, and succeeded in stabilizing the economy and the political situation. The International Monetary Fund in 1985 gave the country a financial parachute in the form of a $300 million loan, called an extended fund facility, and got foreign bankers and governments not only to agree to a restructuring of the Philippines' debt to them, but to extend a new $200 million loan so it could service its maturing debts.

Marcos' plan for a transition from a formal dictatorship to a *de facto* one mimicking Lee Kuan Yew's 31-year one-man rule in Singapore was making headway: the Parliament (Batasang Pambansa) which had 180 members, 55 of whom made up the opposition, convened in June 1984 and elected Marcos' chief technocrat Cesar Virata as Prime Minister.

By that move, Marcos sent a message to the world that there was a clear line of succession, Virata — whom the local and foreign business community, and even the IMF and the World Bank had confidence in — and not Imelda — would be his political heir. The anti-Marcos forces were outmaneuvered. At the time of the economic crisis, Virata appeared to be the most capable to lead the country.

US decision

By this time though, the US State and Defense Departments had decided that Marcos had to be toppled, despite President Ronald Reagan's support for him.

Reagan, a fierce anti-communist, was said to have been convinced by mid-1985 to abandon Marcos when told by the CIA that the growth of the communist insurgency (whose propaganda claimed it was fighting for democracy and against the dictatorship) could only be stopped if Marcos was overthrown and "democracy restored".

If the communists with their allies captured power, the CIA had argued, the US military bases in Clark and Subic would be booted out, endangering Reagan's crusade against "The Evil Empire," the USSR. That of course made Reagan, obsessed with destroying the Soviet Union, change his mind instantly.

Marcos survived the 1983 Aquino assassination and the country's worst economic crisis ever. But he would fall only two and a half years later because of events triggered by a clever US move — it forced Marcos to call for a "snap" elections, which the Constitution didn't require, the conduct of which triggered the events that led to his fall.

Here is how the US executed that move, as narrated by Reagan's personal envoy Senator Paul Laxalt, in the Summer 1986 issue of the conservative magazine *Policy Review.* It wasn't Mama Mary that created events that led to the dictator's downfall, but Reagan and the US government.

In his article, Laxalt described in detail how he relayed to Marcos Reagan's wish for Marcos to undertake "credible" elections to prove that he still had Filipinos' support, an idea that was, to quote the senator, "previously broached to him by CIA director William Casey."

Laxalt even told Marcos in mid-1985 that the announcement for such an election could be dramatically made in his scheduled interview in the American TV talk show, 'This Week" with David Brinkley. Marcos did make the announcement, which surprised the country, on November 4, when interviewed by Sam Donaldson and George Will in that show.

US officials surely were aware of the consequences of that snap election. The rest is history, to use that cliché: it was Juan Ponce Enrile and the RAM's failed coup attempt, the huge crowds that formed around the coup plotters' last stand in Camp Crame, and Marcos' hesitation in using force against the protesters that led to the dictator's fall.

Laxalt's account

It is spine-tingling though to read Laxalt's account, how matter-of-factly he narrated how the president of the Philippine Republic was made to step down from power:

"On February 24, President Marcos phoned me at the Capital, where I was being briefed by Secretary of State George Schultz and Philip Habib, the President's special emissary, about the latest events in the Philippines. Marcos asked me whether a message he had received from the White House calling for a "peaceful transition to a new government was genuinely from President Reagan. I told him it was... President Marcos was terrified by reports that the US Marines were on the way to join the rebels...

"After this phone call (from Marcos at 3 a.m. February 25), Secretary Shultz and I were driven to the White House, where we met with the President, Admiral Pointdexter, the national security adviser, and White House Chief of Staff Donald Regan. The President said it would be impractical and undignified for Mr. Marcos to share power with Mrs. Aquino...

"I then called President Marcos from Admiral Pointdexter's office in the White House. It was 5 a.m., Manila time... President Marcos asked me the gut question—what I thought he should do... I concluded that it was in the best interest of all that he leave. If he did not, I feared a civil war with a lot of bloodshed. I said, 'Cut and cut cleanly. The time has come.'

"We have talked a few times since he came to Hawaii... It's important to understand too that (Marcos) didn't believe he was going to have to leave the country when he agreed to leave the presidential palace. He thought he was going home to northern Luzon. Otherwise, he told me, 'I would have never taken all that currency out of there. That was a violation of our law. I thought I was going home.'

"Apparently, negotiations to permit the Marcoses to go home were still under way when their entourage was flown into Clark Air Field from the presidential palace... Mrs. Aquino and more particularly General Ramos feared he would be a very bad force if he stayed in the Philippines, and so the Marcoses were taken to Guam."

The US made the crucial move that would lead to Aquino's capture of power in 1986. EDSA 1 provided the dramatics with RAM, Enrile, Ramos, and Cardinal Sin the supporting characters of the drama. The US even helped Cory's propaganda by deploying several PR firms to help her, especially the Sawyer-Miller Group.

The US also saved Cory from being overthrown by military mutineers in November 1989. I wonder what role the US had in reinstalling another yellow regime in 2010.

(December 19, 2016)

HIDDEN FACTS ABOUT EDSA

PERHAPS IT WAS BECAUSE of something like the so-called fog of war or an instance of the adage that history is written by the victors. But there were facts — now indisputable — that we didn't know, or were hidden from public knowledge, during the February 1986 People Power Revolt and even three decades later.

Perhaps because of the disillusionment with the presidency of the son of the so-called heroine of EDSA 1, the facts have been ferreted out, or have simply become clearer.

Fact 1: Cory Aquino had little to do with EDSA 1.

Ironically, it was Marcos' legal and military pillar, his long-time defense minister Juan Ponce Enrile who — in a last stand to defend himself and his "RAM boys" from certain doom — was mainly responsible for EDSA 1.

The events that led to it were triggered by the botched coup attempt by the Reform the Armed Forces Movement (RAM) cabal of colonels under Enrile's aegis. It was to have been a classic coup by colonels as what happened in many Latin American countries and other Third World nations. The colonels included Gregorio Honasan, Tirso Gador, Rex Robles, Tito Legaspi, Red Kapunan, and Felix Turingan.

As revealed, more recently in Juan Ponce Enrile's biography published last year and articles written by the colonels since 1986, the conspirators after months of planning, decided to attack — boldly or foolishly — Malacañang Palace at 2 a.m. of February 23, 1986, and capture Marcos and his family, for its coup d'etat to take over government.

Talking incessantly to foreign and local media for months about their opposition to Marcos, it is astonishing that the RAM was so confident, or naïve, that its plot wouldn't be uncovered.

Enrile only realized their plot had been uncovered when a hysterical Trade Minister Roberto Ongpin on the morning of February 22 called him to complain that his military security detail had been arrested by the Marines that night. Ongpin wasn't aware that his security detail were RAM members. They were, rather ineptly, reconnoitering the residence of Marine commander General Artemio Tadiar to prepare for their planned attack on him the next day, when they were spotted by Military Police and arrested.

After lunch that day, Enrile, realizing that his and his RAM boys' plot had been uncovered or had been perhaps long known by Marcos, decided that rather than being ignominiously arrested and even probably executed, decided to take a "last stand" at his headquarters in Camp Aguinaldo.

Several of the RAM boys had been in close contact for months with foreign correspondents — a favorite source of assets for the US Central Intelligence Agency. A 2015 newspaper article by three RAM colonels revealed that an emissary from the Pentagon promised the RAM American government protection from arrest if it "refrained from employing violent methods in pursuing its reformist goals."

Did Enrile and his RAM boys simply expect that the Pentagon would keep its word and intervene in some way to save them from Marcos' wrath?

Enrile though was clever enough to immediately call foreign correspondents to Camp Crame to cover what he thought was his last stand, after then Vice Chief of Staff and long-time PC Commander Fidel Ramos agreed to join him in his mutiny.

Another brilliant move of Enrile was to call Cardinal Sin to ask his faithful to surround Camp Crame to form their human shield. People Power, or People Fodder?

Fact 2: Only a small faction of the military supported the mutineers.

Enrile's RAM boys consisted mostly of the colonels he had taken under his wing as defense minister. Air Force Commander Vicente Piccio, Army Commander Josephus Ramas and Marine Commandant Tadiar were all loyal to the chain of command. The Philippine Constabulary surprisingly though, as it was headed for more than a decade by Ramos who was succeeded by his protégé Renato de Villa, was divided in its loyalties.

The Marcos military succumbed to the EDSA forces because they realized that they were helpless facing the huge crowds. Marcos had given them the categorical order which was impossible to implement — "Disperse the crowds but do not shoot them."

Isn't it Marcos therefore that made it possible for EDSA to be a "peaceful revolution"?

Contrast that to the political will and ruthlessness of the Chinese

Communist Party, which ordered the dispersal of thousands of protestors trying to mimic EDSA 1 in 1989 in Tiananmen Square. China's government deployed battalions of soldiers and police and even columns of tanks in order to crush the rebellion.

Fact 3: Marcos had negotiated with the US to evacuate him and his family by helicopter from Malacañang to Laoag City, the capital of his home province of Ilocos Norte.

We'll never know what Marcos — who even his archenemies concede was a brilliant strategist — intended to do in the North: To rally his army to defend him and re-take Malacañang, or to negotiate a peaceful retirement?

The Yellow propaganda, of course, made a joke out of it, that Marcos thought he was going to Paoay, but was instead brought to Hawaii. That joke made most Filipinos conclude that Marcos fled to the US in fear of his and his family's life. Paoay, however, is a fourth-class municipality that didn't have any emotional links to Marcos, who was born in Sarrat.

The truth is that testimonies in hearings in the US Congress (which investigated what funds were used for the Marcos operation) incontrovertibly show that the US military had orders to take Marcos and his party to Laoag.

The helicopters, however, decided to land at Clark Air Base, as it had become dangerous to fly to Laoag City since they had arrived right after dawn, and the airport there didn't have runway lights. However, the US military received a request from Cory Aquino for Marcos to be evacuated to Hawaii, which it immediately did, after clearance from the White House itself.

Fact 4: Under both the 1935 and 1973 Constitution, Corazon Aquino was not qualified to run for president in the 1986 "snap elections".

Both the 1935 and 1973 constitutions specified that a president must be a "resident of the Philippines for at least 10 years immediately preceding the election." Cory had left the Philippines together with her husband — voluntarily — to live in Boston in 1980. I myself learned about this fact only the other week when an old friend Cecilio Arillo gifted me with his latest book, **The Marcos Legacy.**

So why didn't Marcos, a lawyer, and his stable of the country's brightest legal minds raise this objection to Cory's candidacy?

Perhaps he was confident that there was no way for Cory to win the snap elections. Or perhaps the Americans demanded that he prove his legitimacy in an electoral contest with Aquino's widow. The country's fate at that time was in the hands of the US-controlled International Monetary Fund and the World Bank and a group of foreign banks, mostly American, that agreed to the orderly rescheduling of the country's foreign debts. Without US support of the program, the country would have been plunged into an economic meltdown.

The Comelec count had Marcos winning by a margin of 1.5 million votes. The partial unofficial tally of Namfrel — which was then headed by Jose Concepcion who became Aquino's first trade secretary — had Cory winning by half a million votes.

All these data became irrelevant of course when Cory imposed just a month after Marcos fell, on March 25, 1986 a revolutionary government, which made her a dictator monopolizing executive, legislative, and judicial powers until the 1987 Constitution was ratified.

Fact 5: Cory's 1986 electoral campaign was handled by Western PR men.

Sawyer Miller, an American public relations and political strategist firm that would be in the 1980s and 1990s, the most expensive and most sought-after outfit in the world after EDSA 1, handled almost in its entirety Cory Aquino's public performance in the 1986 snap elections. This is confirmed by US documents that Sawyer Miller submitted in compliance with the Foreign Agents Registration Act.

Its operations during the electoral campaign to transform Aquino's bland widow to a fiery candidate has been revealed in detail in the James Harding's book **Alpha Dogs: The Americans Who Turned Political Spin into a Global Business** (2008: Farrar, Straus, and Giroux). The blurb in the book's jacket described the firm: "A political powerhouse, directing democratic revolutions from the Philippines to Chile, steering a dozen presidents and prime ministers into office."

Sawyer Miller's man on the ground who coached Cory and wrote nearly all of her speeches was one British citizen Malloch Brown, disguised as correspondent of the British newsmagazine *The Economist*. Brown, the book reported, even had to sit on the floor of Cory's campaign bus to hide him from public view.

After Sawyer Miller, Brown would two decades later become United Nations Deputy Secretary-General, and then a UK government minister. Brown was knighted in 2007, after which he has been addressed as Lord Malloch Brown.

I suspect Brown tried to intervene again in Philippine history. He became in 2014 chairman of Smartmatic, the Venezuelan company that provided the vote-counting machines for the computerization of the 2016 presidential elections. Brown reportedly was in Manila in 2015 and allegedly persuaded Comelec chairman Andres Bautista to purchase Smartmatic's vote-counting machines for the 2016 elections.

According to the book, it was Brown who got Cory to stick to a single message "with bumper-sticker simplicity: Marcos is corrupt. Marcos is a dictator."

Brown's message has defined the Yellow thinking to this day.

(February 26, 2018)

WHY CELEBRATE A DIVISIVE EVENT?

THERE HAVE BEEN 20 COUNTRIES in the post-war era that had peaceful "revolutions" similar to our EDSA uprising in 1986 — non-violent, extra-constitutional regime changes, especially transitions from dictatorship to democracy. Thirteen of these were the so-called "color revolutions," said to have been inspired in some way by the EDSA "Yellow Revolution."

But it is only the Philippines that celebrates such an event, and as a national holiday, with all the stage spectacles, speeches, and parades.

As examples, in our neighborhood there had been two ruthless dictatorships. First was the 31-year regime of Indonesia's Suharto, who was rated in 2004 as the most corrupt political leader in the 20th century by Transparency International. Respected historians estimated that 500,000 Indonesians, mostly Chinese, were killed by the pogrom he ordered when he wrested power from Sukarno in 1965. About 1,000 Indonesians were killed by the police in people power-like demonstrations that led to Suharto's fall in 1998.

Does Indonesia have a holiday to commemorate this "people power" revolution? Nope.

Sukarno wasn't even arrested or forced into exile to the US. He died in 2008 at 86 years old after a quiet life in a posh neighborhood in Jakarta, of heart and kidney complications. He was buried in a state military funeral with full honors, with the Indonesian commandos as his honor guard.

The second iron-fisted dictator in Asia was Korea's Park Chung Hee, who ruled for 17 years. His Korean Central Intelligence Agency (KCIA) was so bold and ruthless that it was known to have even kidnapped opposition Koreans abroad.

Ironically, Park was shot point-blank and killed in a banquet by the KCIA director in 1979. After a two-year transition in which another military man ruled as an unelected leader, Korea went on to become a fully democratic state. Does Korea celebrate this transition, demonize Park, and consider as hero the KCIA director who killed him?

Nope. Park's daughter, Park Geun-hye, was even elected as South Korea's 11th and first female president in 2012.

Lech Walesa during a visit to the Philippines told Corazon Aquino that the movement that overthrew the communists in Poland in 1989 was "inspired" by the People Power uprising she led in 1986. Does Poland have its version of our People Power celebration? Nope.

Fighting during the 1989 Romanian revolution (Revoluția Română) led to more than 1,000 killed, and after a two-hour kangaroo court, Nicolae Ceaușescu, who ruled the country with an iron fist for 42 years, was executed, together with his wife.

Does Romania commemorate this historical people power event? Nope.

We can go on and on, with data on each of the 20 countries that had people power-like peaceful revolutions. Not one celebrates its extra-constitutional, non-violent regime change. Significantly, what Indonesia, South Korea, Poland, and Romania, as well as most of these 21 countries, celebrate as national holidays is Constitution Day.

In our case, Constitution Day is a "working holiday" and thus passes unnoticed. No wonder then that the Philippine Constitution is routinely flouted and disregarded.

What these countries mostly celebrate (other than religious days) are their independence dates from foreign masters. None of them celebrates the fall of their strongmen or dictators, cognizant that these men, whatever their failings, were one of their own citizens.

US template

There are three major reasons our governments have celebrated the People Power event since 1987.

First is that EDSA 1 was such a good template for Cory Aquino's master, the United States, to disseminate worldwide in order to rouse people under communist dictatorships to stage revolutions.

The EDSA template would have been swiftly forgotten if there were no EDSA 1 commemorations yearly, complete with videos of nuns and priests seemingly stopping tanks.

The United States' first target was China's democracy movement, which however, failed. Where do you think that young Chinese got the idea to stand ramrod in front of a tank in that iconic Tiananmen Square uprising of 1989?

Remember also that the 1980s was the height of Reagan's crusade against the "Evil Empire," the Soviet Union. The US had actually first focused on Poland, and the Central Intelligence Agency funneled, starting in 1980, a total of $1 billion to Lech Walesa's "Solidarity" trade union that was the vanguard of the Polish revolution. Televised scenes and press photos of EDSA 1 proved a much cheaper way to rouse the Poles into action.

Indeed, even the US officials and the Yellow Cult have boasted that EDSA 1, the "Yellow Revolution," had inspired the peaceful revolutions, especially the "color revolutions" (e.g., Czechoslovakia's 1989 Velvet Revolution), which overthrew communist regimes in Eastern Europe and the Balkans.

The inspiration wasn't just on the level of boosting morale. Formulating and executing the political tactics for Cory and the People Power movement was the political consultancy group Sawyer Miller (see James Harding, **Alpha Dogs: The Americans Who Turned Political Spin into a Global Business.**)

After EDSA, the firm's prestige shot up, and their "technology" — even if described as "the art of the political spin" — was studied, their political consultancy business model adopted by a host of new Washington-based lobbying and communications firms.

I suspect that Sawyer Miller was even directly contracted by the CIA, as that Harding book read: "When the firm's principal David Sawyer died in 1999, (US) Sen. Daniel Moynihan stood up on the floor of the US Senate to mourn him, saying, among other things, that Sawyer 'helped to open up the governments of Eastern Europe and Latin America by introducing mass communication into their electoral processes.'"

The US also realized in EDSA 1 how the media could be so powerful in fomenting revolutions, especially with the emergence of the then new media: the 24-hour Cable News Network (CNN).

EDSA would be the first revolution covered live on TV. Exhilarated after helping a revolution in the Philippines, journalists lusting after a Pulitzer Prize, would rush to whatever country seemed on the verge of a revolution.

While the EDSA template failed in China, it was remarkably successful in Eastern Europe and even in the Middle East, starting with Poland and Romania in 1989, up to the "Arab Spring" revolts in the 21st century.

False portrayal

There's a second reason why we have been forced to celebrate the 1986 EDSA 1. Through its constant demonization of Ferdinand Marcos and deification of Cory Aquino, the Yellow Cult created the false scenario of a national consensus to remove the strongman from power.

The US played the most important role in the "revolution". It had fooled Marcos into thinking that he would be flown to his home province of Ilocos Norte. Instead, he was taken by the Americans to Hawaii in a forced exile.

The scenes of former National Defense Secretary Juan Ponce Enrile and then Armed Forces Chief Fidel V. Ramos staking their lives at Camp Crame, preparing for Marcos' attack, of the helicopter squadron defecting just as they were thought to be positioning to attack Camp Crame, the crowds stopping the tanks in the street — all these images of high drama had to be shown on TV again and again to justify the revolution, to create the illusion that this was a national revolution.

But the first presidential election after EDSA 1, in 1992, provided hard proof that in reality the country was so divided over EDSA 1 and Marcos' subsequent downfall.

Ferdinand's widow Imelda Marcos garnered 10 percent of the votes, while his top crony, Eduardo Cojuangco, received 18 percent. If the two had united instead, they would have gathered 28 percent of the votes, bigger than Ramos' winning 24 percent or Miriam Santiago's 20 percent.

Doesn't that point to the fact that a big part of Philippine society didn't support EDSA 1 and wanted the Marcos regime back, even if just through his wife and top crony? Thirty years after, Marcos' "Solid North" and Imelda's Eastern Visayas, and swathes of Mindanao continue to refuse to be part of the "people" of the People Power uprising.

Ferdinand "Bongbong" Marcos Jr.'s strong showing in the 2010 and 2016 elections is another proof that for many Filipinos, Martial Law wasn't the era of the Dark Lord, as the Yellows Cultists have portrayed it.

The third reason for People Power celebrations: It conceals the reality that the ruling Philippine elite continues to screw the masses, regardless of whether the nation is ruled by a democracy or a dictatorship.

It is not coincidental that the EDSA 1 celebrations have religious undertones.

In ancient and medieval times, religion served to conceal the fact that the pharaoh, the king, or the emperor, together with their clans, exploited the broad masses of the working classes through the lie that these rulers were anointed by, or even sons, of their deity.

The EDSA 1 celebrations portray the fiction that we are a nation of equals, and we have become poor ("condemned") only because of Marcos ("the devil'), and were saved by Cory ("the Messiah").

On the other hand, countries that had people-power types of regime changes don't have such annual "celebrations" because they were honest and clever enough to realize that such would only exacerbate the division in their countries. After all, even dictatorships that had lasted long had to be supported by a significant section of their nation, and their fall would, of course, alienate those sections.

The EDSA 1 celebrations have only been divisive for our country. We should stop this inanity if we are to be united as a nation in the years to come.

(February 26, 2016)

CHINA'S FAILED "EDSA 1"

FRONT PAGE NEWS the other day: China has overtaken Japan as the world's second biggest economy. Then, recall what happened in the so-called Tiananmen Square Incident or Tiananmen Square Protests in China in June 1989.

The West at that time had thought that the Tiananmen protests would be the earth-shaking version of the Philippines' People Power Revolution that occurred only three years back. It wasn't and China was better for that.

In the scale of protests and the number of people participating, the Tiananmen protests dwarfed EDSA 1 many times over. Through seven weeks from April to May 1989, an estimated 100,000 students made a "freedom commune" out of Beijing's Tiananmen Square, sacred ground for the Chinese, where Mao Zedong declared the establishment of the People's Republic of China, and where his preserved body lies in a mammoth mausoleum.

A hastily-made, 10-meter high foam and papier-mâché statue of a "Goddess of Democracy" was erected in Tiananmen Square, irreverently facing Mao's huge portrait at the entrance.

The protests peaked to a crowd of over 1 million, which included ordinary people of Beijing. The students declared that their goal was for more democratic rights, such as free media and increased education budget. China's leadership, however, saw it at first as leading to political and social chaos, and then as a clear and imminent danger to Communist Party rule.

Indeed, the Western media were expecting a cataclysmic event that could result in the overthrow of the party, or at least China's move into Western-style representative government, following the pattern of the Soviet Union's implosion.

Events though didn't turn out the way it did at EDSA 1, or in the democracy movements in South Korea, Chile, and Poland in the years after 1986.

In the wee hours of June 4, 1989, crack troops of the People's Liberation Army entered from all corners of Beijing and forcibly cleared Tiananmen Square of protesters. Battle tanks and armored personnel carriers rammed the protesters' obstacles and destroyed the Goddess of Democracy statue.

Remember the iconic photo of the so-called "Tank Man," the strangely equable man holding a plastic shopping bag, blocking, by simply standing there, a column of tanks on the way to the Square? But this wasn't EDSA 1, when flowers and rosaries made tanks turn around. Two bystanders just pulled the Tank Man away into a nearby crowd, never to be heard of again, with no one, even up to the present knowing his name.

The tank column roared on to the square, a key force that dispersed the demonstrators. Hundreds of student leaders were reportedly put on trial and jailed.

It is to "Paramount Leader" Deng Xiaoping's eschewing Marxist dogma that China unarguably owes its dramatic growth to become the world's second biggest economy today. And it was also Deng who ordered the Tiananmen Square crackdown.

Two decades after the 4th June Movement, it is an intriguing question whether China would have continued its growth if the pro-democracy movement had won. The question is not a purely academic exercise.

Yes, the immediate economic costs of the Tiananmen crackdown were enormous, as Western countries retaliated through sanctions and the suspension of multilateral official loans, to protest what they considered the brutal suppression of the student protesters. China's GDP growth slowed down to 3.8 percent in 1990, a fall from the 9.5 percent average the previous nine years. But then it very soon rebounded, and grew by an unprecedented 10 percent annually from 1990 to 2008.

Was it the decisive military action against the "democracy movement" that, by settling once and for all the issue of stability in China, finally put that country on the expressway towards becoming the world's second biggest economy?

Compare China's growth to the annual 6 percent GDP decline of the Russian Federation in the 1990s when its Communist Party yielded to a chaotic multi-party political set-up. It was only from 2000, when former KGB officer Vladimir Putin ruled with an iron fist, that Russia posted a very respectable 7 percent annual growth.

Maybe better, compare China's record to ours. The turbulence that led to EDSA 1 and the coup attempts after that resulted in a very weak 2 percent annual growth. In an article in this newspaper in August last year, "Why we are where we are," I presented data to argue that our country remains poor to a great extent due to the political instability we went through in the years immediately before and after EDSA 1.

Welcome to the real world where blind economic forces always triumph. It isn't rocket science to know why this is so: Only when things are stable and predictable would businessmen take risks and invest. And it is not selfish ideas I am presenting: in this day and age, the people's well-being is bound to that of the nation-state they belong to. The costs of poverty in terms of lost and wasted human lives are certainly not an abstraction.

We certainly cannot change the past. But maybe, with the rut we have been in for so long, we should start reconstituting our priorities: Political stability or a wild free-wheeling kind of democracy?

(August 18, 2010)

DID PEOPLE POWER MATTER?

EVERY YEAR IN FEBRUARY, the Philippines commemorates the 1986 People Power revolution, which had become a morality play of a Martyr's Widow leading the people to overthrow the Dark Lord.

Indeed, the Philippine morality tale was so powerful that it inspired people in other countries to stage peaceful protests against their own authoritarian regimes.

Huge people's rallies challenged South Korea's strongman, Chun Doo-hwa, just a year after EDSA and eventually led to democratic reforms including the direct election of the president. Chile's strongman Augusto Pinochet called for a referendum in 1988, triggering events that eventually led to his downfall in 1989.

Poland's "Solidarity" movement gained momentum after 1986, with Lech Walesa assuming power in 1989. In his visit to Manila in 1995, Walesa said: "Your peaceful People Power Revolution was an inspiration to us for our own revolution."

From then on, it was a democratic domino effect: Poland's people power revolution; the Singing Revolutions in Estonia, Latvia, and Lithuania in the Baltic states in 1989; the East German democracy movement that eventually tore the Berlin wall down; and, Czechoslovakia's "Velvet Revolution," which all contributed to the demise of a powerful totalitarian state. Even South Africa's Nelson Mandela was inspired by our "people-power" revolution.

Did the events in EDSA in 1986 actually change the lives of tens of millions of Filipinos trapped in poverty? Sadly, no, at least in terms of the nation's and their economic levels.

The chart (left page) confirms the fact that EDSA hardly made the Philippines better off, for so many reasons.

The chart tracks the Gross Domestic Product per capita — a rough measure of the average income of the people in particular country — at constant 2005 US dollars, in order to account for inflation in each country.

The Philippines has the lowest GDP per capita now, at $1,501.

Twenty-eight years after EDSA, Malaysia, Thailand, and Indonesia and other members of the Association of Southeast Asian Nations (ASEAN) have overtaken the Philippines. Malaysia's GDP per capita of $6,786 is a 4.5 times the Philippines' $1,501 while Thailand is more than double at $3,353.

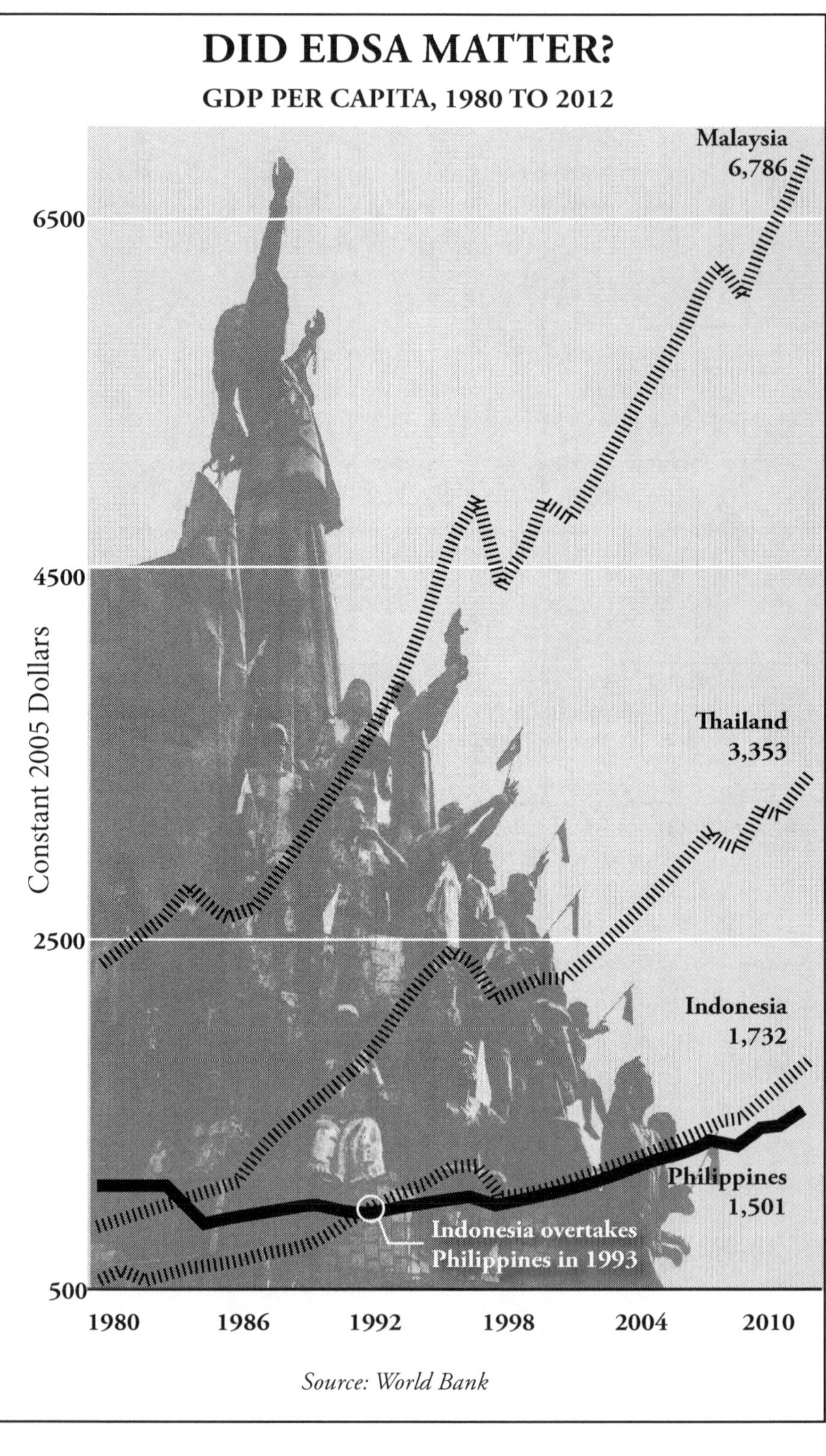
DID EDSA MATTER?
GDP PER CAPITA, 1980 TO 2012
Malaysia
6,786
Thailand
3,353
Indonesia
1,732
Philippines
1,501
Indonesia overtakes
Philippines in 1993
6500
4500
2500
500
Constant 2005 Dollars
1980
1986
1992
1998
2004
2010
Source: World Bank

To put it in another, albeit no less dispiriting way: Philippine GDP per capita of $1,501 in 2012 was roughly that of South Korea in 1961, Malaysia in 1972, and Thailand in 1990. In effect, the country is behind South Korea by half a century, Malaysia by four decades, and Thailand by two decades.

The poverty data for four ASEAN countries also show the Philippines lagging far behind its neighbors.

Malaysia and Thailand have nearly miraculously reduced their poverty incidences (measured as the percentage of population living below $2 per day) to single rates since the 1980s: 2 percent for the former and 4 percent for the latter. No wonder that in the past several years Filipino domestic workers have been leaving the country to serve the Malaysian rich.

POVERTY INCIDENCE:
(PERCENT OF POPULATION LIVING BELOW $2 A DAY)

	1980s	1990s	2000s
Malaysia	11	7	2
Thailand	41	18	4
Indonesia	91	82	43
Philippines	57	44	42

Source: World Bank; for each decade, the latest year data is available.

After nearly three decades, the Philippines reduced its poverty incidence only by 15 percentage points and appears to be stuck in the 40 percent levels.

These statistics, however, could never capture the tragedy and horror of poverty, of children living miserable lives and dying of diseases that have been wiped out in developed countries, of men and women wasting away in slum areas, just waiting for death.

What happened? Why was the Philippines left behind when other nations in Asia showed tremendous growth? Some analysts even think that Vietnam, nearly destroyed by the United States in the 1960s and early 1970s, could soon overtake the Philippines.

The short explanation is that the EDSA Revolution restored the power of Filipino oligarchs, and the oligarchic structure created by colonial powers, and of course, its ideological superstructure, Spanish

Catholicism.

The religious spin given to the Revolution — the Virgin Mary was claimed to have willed it — even strengthened the backward, medieval version of Hispanic Catholicism that partly explains the backwardness of nearly all nations that had been colonized by the Iberian colonialists.

No wonder the Philippines has been unable to undertake even the weakest program for population control, burdening the country with the fastest-growing population of mostly young yet poor people.

Years after EDSA, many of the Marcos cronies have regained their places among the country's cultural-political elites. Even such a prime architect of martial law's economic structure such as Marcos' Finance Secretary Cesar Virata was given by the government-financed University of the Philippines the honor of having its business school named after him.

UP, which has prided itself on being anti-Marcos, appears oblivious to the fact that Philippine business collapsed from 1983-1985 when Virata was Marcos' Prime Minister.

What the heroine of EDSA did was basically to restore the country's political and economic structure, except for its provisions making one-man rule very difficult. It also turned over the control of mass media to its allies, the firm believers in the Yellow Cause, such that today's media has been antagonistic to any administration not allied with the Aquino-Cojuangco family.

Weak state, strong elite

The Philippine state since 1986 has been a weak one, standing not for the nation as a whole but for the strong elites that control it.

In crucial junctures — for instance, the recapture of the Meralco monopoly by the oligarchic Lopez clan right after EDSA or the skirting of land reform through "corporatization" of the Aquino clan's Hacienda Luisita until the Supreme Court stopped it — the elites get what they want, at the expense of reforming the social structures that would have made the country more productive.

The Philippine state has become so weak, its elite so lacking in patriotism, that a foreigner, an Indonesian magnate has been able to capture Meralco and other strategic industries.

Some even say that it would have been probably better if EDSA were a violent bloody revolution.

In such a scenario, the oligarchs would have been wiped out, or the horror of a bloody revolution would have been such a catharsis that it would have forced Filipinos to embark on serious nation-building.

This after all was the case in the French Revolution, America's Civil War, the Korean War, the Malayan Emergency and its ethnic strife that led to the rise of Singapore and Malaysia, and Thailand's bloody extermination of its communists.

Is that such a cruel thought? Maybe, but then how many millions of Filipinos have died or will die of hunger and diseases or would live miserable lives because the Philippines failed to forge a strong nation?

That idea, that strong states emerge from the blood of its people, is worrisome because if that were the case, Vietnam, with three million of its people killed in the war, would soon overtake the Philippines.

The economic chart above is a stark reminder that something is so deeply wrong with the Philippine state. Also: Indonesia's rate of growth suggests that it will become a major economy in the ASEAN, especially since it is a major oil producer.

The sad reality is that despite this seemingly glorious moment in history, EDSA didn't improve much the lives of most Filipinos. Change is needed fast and EDSA was not the answer.

(February 21, 2014)

Benigno Simeon Aquino Aquino

BENIGNO SIMEON AQUINO AQUINO

I'M SURE MOST of my readers will wonder at the title of this column, and see it as familiar and strange at the same time.

While he has been widely known as "Benigno S. Aquino, Jr.", "Ninoy's" official name, going by the Filipino convention, was Benigno Simeon Aquino Aquino. His middle name, or mother's name, was also "Aquino" as his mother was Aurora L. Aquino, a third cousin of his father Benigno Simeon ("Igno") Quiambao Aquino. The "S" was Ninoy's second given name, Simeon.

Ninoy's father had married into two rich clans. In 1916, he had married Maria Urquico, the youngest daughter of a prosperous rice merchant in Tarlac. Two years after Maria died in 1928, he married Ninoy's mother Aurora, 16 years younger, and the youngest daughter of the related hacendero clan, the Aquinos of Concepcion, Tarlac.

"Igno" was a professional politician who rose to become a senator during the pre-war Commonwealth, and then especially since he was a high official of the pro-Japanese Kalibapi, Speaker of the Japan's puppet government's National Assembly during World War 2.

Ninoy in a way followed in his father's footsteps, when as a politician, he would marry Corazon, a scion of another landlord class ascendant at the time, the Cojuangcos. Both would be classic cases, as political scientists would put it, of a country's political class—the unique creation of an electoral democracy—linking up with the economic elite to create an oligarchic clan.

Ninoy's son "Noynoy," the inept President, followed his father's practice and officially used Benigno S. Aquino 3rd. Although Philippine convention would have him named Benigno Simeon Cojuangco Aquino, since his mother was Corazon Sumulong Cojuangco, scion of two powerful politico-economic clans. Noynoy technically cannot be the "3rd", as his father's name was different, Benigno Simeon Aquino Aquino, while his grandfather's was Benigno Simeon Quiambao Aquino.

I haven't found any explanation from Ninoy's family why he chose as his public name Benigno S. Aquino, Jr., which is even engraved on his tombstone. His brothers Agapito and Paul have all followed the Filipino convention of using as their middle name, their mother's maiden name.

Since his given name was Benigno, did he simply choose to emulate his father's name, and be the "junior'?

Having done a stint as a newspaperman, did he think that someday, a headline with "BAA" to refer to him could be made fun of? Was it his way of burying the widespread belief at the time that marriage among cousins, even distant ones, could result in progeny with mental disabilities?

One explanation is that Ninoy followed what President Manuel L. Quezon, one of the most popular leaders of that era, did, which was not to use his mother's name, Molina, as his middle name but his second given name, Luis.

As senator, did Ninoy already believe he would be the country's president someday, and that it would be fitting for him to follow the convention of a popular president?

I would think so. In the late 1960s he was a political superstar, and that hands down, with even a student uprising against Marcos and an economic crisis that started in 1970, he would win as president in the 1973 elections. Instead, strongman rule turned his dreams into a nightmare. He was arrested and jailed in 1972, and sentenced to death by musketry in 1980. After Marcos allowed him to go to the US for a life-threatening heart surgery, Aquino had seemed to have decided to settle into a quiet life in Boston.

Until the news of Marcos' kidney disease in 1982 and indications of an impending economic crisis for debt-ridden countries, that is. All of a sudden, his old dream of being president seemed to be within his grasp , as he had what he had described as his "trump card"* so much so that he was to risk his very life.

(August 20, 2018)

---

*See column "Ninoy's Fatal Miscalculation" in this chapter.

HERO OR POLITICAL OPPORTUNIST AND US PAWN?

AFTER THREE DECADES, we can look at Benigno Simeon Aquino Aquino, Jr., the Yellow Cult's central figure it reveres as Philippine hero and martyr, with unjaundiced eyes.

Peruse the following facts and decide for yourself if he indeed is a hero for whom we devote a holiday, as we do for only two other historical figures, Jose Rizal and Andres Bonifacio.

Or you may be shocked to realize that he was the quintessence of a wily and extremely bold Filipino politician who was used as a pawn by the US. Aquino rocketed to the heights of the political firmament — the youngest senator ever at 34 — because of his bold moves. He again made a colossal bet in 1983, and if he had won he would likely have been the strongman replacing Marcos.

In May 1980, Aquino had a life-threatening heart attack. He refused to be put under the knife at the Philippine Heart Center, built by the Marcos regime in 1975.

The hospital was Asia's first specialized center for cardiac surgery, endorsed by the best surgeons in the world such as heart-transplant pioneer Christiaan Barnard. Yet Aquino claimed that since it was a government hospital, Marcos would easily be able to kill him, under the guise of a botched operation.

While that was a slap not really on Marcos but on the Filipino surgeons at the Center, it was a clever move on the part of Aquino for him to escape the country. You couldn't blame him really: he had spent seven years in prison, convicted by a military tribunal of several crimes, including subversion, and sentenced to be executed by musketry.

Marcos, of course, feared that if Aquino died of a heart attack in prison, it would be blamed on him. Dented would be the semblance of stability he had built after the 1978 interim Batasan Pambansa elections, in which the opposition leader ran and lost.

Marcos though extracted from Aquino, in a message relayed personally by his wife, Imelda, two conditions: 1) that he return to the country when he was fully recovered; and 2) that he refrain from speaking against Marcos during his stay in the US. Aquino himself said he told Imelda he accepted these terms.

Pact with the devil

I can just imagine Aquino in his government hospital bed smiling wryly after Imelda left. A month after his operation in the US, Aquino told an American reporter in Dallas: "A pact with the devil is no pact at all."

Aquino managed to stay in the US after being given the status of "Visiting Fellow" at the Center for International Affairs at Harvard University in Cambridge, and then in the nearby Massachusetts Institute of Technology (MIT). A Harvard official explained that such Fellows "pursued their own research and are expected to present their research findings to the other fellows and interested faculty".

But Aquino never did these things during his stay at Harvard and MIT.

Aquino was certainly not an academic and in those times hardly had the kind of stature for Harvard to bend its strict academic rules just to be a refuge for an opposition figure from some Third World country.

I learned though that it was US President Jimmy Carter himself who asked then Harvard President Derek Bok to get some excuse for Aquino to stay in the US as a fellow of the university.

Carter actually had been trying to get Aquino to be exiled to the US much earlier, in 1978, so that the Harvard Law School invited him as a visiting scholar.

The US eagerness to get Aquino exiled to the US could be partly explained by Carter's very well-known human rights advocacy. But the more likely reason is that as has been its practice, the US routinely befriends opposition figures that have the potential of succeeding an incumbent one.

In the Philippine case at that period, there was another more compelling reason: the US military bases in Clark and Subic, the terms for which were scheduled for review in 1983. Marcos had been demanding more concessions from the US for the use of the bases, asking for higher payments that he wanted to call "rent."

CIA knew Aquino was going home

Having Aquino in the US sent the message to Marcos that if he insisted on such high demands, it might just as well help overthrow his regime, in the guise of championing democratic rule, and install the opposition leader whom they were indoctrinating at Harvard.

Harvard had been known at the time to be a locus of the Central Intelligence Agency's activities, with several of its professors fired in the 1980s after being exposed to have accepted CIA money for their projects.

Aquino, in short, became a US pawn in its geopolitical strategies and, smart as he was, he knew this and played his cards.

Aquino was in continuous contact with US officials, most probably even intelligence officials while he was at Cambridge. Proof of this is a "Top Secret" National Intelligence Daily dated June 27, 1983 issued by the CIA head, which reported: "Moderate opposition leader Benigno Aquino told senior US officials on Thursday he plans to leave the US and return to Manila in August." At the time, nobody else knew of Aquino's plans to return home.

Rather than becoming a scholar, Aquino used his fellowship at Harvard and then at the MIT as a cozy refuge, and to build up his network among anti-Marcos opposition groups and more crucially with the US officialdom. While his supporters claimed that he was writing two books at Harvard, no drafts for these were ever found, not even the roughest outline nor an abstract of his possible topic.

Reflecting his non-academic vein, Aquino left no written work at all, except a purported speech he was to deliver on his return to Manila. (I doubt if it is genuine: It surfaced only in 2014 on Ninoy Aquino day, released by Malacañang under his son Noynoy, without any explanation how it was discovered. Why was it publicly released only after three decades?)

A renowned political scientist, the late Howard Wiarda, who shared an office with Aquino at Harvard, wrote in his book **Adventures in Research** (Volume III: Global Traveler): "(Aquino) wanted to talk constantly, while I was at Harvard to write a book, and in our year together I never saw him read or write anything."

It is astonishing that Aquino, who was supposedly a scholar at Harvard and MIT for three years didn't write anything, not even a journal, an essay, or any article for any US publication denouncing Marcos.

No matter, Aquino galvanized the opposition against Marcos there, the Yellow Cult has been claiming.

I haven't seen any evidence or any testimony to support this claim. It was the Movement for a Free Philippines headed by another former senator in exile, Raul Manglapus, that was more active and went around the US rousing the Filipino community there, to denounce the dictatorship. Aquino rarely left Cambridge.

A fawning article on him a month after his assassination, published in the newsletter *The Harvard Crimson* quoted well-known academic Lucian Pye: "He understood the meaning of a university. He did not use [his academic position] to denounce the [Marcos] government."

Another famous academic at Harvard said, "He was not one to offer a sharp, anti-Marcos diatribe."

Aquino appears to have been militant only a year after his heart surgery. The video of Aquino's philippic against Marcos — which was widely distributed after his killing as proof that it was the dictator who wanted him silenced — was recorded February 15, 1981 before a Filipino community. However, in his June 1981 interview with evangelist Pat Roberson, Aquino talked more about his getting closer to God as a result of his incarceration, and said practically no bad word about Marcos.

Another video was sometime in 1981 in Dallas, where rather than ranting against Marcos, he explained his ideas for getting Saudi Arabia to build a gas pipeline in Mindanao. "If I will be able to sell this (idea) to Mr. Marcos, the Philippines will be able to find an end to our insurgency in the South."

I haven't found any video or report of Aquino making fiery speeches against Marcos after 1981. Had the anti-Marcos fire in his belly gone cold as he and his family enjoyed their stay that lasted three years in a fine house in Newton, Massachusetts, an upper-class district near Boston?

In fact, the report by the CIA mentioned above implied Aquino's slide to irrelevancy: "Aquino's political position has been hurt by his long exile. He probably believes (now) he has to return home if he is to play a role in the post-Marcos era."

Other than that reason, there were two major factors that prodded Aquino to leave his tranquil life in Newton, Massachusetts in 1983.

First, the Philippines' economic crisis unfolded that any observer could see was a very serious threat to Marcos' survival, and Aquino knew this. The Latin American debt crisis broke when Mexico

Director of Central Intelligence

Top Secret

OCPAS/CIG

CY# 285

25X1

National Intelligence Daily

Friday
26 August 1983

PHILIPPINES: Speculation About the Assassination

Several theories about Benigno Aquino's assassination have emerged in Manila.

A source of the US Embassy reports that Aquino may have been murdered by one of his numerous enemies from Tarlac Province. In his early political career, Aquino used violence when dealing with political opponents and economic rivals. According to the source, such individuals had the strongest reasons to kill Aquino.

Another Embassy source says most university students and members of the opposition continue to believe that the first family ordered Aquino killed. Several prominent members of the ruling party speculate that low-level government officials had Aquino killed, without the knowledge of President Marcos, because they thought it would serve his interests.

CIA's first report on the Aquino assassination, contained in the Director's Top Secret National Intelligence Daily issued August 26, 1983.

defaulted on its foreign loans in August 1982, and would soon hit the Philippines as well, triggering its worst economic crisis ever. It would have been impossible for Aquino, with his wide network, not have been informed about this.

Second, Aquino thought, and was convinced of the certainty that Marcos was dying. He had to rush home to wrench the leadership from others who were active in trying to topple Marcos, especially Salvador Laurel.

This is disclosed in an audio tape of his conversation with Steve Psinakis a few days before his return to the country.

In that conversation, Aquino said: "Marcos is a man now: Terminal… now that he (Marcos) is about to meet his Maker, I am almost confident that I can talk to him and sell him something."

Aquino told Psinakis his information came from Cardinal Jaime Sin. I suspect it came from his American intelligence friends, which is why he was so confident of his information.

Bullet-proof vest

But still he risked his life, as he was told by Imelda herself that there were serious threats to his life. Indeed, that's been Aquino's well-known trait: He takes huge risks.

Aquino was smart though. He filled his China Airline flight with media men, practically from every continent, with not a single Filipino, though. He calculated that they could be his human shields, and that Marcos wouldn't risk his foremost critic to be killed in front of the world.

In a TV interview in his hotel before the flight, he showed his bullet-proof vest he said he'd be wearing for protection. I cannot fathom why he disclosed that crucial information, which his killers obviously learned about, so that he was shot instead at the head, with a .357 Magnum, one of the most powerful handguns in the world.

Except for his brother-in-law, ABC newsman Ken Kashiwahara, the foreign media men turned out to be as meek as sheep, and didn't question, much less block, the unarmed military men who fetched Aquino to escort him to the tarmac. Nobody tried to be with him as he was brought down. Aquino terribly miscalculated.

Did his death trigger Marcos' fall? It helped, no doubt. It was the last straw that broke the camel's back of our foreign debt, leading to our

October debt default. But after his funeral parade in August 1983 that was attended by a million people, the protest crowds dwindled.

By late 1985, the hyperinflation that started in 1985 was on its way to being tamed, after the central bank gave wealthy Filipinos an irresistible haven for their funds (the Jobo bills, with their astronomical interest rates). A rescheduling plan for foreign debt was also in place.

Marcos became so confident that he was on his way to restoring political and economic stability. He fell for the US ruse to call for "snap" presidential elections, which really had no constitutional basis.

That Ninoy's assassination triggered the People Power revolt that overthrew Marcos is merely a romantic tale, exploiting our superstition for messiahs and fondness for heroes who give up their lives for a nation.

Marcos gave in to the US demand for him to call snap elections to prove his legitimacy. The cabal that planned his overthrow very expertly created the perception that Cory won the elections — by declaring her victory ahead of the official returns, outsmarting Marcos. The strongman's refusal to recognize Aquino as the winner, and the propaganda that she won despite massive cheating, convinced Enrile and the RAM boys to accelerate their plan for a coup.

But Marcos got wind of their conspiracy and jumped the gun, ordering the arrest of Enrile and his RAM conspirators of mostly colonels he had nurtured for a year. Enrile was desperate, convinced that Marcos will kill him or throw him to jail.

He and his RAM decided to take their last stand at his headquarters in Camp Aguinaldo, and die in blaze of battle. He managed to convince Fidel Ramos — who most probably had been told by his US contacts that Ronald Reagan was set to dump Marcos — to join him and together they marched towards Camp Crame, which they thought could be better defended.

Enrile's genius was that he thought of a strategy. They could stop Marcos' forces from wiping them out if there were human shields, which would buy them time to negotiate their way out of their deaths. It was also his genius to beg Cardinal Sin to call on his faithful to go to EDSA and surround Camp Crame, to form a human shield.

Fortunately for those in EDSA in February 1986, Marcos wasn't of the thinking the Chinese Communist Party adopted in the Tiananmen Square uprising in 1989, which was to let People's Liberation Army tanks and battalions of riot police dismantle what really were weak human shields, killing an estimated 10,000 protesters.

Marcos ordered his troops to stand down, and, according to his son Ferdinand Jr. ("Bongbong"), told his generals: "I have served my countrymen for most of my life. I am not about to kill them now."

To this day, many still credit EDSA 1 as due to some divine intervention, although it was due to a failed coup and a cardinal's intrusion into politics.

I suspect that historians of the future would show that it was US intervention that was the key as the Americans had become so worried over the future of their military bases in the country, the lease for which was to expire in 1992.

(August 21, 2017)

NINOY'S FATAL MISCALCULATION

IT WAS RENOWNED scholar Edward Carr who pointed out in his book that is a bible of sorts for historians, **"What is History?"**: "The facts speak only when the historian calls on them: it is he who decides to which facts to give the floor, and in what order or context."

This is so true in the case of two sets of "facts" involving the last days of Marcos-era opposition leader Benigno "Ninoy" Aquino, Jr.

One is Ninoy's last interview with foreign correspondents inside the plane in the wee hours of August 21, 1983, a few hours before the aircraft landed and he was killed by a single bullet to the head.

The second set of facts is his telephone conversation two days before he left the United States on the way to the Philippines, with his close friend, the late Greek-American Steve Psinakis (the husband of Presentacion Lopez, the only daughter of Don Eugenio Lopez, Sr.), who had it recorded.

Philippine Daily Inquirer columnist Amando Doronila, who was also a close friend of the Lopez clan, wrote in August 2008 that Psinakis himself had released a transcript of the tape to his newspaper, and even played the actual audiotape to him.

Why the conversation — which was a scoop for the *Inquirer* — wasn't put on the PDI's front page and was seemingly ignored by the Yellow Cult would be obvious from the rather different portrait of Ninoy it presents, a transcript of which I publish below.

In Ninoy's interview with foreign correspondents, he is the humble opposition leader who decided to return to the Philippines, as he put it, "to help the opposition rebuild its grassroots organization" for the 1984 Batasang Pambansa elections. In his talk with the press, Ninoy is the picture of a reluctant martyr: "I no longer crave for political office. I would like to reiterate: I am not out to overthrow Marcos."

A different Ninoy

He does slip, though, and responds thus to a reporter's question on why he was returning to the Philippines: "I don't think a general should be ten thousand miles from his troops, even if he's leading them from prison." He says what heroes usually say: "I have to suffer with my people, I have to lead them because of the responsibility given to me by my people."

It is a different Ninoy in the Psinakis tape, in which he reveals why he is rushing to return to the Philippines: Marcos is dying, he's said his farewells to his generals, and he's got just three weeks to settle his affairs on earth. "Marcos is a man now: Terminal," he says. Ninoy says that Imelda is moving to grab power.

While Ninoy, of course, doesn't specifically say he is in the best position to be the next president, one senses from his conversation with Psinakis that he is "convinced 100 percent" that Marcos would allow him to be his successor. "Now that he (Marcos) is about to meet his Maker, I am almost confident that I can talk to him and sell him something," Ninoy tells Psinakis.

Ninoy revealed to Psinakis that he has "trump cards," which gave him confidence that Marcos would let him assume power. He said ASEAN leaders would support him to succeed Marcos and so would Japanese Prime Minister Yasuhiro Nakasone, who he said was "willing to send a private envoy" who would use Japanese economic assistance to the country as leverage.

Listening to the Psinakis tape, one would see Ninoy as a political player with nerves of steel, very much aware of the risks of his move to take over from Marcos, even as he cannot let a big opportunity pass him by. Even his tone in the telephone conversation is so different, supremely confident in the way I remember him giving a privilege speech in the Senate.

He explained to Psinakis the three scenarios he was expecting. First, a "100 percent (chance) I will be brought directly to prison; so that I may not get a chance to talk to anybody on the ground." Second, they will "turn back the plane" (to return to wherever it came from). And third, "and this is really iffy, they have two guys stationed to knock me out at the airport."

I find it remarkable that in the Psinakis tape he said nothing that is in the genre of the heroic statements he made in his interview with the press, like he is willing to risk his life, and even die for the country. He is rushing back expecting that Marcos would die in weeks, and he has the support of ASEAN and Japan to assume power.

I certainly don't mean to be facetious, but after listening to the tape, that quote from the TV series *"Game of Thrones"* sprang to mind:

"When you play the game of thrones, you win or you die."

The tape reveals that Ninoy was rushing home believing Marcos would be dying very soon — he mentioned the time frame of three weeks — and he believed that he could talk to the dictator who, with his trump cards, would make him his successor. But he knew there was a risk he could be assassinated.

Ninoy's "trump cards"

Aquino's — or Sin's — information, however, proved to be so wrong. Then president Ferdinand Marcos was indeed hospitalized at the Kidney Center in July 1983. But according to his son Ferdinand "Bongbong" Marcos, Jr., that was when he donated his kidney to his father for a transplant.

(Bongbong in an interview said his father had recovered from the transplant, and was having lunch with them when he received the news that Ninoy was assassinated. Marcos would die not in 1983, but six years later.)

What Aquino did not to mention to either the reporters or to Psinakis was that by early 1983, the country was already moving towards the worst economic crisis ever, to a great extent the result of the global debt crisis triggered by the Mexican default on its loans in March 1982.

Should we classify Ninoy as a hero, with his reasons for returning revealed, and at a period when the economy was already teetering, that only the slightest political trouble would push to the chasm? Or should we classify him as a traditional politician who is seizing the opportunity and his moment for glory?

These are questions that I would really like to be answered in my lifetime and if there are people out there with new evidence or testimony, I am willing to be enlightened.

The following is the transcript of Aquino's telephone conversation with Psinakis on August 13, 1983:

> **Ninoy Aquino:** Hi Steve, I'm at the airport and I cannot leave America without saying goodbye to you and expressing to you my deepest gratitude.

Steve Psinakis: Our prayers are always with you and all I can [say] is, remember that a word from you and anything you want is in your fingertips from me, okay? There's no limit to what I will do for you if you need some help. We are praying for you, for your safety and success and freedom of people, okay?

Aquino: Now this is the latest, Steve, that I can give you. My source is Cardinal Sin. Number one: Marcos checked in at the Kidney Center. The experts went, saw him, they did a test. He flunked all tests and the conclusion was if they operate on him, it would be fatal.

So he went back to the Palace. He is no longer responding to medication and he will have to be hooked up to the dialysis machine now more often. How he will last with that machine on, I don't know. Apparently they are now moving to put Imelda in effective control. And they are going to revamp the Cabinet, with (Roberto) Ongpin most probably emerging as prime minister and finance minister. Danding Cojuangco or [General Fabian] Ver, defense minister. O. D. Corpus possibly foreign minister, and maybe Ayala, I mean Enrique, maybe agriculture minister, I don't know.

But there's a major shake-up. Marcos met with his generals and apparently said goodbye to them last Friday. He was on television in Manila 24 hours ago, commenting on the boxing fight of Navarette and Talbot to show the people he is okay. But it's a matter of time, so he wanted three weeks to collect his thoughts, write his memoirs, complete his book and most probably craft the final stages of his administration.

He's a man now: Terminal. He knows he's going and that's the background I'm coming in.

Psinakis: I [also] heard some of this yesterday.

I got some reports, not of course as authoritative as yours, but pretty much the same that something was wrong and they couldn't operate and so forth. At any rate, the thought that comes to mind is that is good and bad. Good in that he's going and he knows it. He might show some compassion for the country and treat your return with more pragmatic thinking. The bad part may be that hardliners like Ver who are bulldogs without any political savvy, who may think that they're next in line [of succession]. Obviously, such people would look at your return with uh… That's what I'm worried about.

Aquino: Well, there are two reports I received along that line. Well, if they pinpoint the plane I'm coming in. The rumor in Manila is that I'm taking the private jet of Enrique (Zobel) from Hong Kong. But all planes are being guarded and they may close the airport on Sunday or turn back the plane if they would be able to pinpoint which one I'm coming in.

The third, and this is the real iffy. They have two guys stationed to know me out at the airport. And they will try them for murder, they'll convict them, but they have assurances.

Psinakis: Ah…let's not think about that.

Aquino: Yeah, that's the… Those are the things that I've been alerted. So, I don't know what options they will do now. But I am meeting with ASEAN leaders beginning Tuesday, Wednesday, and Thursday. Indonesia — Suharto might receive me. Malaysia is already firm and Thailand is just about firm. Now Japan has sent word that if Imelda is in place [Prime Minister] Nakasone is willing to use his economic clout.

Psinakis: Ah really, huh?

Aquino: Yes… to tell Imelda that if you treat Aquino nicely, we can dialogue.

Psinakis: Oh, that's good news all right. That's damn good news.

Aquino: Nakasone is willing to send a private envoy, a secret private envoy with a personal letter making a plea for me. If am still alive and in prison, that if they will treat me gently, and come up with some kind of an understanding, Japanese economic assistance will continue. Because they are very uptight that if the woman [Imelda] takes over and there will be chaos, you know, it would be bad. Now the ASEAN leaders, on the other hand, feel this way: ASEAN today is already one region. And any instability in one part of ASEAN will scare investors in the entire region.

That's why they are very, very uptight about the possibility of chaos and instability in the Philippines with Imelda. And that is the background of my conversation with them: That I am not going to upset the apple cart but that we can harmonize our movement.

To what extent they will be able to mitigate the hardliners, I don't know. That's the chance we'll have to take. If I survive Sunday, and I get to prison, I'm there in a week's time, I can get the works going.

I'm picking up a letter from [MNLF chairman] Nur Misuari, telling them that if the government will trust me as a negotiator, then they can start talks again. But they will not talk to anybody else.

Psinakis: It sounds to me like you have an awful lot of pluses on your side.

Aquino: Those are the trump cards I'm bringing home, which of course can be negated if one character gets to throw me out.

If I get into prison, there is no doubt, like 100 percent, I will be brought directly to prison. I may not even get a chance to talk to anybody there on the ground. But it's okay. A long as I'm alive and in prison, I can start using my trump cards.

I will try to hold out for a meeting with Marcos. Now that's he's about to meet his Maker, I am almost confident that I can talk to him and sell him something. Although the Cardinal told me that "if you think you can sell Marcos a bill of goods like return to democracy and electoral processes, forget it. You're dreaming."

"He's no longer in that state." This is the Cardinal's idea. I don't buy it. Because I don't think that a man who is about to die will be, you know, too hard-headed.

Psinakis: I hope you are right, but I think the Cardinal is right. I think Marcos… not only because he doesn't want to, that's academic at this point in time. But I think he has just… he's so deep and he has no choice but to stay where he is and leave things as they are. And I certainly hope that that's wrong because we don't want that.

Aquino: Okay. So, goodbye Steve.

Psinakis: One last question…

Aquino: Yes?

Psinakis: Any whatsoever… any indication from the US side that there might be some help on the cooperative or absolutely nothing?

Aquino: No. No indication. Except that they are watching me. They are following all my steps. But I am still hopeful that sanity will prevail, and they will know that eventually, they'll have to come to talk. Because I don't think they're very happy with the woman [Imelda] running the show.

(December 5, 2016)

HE BELIEVED MARTIAL LAW WAS NECESSARY

THE YELLOW AND RED CULTS' NARRATIVE has been that President Marcos imposed martial law solely in order to perpetuate himself in power, as the Constitution then barred him from seeking a third term with his second term ending in 1973.

They claim that the one main excuse Marcos gave why an authoritarian rule was necessary — that the communist insurgency, financed by oligarchs had become so serious that it couldn't be addressed in a democratic system — was false, that the threat had been exaggerated.

However, ironically since he was jailed the day martial law was imposed until his exile in 1980, assassinated opposition leader Benigno Aquino, Jr., Marcos' arch enemy did believe the strongman's explanation: martial law, while it did allow him to continue in power, was necessary to prevent the country from falling into chaos.

This is according to a United States airgram (a top-secret communication sent by courier via the diplomatic bag instead of by telegram) from the American embassy in Manila to the Department of State on September 21, 1972, or two days before martial law was announced.

The airgram was drafted by then Political Counselor John Forbes, who after two tours of duty in the Philippines, has remained here since the 1990s as a permanent resident, and earning reportedly a very good living as a political and business consultant.

It was declassified in 2016 along with about 50 other such confidential diplomatic documents by the US State Department's Office of the Historian, as basic source material for its compilation, *"Foreign Relations of the United States, 1969-1976"*.

The report, which was based on Forbes' and another unnamed embassy officer's conversations with Aquino, reads:

"With rapidly worsening law and order and communist dissident problems added to these economic woes, Aquino believes that Marcos must take strong actions in the near future and that these will include martial law. If the President follows this course, Aquino said that, 'for the good of the country,' he would support Marcos.

"Since the law and order and economic situation is deteriorating so rapidly, in Aquino's view, the good of the country requires strong measures on the part of the central government.

"The growing threat from the dissidents, the worsening law and order problem, the serious economic setback that has resulted from the floods in central Luzon and the probable ill effects of the Quasha decision of the Supreme Court on the country's foreign investment climate, were cited by Aquino as reasons why stronger central government action is needed.

Such action means martial law. Were he President, Aquino indicated that he would not hesitate to take such strong action and would, for example, execute several corrupt officials at the Luneta Park in Manila as a lesson to other officials that 'he meant business'."

Perhaps that was one reason that convinced the US not to protest the country's move towards a one-man rule, that shattered its image as its showcase of democracy in a region where strongman rule — e.g., Suharto of Indonesia, Lee Kuan Yew of Singapore, Park Chung-hee of South Korea, Chiang Kai-shek of Taiwan — were more the norm than the exception:

When martial law was declared at midnight September 22, Deputy National Security Adviser Alexander Haig sent a memo to President Richard Nixon briefing him on the development, and advising him "to refrain comment on Marcos' action, regarding it as a Philippine matter".

Haig noted though that that would be interpreted as a "tacit US support" for Marcos' imposition of martial law. Next to this sentence was a notation in Nixon's handwriting, which read: "K — Low key it."

Haig's memo, taken from the National Archives, Nixon's Presidential Materials, and marked "Secret: Sensitive" was another material in the State Department Office of the Historian's Foreign Relations of the United States, 1969-1976.

Parts of it read, which turned out to be an accurate narrative of events, and far from the Yellow narrative of a Dark Lord imposing his will on the land:

"Embassy Manila estimates that the country will react with resigned acceptance, after the initial shock and uproar. Criticism of Marcos' action would diminish particularly if there were early evidence of movement toward meaningful reform…

"At least in the short term, martial law should pose no direct serious problems for US security and economic relations with the Philippines. In fact, the climate for individual business operations might even be improved.

"As to our position, I believe we should refrain from comment on Marcos' action, regarding it as a Philippine matter. This stance may well be interpreted as tacit US support for Marcos' move, and result in criticism of us, particularly if Marcos does not make good use of his increased authority and the situation deteriorates.

"On the other hand, Marcos probably will appreciate such a stance on our part, and this should result in his continued cooperation in our maintaining effective access to our bases in the Philippines and his assistance in resolving US private investment problems resulting from last month's Quasha* decision."

(January 9, 2017)

---

*The "Quasha decision" referred to the Supreme Court's decision on August 17, 1972 that ruled the termination in 1974 of the so-called Parity Rights Amendment, which since 1947 gave Americans the same property rights as Filipinos, required all US citizens to divest their properties in the country.

The decision panicked US businesses, not only since they owned land where their offices stood but had vast agricultural plantations, as in the case of Dole and Del Monte.

A way out of this quagmire, or at least for an orderly and gradual divestment of American property holdings, had become a major concern of US government itself, and appears to be one major reason why it supported Marcos' martial law.

The main system that Marcos offered US property owners — which is practiced to this day — is for American companies to sell their lands to law firms, which then leased these back to them.

SON DIDN'T CARE TO BRING KILLERS TO JUSTICE

YESTERDAY WAS THE 31st anniversary of the assassination of the Yellow Cult's national martyr, Ninoy Aquino, and again, photos of his son President Benigno Aquino III with his sisters praying before their father's grave hog the newspapers' front pages.

Ninoy's murder on August 21, 1983 was an event that changed the course of Philippine history.

I am still astounded at how its masterminds and conspirators were so daring and precise in their execution of the deed as to kill him in broad daylight. If the killers' timing was just a few seconds late — or if the journalists with Aquino had been a bit bolder as to insist on following Aquino down the tube — the opposition leader's killing could have been witnessed and photographed by foreign media, who would have told the world about it.

As mysterious though as to who were the brains behind the assassination is the fact that Aquino's now powerful son, Benigno III, has done nothing to uncover who were behind his killing, as well as that of Rolando Galman, allegedly the trigger man who put a .357 mm. bullet into Aquino's head.

This, despite Benigno III becoming the most powerful man in the country that he has been able to remove the Supreme Court Chief Justice, incarcerate the former president on flimsy grounds, and have the entire Congress under his thumb.

Aquino is known to be vengeful against those who have slighted him in the most minor manner. This trait certainly doesn't apply to his apparent nonchalance towards his father's murderers. He has done nothing to show that he is interested in finding out.

The highest-ranking officer convicted for the crime was Aviation Security Command General Luther Custodio, who died in 1991. The rest of those convicted consisted of one captain, one lieutenant, and — talk of a class system — 13 enlisted men.

The investigation and legal proceedings undertaken by the Sandiganbayan that led to the September 1990 conviction of these 16 military men were all undertaken at the height of the popularity and power of President Corazon Aquino, who could have left no stone unturned to identify and bring to justice her husband's real killers: the person or the group of persons who ordered the assassination.

What kind of nation are we to fool ourselves that these military men acted on their own, and that there were no powerful personalities who ordered them to undertake an operation perfectly executed, without a single witness even with a phalanx of foreign correspondents accompanying Ninoy?

Masterminds not idle

The masterminds of the assassinations don't seem to have been idle, and have been determined to forever erase all trails of the evil deed that could lead to them.

In the early morning of May 7 this year, discharged Master Sergeant Pablo Martinez was killed in what initially appeared to be an accident along Roxas Boulevard.

An eyewitness claimed that an SUV Montero driven by one Henry Roque, ran over him after he fell from his bicycle which the vehicle bumped. The police initially concluded that it was purely an unfortunate accident. His son Diomedes, also an Air Force sergeant, however, suspected he was murdered.

The latest report I've been able to dig up was a Philippine Star news item dated May 19: "Parañaque police investigators confirmed that Roque could no longer be contacted after three witnesses surfaced and claimed they saw his SUV deliberately run over Martinez after he hit the victim's bike and fell down into the asphalt."

Who is Martinez? He was convicted as one of the conspirators in Aquino's assassination and had served nearly 30 years in jail for the crime. Since his release in 2007, and probably because he had become deeply religious, Martinez had been volunteering to disclose the brains of the murder.

In 1995, he admitted his role in the plot, and testified that it was Galman who killed Ninoy with a single bullet to the head. He said it was he who escorted Galman to a motel to spend the night before the assassination.

Martinez alleged that former Philippine Constabulary Major Romeo Gatan, a businessman named Hermilo Gosuico, former Air Force Col. Romeo Ochoco, and Air Force Capt. Felipe Valerio were in that hotel to tell Galman what he would do the next day. The other 11 officers and soldiers made up the team that allowed Galman to get close to and shoot Aquino in the head, after which they gunned him down.

Martinez' earth-shaking testimony, though, was first narrated in a February 2006 article in the U.S. Time magazine and in an on-camera interview in 2007 by ABS-CBN's Julius Babao with him right after his release from prison:

"I didn't hear any direct order from him, but I asked them [the conspirators in the hotel] who was giving them the orders, and they replied, 'Danding.' "

He was referring to oligarch Eduardo Cojuangco who had controlled until the last few years the giant San Miguel Corp. Martinez's claims were recorded in a formal deposition and submitted to the Supreme Court, which had been asked to reopen the case. The Court, though, ruled that it didn't qualify as "newly found evidence."

Cojuangco has vehemently denied such accusations.

"Valerio is among those who might be able to shed light, but to me, it's Ochoco whom the government should ask because he was the one who ordered me to bring Galman to the airport," Martinez said in 2007.

Captain Valerio was the head of the 10-man team of the Aviation Security Command who collected Aquino from the China Airlines plane to the airport's tarmac, where the former senator and then Galman were shot dead. Valerio and his immediate superior Air Force Colonel Ochoco disappeared right after Marcos' fall in 1986.

Valerio was not included among the 16 convicted or the other 18 accused who were acquitted since he could not be arraigned, as he could not be found and arrested. He was reported to be living in the US.

Ochoco, for some reason was also not indicted, and has been reported to be living in Australia.

Aquino or his officials had done absolutely nothing to get in touch with Martinez or with the other 10 officers and soldiers convicted of the crime, to convince them that they would be placed under his protection if they told everything they knew about the assassination.

Having given everything the Americans wanted, allowing them to have military forward operating sites here, couldn't have Aquino asked them for a small favor of looking for Ochoco and Valerio, and extraditing them here to face justice?

One would have thought the martyr's only son would use all the resources at his command as President not just to seek justice for his father, but also to shed light on what is one of the most ruthless but pivotal killings in our nation's history.

Aquino hasn't.

Aquino's seeming lack of concern over his father's murder convinces me that either there is something deeply wrong in this person's psyche, or that there is something terribly embarrassing in the assassination that has been kept so secret, that even the victim's powerful family has refused to uncover its mastermind.

Aquino's mother Cory also seemed disinterested when she was president in getting to the bottom of her husband's murder. However, this was mostly viewed as an understandable, even laudable, above-the-fray stance of the Saint of Democracy.

More cynical observers felt, however, that she was afraid to discover that the mastermind could be Cojuangco, her cousin, or that she even already knew this.

Political stability's sake

An interpretation kind to her claimed that if she had pursued Cojuangco for the crime, the oligarch could have joined and funded the many coup attempts against her rule, and that she chose to sacrifice her personal wish — to avenge her husband — for the sake of the country's political stability.

The son certainly can't make such justification now for his disinterest in finding out who ordered his father's murder.

A big lacuna in our nation's history remains to be filled, as mysterious as why his widow and the son hadn't lifted a finger to expose who ordered the head of their family killed.

In the case of the also mysterious assassination of another president, the US's John F. Kennedy, the trail had gone totally cold after nightclub owner Jack Ruby, who killed the alleged assassin Lee Harvey Oswald, died in prison four years later in 1967.

In Ninoy's case, Martinez had provided enough leads to solve the mystery, and many of the soldiers convicted are still alive and can be persuaded to tell everything they know. They can even be convinced to disclose, who reportedly has been generously taking care of their families financially in the 30 years they've been in prison.

The crimes' planners — Ochoco and Valerio, Martinez alleged — can still be tracked down. (Businessman Gosuico and Major Gatan reportedly died several years ago by natural causes, although I have been unable to confirm this.)

How can Aquino keep wearing that yellow ribbon on his chest, when he has done nothing to solve the crime it signifies?

How can we be proud of a nation whose two presidents, one the widow and the other the son, had not bothered to bring justice to a hero, who had declared that the Filipino is worth dying for?

Or maybe it would be more realistic to hope that Senator Ferdinand Marcos, Jr. — who aspires to lead this nation — would provide evidence to prove that it wasn't his father who ordered Aquino's murder, as many Filipinos believe.

(August 21, 2014 and August 20, 2015)

POSTSCRIPT:

For such a serious accusation made in two columns published in two years, that Aquino had done nothing to solve his father's murder, and especially as these two articles went viral, garnering more than 70,000 likes and shares, I was expecting that the President or his many spokesmen would reply to the points I raised. They were silent as the grave: nothing.

The Jabidah Hoax

JABIDAH: THE YELLOWS' FIRST BIG FAKE NEWS

THE SO-CALLED Jabidah "massacre" of March 1968 — about which an ignorant writer in another newspaper complained why there was no commemoration yesterday on its 50th anniversary — was the Yellow Cult's first colossal fake news.

If there was any killing, it was of President Ferdinand Marcos' covert plans to forcibly take over Sabah over which we had, and continue to have, legitimate claims under international law, but which Malaysia arrogantly ignored and continues to ignore.

The episode only revealed the utter lack of nationalism and deviousness of the Liberal Party and its most articulate leader, Benigno Aquino, Jr., to advance their political ambitions.

Under the guise of investigating reports of a so-called massacre in Corregidor island, of young Muslims being trained by the Army Special Forces to infiltrate Sabah, the Yellows in effect ratted on Marcos and his plans to Malaysia.

By doing so, they thought they could torpedo Marcos' re-election in the coming year, 1969, especially since he had become popular, even successful in portraying himself and Imelda as the Filipino version of the Kennedys. Even the powerful oligarchic clan, the Lopezes with their media empire, at the time was supporting Marcos whose vice president was the patriarch Fernando Lopez.

The Jabidah hoax nipped in the bud what would have been a tremendous nationalist accomplishment for Marcos: reclaiming Sabah, a resource-rich territory just a bit smaller than Mindanao.

According to the armed forces plan called *Operation Merdeka* ("Freedom"), Muslim Tausug recruits were to be trained by the military to infiltrate Sabah, and foment there an uprising among their ethnic group against the Malaysian government. The uprising would be the excuse for the Philippine military to invade Sabah and claim it as part of Philippine territory.

That wasn't a far-fetched plan. At the time, our country had a more powerful military than Malaysia, which was founded only in 1963, and needed only an excuse to forcibly take over Sabah.

By exposing the plan, the Yellows calculated Malaysia would retaliate, and get the one-year old Association of Southeast Asian Nation (ASEAN) to condemn Marcos, thereby blackening his image in the country.

The Yellows' Jabidah hoax was the key event that doomed our plans for reclaiming Sabah. All the talk over a purported massacre made the issue of reclaiming Sabah so unpopular, that Marcos shelved the idea. The young nation, Malaysia, strengthened its administration of the vast territory, and scrambled to convince the international community that it was the legitimate owner of Sabah.

The Jabidah hoax would have one huge negative consequence for the Philippines, which hounds it to this day: the growth of the Muslim insurgency, which currently, under the subterfuge of having a Bangsamoro Basic Law, threatens to dismember the country.

MNLF exploited the hoax

Without the Jabidah hoax, the Moro National Liberation Front (MNLF) and its breakaway and now the bigger and deadlier organization, the Moro Islamic Liberation Front (MILF) would not have grown into insurgencies that actually threaten the Republic.

The MNLF exploited the much-publicized allegation to rouse the Muslim youth's anger so they would rally to the fledgling organization, which the more powerful Muslim traditional politicians had earlier refused to support.

Contrast this with the communist movement, which was jump-started by the so-called First Quarter Storm (FQS) of 1970. These massive student demonstrations against Marcos radicalized the Manila-based youth and drove them to join the New People's Army.

The impact of the Jabidah hoax on the Muslim youth was 10 times that of the FQS.

The MNLF propaganda machine mythicized Jabidah to become, as one gullible academic put it, the "sacral moment invoked from time to time to mobilize the Muslims to the movement's cause."

It portrayed the alleged massacre as the culmination of genocidal century-long attacks against the Moros: therefore, a Bangsamoro or an independent nation-state of the Moros was seen as necessary.

Another consequence of the Jabidah hoax was that Malaysia expectedly retaliated against Marcos' plans. If the Philippines' game-plan was to foment revolution against Malaysia among Muslims in Sabah, our neighbor's tit-for-tat was to foment revolution in Mindanao against the Marcos regime.

Malaysia financed MNLF

When the Yellows exposed Marcos' plans, Sabah's first Chief Minister Tun Mustafa was livid. He gave huge finances to the MNLF and allowed its members to use Sabah as their refuge and base. Mustafa arranged for several 90-man batches of MNLF cadres to undergo military training in Malaysia conducted by top-notch former British Special Action Service officers.

The training in Malaysia was crucial in the growth of the MNLF since despite their vaunted bravery and martial tradition, the Moros were practically medieval in their military outlook and skills. Among these young Moros were the present chairman of the MILF, Murad Ibrahim, and most of the organization's officers corps.

Malaysia's support for the MNLF indeed makes up one most important ingredient for an insurgency to grow, as in the case of the Viet Cong: a supportive country to provide logistics and arms as well as physical refuge.

I have written six columns to prove, without a shadow of a doubt, that the Jabidah massacre was a hoax, and nobody, not even the MNLF and the MILF has questioned my assertions. I wonder why those still claiming it was real haven't bothered to read the voluminous transcripts of the Senate and House of Representatives hearings on the issue, as well as the decision of the Military Commission that tried the case originally filed by the sole witness — all of which show there was no massacre of Moros in Corregidor.

Former President Benigno Aquino III, very ignorantly claimed that it was his father who exposed the Jabidah "massacre." On the contrary, in a speech even available online, Aquino very categorically said he himself interviewed in Jolo the young Muslims who were reported to have been killed. There was no massacre at all, he concluded.

It is has been part of Moro culture to avenge their kinsmen, even if it takes decades to do so, resulting in the so-called, notorious rido, or clan wars, that explains much of the violence in Muslim Mindanao.

Not a single casualty

Yet after 50 years, not a single casualty of the "massacre" has been identified.

No one has claimed that his brother, husband, son, a kinsman of the nth degree, or even a friend was among those killed in the purported massacre. Moro propagandists would not even dare pay a scoundrel to claim to pretend he had a Jabidah-massacre relative.

This is astonishing, especially because of the well-known and feared practice of rido among Muslims in Mindanao. Either based on religion or just tribal culture, this tradition requires the family of a murdered person to exact vengeance, even against the relatives of the perpetrator and across the generations.

After the issue died down, the sole alleged witness of the "massacre," Jibin Arula, evaded going back to his Sulu home province and settled in Antique. The MNLF and the MILF never took him under their protection, and official documents of the two organizations have never officially asserted that the "massacre" occurred.

The MILF's official website posts absolutely nothing about Jabidah. The website features 32 of Misuari's speeches since 1997. Not one of these speeches mentions a "Jabidah massacre".

In fact, Misuari has written only one book, actually a lengthy pamphlet, in 1989: "The Unbroken Thread of Genocide in the Bangsamoro Homeland." There is not one word in that pamphlet on the Jabidah Massacre, even if the MNLF rode the outrage over it in 1968 by having its foundation day on March 18, when the supposed massacre occurred.

Impoverished, Arula went to Naic, Cavite in the late 2000 to be given odd jobs by the son of Melencio Sagun, the chief of police of the town in 1968 who purportedly "found" him after his alleged dramatic escape from Corregidor.

The villain portrayed by the Yellows, Air Force Major Eduardo Martelino, who headed the Merdeka plan, after becoming a full colonel and retiring from the service, settled in Tawi-Tawi to live with his Muslim wife in a Tausug village where he had recruited the young Moros for his Sabah operation.

Would he have done that if he, as the Yellows publicly alleged, ordered the Jabidah "massacre"?

There was one unintended consequence of the Jabidah hoax that affected in a big way the course of our nation.

The military became so incensed over the investigations, and the Yellows' hidden agenda, which was to expose their strategy to take over

Sabah. Its top brass and those accused in the investigations even took out front page advertisements in newspapers condemning Congress for its "politicking" at the expense of the armed forces' prestige.

Four years later, it didn't take much for Marcos to convince the military that representative democracy was failing, and that he had to declare martial law.

One factor that convinced Marcos to go ahead with his strongman rule, was the fact that the Jabidah episode exposed an opposition so unpatriotic that it even exposed his plan to reclaim Sabah for the Philippines.

In Marcos' mind, whether self-serving or not, he had the right to wipe out such an unprincipled opposition, through martial law. Indeed, his declaration of martial law on September 22, 1972 was justified as a move not only to protect the Republic from the communists and the rightist opposition, but to stop the "secessionist movement in Mindanao."

Karma certainly has been a bitch for the Yellows. Marcos' 13-year rule would nearly wipe them out.

(March 20, 2013; March 22, 25-26, 29 and 31, 2015)

CLEAREST INDICATIONS OF A HOAX

THE CONTRASTING FATES of the alleged perpetrators of the "Jabidah massacre" and its supposed sole witness, Jibin Arula, are a strong testimony to the fact that "Jabidah" was nothing but a hoax.

Although Air Force Major Eduardo Martelino headed the entire operation to reclaim Sabah, the training of recruits was undertaken by the Army's Special Forces, its elite unit established by then Captain Fidel Ramos.

Other than President Marcos himself, therefore, command responsibility for *Operation Merdeka* would have been on the armed forces chief of staff at that time.

Who was he? General Manuel Yan, the youngest to be appointed to the post, and considered to have been the best and most principled Chief of Staff the country ever had. He resigned his post when martial law was imposed, declaring that he could not implement it as he thought it unconstitutional.

Because of his prestige, though, Marcos convinced him to become ambassador to Thailand. President Corazon Aquino subsequently appointed him as ambassador to Indonesia and then to the UK Court of St. James.

Distinguished as Yan was, would he have allowed a whitewash of an alleged Jabidah "massacre"?

President Ramos recruited Yan in 1992 as his Presidential Adviser on the Peace Process, his chief negotiator with the Moro National Liberation Front (MNLF) that led to the 1996 peace settlement. Would the MNLF have talked to the ultimate commander of the Army Special Forces that massacred Muslims in Corregidor in 1968? I don't think so.

Well maybe, it was the Army commanding general who was the rascal?

The Army commander then was as distinguished as Yan — General Romeo Espino, who went on to become the armed forces' longest-serving chief of staff, from 1972 to 1981.

Espino was chief of staff for most of the martial law era and had not been tainted by the allegations of human rights abuses. Do you think such a principled military officer would have covered up for his men's atrocities? I don't think so.

What happened to the officers accused by the sole witness of murdering or having ordered the killing of at least 24 Muslim youths in Corregidor?

If there were really a massacre of Muslims, you would think that Major Martelino — whom then Senator Aquino demonized as an evil kind of James Bond, the blockbuster movie at that time — would have emigrated to the United States or anywhere in the world to escape Moro wrath. After all, the thousands of MNLF fighters and relatives of those allegedly killed in Corregidor would be going after him, a fatwah in effect declared on him, right?

Far from that. Martelino, after his acquittal by the court martial, went on with his military career, becoming full colonel. Even years before Jabidah, he had married a Muslim, Sofia, and converted to Islam, taking the Muslim name Abdul Latif.

After retirement, of all places to live for a man who was supposedly responsible for the Muslim youths' massacre, Martelino settled down with his Muslim wife in the midst of the Tausugs in Simunul island in Tawi-Tawi, where he first recruited and trained for the Merdeka Muslim infiltrators.

His involvement in *Operation Merdeka* apparently wasn't just another military assignment for him, but was part of his life's cause.

He wrote a book in 1959 entitled **"Someday Malaysia,"** published in New York, which even United Nations General Secretary Carlos Romulo prefaced and called a "valuable contribution" to scholarship.

By "Malaysia," Martelino wasn't referring to the Federation of Malaysia, which would be founded only in 1963. He referred to a "Union" he said President Manuel Quezon first conceived:

"A prosperous world unit comprising the nations of Southeast Asia inhabited by the Malayan race. Burma, Thailand, Annam, Malaya, Indonesia and the Philippines leagued in an integrated commonwealth."

And the other officers who were accused by the sole whistleblower Arula of killing the Muslim recruits?

They all went on to have distinguished military careers, the Jabidah accusations against them forgotten. Other than Martelino, Arula — a barely literate former farmer — had filed charges against five officers, who were then tried in a court martial and acquitted. We were able to trace what happened to each.

Captain Teodoro Facelo, whom the alleged witness Arula claimed recruited him, became a full colonel, and served as the second commander of the Army's 503rd infantry brigade in the late 1980s. This brigade had been distinguished for its successful campaigns against the New People's Army, with not a single human rights case filed against its members.

Captain Oropesa rose to the rank of general. Following is the last report on him that I obtained, dated June 26, 2014:

"The 11th Special Forces team, composed of Gen. Cirilo O. Oropesa AFP (Ret.), Maj-Gen. Jose Magno Jr. AFP (Ret.), Maj-Gen. Rodolfo Canieso AFP (Ret.), Gen. Rodrigo Ordoyo AFP (Ret.), was honored for their significant role in the training and organization of the 1st Special Forces Company led by then Capt. Fidel V Ramos."

Lieutenant Eduardo Batalla got to be brigadier general, and in 1989 was the Philippine Constabulary Commander for Western Mindanao. He was murdered, together with several other officers, by Muslim rogue cop Rizal Alih who took them hostage in a prison break.

Captain Ruperto Amistoso became a full colonel when he retired, and was recruited in 1990 by General Jose Almonte as the Intelligence and Investigation Services chief of the crack anti-smuggling unit at that time, the Economic Intelligence and Investigation Bureau.

Captain Alberto G. Soteco wasn't really a military man but a doctor, who, after volunteering for the Philcag contingent in Korea was assigned to the Special Forces' detachment in Corregidor. He left the military right after they were acquitted by the court martial.

Are these the kind of officers who would undertake a ruthless massacre in Corregidor in 1968?

How about Abadilla?

That a Lieutenant Rolando Abadilla was one of the accused, has been taken by Jabidah propagandists as an indication of the ruthlessness of those who were supposed to be guilty of the alleged massacre, since he became notorious in the 1980s as Marcos' Metrocom chief. But in Corregidor he was merely a supply officer.

Would Marcos have taken as his top henchman a military man whose head would have been put by the MNLF on a bounty because of "Jabidah"?

Poor Jibin Arula

The only really pathetic figure here in this entire saga is Jibin Arula, the only one who claimed he was an eyewitness to a massacre.

When the Jabidah controversy waned, in part because of the ridicule later heaped on it as "a massacre without the massacred," Arula's patron, Cavite governor, Liberal Party stalwart Delfin Montano, discarded him like a used rag after Marcos won the 1969 elections.

According to Arula's own account, Montano gave him P20,000 to leave and fend for himself.

As the sole witness to what was supposedly a historic event that fueled growth of the Moro rebellion, he would have been taken in by the MNLF, even secured him in Malaysia, or for the MILF, to relocate him to one of its many camps in Maguindanao, right?

Nope. He settled in Antique with another woman, leaving his wife in Bonggao, an island in the Sulu archipelago. He would have seven children on that Visayan island and people there didn't even know he was Muslim as he regularly attended mass in the village's church.

That the MNLF, MILF, Senator Aquino and the entire opposition Liberal Party cared little for Arula, the only person who "exposed" the "Jabidah massacre" obviously means that they knew something the rest of the country didn't.

MNLF chairman Nur Misuari, when he got to be ARMM governor, recruited him in 1997 for an assignment with a monthly salary of P7,000, to narrate when asked his Jabidah allegations at forums on the Moro issue. He spoke only at a few of those forums, though. He became jobless when Misuari ended his term in 2000.

Arula resurfaced in 2007, and was interviewed by several obviously gullible journalists (even featured in a documentary by Al-Jazeera) and invited to forums by NGOs at that time during the propaganda campaign for a peace settlement with the MILF.

When his wife died sometime in the mid-2000s, he went to Cavite and was given odd jobs by the son of Melencio Sagun, the chief of police in Naic, Cavite in 1968 who purportedly "found" him after his dramatic escape from Corregidor.

Arula died in a vehicular accident in 2010, which Aquino's organizers of a planned Jabidah commemorative event found out only in 2011, when they were looking for him as their star participant.

Nobody even knows where he is buried; no relative of his has come out. Neither the MNLF, nor the MILF has ever mentioned him again.

(March 27, 2015 and March 30, 2015)

POSTSCRIPT:

It is the National Historical Commission that by law is the sole government agency with the "authority to determine all factual matters relating to official Philippine history". Aquino in 2013 ordered it to officially acknowledge the purported atrocity, "to recognize it as part of our national narrative."

To the credit of its chairman Ma. Serena Diokno the NHC refused to follow Aquino's order. However, buckling under intense pressure by Aquino and his officials striving to get the Moro Islamic Liberation Front to sign a peace agreement they thought would win them the Nobel Peace Prize, the NHC found a way out: It authorized a site in Corregidor named as "Mindanao Garden of Peace."

The Filipino text of the plaque at the Garden of Peace reads;

"(This site) served as a camp for the training of Moro youth headed by staff of the Armed Forces of the Philippines. This started in Simunul (now a town in Tawi-Tawi province) 17 December 1967, and transferred to Corregidor, 3 January 1968. The reports of killings of several members on 18 March 1968 served as a fuse for the dispute in Mindanao that led to the national crisis in the decade of the 1970s. This Mindanao Garden of Peace symbolizes the goodwill among Filipinos to attain peace and progress in our country."

Diokno explained to this writer: "As you can see, the NHC Board worded the text of the historical marker very carefully, mindful of the conflicting accounts of the events: from the personal account of Mr. Jibin Arula to the congressional investigations, including the thorough investigation led by Senator Benigno "Ninoy' Aquino, Jr. in the Senate, and the Military Court formed to try the military men involved in the secret training.

She added: "While the purpose of the mission was perceived differently, and the events that led to it and the actual occurrence in the morning of 18 March 1968 were never really ascertained, the reports agree on the facts stated in the historical marker."

In plain language, what Diokno is saying is the following: "There was no Jabidah massacre, as far as we can determine at this time, since there are conflicting accounts of whatever happened. However, it is a fact that the "reports of killings" in Corregidor "served as a fuse" for the Mindanao conflict.

AQUINO LEAKED MARCOS' SABAH PLAN

CONTRARY TO MANY accounts, senator Benigno "Ninoy" Aquino Jr. did not expose the so-called "Jabidah massacre," a bogus incident that nonetheless was mythicized by the Moro National Liberation Front (MNLF), in order to rally Muslims to its secessionist cause.

What Aquino revealed to the world, was the secret plan of his political arch-enemy president Ferdinand Marcos to train and send Muslim commandos to Sabah to organize a revolt against Malaysia, the first step for the Philippines to take back its territory.

According to the plan called *Operation Merdeka* (Freedom), hatched by Marcos' armed forces, the uprising would be the excuse for the Philippine military to invade Sabah, which the Philippines had declared to be part of its territory (through the strong claims, backed up by documentary evidence, of the Sultanate of Sulu).

At the time that Marcos planned to take over Sabah, the Philippines had a more powerful military than that of the new nation Federation of Malaysia, founded only in 1963.

The so-called "Jabidah massacre" was the purported murder on Corregidor Island on March 18, 1968 of 24 Muslim Tausug recruits being trained by the military to infiltrate Sabah.

But there was no murder or massacre. Ninoy Aquino actually debunked the allegations of a massacre from the start and his statements on this are preserved in the annals of the Senate as his privilege speech delivered March 28, 1968.

In his privileged speech, misleadingly titled ""Jabidah! Special Forces of Evil?", Aquino didn't jump in to demonize Marcos over the alleged massacre. His intention obviously was only to disclose to the Malaysians that Marcos was moving to forcibly take over Sabah, and he didn't want to dent his credibility by making allegations of a massacre that later would be prove to be untrue.

Aquino related that he himself went to Jolo and Tawi-Tawi to find the alleged victims' relatives and even interviewed the sole "witness" Jibin Arula.

Aquino in his speech concluded: "After interviewing the self-asserted massacre survivor, Jibin Arula, doubt nagged me that there had indeed been a massacre."

Aquino explained his doubts:

"Arula must have made a dash for his life, thinking that they had been brought to the airstrip for the 'slaughter.' Told to halt by his escorts, he kept running. His escorts shot him in the leg to force him to stop. He kept going — and the rest is his story. But what happened to his eleven companions? Were they really ' massacred?'"

Aquino went on: "Some say that when the firing started with Arula, his companions ducked. So that Arula was correct when he said that he saw his companions fall to the ground. But were they shot? Or did they duck because of the firing?"

Recruits were alive and well

The alleged "slaughter" Aquino referred to was Arula's claim that he had suspected that 24 recruits who left two days earlier, whom their military superiors said were being brought to Sulu to be deployed to Sabah, were actually killed.

But Aquino pointed out: "In Jolo yesterday, I met the first batch of 24 recruits aboard [Navy Vessel] RP-68. This group was earlier reported missing — or, even worse, believed ' massacred' . . . William Patarasa, 16 years old [one of the recruits] denied knowledge of any massacre."

Aquino in his speech elaborated his view: "This morning, *The Manila Times*, in its banner headline, quoted me as saying that I believed there was no massacre on Corregidor. And I submit it was not a hasty conclusion, but one borne out by careful deductions."

What were these deductions? According to Aquino:

• "What would have been the motive for the 'massacre'? Some quarters have advanced the theory that the trainees were liquidated in order to silence them. But then, 24 boys have already shown up in Jolo safe and healthy. To release 24 men who can spill the beans and liquidate the remaining 24 'to seal' their lips would defy logic."

• "Arula's fears, which in his place may be considered valid, may not be supported by the recent turn of events. Twenty-four recruits have turned up."

Aquino emphasized that only a rigorous investigation of Arula's allegations would arrive at the truth. He asked the military to "produce the eleven recruits" the lone survivor allegedly killed.

But if the eleven merely resigned and like the first twenty four returned to Sulu, or even deployed to Sabah, could the military have traced them and asked them to testify?

Fifty years after the alleged massacre occurred, there hasn't been a single victim of the identified. For an ethnic group known for its close yet expanded kinship system, no relative has ever claimed his brother, son, cousin, or husband was killed in Corregidor.

So what was Aquino's speech all about? Only 20 percent, of Aquino's 5,734-word speech, discussed the alleged massacre.

The biggest part of his speech exposed details regarding the Jabidah plan he boasted he uncovered, through his investigation and disclosures by his moles in the country's intelligence services.

"It is the codename for a supposedly super-secret, twin-goaled operation of president Marcos to wipe out the opposition . . . — literally, if need be — in 1969 and to set this country on a high foreign adventure," Aquino said in his speech. Careful not to mention "Sabah", Aquino said: Jabidah "is the codename for Mr. Marcos' special operation to . . . achieve territorial gains."

Arula's dubious story

An indication of what the Jabidah issue was really all about is the involvement of Marcos' most vociferous critic Cavite governor Delfin Montano. The governor was the one who shepherded Arula to file charges at the Cavite Court of First Instance against Army Major Eduardo Martelino and 10 other officers and soldiers, whom he alleged were involved in the purported atrocity.

Arula claimed that together with about a dozen of his fellow Muslim trainees, he was ordered to line up at the airstrip in Corregidor in the wee hours of March 18, 1968, and then shot by their trainers. He alleged that he was hit in the leg, so he managed to run, hide in the bushes, and then escape to the sea to be rescued hours later by fishermen.

Arula's account was so fantastically dubious, reminding one of a B-grade action movie. It was so obviously scripted to be a key element of a political plot against Marcos and his *Operation Merdeka*.

How could a poor, illiterate Muslim who was wounded in the leg on March 18 swim 25 kilometers from the deep and rough waters of Corregidor, towards Manila Bay and then Naic town in Cavite? This in itself is physically impossible.

How could he go through that exhausting ordeal, a purported near-death trauma, a wounded leg, and then just five days later file a case against the military in a Cavite court? Even rich victims of crimes take months to file a case against ordinary citizens, and even longer against those in power, such as the military.

National artist Nick Joaquin (as Quijano de Manila), then a journalist writing in the most respected magazine at that time, the *Philippine Free Press*, wrote:

"Upon interviewing Arula, the sole witness to the alleged massacre, Aquino 2nd realized that for a second-grade dropout, this self-styled survivor of an alleged massacre had an amazing 'photographic memory' — he cited a litany of 48 names in full and retraced the elaborate unfolding of events, including the departure of the exact number of men from the camp, batch after batch."

Still though, the allegations became a burning issue in the country with the two major newspapers at that time, both stridently anti-Marcos, *The Manila Times* and *The Manila Chronicle*, portraying Arula as a hero.

Four congressional investigations by different committees were undertaken, all of which couldn't establish that there was a massacre. These were four years before Martial Law, when the country's democratic processes were so vibrant, and the opposition was powerful both in Congress and in media.

Then congressman Rashid Lucman of Lanao del Sur, claimed that the massacre was motivated by Marcos' greed to claim Sabah for his personal property. Lucman months later would organize the Bangsa Moro Liberation Organization, the MNLF's precursor, and, after the hearings, got Malaysia to secretly train its recruits.

Two dozens of the Muslim youths who were recruited for Merdeka were purportedly killed because they complained of poor food and low salary, and decided to resign.

In the MNLF's myth-making though, the reason was changed into a noble one, that the Muslims refused to fight their brother Muslim Malaysians. It was a clever revision of the fictional story.

Malaysia's angry response

When the top-secret *Operation Merdeka* was exposed to the public, Sabah's first Chief Minister Tun Mustafa was livid, and in retaliation, would fund the MNLF and allow them to use Sabah as their refuge and base.

Mustafa even arranged for 201 MNLF cadres, including the present chairman of the Moro Islamic Liberation Front, Murad Ibrahim, to be trained in Sabah by former British Special Action Service offices, which formed the Muslim organizations' officers' corps.

The growth of the Muslim insurgency is, therefore, to a very large extent, due to Malaysia's help.

In a demonstration of the law of unintended consequences, the MNLF founded in 1972 would use the allegation to rouse Muslim youth's anger so they would rally to the fledgling organization, which the more powerful Muslim traditional politicians earlier refused to support.

The MNLF (and its breakaway group the Moro Islamic Liberation Front) mythicized Jabidah to become, as an academic put it, the "sacral moment invoked from time to time to mobilize the Muslims to the movement's cause." Misuari portrayed it as the culmination of genocidal attacks against the Moros; therefore, a Bangsamoro — an independent nation-state of the Moros — is necessary.

The mythicization of Jabidah has been so successful that even Ninoy's son, the former president Benigno S. Aquino III and supporters of his Bangsamoro Basic Law have falsely, cruelly compared the Mamasapano massacre of 44 police commandos to the non-existent "Jabidah massacre." In their ignorance and stupidity, they are spitting on the graves of real heroes who fought for the Republic.

Aquino III obviously did not read his father's speech at the Senate. Ninoy Aquino actually debunked the allegations of a Jabidah Massacre from the very start.

Given his wily political nature, the elder Aquino gave his speech the misleading title, "Jabidah! Special Forces of Evil?" But there was no massacre and even Ninoy said he doubted it after having met the Muslim recruits who turned out to be alive and well.

But the damage had been done. After Aquino's speech exposed the military's secret *Operation Merdeka* (which could have been successful, given the strength of the Philippine military then) Marcos decided to scuttle all plans — militarily or diplomatically — to reclaim Sabah.

(March 20, 2013 and March 23, 2015)

BEHIND THE FAKERY: WARLORD VERSUS WARLORD

BEHIND THE FAKE INCIDENT called the "Jabidah massacre" was, as Filipinos term it, *"pulitika,"* or politics in its most pejorative sense. Jabidah started as a propaganda weapon in the political war between two warlords, for control of Cavite in the 1971 elections and consequently the Philippine presidency.

How exactly did the allegations of a Jabidah massacre come about?

The sole person who alleged (and even claimed to have witnessed) that Muslim commando trainees bound for Sabah were killed in 1968 in Corregidor was Jibin Arula, who dropped out of a Tawi-Tawi school when he was in second grade.

Arula's far-fetched story was that after escaping into the sea, wounded, while his comrades were mowed by down by the military, he was rescued off Corregidor by Cavite fishermen, who brought him to the province's chief of police Melencio Sagun.

He claimed that after telling the police chief his story, he was brought to provincial governor Delfin Montano.

The governor, from a clan accused of the so-called 1952 "Maragondon Massacre" of its political enemies, became an instant and ardent human rights champion, if one believes this yarn. He put Arula under his protection, sustained him financially, and had him file the case at the Cavite Court of First Instance against the military men responsible for the alleged killings.

That the governor was keenly interested in the case, and funded it, is obvious in that Arula, a poor Muslim, even got to file a case at the Supreme Court asking it to rule illegal the military assumption of jurisdiction over his Jabidah allegations, that he had filed in the Cavite court.

Who was this "human rights champion" Delfin Montano who took on not only the Armed Forces of the Philippines but President Ferdinand Marcos himself?

Montano was the scion of the most powerful warlord clan that ruled Cavite until martial law. His father, the clan's patriarch Justiniano Montano was a Liberal Party pillar, who was the lone congressman of Cavite from 1955 until Congress was abolished under martial law in 1972. His son Delfin was governor during the same period, the longest-serving governor ever of the province.

The Montano warlord clan was one of Marcos' political arch-enemies before martial law. After the 1965 presidential elections in which he lost heavily in Cavite to his rival Diosdado Macapagal, Marcos laid siege to the Montanos' kingdom, attacking the smuggling businesses that were under their protection and even getting criminals such as the legendary "Nardong Putik" out of jail as a counter-force to the warlord's "private army".

Matters came to a head for the Montanos in the 1967 local elections. Marcos threw everything against them. Their men were disarmed while their rivals were allowed to keep their arms; the entire province was placed under Comelec control; and massive funds were given to the anti-Montano candidates.

For the first time in decades, the Montanos' grip on Cavite weakened and they lost several of their municipal bastions.

A Marcos coup was the defection of the Montanos' richest crony, the infamous "smuggling lord" Lino Bocalan to his camp. In exchange for being allowed to continue his smuggling business, however, Marcos required of him certain services.

These were dramatically described in a 2000 book that has pandered the myth of a "Jabidah Massacre", but whose authors were unable to connect the dots in front of them:

"Bocalan had also been among the financiers of *'Operation Merdeka.'* In his coastal home in Cavite in 1998, Bocalan, 70, hesitates to talk about his participation in Operation Merdeka.

"Halfway through a bottle of whisky on a Sunday midmorning, he relents a bit. 'Marcos told me he needed help for Sabah,' Bocalan says in Filipino." My duty was to finance the operation. I spent millions (of pesos)… I fed the Filipino trainees in Sabah, paid their salaries. I supported them. I sent my brother and my people to Tawi-Tawi and Corregidor to give food and money (to the recruits)."

The Montanos learned of Bocalan's involvement in Operation Merdeka. But exposing to the public the government's plan for the Philippines to take over Sabah would sound unpatriotic, pro-Malaysian, and even treasonous.

The Montanos found a way to go around this problem to hit at their ungrateful crony Bocalan and even politically wound their enemy Marcos for the 1969 elections, by using Arula's allegations of a massacre in Corregidor.

The smuggling lord who reportedly financed the secret operation could have been implicated and indicted if the case had been tried at the Cavite Court of First Instance. But the Supreme Court upheld the military's move to have the case tried by court martial.

The Liberal Party, with the help of the Lopez media entities, *The Manila Chronicle* and ABS-CBN, went to town with the issue. A University of the Philippines (U.P.) Muslim instructor named Nur Misuari and his colleague in the university, master propagandist Jose Ma. Sison, together with the student organizations they controlled made it so much of a cause célèbre, they actually radicalized young Moros to join the Muslim insurgency.

But there was no Jabidah massacre. It was a hoax, a ruse, a sham, and the deception continues to this day.

(March 25, 2013)

Ferdinand Edralin Marcos

A BRIEF HISTORY OF MARTIAL LAW

WHEN PRESIDENT FERDINAND MARCOS declared martial law in September 1972, I was then a 19-year-old Ateneo college dropout heading the Manila and Rizal organization of the Communist Party of the Philippines.

For its sinister reputation even at that time, the party was actually a rag-tag band of dreamy-eyed baby boomers who thought they could replicate the Chinese revolution: founder Jose Sison was then 33 years old and the legendary Kumander Dante, 29.

The fledgling party was giddy over the revolutionary flow of the student demonstrations in 1970, and thought it could artificially create such revolutionary fervor again. At the same time, it thought it could provoke the ruling class to internecine strife that would implode its rule.

Two teams of activists from the urban poor slums of Tondo and Caloocan — specially recruited for the operation by Sison and his five closest cadres — hurled three grenades at the stage of the Liberal Party's *miting de avance* in August 1971, injuring nearly all of the party's senatorial candidates and killing nine people, including photojournalist Ben Roxas and a five-year old child.

A veteran guerilla from Tarlac who had joined the newly formed New People's Army, and who had been close to the Liberal Party's superstar Senator Benigno Aquino, Jr. was responsible for the opposition leader's escape from the carnage. Aquino was told to delay his arrival in Plaza Miranda at the rally until "something important" happened.

The bombing was blamed on Marcos, who had become unpopular because of the massive student demonstrations against his administration and the opposition's unrelenting muckraking against him through their powerful media outlets the *The Manila Chronicle* and the ABS-CBN radio-television network.

The party's calculation at that time was that the Plaza Miranda bombing would intensify in what in Leninist jargon was "the split within the ruling class," so much so that Marcos would soon declare a hated martial law — and create a revolutionary situation chaotic enough for the communists to take over power.

However, the bombing finally convinced Marcos to impose martial law, the legality of which he had asked his then justice secretary Juan Ponce Enrile to study as early as 1969. Marcos imposed martial law in 1972, after a year of meticulous preparation, during which he convinced the military establishment and his closest allies in the ruling class that it was the only way to save the Republic "from the Left and the Right."

Split the ruling class

The party was caught flat-footed when martial law was imposed. Many of its top leaders were arrested or killed in a few months' time. In my case, after romanticizing urban guerilla warfare, my comrades and I found ourselves armed exactly with one rusty Thompson and two carbines of World War II vintage.

With my late wife Raquel and our 18-month-old daughter, I was captured six months later in a dawn raid by the Philippine Constabulary's 5th Security Unit, to spend two years in Marcos' prisons.

That expectation that the "split within the ruling class" would intensify turned out to be monumentally inaccurate.

Marcos suppressed only a small faction of it that was his avowed enemy years before. This consisted mainly of the powerful Lopez, Osmeña, and Roxas-Araneta political and economic elite.

Few among the elite sympathized with the Lopezes, which owned the Meralco monopoly, and arrogantly wielded its deadly media weapons as well its political power (Fernando Lopez was Marcos' vice president).

Even the big guns of the Cojuangco clan, Ramon and Eduardo, cousins of Corazon Aquino, the figurehead of the anti-Marcos revolt a decade later, were among Marcos' loyal supporters.

Ramon Cojuangco even allegedly dummied for Marcos's controlling shares in the telephone monopoly PLDT, which Marcos acquired when the American owners sold the firm to Filipinos in 1967, two years after he became president.

Ramon's son Antonio, however, would later (after Marcos fell in 1986) claim that his family was the real owner of the shares. The Supreme Court in two separate decisions would rule that a part of the shares were indeed the Cojuangcos' but another part was owned by Marcos.

Eduardo, the political kingpin in Central Luzon, was given control of the vast though backward coconut industry, in order to modernize it.

This project was aborted in 1983, but it led him to buy in 1983 from the Ayala-Soriano clan the controlling shares of then beer monopoly San Miguel Corp.

Most of the Philippine elite embraced and supported Marcos' "constitutional authoritarianism", a drastic departure from the US-imposed system of electoral democracy that had largely failed the nation. After all, strongman or single-party rule was the norm in Asia in the 1960s and 1970s, which was seen as necessary to enable these countries to develop swiftly, as in fact the so-called East Asian tiger economies did.

Economy surged

As such, Marcos' strongman rule was not so strange, and certainly not abhorrent to the ruling elite that preferred peace and order rather than democratic rituals, which after all were simply intramurals among the political elites and the politically-involved magnates.

Whether it was because of Marcos' "Green Revolution" or simply because the International Rice Research Institute was luckily located in the country, production of the high-yielding Masagana 99 rice it developed zoomed during martial law. The yields were so high that the prices of this staple food fell, the most important factor for a contented populace.

Most Filipinos acquiesced to martial law for the "peace and order" it achieved so quickly in its first years, as the economy surged from 1972 to 1980 at an average annual growth rate of 6 percent. The growth rate for 1973, the first full year of martial law, as well as for 1976, was 9 percent, an astounding pace never beaten to this day.

Vicente Paterno, chair of the Board of Investments, then trade and industry secretary and finally public works secretary, was at the forefront in rallying the support of ethnic Filipino big-business groups for Marcos.

The revered Carlos Romulo, the only Filipino elected president of the United Nations General Assembly, was Marcos' foreign secretary until his retirement in 1984. His two sons Ricardo and Roberto would become legal and business luminaries during martial law through the post-Marcos period. Many of the Supreme Court justices since 1980 had their legal careers jump-started during martial law.

Marcos plucked from the UP academe Finance Secretary Cesar Virata and Budget Secretary Jaime Laya, who would lead a corps of technocrats in the bureaucracy. They were given almost full authority and autonomy in running the economy, to the hosannas of the business sector.

Marcos recruited a core of ideologues and eminent writers — respected academicians and columnists now — who fleshed out his vision of a "New Society" and wrote his speeches as well as his history of the Philippines, *"Iginuhit ng Tadhana."*

Fr. Jose Cruz, S.J., president of the Ateneo for most of martial law, was Marcos' spiritual adviser. UP president Onofre D. Corpuz got poorly paid academics fat paychecks working for Marcos' think-tanks such as the Development Academy of the Philippines.

AIM and Opus Dei

Philippine businessmen's revered "Yoda," Washington SyCip, recommended to Marcos his protégé, Roberto V. Ongpin, who would be the strongman's very effective trade and industry head. It was during martial law when SyCip's brainchild, the Asian Institute of Management, established in 1968, grew as a center for Philippine technocrats and big business executives.

Funded by the richest tycoons during martial law, AIM trained an entire corps of military officers in management, not only improving the efficiency of Marcos' apparatus for rule but also giving these officers second careers in top management positions in the private sector after their mandatory military retirement at 56.

It was also during martial law that Opus Dei's Center for Research and Communications grew to become the University of Asia and the Pacific, because of the support, especially financial, of three Opus Dei stalwarts who ran the corporations of Imelda's brother Benjamin "Kokoy" Romualdez.

It was our economic and ideological elite that embraced and supported the martial law regime, and made up its main pillar, as much as the military did.

The communists had not at all expected that the economy would surge up to 1979, which would allow Marcos to crush his enemies, and rule for so many years.

The Philippine ruling class junked Marcos only when the economy collapsed in 1983 and their wealth shrank.

But the sparks of the eventual economic conflagration began much earlier, in the 1970s, after the Arabs took back the oil fields from the Western "imperialists" and found themselves awash in what would be dubbed "petrodollars".

Western bankers recycled this new money into quick and cheap loans to Third World countries. For the first time, poor countries such as those in Latin America and in Asia were deluged with easy loans purportedly needed to finance their development.

But then, the Iranian Revolution broke out in 1979 and the Iran-Iraq War in 1980. These triggered an oil crisis that pushed up interest rates worldwide.

In 1981, a banking crisis broke out when textile tycoon Dewey Dee absconded on his loans from private as well as state banks. The second global oil crisis broke out in this same period, eventually leading to the 1983 debt default, and an economic conflagration that had the GDP shrinking by an unprecedented 7 percent annually.

Global Debt Crisis

Countries in debt, including the Philippines, had to take out new loans just to pay interest on previous loans, thus falling deeper and deeper into debt. In 1982, Mexico and several other Latin American countries defaulted on their loans, creating the global debt crisis.

Aquino's return in August 1983 to the Philippines couldn't have been made at a worse time — and he was keenly aware of this, thus the huge risk he took in returning to Manila. Interest rates were going through the roof, eating into the country's dollar reserves so fast that the Central Bank falsified data to conceal their low levels.

The political instability in the wake of Aquino's assassination accelerated the economy's collapse. In October 1983 the country ran out of dollars to service its loans, and defaulted on its debts, financially isolating it from the world.

The GDP collapsed by an unprecedented 7 percent in 1984, and in 1985, the peso's value crumbled from P9 to P20 to the dollar, and inflation surged by a riot-in-the-streets rate of 50 percent in 1984. No president could have survived such an economic catastrophe.

The elite suddenly became freedom-lovers, donning yellow Lacoste shirts and joining street protests, to demand that Marcos step down. People power was based on a bad economy's propensity to convince people to overthrow their government.

The US junked its support for the strongman and undertook clandestine moves to put Cory Aquino into power. It feared that the internecine fight between the pro-Marcos and the anti-Marcos factions would give an opportunity for the communists to grab power.

The Americans calculated (wrongly as it would turn out) that its support for the revolt against Marcos would create so much goodwill for it that the Philippines would allow its military bases (deemed crucial in the Cold War with Russia and in the wake of China's rise) to remain in the country past the Military Bases Agreement's expiration in 1992.

Just like the US government, the Philippine ruling class cleverly, and rather swiftly, abandoned its support from Marcos just as the Cojuangcos were set to capture political power in 1986.

Same oligarchs

The narrative of the House of Cojuangcos and the Yellow Cult regarding the martial law era comprises a Dark Lord imposing his will on a hapless people, with a Messiah sacrificing his life to embolden Filipinos to topple that regime in 1986.

That's an utter fairy tale. It is an old, overused storyline of the Lord-of-the-Rings kind of movies, believed as true by small minds to explain the past. But reality is always, and in all ways, more complicated.

After 42 years Filipinos have grown up, and have become tired of that old fairy tale. We are even often depressed at the unhappy reality we face:

We see mainly the same oligarchs, or their children or grandchildren, ruling the land, even as a fourth of the nation's citizens live in utter poverty and abject misery, while those just above their station in life are killed in broad daylight or in their homes in a country run by incompetent buffoons.

They have even become more powerful.

Just take a look at the latest Forbes' list of Filipino billionaires. They are mostly the same tycoons you would read in the business pages of newspapers during the Marcos era.

Yes, there are entirely new faces, even dwarfing in power these pre-martial law tycoons, the most prominent of which is Manuel V. Pangilinan, who controls the country's strategic utility firms in power, communications, water, and infrastructure despite this being a clear violation of the Constitution.

Pangilinan though is not a brown taipan, but an executive of the regional conglomerate built by Indonesian strongman Suharto's crony Sudono Salim (Liem Sioe Liong) and his son Anthoni after they fled their country when it was going through its own kind of "EDSA 1" revolt in 1997.

Before martial law, we had the oligarch clan, the Lopezes, controlling Meralco. During martial law it was Marcos who controlled it. The People Power Revolution handed it back to the Lopezes, who gave it up to a group controlled by the Indonesian Salim, who has had no qualms remitting its huge profits first to Hong Kong and then probably to the Salim's British Virgin Islands and Liberia holding companies.

And what about the rest of Filipinos? Because of relentless population growth, the number of dirt-poor Filipinos, or those living on $1.25 or P55 per day, presently stands at 17 million. Only 2 million were lifted out of abject poverty since 1985.

This is what we have achieved as a result of electoral democracy?

(September 21, 2011, October 3, 2012, and September 24, 2014)

THE ELITE AND THE MILITARY SUPPORTED MARCOS

IF THAT ADAGE that "history is written by the victors is right' we have to posit that in the case of the Marcos' 13-year one-man rule, the victors — or the vanguard of the victors — were that faction of the elite the Ilocano politician had warred with, led by the Aquino-Cojuangco, Lopez, and Osmeña clans.

But what about People Power? After all, what radical regime change in history by a faction of the ruling class wasn't undertaken using the people, and purportedly by the people.

The rough drafts of history are to a great extent written by media. The Lopezes, the epitome of the landlord class Marcos suppressed through martial law, set up immediately their ABS-CBN broadcast network and the newspaper *The Manila Chronicle* a few months after Marcos' fall.

Journalists imprisoned and made unemployed for more than a decade by the strongman, their careers and high-standing in society suddenly cut short in 1972, rushed back to the scene with a vengeance and set up what would be the mainstream newspapers of today, which now largely form what people think.

The victors' narrative is that Marcos knew the 1935 Constitution barred him from running for a third term in 1973 so he declared martial law to extend his rule.

This narrative would be bolstered after Marcos fell when, with US help, his alleged Swiss bank accounts, Manhattan properties, and his ownership of shares in Philippine Long Distance Telephone Co., and other firms through dummies were uncovered.

Marcos purportedly parlayed for US support for martial law - his assurances that there would be an orderly withdrawal of US investments after the Laurel-Langley Agreement ended in 1974, with American companies even given legal loopholes to hold on to their lands.

Political fox that Marcos was, he knew the US would support his strongman rule since the American military bases in Subic and Clark were crucial to the US aggression in Vietnam, at its height at that time.

However, few remember that, unlike today, strongman rule was the norm in Southeast Asia at that time. This was seen as the only way to put in check the unwieldy democratic systems and then move swiftly into developing their economies. When Marcos declared martial law in 1972, South Korea's Park Chung-Hee was on his 10th year as dictator; Taiwan's Chiang Kai-shek on his 22nd year; and Singapore's Lee Kuan Yew on his 13th year. Indonesia's Suharto was on to his 5th year. Even the most developed country in Asia, Japan, was governed by a single party, the Liberal Democratic Party, which has held power from 1955 to this day (losing control in just two short periods).

Thailand had martial law — the real one in the classical sense of a country being ruled by the highest-ranking military commander — from 1963 to 1973 under Field Marshal Thanom Kittikachorn.

In this age of reason, however, we can spot anomalies in the victors' narrative to question some of its elements, hopefully to learn from history.

That most of the elites and their ideologues supported martial law, including the Ayalas, Sorianos, Concepcions, the Chinese-Filipino businessmen, local and foreign chambers of commerce, the Opus Dei, the Catholic Church then headed by Cardinal Jaime Sin, is a fact hardly mentioned in the current narratives. The cover story of the October 1977 issue of *Business Journal*, the official publication of US companies in the country was headlined: "New Society Provides Positive Atmosphere for Foreign Investors."

The Spanish-descended elite such as the Ayalas and the Sorianos were happy with their beer-monopoly San Miguel Corp., as well as their real estate business that boomed in the years after martial law was declared.

It was during martial law that the Ayalas' Makati became the country's premier business district. The Ayalas' first big push outside Makati, which energized it, was its development in 1980s of Ayala Alabang Village and commercial complex, the pet project of Enrique Zobel, who had not kept secret his support for Marcos.

What made that area attractive to the rich, in a dusty place known to be in the general area of the Bilibid National Prison? The South Superhighway, now known as SLEX, built in the 1970s and which opened up Las Piñas, Laguna, and even Cavite to gated-village developers who are now the country's richest property tycoons.

Note, too, it was the Ayalas with the Sorianos who sold at a premium over market prices in 1983, the country's premiere industrial corporation SMC to Eduardo Cojuangco, labeled by the anti-Marcos crowd as the dictator's principal crony.

Chinese-Filipinos

A Marcos policy helped create a new elite in this country: the wealthy Chinese-Filipino businessmen. Before martial law, acquiring Filipino citizenship had required substantial bribes, political connections, and many years of tedious legal procedures.

Marcos' Letter of Instructions No. 270 of 1975 changed all that. It allowed ethnic Chinese to become citizens in a few months' time, simply upon the President's signature, empowering them to own lands and enter industries constitutionally banned to foreigners, thereby releasing their entrepreneurial energies.

Indeed, Marcos' "instructions" led to the rise of today's new generation of Filipino taipans such as property and liquor billionaire Andrew Tan and plastics king William Gatchalian.

A Chinese-Filipino shoe merchant, Henry Sy, built his first department store in the 1970s. This became the prototype for his huge malls, the first of which, SM North EDSA, was opened in 1985, at the height of the Philippine economic crisis.

The Cebu-based Chinese-Filipino John Gokongwei moved to the booming metro Manila area to set up food processing factories and agribusinesses, and then quickly diversified to the building of shopping malls.

Why, even the Araneta Center, owned by the Roxas family that was supposed to be a Marcos enemy, was given a boost in 1975 when it staged the world famous Ali-Frazier fight "Thrilla In Manila."

One visible symbol of the business elite's support for Marcos was the Asian Institute of Management, founded in 1968 by Washington SyCip. Funded by the richest tycoons at that time, its glory days were during martial law.

AIM trained not just a new generation of executives but a corps of military officers that are now skilled in management. This not only improved the efficiency of Marcos' apparatus for rule but gave these officers second lives (top management positions in the private sector) after their mandatory retirement from the military at the relatively young age of 56.

Opus Dei institutions that became first the Center for Research and Communications and then the University of Asia and the Pacific, flourished with huge donations from three bankers who ran the corporations of the Imelda's brother Kokoy Romualdez.

The ruling classes are always opportunists and protective of their wealth. The global economic crisis broke out in 1981 following Latin American countries' default on their foreign loans. This event triggered our own debt default in 1983 and the ensuing economic holocaust that was so terrible the elites started to hate Marcos.

"Rolex 12"

Other than the elite's support for martial law, one important question is: Why did the military and police embrace Marcos' one-man rule?

Why did they support him for 13 long years, and abandoned him only in 1986, when it joined the elite who saw the strongman's downfall as the only viable exit out of the steep economic recession, and after the US got worried that Marcos had become the communists "biggest recruiter"?

The question is valid when one considers that the military's officers corps, mostly from the lower-middle classes from all over the country, were steeped in democratic principles. They were schooled in the Philippine Military Academy, which is patterned after the US West Point (its curriculum even has liberal arts subjects).

This is so unlike the officers' corps in many old European and Asian countries, which emerged from the feudal, warrior elites.

The victors' narrative was that a group they dubbed "Rolex 12" planned the imposition of martial law, because allegedly, Marcos gave them in gratitude gold Rolex watches on the eve of the historic event. The narrative's intent was to depict the group as a shadowy conspiratorial group that Marcos lavished with luxury watches.

But according to a December 1974 cable which was among the thousands released in wikileaks.org, then US Ambassador to Manila William Sullivan reported that Marcos gifted the 12 with personally-inscribed Omega watches during a ceremony in 1973. "Marcos chose to decorate the twelve men of defense establishment whom he described as instrumental in deciding and implementing martial law," Sullivan reported.

The other members of the group other than Enrile and Marcos' confidante Eduardo Cojuangco were AFP Chief of Staff Romeo Espino, Army Chief Rafael Zagala, PC chief Fidel Ramos, Air Force Chief Jose Rancudo, Navy Chief Hilario Ruiz, AFP Intelligence Chief Ignacio Paz, PC Metropolitan Command Alfredo Montoya, PC vice chief Tomas Diaz, National Intelligence Coordinating Authority chief Fabian Ver, and PC Rizal head Romeo Gatan.

That isn't at all a shadowy conspiratorial group, but the formal AFP leadership, the top brass of the military establishment, which undertook a precision planning for martial law.

Contrary to the caricature of drunk military men torturing innocent civilians suspected to be going against Marcos, the military that ran martial law was led by officers of the highest integrity.

Name any respectable, patriotic, and freedom-loving former military man you can think of, and he did the duty assigned to him in the operation that imposed martial law on the wee hours of September 23, and all other tasks assigned to him — for more than a decade until February 22, 1986 — when some elements of the Armed Forces mutinied.

Respected officers

The head of the military establishment was AFP Chief of Staff Romeo Espino, who became the longest-serving AFP head, from January 1972 up to 1981 when he retired. Espino has remained as one of the most distinguished and most respected generals in AFP history, with not a single corruption or human-rights case brought against him.

Former president Fidel Ramos headed almost during the entire period of Marcos' dictatorship, practically half of the country's armed forces that enforced martial law on the civilian population: the Philippine Constabulary, or what's now our Philippine National Police.

While Marcos appointed his cousin Fabian Ver as AFP Chief of Staff in 1981, he still made Ramos the AFP Vice Chief of Staff. It wasn't Marcos who issued the now-infamous Arrest Seizure and Search Orders (ASSO) against his perceived enemies. It was Ramos: I still have mine with his signature. The most effective unit that captured leaders of the opposition and the Communist Party was the PC's 5th Constabulary Security Unit, my captors.

Ramos' counterpart in the Army was Fortunato Abat, commanding general from 1976 to 1981, famous for "saving Mindanao," as is his book's title, from the Malaysian-funded Muslim insurgents. He is a respected ex-military man to this day. One of Ramos' most trusted deputies was the much–respected Renato de Villa who had been considered as the viable presidential candidate to succeed him as president.

Look at this short list: Jose Almonte (Philippine Military Academy, Class of 1956), Eduardo Ermita ('57), Rodolfo Biazon ('61), Angelo Reyes ('66), Reynaldo Wycocò ('68), Voltaire Gazmin ('68), Hermogenes E. Ebdane ('68), Gregorio Honasan ('71), Panfilo Lacson ('71), Edgar B. Aglipay (71), Jaime de los Santos ('73), Alexander B. Yano ('76), and Delfin Bangit ('78). These are just some of the military men of unquestionable integrity that were in the armed forces in various levels of command during martial law.

Most, if not all, of the generals who bravely signed that recent open letter to President Benigno Aquino III, explaining to him that the Bangsamoro Basic Law will dismember the Republic, were with the military that supported Marcos' one-man rule.

Marcos had justified martial law on grounds that the Right (by which he mainly meant the Aquinos, Lopezes, and Osmeñas) and the Left (the nascent Maoist Communist Party of the Philippines) had formed an alliance to topple the Republic. He was duty-bound, as his Proclamation 1081 itself put it, to save the Republic.

The reason why the military supported martial law was that it believed that justification by Marcos.

Among others, two developments convinced them Marcos was right in claiming that the Republic was under siege from the extreme Right and the extreme Left: the Jabidah Massacre Hoax and the Plaza Miranda Bombing. The author of the first was the Liberal Party and the second, the Communist Party.

(September 20, 2015)

LIBERAL AND COMMUNIST PARTIES PROVOKED MARTIAL LAW

FOR ALL THEIR self-righteous "Never Again" mantra and their odium against Ferdinand Marcos, it was the Liberal Party and the Communist Party of the Philippines that provided the excuse for the strongman to impose martial law, and to perpetuate himself in power beyond his constitutional term.

How?

The Liberal Party's so-called "Jabidah" investigations in 1968 and the Communist Party's bombing of that party's *miting de avance* on August 21, 1971 convinced the military — and most of the Filipino body politic — that our democratic institutions were an utter failure, and the elites a traitorous and opportunistic group.

I explained in minute detail in previous columns why the so-called "Jabidah Massacre" of March 1968, supposedly of several young Muslims who were being trained to infiltrate Sabah and who mutinied against their Special Forces army officers and were allegedly executed, was all a big lie, a giant hoax.

Dozens of hearings both in the Senate and in Congress in March and April were undertaken to uncover the supposed killings. The Liberal Party's brightest minds such as Jovito Salonga, Ambrosio Padilla, and Benigno Aquino Jr., and aggressive Muslim congressmen such as Speaker Pro Tempore Salipada Pendatun and Lanao del Sur representative Rasid Lucman grilled the military to admit to the massacre.

Even AFP Chief of Staff Manuel Yan and then Army commander Romeo Espino (who would become Chief of Staff in 1971) were summoned to the hearings.

If one reads the transcripts of the investigations at the hearings in 1968 in the Senate and House of Representatives, it was a circus as much as they were a kangaroo court.

In the end, when it was obvious that there was no such massacre, the Liberal Party quietly distanced itself from it, and the entire affair vanished from the front pages replaced by the heat of the 1969 elections.

Members of the Senate committee investigating the Corregidor incident, left photo, question Capt. Jose O. Sta. Romana of the judge advocate general's office at the resumption of the hearing yesterday. Sta. Romana submitted to the senators a copy of the Corregidor trainees' petition for pay, which reportedly touched off the alleged "mutiny." On panel are, from vito R. Salonga, Magsaysay, and na.

3 'lost' trainees alive

They deserted training camp, Almendras says; all named

By Isagani Yambot

Three of the missing 26 Muslim trainees deserted camp and are alive.

This was disclosed yesterday by Sen. Alejandro

Dugasan, was with them when they left but he returned to army control la

Benigno S. Aquino Jr and former Ambassador Amelito Mutuc, counsel for

proper time he would present before the investigating committees the man who took the four Muslim trainees in a banca from

Manila Times article, when the hoax started to be uncovered.

The press then was worse than today and sensationalized every single allegation. A *Manila Times* banner story on April 18 screamed, "I was there: Witness Bares Killings," which even identified seven supposed military executioners of the Muslim recruits. The next day, in smaller headline types, appeared the story: "Ahid [the "witness"] changes story." He never saw any killings, he just heard three shots in the evening.

The Liberal Party wanted to prove in the Jabidah hearings that the Army's Special Forces massacred "many" Muslim trainees, even after searches could not find a single corpse.

Only a lone dubious witness claimed there was such a massacre in the botched military operation called "Merdeka." The operation was purportedly to infiltrate commandos into Sabah to organize its Tausug residents to rebel against the Malaysian Federation.

Why would they do that? In 1968, Marcos became aggressive in pushing the Philippine claim that Sabah is part of its territory.

The Sultan of Sulu gave Marcos the authority to pursue his proprietary claims, and talks with Malaysia were scheduled later that year on the claim, the last attempt before it would file a suit at the International Court. Marcos just was about to sign a bill that redefined the Philippines' territorial baselines to include Sabah.

It was a 180-degree turnaround however for Marcos, who earlier seemed disinterested in the Sabah claim, compared to his predecessor Diosdado Macapagal whom he had defeated in the 1965 elections.

Marcos in 1968 now projected himself as a nationalist and as the Philippine president who would win back Sabah for the nation. That would have foiled the Liberal Party's campaign (with the help of the Lopez media entities after his vice president Fernando Lopez broke ties with him) to portray him as a corrupt leader.

The Jabidah "scandal" torpedoed Marcos' project to take back Sabah. Allegations that Muslims were killed when they refused to infiltrate Malaysia — a lie, as it turns out — reached such scandalous proportions that Sabah's first governor Tun Mustapha was able to convince his Malaysian superiors to refuse all talks to settle the Sabah dispute.

Worse, Mustapha retaliated by financing and training militarily the first officers' corps of what would become the top Islamic secessionist group, the Moro National Liberation Front.

Sabah claim forgotten

After the hoax was exposed, Congress and the Press mostly controlled by the opposition lost all interest in anything involving Sabah and the Philippine claim.

The Liberal Party, which portrayed itself as the nation's hope at that time to defeat a corrupt president in the 1969 elections, demonstrated to Filipinos that they were willing to sacrifice national interests for their political ends. They willingly threw the country under the bus, so long as they were able to blacken Marcos' reputation and foil his chances of winning as a re-electionist.

Aquino Jr. was cunning: Even as he knew that there was no massacre as he himself interviewed the young Muslims who were supposed to have been killed, he still gave a sensationalist speech in the Senate, which bared to the world, including Malaysia, that there was an army operation to claim Sabah by force.

That the military was disillusioned with democracy's institutions was demonstrated in a full-page advertisement in newspapers in April 1968 that expressed the accused military men's anger and frustration, in the form of an Open Letter to the President. That such a manifesto was made public was something never before done by active military personnel.

Dramatically titled, "Last Will and Testament of a Soldier," the letter among other points, called the Senate an "Inquisition" that judged them guilty without fair hearings, and that the "probes were pre-set" to make them look like "scoundrels." It said that the Senate had put the entire "AFP on trial" and perhaps ominously that they would rather "accept death, not dishonor."

With military men feeling that way, angry with the Senate, which is supposed to be a pillar of democratic government, it wasn't really difficult for Marcos to convince them to destroy that institution four years later.

After Marcos won re-election in 1969, and the "Jabidah" issue as well as our Sabah claim were all but forgotten, massive student demonstrations on a scale never before seen rocked the country at the start of 1970.

It was called the First Quarter Storm. Communist Party Chairman Jose Ma. Sison plagiarized the name from Mao Zedong who called the capture of the Shanghai municipal government by his Red Guards in 1967 at the height of his Great Proletarian Cultural Revolution "the January Storm."

However, unlike the Cultural Revolution that would continue for two more years, the revolutionary flow launched by the First Quarter Storm ebbed towards the end of 1970.

Sison was faced a with a huge problem. He had convinced Mao through his official in charge of exporting revolution, Vice-Chairman Kang Sheng, that the Philippines was ripe for revolution and just needed arms.

Kang ordered the country's fledgling arms industry to reverse-engineer and then manufacture 100,000 US M-14 rifles (which couldn't be traced to China) for delivery to the communist armed wing, the New People's Army. The test run for the arms shipment was scheduled in 1972.

But who would use the rifles? Only a small part of the youth of the First Quarter Storm embraced communism and joined the New People's Army (NPA). With things normalizing by the end of 1970, and so many "reformist organizations" rather than radical ones emerging out of that First Quarter Storm, the NPA wasn't exactly expanding by leaps and bounds.

Sison's solution: Following Lenin's teachings, exacerbate the "split within the ruling class" and help worsen their internecine strife so as to create a chaotic situation that would push the youth to the folds of the proletarian vanguard, and its army, the NPA.

That "operationally" meant worsening the fight between Marcos and his Nacionalista Party, on one hand, and Aquino and his Liberal Party on the other hand. The timing was perfect as senatorial elections were scheduled in November 1971, and the political climate was heated.

Communists bomb Plaza Miranda

On the evening of August 21, 1971, just as the Liberal Party was having its first speakers for its *miting de avance* for the senatorial elections that year, three two-man teams made up of urban-poor activists recruited into the Communist Party lobbed grenades to the stage.

The explosives killed a 5-year-old child and *The Manila Times* photographer Ben Roxas. They also wounded most of the Liberal

Party's candidates; except of course its star candidate Benigno Aquino who mysteriously wasn't around.

The Communist Party the very next day had leaflets and posters distributed which had cartoons of Marcos wearing a Hitler-moustache and dubbed "the mad bomber." The Liberal Party of course blamed Marcos, and only one senatorial candidate, Eddie Ilarde, was intelligent enough, or had the integrity, to claim that Marcos couldn't have been so stupid to do something he'd be blamed for.

When the arms shipment on a rickety ship M/V Karagatan sent by Mao arrived in July 1972, the NPA could muster only two squads to get them so that they were easily beaten back by Philippine Army troops and had to escape with only 200 of the 1,500 rifles landed.

Instead of creating another "revolutionary flow" as Sison had planned, what the Plaza Miranda bombing did was to convince the military establishment that the communists had become so ruthless and so cunning it could not be defeated through the democratic system.

How could they exterminate the NPA when it could use Hacienda Luisita as a refuge, when it could forge alliances with anti-Marcos political warlords, when media was controlled by a faction of the elite that was against Marcos, and with the very popular senator Ninoy reportedly being the communists' patron and who was allowed to evade the Plaza Miranda bombing?

By early 1972 the military establishment — which included AFP Chief of Staff Romeo Espino, Philippine Constabulary chief Fidel Ramos, Army Chief Rafael Zagala, Air Force Chief Jose Rancudo, and Navy Chief Hilario Ruiz and five others who were with the group dubbed the "Rolex 12" — had already agreed to impose martial law in the second half of the year.

Marcos though was clever enough, with the help of intellectuals like Onofre Corpuz and Adrian Cristobal, to formulate a bigger vision for the country beyond the need to defeat the communists.

As one who identified himself as Emilio Marayag wrote in the comments section of one of my columns:

"I was a new cadet when Martial Law was declared. Looking back I believe the main reason why the military supported Marcos was that he had a clear strategy to make the country great again: the revolution from the center strategy. Military men love to follow leaders who have a clear strategy to attain a noble objective."

Sison's Plaza Miranda bombing gave Marcos the perfect immediate excuse to impose martial law on September 21, 1972 (it was announced to the public on September 23).

By 1979 at the peak of his power, popularity, and wealth, Liberal Party leader Ninoy Aquino was in jail and so was Sison, thanks to the martial law they helped provoke.

(September 23, 2015)

HELPED BY COMMUNISTS, OLIGARCHS DEMONIZED MARCOS

I'VE WRITTEN SEVERAL columns debunking the Yellow Cult's distortion of the history of the Marcos era, certainly not to defend the strongman.

Rather, by exposing their deception over Marcos' demonization, the basic problems of the country can be revealed as clear as day: a greedy oligarchy unconcerned over, even blocking, the redistribution of assets and radical basic reforms that could improve the lives of majority of Filipinos.

Other strongmen in Asia who had much worse human rights records had not been similarly demonized.

Two of these are Indonesia's Suharto, whose 32-year regime was responsible for over 500,000 Indonesians of Chinese ethnicity killed in an anti-communist pogrom and South Korea's Park Chung Hee, with his infamous, dreaded Korean Central Intelligence Agency that was notorious for its torture and kidnapping of those who opposed the strongman.

After Suharto was forced out of power in 1998, he lived a peaceful retirement unbothered, until his death in 2008, at the age of 86. Singapore's Lee Kuan Yew, and Mahathir Mohamad of Malaysia and other Asian leaders paid their respects at his deathbed.

Assassinated after 16 years in power, Park has been revered in his country with even a Presidential Library and Museum set up in 2012 to honor him. His daughter, Park Geun-hye, was elected the first female president of South Korea in 2013 serving until her impeachment and removal four years later.

Why, in contrast, has Marcos and his rule been painted so black, that none of his accomplishments are recognized, and that there is even opposition to his remains' burial at the military's official cemetery? (That martial rule wasn't all bad is indisputable: the average GDP growth rate during Martial Law — excluding the recession from 1983 to 1985 — was 5.6 percent, higher than under Cory Aquino, when the pace of growth was at 3.4 percent and Ramos, at 3.5 percent.)

There has been a practical reason for Marcos' demonization. It was a major project, ironically, by both the Communist Party of the

Philippines and the oligarchy, to advance their respective agendas.

The communists' objective was to expand the organization and get sympathizers in a country extremely anti-communist because of Catholic Church dogma (that the communists were atheists) and the US cold war propaganda. And to them the only way to achieve that was to portray the Marcos regime as a ruthless, fascist state.

Mao plagiarized

Sison realized early enough that its political program, encapsulated by the slogan plagiarized from Mao Zedong's writings, to wit, the toppling of "US imperialism, feudalism and bureaucratic-capitalism" would never rouse the masses to revolution.

The massive student demonstrations in the first quarter of 1970 were a big lesson for the communists. These broke out not because of protests against the US bases, landlordism, or corruption, but because of the alleged police brutality against student demonstrators that occurred at Congress right after Marcos delivered his 1970 State of the Nation Address, gaslighted by sensationalist media coverage.

Learning from that episode, the Communist Party undertook the Plaza Miranda bombing of the Liberal Party's *miting de avance* in August 1971, and blamed it on Marcos to depict him as a ruthless fascist. The Liberal Party knew it wasn't Marcos, but played to the communist's script because that portrayed them as the helpless victims of Marcos' ruthlessness. As a result, the Liberal Party won five of the eight senatorial elections seats in the elections two months later.

Middle-class organizations and clerics supported the Communist Party and its front organizations, not because they believed in Marxism-Leninism, nor in the communist-led "National Democratic Revolution," but because they were hoodwinked by communist propaganda that Marcos was a fascist in the same mold as Hitler or Mussolini, and that it was their moral duty to fight the regime.

Most of the reports on Marcos human rights abuses have been by communist cadres.

One "victim," who seems to delight in relating his torture story of how his penis was electrocuted, headed the Party's dramatically called "Explosives Movement," which developed the NPA's lethal mines that horribly killed or maimed Philippine Army troopers. Lethal mines are now considered by the civilized world as weapons against humanity.

The Indonesian communists couldn't do what the Filipino communists did — exploit Suharto's human rights abuses — because they were literally exterminated by the strongman in 1965-1966. Suharto's atrocities would come to light only in the 1980s.

In contrast, except in cases where they were killed in firefights with the military, most Filipino communists were released from the Marcos prisons to rejoin the armed struggle or head up the legal fronts of the CPP.

Significantly, CPP head Jose Ma. Sison, a former English teacher and frustrated writer, wasn't a communist theoretician or a mass leader. His skill was in demagoguery and propaganda.

Thus, the Party's propaganda and intellectual assets have been fixated almost totally on projecting Marcos and his successors as American-supported fascist regimes: e.g., US-Marcos, US-Aquino, US-Ramos, which must be overthrown by force. So much so that apart from the slogans on "agrarian reform" and "anti-imperialism" few people know what they stand for now.

The Left has even practically abandoned the working class, allowing President Benigno Aquino III to boast that there had practically been no labor strike and that the communist movement had gained no amount of significance under his term (excluding Hacienda Luisita, of course.)

Class rule

Why would the oligarchy want to demonize Marcos? Because that conceals their greedy class rule, unchanged since the nation was born. Blaming has distracted us from looking at the real basic problems of the nation, which is the oligarchs' unequal hold over productive assets.

A perfect example is the Ayala clan, who cleverly portrayed themselves as being anti-Marcos after 1986, with its propaganda coup having its patriarch Don Jaime Zobel de Ayala joining Cory Aquino's rallies in 1985-1986. But it had as well Enrique Zobel, an avid Marcos supporter, the one who actually led the Ayala conglomerate's phenomenal growth during Martial Law.

Why wouldn't the Ayalas have supported Marcos? The South Luzon Expressway Marcos built opened up the vast Alabang areas, which the Ayalas owned, for Ayala's residential and commercial development.

Without their monopoly status (Marcos classified the beer industry as "overcrowded"), San Miguel Corp., which the Ayalas with the Sorianos owned until 1983, couldn't have become the country's biggest conglomerate at that time. (And when for some reason, Marcos allowed Lucio Tan to enter the beer industry in 1982, the Chinese businessman was called a crony by the oligarchs!)

These are only glimpses of the oligarchs' support for the Marcos regime: most of them, of course, condemned him when he fell.

The Lopezes, the country's epitome of the country's political-economic-cultural elite, were one of the few oligarchs Marcos attacked, as they were the most involved in politics and had the resources to overthrow him.

In just weeks after they returned from exile, President Cory Aquino turned over to them the power distribution monopoly, Meralco, payment for which allegedly did not include its huge martial law capital investments. They moved fast into power-generation and water services with huge loans from the state-owned Development Bank of the Philippines (DBP). The DBP wrote off P1.6 billion in loans to Lopez firms in the last decade.

The Lopezes' ABS-CBN Network has been a powerful molder of the Filipino mind since 1986, and, therefore, a most effective tool for Marcos' demonization. It was sweet revenge for the Lopezes: How dare a politician from the poor North, married to a commoner from Leyte, which was the source of the sugar industry's near-slaves called sacadas, imprison the Lopezes and the Osmeñas, the vanguards of the country's sugar oligarchy?

In contrast, Indonesia's Suharto had not attacked any oligarch when he grabbed absolute power in 1965, except his predecessor's military men and the Indonesian Communist Party. Although his regime killed thousands of Indonesians of Chinese ethnicity suspected of being communists or communist sympathizers, Suharto made cronies out of the rich Chinese, such as Soedono Salim, giving them lucrative monopolies. As a result, when Suharto fell in 1998, there were no powerful oligarchs like the Lopezes in our country who went after him, in life and in death, and demonized him.

Aquino-Cojuangco oligarchy

What kind of oligarch rule was restored? The Aquino-Cojuangco oligarchy managed to impose a fake agrarian reform option, "corporatization," or the fraudulent transformation of farmers into shareholders of a firm "owning" the hacienda. The clan would block its hacienda from being put under real agrarian reform for 25 years, until the Supreme Court ruled against it in 2011 and 2012 — costing Renato Corona his Chief Justice post. Such has been the power and greed of the Philippine oligarchy.

Because of their demonization of Marcos, the oligarchs made us believe that the country's basic problem involves entirely the President, whether he is corrupt or not. Most Filipinos still have that view.

Prodded by Western governments and big businesses, the oligarchs have succeeded in creating an economic policy environment, in which they were basically allowed to do what they wanted, justified under the ideology euphemistically called "neoliberalism," but which means nothing but unbridled capitalism.

This has resulted in such things that hinder our development as weak government revenues, because of massive tax evasion by the oligarchy, and the consequent underinvestment in quality education for the masses and infrastructure.

Under oligarchic rule, there has been, of course, a dearth of reform that would have converted part of their super-profits into better wages and living conditions for workers. The country's inheritance laws merely transfer one oligarchic generation's wealth intact to the next generation, perpetuating their rule.

It has resulted in the weakening of the state apparatus so much so that oligarchs had for decades captured regulatory bodies, among them the Energy Regulatory Commission, the Securities and Exchange Commission, and the National Telecommunications Commission.

The most scandalous instance of such regulatory capture has been the Indonesian oligarch Anthoni Salim's building of a Philippine conglomerate in the public utilities sector — a sector in which foreign ownership is limited, as mandated by the Constitution.

President Fidel Ramos had deregulated the telecoms industry in 1992, leading to its turnover to Indonesia's Salim and Singapore's Singtel.

(September 29, 2016)

MARTIAL LAW HISTORY IS THE PROPAGANDA OF THE VICTORS

IN A SPAN OF a lifetime, and with regard to the Marcos era, we are seeing the truth of a quote attributed to Bavarian playwright Ernest Toller: "History is the propaganda of the victors."

Winston Churchill revised that to the more well-known: "History is written by the victors."

Consider what happened right after EDSA 1 in February 1986.

The Marcos camp was so stunned at how quickly the US, as well as military leaders Juan Ponce Enrile and Fidel Ramos, abandoned the strongman they supported for more than two decades, that they had to abandon their dinner and leave Malacañang. Even Eduardo Cojuangco, the most capable to lead the Marcos camp, joined the strongman in his flight out of Manila — to their Ilocos redoubt they very mistakenly thought.

They ended up in Hawaii, all treated as stateless refugees, with Marcos given a small slip of paper by the Immigration Service declaring he was the "State Department's guest". Gratitude isn't a value in US foreign policy.

Enrile and Ramos led the defection of the entire armed forces to Cory Aquino's camp. Without a leader (except perhaps for the aging Arturo Tolentino, who won the vice-presidential post in the 1986 elections), the "Solid North" acquiesced to the victors. After a few days insisting he was Marcos' legitimate successor, as he had been elected prime minister by parliament, Cesar Virata just stayed home, and started asking his World Bank and big business cronies for consultancy jobs.

The many, many businessmen, local politicians, and government officials that made up the political base of Martial Law all went home or abroad to enjoy their wealth.

Enter the victors, led by the houses of Cojuangco and Lopez.

Having run the biggest media empire before martial law as well as having been consummate politicians, the Lopezes were experts in propaganda, or rather, how to mold a nation's consciousness for its benefit.

Even Marcos had not been as skilled in, or as appreciative of, the value of propaganda as the Lopezes. When he was the victor after declaring Martial Law, his accusation that the Lopezes led the "extreme Right" that allied itself with the "extreme Left" never got traction.

The Lopezes in contrast were propaganda masters. The Marcos era was portrayed as an Asian equivalent of Nazi Germany, so that Filipinos forgot that it was oligarchs like the Lopezes who gave the strongman the excuse to impose martial law, and that it has been, and still is, a greedy oligarchy that is the root problem of the country.

The Lopezes financed the building of the Bantayog ng mga Bayani, which supposedly is where the heroes of the anti-Marcos struggle are commemorated in a monument mimicking the US Vietnam Veterans Memorial. Commission on Human Rights chairman Chito Gascon wants it to be converted into a P500 million museum on anti-Marcos "atrocities," to ape the many Holocaust Museums all over the world.

"The root of the Philippine quagmire is the Marcos era, and now his ideological descendant, which President Duterte allegedly is, not the rule of oligarchs." That has been the Martial Law history as written by the Yellow Cult.

The Yellows' "Never Again" slogan was even copied from the Jewish Defense League's now universal chant to protest the Holocaust in which six million Jews were exterminated by the Nazis. The principle of propaganda of course is to exaggerate to the extreme.

The heyday of the Marcos era — from 1972 to roughly 1979 — when GDP grew at an average of 6 percent, rice self-sufficiency was achieved, and massive infrastructure never before seen built was deleted from Filipinos' memory.

The Lopez-Cojuangco elite didn't find it so difficult to write their martial law history as propaganda, thanks to three groups.

The first group was the US "Deep State", which had scrambled to oust Marcos on the calculation that a grateful Cory Aquino would extend the presence of US military bases in the Philippines, when the bases treaty expired in 1991.

This group also used the EDSA 1 Revolt as its "Down-with-Dictators" template for getting the former Soviet Union satellite states into its camp: Poland's Lech Walesa and his Solidarity movement wrested power in 1989; Singing Revolutions broke out in Estonia, Latvia, and Lithuania in the Baltic states; an East German democracy movement surged that finally tore the Berlin wall down; and Czechoslovakia's Velvet Revolution erupted in late 1989. The template even nearly toppled

Chinese Communist Party rule through the so-called Democracy Movement that peaked in the Tiananmen protests, also in 1989.

US media and academia followed the US Deep State's wishes, with nearly all books on Martial Law, except those of Carmen Pedrosa and Primitivo Mijares, written by Americans.

Manufactured figures

In much the same way that the foreign-financed website Rappler spread its manufactured figure of 7,087 killed in Duterte's war against drugs (as of September 2016), it was an American scholar Alfred McCoy who had succeeded for three decades in propagating the lie that 3,257 people were summarily executed during Martial Law.

McCoy fabricated that figure, pretending to use empirical data.

Philippine academia has mostly been US academia's monkey, since those who occupy the highest posts in universities, get their PhDs from US universities. You don't get that degree and have your dissertation approved if you don't subscribe to their worldview. Strangely though, no Filipino academic has managed to write a history of the Martial Law period.

The second group that has helped the oligarchs in the manufacture of anti-Marcos history is media, more precisely a group of media men of the last generation. Media men, especially columnists, who occupied high standings in society suddenly found themselves out of work when Marcos closed down their newspapers and TV stations, with a few fleeing abroad, even to Australia.

Several wouldn't have reached such high standings in the profession after martial law, and would have been only feature or lifestyle writers, if they had not boldly written anti-Marcos articles during martial law.

Can you blame them if, after the dictator fell, they would come back to media with a vengeance? From 1987 to just a few years ago, Philippine print media has been dominated by the *Philippine Daily Inquirer* and the Philippine Star, both founded by anti-Marcos journalists whose editors don't hide how much they hate Marcos even as they idolize the Aquino-Cojuangco clan.

The third group responsible for the vitriolic anti-Marcos propaganda is the Communist Party and its fronts, whose dogma maintains Marcos was a ruthless dictator in the mold of Hitler, Mussolini, and banana-republic strongmen.

I frankly cannot understand why three decades after Marcos fell, the Left continues to be so fixated on Marcos. Is it because most of those they claim were human rights victims were in truth their members who were deeply involved in the armed struggle to topple Marcos, such as myself? Is it because they think that by invoking Marcos as a ruthless tyrant they fought, they can claim to be patriots and lead this generation of Filipinos?

Maybe we are a people after all who don't seem to care about history, as truthfully written. That has been, and could be our tragedy.

(September 20, 2017)

DAYS OF SHAME: AUGUST 21 — 1971 AND 1983

AUGUST 21 IS ONE of the most significant dates in our post-war history, when two historic, connected events happened, the consequences of which have made up our messy present.

Two dastardly crimes were committed on the same day, August 21. Two Aquino presidents, despite their huge resources and popularity when they were in office, refused to investigate to bring the killers to justice.

One incident on August 21, 1971 triggered events that led to the imposition of martial law and the start of Marcos' 13-year dictatorship. Another on the same calendar date 12 years later in 1983 triggered events that led to the fall of that dictatorship.

First Crime: Plaza Miranda bombing, August 21, 1971

Four grenades were hurled at the stage of the Liberal Party' grand *miting de avance*, killing nine and wounding 95 others. Many of the party's leaders and all of its senatorial candidates were seriously injured — except its "star" Benigno Aquino, Jr.

The bombing was blamed on President Ferdinand Marcos, and with his popularity already declining amid constant media attacks, public opinion largely believed so. As a result, most of the senatorial and congressional candidates from Marcos' party lost in the elections that year, drastically weakening his political strength.

Kept secret for decades, the bombing was revealed to have been the idea of, and ordered by the Communist Party of the Philippines chairman, Jose Ma. Sison, and executed by his most inner circle, called the party's Executive Committee of the Political Bureau.

Only Sison's inner circle (and the young activists who undertook the bombing, believing it was for a just cause) knew it was a Communist Party operation. Current Communist Party Chairman Benito Tiamzon, as well as everyone in the top leadership now, didn't know that the Plaza Miranda bombing was Sison's secret operation. (See, among other accounts, Gregg Jones' **Red Revolution: Inside the Philippine Guerrilla Movement** and the more recent **Secrets of the Eighteen Mansions** by Mario Miclat.)

Sison's motive: In the words used by communist party documents at that time, "to intensify the split within the ruling class" in order to create another "revolutionary flow." In ordinary language, the bombing would push the opposition Liberal Party and their supporters to strike back, even violently, at Marcos.

The country would be plunged into civil war, which the Communist Party as a very organized and armed force could take advantage of to capture power.

The Plaza Miranda attack was one of the events that convinced Marcos, and the military establishment to plan carefully and eventually impose Martial Law 13 months later.

Marcos, Defense Secretary Juan Ponce Enrile, the Armed Forces Chief of Staff Romeo Espino and all other service commanders were convinced that opposition leader Ninoy Aquino had allied with the communists and their armed wing, the NPA.

How else could one explain that Aquino was the only Liberal Party senatorial candidate who was spared from the attack since the grenades were exploded while Ninoy was still far from the Plaza?

He claimed later, according to one report, that he was with the powerful Laurel family in a nearby restaurant who were having a birthday celebration. He said he was delayed in going to Plaza Miranda since he was waiting for Cocoy Laurel's singing number to end.

There have been rumors though that the notorious NPA commander "Pusa," a Tarlac-based hit man known to be close to Aquino, warned him to delay his arrival at Plaza Miranda.

Few believed the most commonsensical question then: Why would Marcos, whom even his enemies credited as a brilliant strategist, undertake such an attack that obviously would be blamed on him?

Aquino and the Liberal Party didn't bother to pursue an investigation into the carnage, and instead roused public opinion against Marcos, as "The Mad Bomber," even after they took control of the Senate in the elections three months later.

Second Crime: Aquino assassination, August 21, 1983

The political instability triggered by that assassination combined with the economic downturn at that time, due to the global debt crisis, led to the country's worst recession ever.

With GDP contracting by seven percent each for 1984 and 1985,

Marcos' overthrow in 1986 became wellnigh inevitable, although it was obviously the aborted coup attempt against him and the massing of people at EDSA to defend the military rebels that plunged the dagger into the regime's heart.

Worse was that Marcos, largely unknown to the public, was suffering from kidney problems. On July 1983 he had a kidney transplant operation at the Kidney Center with his son Bongbong as the donor. According to Juan Ponce Enrile's biography, Marcos emerged from his bedridden state only on August 15, 1983.

For the first time in Marcos' eleven-year strongman rule, there emerged a major possibility that his life could abruptly end. This happened in a period when political and economic instability were building up, and his party sharply divided between the Enrile faction, and those of Imelda Marcos and Fabian Ver.

And it was during this time that Ninoy Aquino made moves for his return to the Philippines, as Jaime Cardinal Sin tipped him off that Marcos was dying. His journey ended with his assassination on August 21, 1983.

Few believed the most commonsensical question then: Why would Marcos, whom even his enemies credited as a brilliant strategist, undertake such an assassination that obviously would be blamed on him?

I find it astonishing that Aquino was killed with such precision, by a single bullet to the head. The habit taught to anyone who uses a gun, is to shoot at least three times, to make sure the target is incapacitated. But that's probably for amateurs.

I find it astonishing that it was done in broad daylight, even risking so many eyewitnesses (there was only one, the so-called "crying woman"). I find it astonishing that the alleged killer, Rolando Galman, was killed even before Aquino's body slammed on the tarmac.

It was an operation of such precision and utmost secrecy that Filipinos are not known for. Is it possible that the US CIA was involved in a covert operation? The CIA's documented record of interference in Latin American nations makes this not an impossibility.

What is also astonishing is the fact that despite the 12 years when Ninoy's widow Corazon Aquino and his son Benigno Aquino III wielded the tremendous powers of the Philippine presidency, they did nothing to unmask the murders' brains.

How difficult would it have been for the two powerful Aquino presidents to fund a crack group of investigators to unearth the truth?

A special three-judge court convicted in 1990 officers and soldiers, the highest ranking of whom was Brigadier General Luther Custodio, who headed the Aviation Security Command in charge of the security of the Manila International Airport, where Aquino was assassinated. The two other officers and the 13 enlisted men were convicted for life and jailed in the National Penitentiary in Muntinlupa.

Why couldn't then President Cory Aquino and then her son Benigno III offer them pardon — and maybe even money to live in security and comfort abroad — in exchange for identifying the brains of the murder that shaped our history?

Cory in a speech at the commemoration of the 19th death anniversary of her husband in 2002 in fact said: "Some of those behind the killing are holding positions in government." She did not give more details.

If she believed so why didn't she and then her son move heaven and earth, which they had the capacity to do so, to uncover the masterminds?

The only logical explanation I could think of is that the two Aquino presidents (in Cory's case as early as 1986) were informed, maybe even provided indisputable evidence, on who or what group, was the mastermind of Ninoy's murder.

But if it were Marcos, why did they not disclose this to the nation and provided the body of evidence, in order to totally demonize him beyond any historical revision?

Or was Cory told that if she made public the brains of her husband's murder, she would be so easily toppled by Enrile's RAM rebels, so that she just had to suffer quietly? After all, she probably would have been advised, her entire narrative of the widow going after her husband's murderer would collapse if she were to disclose the real mastermind.

There is another question that bothers me a lot. Was it just sheer coincidence that two historic events occurred on the same date?

I wonder. In what would be his death voyage, Aquino arrived in Taipei on August 19, 1983. But he booked his flight to Manila for two days hence, August 21.

Was the date of his return to the country some secret message to the dictator, one that only he and Marcos would understand?

(August 20, 2013 and August 21, 2016)

THE TRUTH BEHIND THE HUMAN RIGHTS ABUSES

AFTER FERDINAND MARCOS' downfall in 1986, it had been an unchallenged dogma that one of martial law period's horrid aspects was its human rights abuses. This again appears to be another instance proving true that adage: "The victors write the history."

This despite the data in an anti-Marcos book, **Rebellion and Repression in the Philippines** (1989: Yale University) by Richard Kessler that show human rights abuses during the regime of Corazon Aquino was just as bad as Marcos' record.

Ironically, Kessler's data have been the basis of the oft-repeated claims by a more rabid anti-Marcos American historian, Alfred McCoy, that the human rights abuses during the Marcos regime were worse than those in the infamous Latin American dictatorships.

McCoy wrote, "Marcos' tally of 3,257 killed exceeds those under the Brazilian and Chilean dictatorships." That 3,257 number had become the most-used figure to allege the ruthlessness of the Marcos rule.

An attention-hungry blogger turned cut-and-paste writer for instance, referred to McCoy's figures when she arrogantly asked Marcos' son Ferdinand Jr., when he ran for vice-president in 2016, that he first needs to apologize for "the 3,257 murders during his father's regime." Yellow believers have such a fixation on that number with one inane columnist writing that "3,257 is a number that chills the blood."

What these Marcos critics didn't bother to examine was Kessler's data, on which McCoy almost completely relied on for his report.

Quite ironically, Kessler presented his data in his book published in 1989, in order to hammer his point that human rights abuses had not at all subsided even when Cory Aquino assumed power until 1988, the last year for which data was available.

Kessler wrote (p. 136): "International groups, such as Amnesty International and the Lawyers' Committee for Human Rights, issued reports in 1988 that suggested that the human rights situation (under the Aquino regime) was at least as bad as it had been under Marcos. As table 5.1 indicates, human rights violations — always a problem in the Philippines — did not cease with democracy's return."

Demonstrating either his bias or his utter lack of real academic rigor,

McCoy did not even mention that Kessler presented his data mainly to show that human rights violations continued under Cory. The table (5.1) below, scanned directly from Kessler's book, shows the following: *(Table is unedited except for the arrows to emphasize that the data involves both the Marcos and Aquino regimes.)*

Insurgency and Counterinsurgency 137

TABLE 5.1
Human Rights Violations in the Philippines, 1975–1988

Year	Arrests	Disappearances	Extrajudicial Killings	
1975	—	9	3	MARCOS
1976	—	44	12	
1977	1,351	17	51	
1978	1,620	10	86	
1979	1,961	48	196	
1980	962	19	218	
1981	1,377	53	321	
1982	1,911	42	210	
1983	2,088	145	368	
1984[a]	3,038	137	445	
1985	7,253	213	517	
1986	1,712	43	197	AQUINO
1987	7,444	50	242	
1988[b]	1,726	82	117	

a. Figures for 1984 exclude Mindanao during November-December.
b. Preliminary figures, January 1–June 30.
Note: Figures do not include NPA killings.
Source: Task-Force Detainees–Philippines, *Philippine Human Rights Update* (Manila, monthly issues for periods covered).

Chart from ***Rebellion and Repression in the Philippines*** *(1989: Yale University) by Richard Kessler*

The figures show that human rights abuses continued under Cory Aquino. The 7,444 arrests in 1987 were even the highest recorded in the 14-year period.

Extrajudicial killings continued even during the regime of Aquino, data confirms, which flies in the face of her manufactured image as "squeaky-clean" and even "saintly" compared with the demonized Marcos.

The academics' partisanship and betrayal of their discipline is demonstrated, though, by the fact that they merely added all the cases during Martial Law. The number of disappearances and extrajudicial killings, therefore, from 1975 to 1985 totaled 3,164.

Again showing his anti-Marcos' bias, McCoy obviously thought this figure was low, so he looked for another source claiming a bigger number.

This was provided in another book by known leftists Verne Mercado and Mariani Dimaranan showing 93 more. Not explaining why he chose this higher figure, McCoy came up with that now infamous figure of 3,257 people killed under the Marcos regime.

But this figure means nothing if not compared with anything else. Kessler, in fact, presented his data for comparison with the first three years under Aquino, which I summarize in the following table:

HUMAN RIGHTS ABUSES UNDER THE 2 REGIMES		
	MARCOS: 1975-1985	AQUINO: 1986-1988
Total disappeared and extra judicial killings	3,257	731
Average per year	296	244
TOTAL arrests	21,561	10,882
Average per year	1,960	3,677

We would just be making an inane apples-and-oranges comparison if we just looked at the totals, since these do not take into account the fact that the Marcos cases span 11 years against Cory's three years.

To evaluate how bad the human rights situation really was during the comparative regimes, the average per year should be taken for the years under Marcos and those under Aquino.

The figures are shocking.

There were three times more arrests per year under Cory than under Marcos: 3,627 against 1,960. The average of those killed and disappeared during Cory's watch was 244 annually, which isn't too far from Marcos' 296.

Now, as they want Marcos Jr. to apologize for the human rights abuses under his father's government, shouldn't they ask President Benigno Aquino III and his sisters to apologize for the abuses during their mother's time?

This is, in fact, the reason why Kessler presented his statistics, to show that human rights violations continued under Cory, and may have even worsened.

In fact, before he presented his "dry" statistics, Kessler gave vivid examples of human rights abuses under Cory Aquino:

"In April 1987, a member of the United Farmers' Organization was kidnapped by a local vigilante in Cebu City, her body, with her head and leg hacked off, was recovered over a week later.

"In May, a thirty-year-old woman, eight months pregnant, and another young woman, disappeared. Their bodies were later discovered, headless and stabbed multiple times. That pregnant woman's abdomen had been slashed open and the fetus ripped out.

"One day in June, a farmer hoeing his field in Negros was attacked by several vigilantes, who accused him of being a Communist rebel. He was decapitated and disemboweled. They took the head of the local military commander who told them that the man was innocent. The head was abandoned in a ditch, to be recovered later by the man's wife." (Kessler, page 136)

As that blogger melodramatically claimed she cried as she cut and pasted reports of human rights abuses under Marcos, I hope she also shed a tear or two for such horrible killings under Aquino.

Vigilantism is the main fomenter of human rights abuses under any government. As Kessler explained in 1989, observing the first three years after Marcos fell:

"Vigilante groups had sprung up all over the country with the tacit or direct support of the military and the government during 1987 after a year of relative calm in the insurgency.

"In Mindanao were the Alsa Masa in Davao City, the Eagle's Squad, the United People for Peace; in Negros, the Philippine Constabulary Forward Command; and in Cebu, the Tadtad and the Citizens' Army against Communism; and even in Manila, the police began giving weapons' training to civilians forming neighborhood patrols."

Kessler concluded of the Cory Aquino regime: "The government appeared powerless to restore the rule of law."

Many Filipino academics have become highly partisan and too gullible that they believe all of McCoy's allegations and distortion of Kessler's data. Lacking academic vigor, they are too lazy to question McCoy's data and even accuse journalists like me who are seeking the truth that we "insult the memory of those thousands who were savagely killed."

Such attribution of motives to seekers of truth is so blatantly unacademic, a sign of an indolent mind. No wonder our academe is in such a sorry state.

(April 18, 2016)

NOTE:

Kessler is also a bit intellectually dishonest in that he claimed that the source of his table was the *"Task Force Detainees-Philippines, Philippine Human Rights Update"* (Manila, monthly issues for the periods covered).

This isn't accurate, as exactly the same table had come out in TFD's publications. This means that it wasn't Kessler who compiled the data for that table by poring over the TFD's monthly "Human Rights Updates." He simply copied the summaries provided by the TFD, and assumed the group was objective in its reports.

This is the bigger problem in estimating the real extent of human rights abuses during the Marcos era. There is no way now really to determine if the TFD's data, its sums for each year, are accurate and objective.

This is because TFD wasn't an objective observer. During Martial Law it was totally controlled by underground cadres of the Communist Party of the Philippines (CPP).

Communist activists released from prison routinely manned its offices before they went underground again in the 1980s. Trust me, I was a cadre at that time. The TFD is not an impartial or "highly regarded Catholic body" and instead is one of the legal fronts of the Communist Party.

Because Filipinos are rabidly anti-communist (due to US influence), the only way for the Communist Party to get them as allies was to portray Marcos' regime as so ruthless and evil. With the help of indolent and partisan academics, it seems the communists have succeeded.

INSIDE THE MARCOS PRISONS: A PERSONAL STORY

ANTI-MARCOS WRITERS routinely claim, in order to portray that human rights violations during martial law was horrific, that 50,000 Filipinos were detained during that regime. That figure is not supported by facts at all.

While thousands were indeed detained immediately following the declaration of martial law, most were held for only for a few days since the government wanted to make sure that there was little resistance to the new order. There is no evidence that the cumulative total of those detained (with most released) ever reached 50,000.

On the other hand, reports of the Amnesty International which has always been critical of martial law, point out that many of those detained in those first months were released a few months after, that by 1980 (the year for which data are available) there were only 1,913 political prisoners, and by 1981 — in the regime's effort to prove that martial law was indeed lifted — only 243.

I myself practically witnessed the drastic reduction of political prisoners after martial rule was stabilized. In December 1974, I was among about a thousand out of the 2,000 detainees released from detention centers in military camps in the "spirit of Christmas," according to Marcos.

The reality was that the populace already supported martial law by that time, Marcos' one-man rule was already entrenched, and there was no need for that many detainees.

Many of those released, like myself, chose to abandon the armed revolutionary movement, although many returned to the underground, even becoming top communist leaders and NPA commanders.

The related notion to the claim that 50,000 Filipinos were in prison during martial law is that Marcos' detention camps were so horrible that one crackpot author, who never saw an actual facility, claimed these were similar to Soviet's alleged horrific "gulag archipelago," the system of forced-labor camps mostly located in Siberia.

That is total rubbish, and I know what I speak of.

I was incarcerated in five Marcos detention centers for about a year and half, together with my late wife Raquel, from 1973 to 1974: the Philippine Constabulary's (PC) 5th Constabulary Unit in Camp Crame; that of the Intelligence Service of the Armed Forces of the Philippines (ISAFP) in Camp Aguinaldo; that of the National Intelligence Coordinating Authority in its headquarters at V. Luna Road in Quezon City (where it still is); as well as the Ipil Youth Rehabilitation Center and the maximum security Youth Rehabilitation Center, both in Fort Bonifacio — the latter two being the biggest during the martial law period.

For me and most other political prisoners of that time, the horror part of our saga, from which much of the tales of "torture" emanated, was our "processing period". These were the days right after our arrest when Marcos' intelligence services raced to extract from us information that could lead to the capture of our other comrades, especially the big fish.

I was arrested in July 1973, together with nearly all of the Communist Party's Manila-Rizal Regional Committee, which I headed. Several of the committee's members would, three decades later, constitute the core of the revolution's leadership, among them the party's chairman, now Benito Tiamzon, his wife Wilma, and secretary-general Adelberto Silva.

We were jailed for several weeks at the 5th Constabulary Security Unit's (CSU) headquarters in Camp Crame, all 20 of us in a cell roughly half the size of a regular classroom. A bucket at a corner was our urinal, so small that you had to kneel to piss in it and which got to be so stinky in the morning.

The cell was so cramped that we got into each other's nerves: I once lunged at Tiamzon for making fun of me meditating in the lotus pose, which I credited for keeping my sanity.

Such cells shocked our middle-class comrades, especially writers romanticizing themselves as glorious heroes of a Revolution, as they, of course, had seen nothing like those circumstances in their cloistered lives.

I, and my lower-class comrades, knew better. The PC cell was actually much better than the horrific bug-infested and crowded Marikina City Jail, where I spent three nights in 1970 when I was arrested, together with several other Atenean activists, for joining a labor strike at the Goya Chocolate factory in Marikina.

Class system in jail

Detention cells during Martial Law and after Martial Law are the same, with many in a much worse state than before, as seen in recent television news footages of crowded prisons in Quezon City and elsewhere.

Our society's class system, of course, was followed at the 5th CSU jail, as it is in every other prison. After several punches to my solar plexus and liver by soldiers who, I learned later, routinely slug a bottle of gin to fight off fear in operations against communists, I wasn't touched again, other than through a truth-serum session later at the headquarters of the army's intelligence services.

However, my bodyguard and other staff who were from the poorer classes were beaten up badly, sometimes just for fun by these soldiers to relieve their tension.

Again middle-class political prisoners are shocked by such beatings, which however, routinely occur today in detention cells in police precincts.

After a month, when the military felt they couldn't get any useful information from us, we were taken to join about 2,000 other detainees to the Ipil Rehabilitation Center at Fort Bonifacio, which was the regime's biggest detention center. As I entered Ipil, with its huge grounds, and seeing our other comrades, I think I heard choirs of angels singing hallelujah.

Ipil was nothing like the horrible detention centers ignorant anti-Marcos writers describe. I think this is the reason why the Yellow Cult, even with their absolute power in 1986, had not preserved — in the manner they have done with Ninoy's cells in Fort Magsaysay in Laur, Pangasinan — any detention center during Martial Law as these would conflict with their horror tales. I haven't found even a single photo of these centers.

Ipil was converted from a training school for non-commissioned officers, and consisted of five buildings, two of which were our barracks, another for the women detainees, which was separated by a gate from ours and closed in the evening. The fifth building, which had an elevated stage (for graduation ceremonies mainly), was our dining hall.

It reminded me of the Ateneo High School complex, with the desks, of course, replaced with two-level bunk beds. What would be a more familiar analogy would be that Ipil looked like the public elementary schools in the provinces, but with higher ceilings. And like these schools, Ipil had vast grounds, where we tilled huge vegetable plots encircled by a jogging path. There was a regulation-size basketball court, the scene of not a few fisticuffs between the detainees' and the guards' teams.

The bunk beds were in high-ceilinged halls of the three buildings.

It wasn't really so bad, after one has gotten used to sleeping deaf to the orchestra of snores all around you.

Not a few comrades decided to bring in their children into Ipil — as my wife and I did with our daughter Andrea, who stayed at the women's quarters for months. A comrade of ours we called Dolphy, from a poor area of Tondo, set up in one corner of the hall his very own territory, surrounded by two bunk-beds covered by banigs, where he, his wife, and child lived.

"Revgov" in prison

We were left mostly on our own, and we set up our own covert "revolutionary government" of sorts in our prison, which I led being the highest ranking communist there, until I resigned from the party. We had communal vegetable production, a store, a cultural group, a medical group (which, unfortunately administered bad acupuncture) and even our own security unit, which on one occasion beat up a detainee whom we suspected was a mole.

We set up a library, which I volunteered to run with now-famous scriptwriter Ricky Lee, as this had the privilege of living with private space in the Quonset hut were the library was housed.

Ipil's warden was a grandfatherly Master Sergeant we called "Master." He often practically begged us not to do anything that would mar his service record, since he was to retire soon. His two main assistants were young army privates from some distant provinces who were so self-conscious like awkward teenagers and apologetic when they held the morning assembly to check if no one had escaped.

The food was bad, of course, especially if you came from the middle or upper classes that accounted for probably 70 percent of the detainees. But I later learned it was the same chow distributed to all soldiers in Fort Bonifacio. Our relatives brought the best food they could every time they visited, and we shared these with our poorer comrades.

I was transferred to the Youth Rehabilitation Center (YRC), also in Fort Bonifacio, where I stayed for a few months, because I led (with a priest) a hunger strike at Ipil for reasons in hindsight so trivial I forget now what it was.

YRC was supposed to be a higher-security prison where high-ranking communist leaders such as Nilo Tayag and NPA commanders were detained, together with rich people Marcos thought were financing the movement to oust him, such as the Araneta brothers, Antonio and Enrique. YRC was in an old castle-like building and had fewer detainees, perhaps about 100.

After a week in a solitary cell like you see in the movies — the worst episode in my detention —I was "released" to join the other detainees. While YRC was dreary, and didn't have the open spaces of Ipil, detainees had more privacy, with most of them living in two-person cells, which in my entire stay there I never saw locked.

It is understandable for those detained during Martial Law, who are now in their 60s, to try to give meaning and drama in their lives through narratives that they heroically fought dictatorship, and suffered terribly under detention.

Communist cadres

What isn't mentioned at all in such narratives is that many, if not most, of them were cadres of the Communist Party that tried to overthrow the government through arms and to install its own dictatorship.

In my case, I not only headed the Party's organization in Metropolitan Manila, but I was also organizing the first armed group intended to operate in the metropolis, the prototype of which would later be the dreaded Alex Boncayao Brigade. Why shouldn't the state arrest and detain me?

How many of the political prisoners during Martial Law, who spent years in detention centers, were cadres of the Party, or instead were — as a common Filipino joke always says of innocent young victims of circumstances, which was popular in detention camps — merely sent out by their mothers on an errand to buy vinegar from the store when they were arrested?

We dramatically portrayed ourselves as freedom fighters, a concept which our non-communist supporters (especially gullible clerics looking for some meaning in their otherwise empty lives) fell for, hook, line, and sinker.

Yes, we were fighting a dictatorship, but we were also fighting to install a dictatorship of the proletariat, represented, of course, by the Communist Party. We were waging, as Party Chairman Jose Maria Sison repeatedly wrote, a people's war. For Marcos' military at that time, they were waging a war against Communists and Moro secessionists.

There were, of course, torture, rape, and summary executions by Marcos' military. But what war has there ever been in the world in which there were no atrocities by the sadists, the cruel rogue elements from both protagonists? Even the Communist Party in the 1980s committed such atrocities, even against their own comrades, in their paranoia that spies and moles had massively infiltrated the revolution.

The crucial question really is whether there was a Marcos policy to undertake such horrific human rights abuses and if these occurred in such scale as the Suharto regime's genocide of at least 500,000 Chinese-Indonesians in 1965 or the institutionalized torture by the Chilean state under Pinochet in the 1970s.

I don't think there was.

That Filipinos voted Fidel Ramos as President and Juan Ponce Enrile as senator for several terms — the two men who supervised the military and the police during Martial Law — implicitly provides us with a resounding answer to that question.

(September 23 and 26, 2016)

IT IS RAMOS WHO SHOULD APOLOGIZE OVER THE 'ABUSES'

ONE OF THE BIGGEST contradictions in the Yellow Cult's narrative of the martial law period is its dogma that the Marcos regime's human rights violations were horrendous.

Yet the organization alleged to be mainly responsible for such crimes, the Philippine Constabulary, was headed by a pillar of the Yellow Cult, General Fidel Valdez Ramos, who was Marcos' cousin and one of the most powerful figures of that regime.

Cory Aquino hand-picked him to be her successor in the 1992 elections, pushing aside House Speaker Ramon Mitra, an opposition leader since the 1970s who had been chosen by her ruling party Laban ng Demokratikong Pilipino as its presidential candidate.

The Yellows' dogma is that Ramos' crucial role in toppling the dictatorship has exculpated him from the sins of martial law.

Are they right? Or is it just because Cory anointed him as her successor that he has been absolved of any responsibility over the human rights abuses?

I prefer though a simpler explanation. Human rights violations during the martial law have been exaggerated. They were made to appear worse than they were in order to serve the propaganda needs of the yellow regime. Ramos indeed was a pillar of martial law, but he couldn't have been responsible for human-rights abuses during that era, as these weren't really as bad as the Yellows have claimed.

There was no state policy to ride roughshod over Filipinos' human rights, in contrast to what happened in dictatorships elsewhere such as Indonesia under Suharto, South Korea under Park Chung Hee, or Chile under Allende.

It is his being political opportunistic and even untruthful that Ramos publicly demanded that the Marcos family apologize for martial law and its abuses, and that the dictator's corpse should not be buried at the Libingan ng mga Bayani. This is plainly wrong on three dimensions.

First, Ramos was one of the main pillars, even the strongest pillar, of the Marcos dictatorship, since he headed the national police — called the Philippine Constabulary from 1972 to 1981 — the apparatus that enforced martial law over the civilian population.

Shouldn't he apologize for that instead of asking Marcos' widow (what wife would testify against her husband?) or his children who were in their teens at that time to do so?

Second, if he wasn't really in control of the PC, and wasn't responsible for its alleged human rights abuses, then why didn't he resign early during the dictatorship, as a strong protest against Marcos? That would have been big news and could have hastened Marcos' fall and spared the country the political-economic crisis of 1983-1985, which was the real cause of our underdevelopment for a decade. Shouldn't he apologize for that?

Third, if the extent of alleged human rights abuses were actually exaggerated, the product of communist propaganda that demonized Marcos as a fascist in order to ally the people behind their hidden goal to establish a one-party dictatorship, then why hasn't Ramos — the best living witness of the martial law years — told us what really happened?

He has published perhaps two dozen books containing his speeches, and yet he has not written a single article on alleged human rights abuses during martial law, or what he witnessed during that era.

Marcos in a rare photo with his defense secretary and Martial Law Administrator Juan Ponce and Enrile and Philippine Constabulary Chief Fidel Ramos.

Shouldn't he apologize for our difficulty in having an accurate, balanced picture of that crucial period of our history, and even worse, for supporting the communist narrative versus Marcos?

If Ramos just revealed what he knows, we would be able to decide conclusively whether or not the alleged human rights victims were, in reality, casualties of a war that the communist party chief Jose Ma. Sison himself declared as the "people's war" to topple what he called then the US-Marcos regime.

Of course, Ramos had kept silent on this, since this would have made him appear sympathetic to the strongman, so that Corazon Aquino wouldn't have anointed him as her successor to the presidency in 1992.

If he had talked about martial law, the anti-Marcos activist candidate Ramon Mitra or the fiery Miriam Defensor-Santiago would have roundly defeated him by labelling him with the Marcos camp, along with Eduardo Cojuangco and Imelda Marcos. Shouldn't Ramos apologize for his political opportunism?

It was the PC, and not the three services of the armed forces, that was Marcos' network for enforcing martial law. Not only was the armed forces legally banned from dealing with civilians, but it was tied down during martial law fighting the Malaysian- and Libyan-supported Moro National Liberation Front in Mindanao.

Nearly all of the human rights abuses Marcos has been accused of were undertaken by PC units, especially through its national network of "Constabulary Security Units," whose heads reported directly to Ramos.

The most dreaded (or successful) of these was the Manila-based 5th CSU, credited with capturing most of the Communist Party leaders, including Jose Ma. Sison and the Manila-Rizal Regional Committee, which I had headed as teenaged communist.

The cruelest case of human rights abuse during martial law that the Left always presents to media as its Exhibit A against Marcos was student activist Liliosa Hilao's torture, rape, and murder, with her sister Marie also sexually abused while in detention.

But the unit Hilao's sister Marie herself said was responsible for this was the PC's dreaded Constabulary Anti-Narcotics Unit, the CANU, which was even worse than the death squads killing drug pushers all over the metropolis now.

Were the CANU officers, and Ramos who had command responsibility over the crime, charged? No, the American lawyers cleverly indicted Marcos, as hundreds of millions of pesos compensation could be extracted from him because a Swiss bank account he allegedly owned had been confiscated, and was in government hands already. I doubt if they could have extracted a centavo from Ramos or the CANU offices.

I find it astonishing that two top communist cadres almost every year on the anniversary of martial law's declaration seem to relish giving media details of their torture (one that his penis was electrocuted, the other that a tingting, or thin stick, was inserted), and then condemning Marcos for their fate.

Yet they seem to be afraid to mention that it was PC units, over which Ramos had command responsibility, that were responsible for their torture.

Take my case. I was arrested together with my wife Raquel and most of the party's Manila-Rizal Regional Committee, and we spent two years in Marcos' prisons. Who arrested us, and beat up many of my comrades? The PC's 5th CSU. I was sent to the 5th Military Intelligence Group only for a few days, for interrogation aided by an injection of sodium pentothal.

That was it though from the military intelligence guys — no beatings at all, no psychological torture. I was also sent to the National Intelligence Coordinating Agency, headed by General Fabian Ver to be, to use their term "tactically interrogated". To my surprise, I was "interrogated" by bored-looking civilian bureaucrats, who looked more frightened of me than I was of them.

I don't think Marcos ever heard of me. After Sison, Kumander Dante, and renegade Army lieutenant Victor Corpus, I don't think he even knew of the names of the other communist leaders.

But I'm sure Ramos knew me by name. My father, a lawyer, after he was told I was arrested by the PC, wrote probably a dozen letters to the PC chief Ramos asking for my release, pointing out that I had not been charged in court. Ramos didn't bother to reply.

Only when my exasperated father decided to write Defense Secretary Juan Ponce Enrile did he get a reply from Enrile himself (or maybe he just signed a pro-forma letter) explaining that Proclamation 1081 had given the state the authority to arrest anybody without charges.

It was only when we were released two years later that I learned that it was Ramos who issued the so-called ASSOs (Arrest, Search, and Seizure Order) against me and for all political detainees.

Shouldn't Ramos apologize for that?

Those who didn't participate in the anti-dictatorship movement, or didn't care what was happening at the time, are unaware of Ramos' crucial role that enabled Marcos to rule as a strongman for 13 years.

Marcos' cousin

Ramos' hold on the PC was as strong and indisputable as his loyalty to Marcos for one major reason: he was Marcos' cousin. His grandmother, Crispina Marcos, was the sister of Fabian Marcos, the strongman's grandfather. While that may seem a distant link, it means nearly being brothers among the clannish Ilocanos. Did that embolden the PC to commit human rights abuses?

Ramos' father was also one of Marcos' most trusted diplomats, whom he appointed as his foreign secretary when he won the presidency in 1965.

Marcos trusted Narciso Ramos so much that he was his representative in negotiating with the Americans, the reduction in the tenure of military bases from 99 years to 25. Nationalists should applaud that Marcos-Ramos feat, as the new treaty, called the Ramos-Rusk Agreement, shortened the lease that originally was to expire in 2046, so it would end in 1991 — when the Senate voted to junk it.

Narciso was also Marcos' representative in the founding of the Association of Southeast Asian Nations (ASEAN) in Bangkok in 1967. Ramos' sister, Leticia Ramos-Shahani, followed in their father's footsteps, and was appointed ambassador to Australia in 1981.

Because of his blood relationship to Marcos and his never-contested hold on the PC, Ramos was perceived during martial law as the regime's most powerful man, next only to Marcos. Defense Secretary Enrile was Marcos' official Martial Law Administrator, only since the strongman wanted his dictatorship to be portrayed as built on solid legal grounds.

But Enrile was just, well, the lawyer and administrator; it was Ramos who was the muscle, his PC the organization that made the country follow the dictatorship.

The myth Ramos probably deliberately disseminated was that it was General Fabian Ver, the commander of the Marcos Presidential Guards and head of the National Intelligence Security Authority, who ran the security apparatus.

But Ver wasn't related at all to Marcos but was just a Sarrat townmate, and from an unimportant clan. Ver was Marcos' chief bodyguard who had no business outside of securing Marcos. Even Ver's sons, PMA graduates Irwin and Rexor, were limited in their role as commanders in the PSG, assigned nowhere else.

The NICA was, as it has been through the years until today, a weak agency run by civilians with hardly any muscle or brains. Even the most vitriolic critic of martial law hasn't accused Ver or his NISA of any human rights abuses.

Other than his being Marcos' cousin, Ramos had another strength. He was perceived to be close to the US military establishment, having studied at West Point, with many of his classmates advancing to the top brass of the American armed forces.

Was it coincidental that he abandoned Marcos, when the US military establishment and President Ronald Reagan as well (who had been firm supporters of Marcos), bowed to the State Department's lobbying to jettison the dictator in February 1986?

Was it coincidental that Cory Aquino, who was backed by the US and even saved by US Phantom jets in the 1989 coup, unexpectedly picked Ramos as her successor, instead of Mitra who was her party's choice?

Was it coincidental that Ramos became so critical of President Rodrigo Duterte after he announced a policy of separating from the US?

Why does the Yellow Cult keep on condemning somebody who is not only out of power, but is dead, while praising — or just keeping quiet — about someone whose political opportunism got him the top prize?

(November 16, 2016)

NOTE:

This column was written at the height of the controversy over President Duterte's decision to allow Marcos' body to be buried at the Libingan ng mga Bayani. Ramos had publicly opposed it, and demanded that the Marcos family apologize for the strongman's abuses during martial law.

Cesar Virata, Marcos finance secretary and chief economic tsar, and from January 1981 to February 1986, Prime Minister.
(Image from Robert Turner/ArtDirectors, UK)

VIRATA AND TECHNOCRATS RAN THE MARCOS ECONOMY

IN ITS VITRIOLIC anti-Marcos manifesto in 2016 protesting President Duterte's approval for Ferdinand Marcos' remains to be buried at the *Libingan ng mga Bayani*, Ateneo de Manila teachers issued a manifesto that pontificated, "The Marcos regime's economics of debt-driven growth was disastrous for the Philippines."

An earlier opinion column by a respected UP economist made the same point, that the economy had a "dismal performance under martial law."

What is astonishing in the condemnation of the Marcos years by the Ateneo and the UP professor is that both pretend — considering that they are supposed to be academics — that they are unaware that it was one Cesar Virata who was almost totally in charge of the martial law regime's economic management. (The UP's College of Business Administration was renamed into Cesar Virata School of Business in 2013, with no protest at all from the academic community.)

Of course, the buck stopped with Marcos, and he had command responsibility. But to blame only Marcos for the purported economic mismanagement during martial law is grossly inaccurate.

Just as Marcos gave full authority to Defense Secretary Juan Ponce Enrile and Philippine Constabulary Chief Fidel Ramos to deal with the two insurgencies (the communists and separatist Moros) and to keep peace and order in the land, he gave Virata, whom he plucked in 1967 from the UP School of Business and groomed to be his top technocrat, as much authority as possible over economic management.

Virata was Marcos' economic tsar and chief technocrat, occupying the crucial post of finance secretary from 1972 to the day the strongman fell on February 25, 1986. Never before and after has there been such a powerful Cabinet member as Virata. Marcos after Alejandro Melchor left in 1974 had weak executive secretaries. Virata reported to no one else but Marcos.

He was one of Marcos' earliest recruits, joining him in 1967 as deputy director of his Presidential Economic Staff, his personal brain trust on economic matters. That he was Marcos' official in charge of the economy is also reflected in the fact that he was chairman or board member of 22 government firms and financial institutions — as many as Imelda's — in which he made P1 million a month, a fortune in those days.

Marcos' economic manager

Marcos trusted him so much he ordered his 200-member Interim Batasang Pambansa and then the "regular" Batasang Pambansa, set up in 1984, to elect him as Prime Minister.

Virata took the prime minister's title so seriously that he refused to vacate his office in the days after EDSA I, saying he was elected to the position, and resigning would have meant "a dereliction of duty".

When I was covering the finance beat for the business newspaper *Business Day* in the early 1980s, all of us in media addressed him as "Prime," an address he preferred. Marcos chose him to be Prime Minister as his message to the country and the world that his economic manager was his political heir.

Virata was to economic management during martial law what Ramos was to the regime's police apparatus, and Enrile to the armed forces.

Marcos ruled as a strongman through a troika: Enrile, Ramos, and Virata. Without this troika, Marcos' strongman regime would not have lasted a year.

Just as the Ateneo statement condemned "Marcos economics" as "debt-driven growth," UP economist De Dios claimed that the "economy suffered its worst post-war recession under the Marcos regime because of the huge debt hole it had dug... collapsing completely in 1984-1985 when the country could no longer pay its obligations...."

But was it Marcos who was poring over the central bank's balance of payments and external debt reports? No.

It was Virata who had that responsibility as finance secretary, chairman of the Monetary Board of the central bank and the head as well of the National Economic Development Authority, during martial law.

As finance secretary it was Virata who asked for, negotiated, and even signed for most of our government's foreign debt. The Monetary Board he chaired was the policy-making body of the central bank that had the sole authority to approve even a dollar of foreign debt.

In 1983 when the Philippines defaulted on its loans, its total debt stood at $24.8 billion. Some $16.7 billion or two-thirds of this, were incurred by, or guaranteed by the national government, and the loans were mostly from the World Bank, the International Monetary Fund and the governments of the US and Japan, or more than half of our total debt.

Was there a single foreign loan Virata didn't want government to incur, yet was forced to get, on orders from Marcos? None.

Virata was chairman or board member of the 22 government firms that had incurred huge foreign debts, a part of which were re-lent to private firms. One case was a $200 million loan from the World Bank purportedly to modernize the country's textile industry.

It was the Development Bank of the Philippines that incurred the loan and the Board of Investments that determined to what firm it would be given. Virata was chairman of the DBP and a member of the Board of Investments.

The program was a disaster, with evidence unearthed years later that the textile firms channeled their funds to other sectors, even real estate and hotels.

Neoliberal technocracy

Virata didn't work alone, but headed the most powerful bloc in Marcos' regime: the technocrats who occupied key economic posts and headed government's biggest corporations. Among these technocrats were the following:

Gerardo P. Sicat, Marcos' economic guru and chief economic planning minister, who organized the Neda in 1973 and headed it until 1984. Sicat was and to this day a true believer of Marcos' martial law "vision," as he reveals in his book **Cesar Virata: Life and Times,** published by the UP (University of the Philippines) Press:

"On September 21, 1972, Marcos declared Martial Law, explaining that he would build a New Society. The immediate effect of this declaration was a major shift in the political and economic climate. Martial Law gave Marcos the power to undertake a clean execution of institutional change. Economic reforms suddenly became possible under Martial Law. The powerful opponents of Martial Law reform were silenced. Now it was possible to have the needed changes undertaken through presidential decree... Marcos was a lawyer and he made sure that the moves he made were covered effectively by current provisions of law or by new legal provisions... The technocrats who occupied high positions under the Marcos administration found themselves in charge of major economic policy... Now they were power wielders within the government."

Roberto V. Ongpin: Marcos' minister of trade and industry throughout his regime, especially credited or cursed, for handling the country's foreign exchange market by controlling the so-called underground "Binondo Central Bank" during the crisis years of 1984-1985. Ongpin was at odds, however, with Virata and Sicat because of his espousal of a Japan- and Korea-type of state-directed industrial development.

Jaime Laya: Marcos' budget secretary from 1975 to 1981, and central bank governor from 1981 to 1984. The IMF and the World Bank asked for his head in 1984 for being responsible for tampering of the central bank's reports on the country's international reserves in order to conceal that it was running out of foreign exchange. Marcos then appointed him as education secretary, a post he held until the Marcos regime's very end. (Another technocrat from UP, Manuel Alba, replaced Laya in 1981 as budget minister, a post he held until the end of the Marcos regime.)

Placido Mapa: A ranking Opus Dei member who headed the Neda from 1981-1983 and at various years during the dictatorship, the Philippine National Bank and the Development Bank of the Philippines.

Arturo Tanco: Agriculture secretary from 1974-1984, the architect of the Green Revolution, which steered the country to rice self-sufficiency. He was succeeded by his trusted deputy, a veterinarian, Salvador Escudero III, father of Senator Francis Escudero.

Geronimo Velasco, CEO of Philippines National Oil Company and the National Power Corp. the country's two biggest corporations. He was Minister of Energy from 1979 when the post was created, up to 1986. Velasco, dubbed as Marcos' "Energy Czar" was in charge of building the Philippines' power system and reducing the country's dependence on imported oil by building geothermal and hydroelectric plants.

If Virata, Sicat, and the other technocrats weren't really running the economy, why did these professionals — known for their integrity, pride, and egoism — stick through the entire Marcos regime? I don't think any of them was the type who would act willingly as Marcos puppets.

Virata, Sicat, and many of the technocrats (except for Ongpin) were early believers in neoliberalism, the dominant ideology in the West and among our economists now, which is basically unbridled capitalism. This is also the economic philosophy of the WB and the IMF.

Their economic philosophy were largely molded in the Ivy-League colleges where they studied: Virata was at Wharton; Sicat, at the Massachusetts Institute of Technology; Laya, at Stanford Graduate School of Business; and Mapa, at Harvard.

They were true believers of neoliberalism and laissez-faire capitalism, and thus also believed that state intervention in the economy should be minimal. This explains why the early growth seen during martial law was not sustained and collapsed readily following the oil and debt crises.

Contrast what these technocrats did or did not do, to the actions of their counterparts in Japan, South Korea and Taiwan. These Asian Tigers supported (and forced in some cases) their local companies into becoming world-class players.

Marcos was demonized after he was overthrown, but surprisingly, his technocrats who ran the economy became highly-respected members of the Philippine society after 1986. Their role in managing the economy under martial law was largely forgotten.

This isn't at all surprising. Filipino elites needed their services, as they knew the ins-and-outs of the financial and business world they presided over during 13 years of Marcos' rule. The Philippine elite assessed that these technocrats didn't do so bad really, with the economy simply a victim of external shocks.

Virata had been consultant to the WB and to scores of private companies, even serving as director in a few others. He was awarded in 2016 by the Emperor of Japan with the Order of the Rising Sun, one of the few non-Japanese who has received such decoration.

The UP, which was a center of the anti-Marcos movement in the 1970s, even named its School of Business Administration, the Cesar E.A. Virata School of Business, the only building or institution in the country's premier educational institution ever to be named after a living person.

Sicat is treated as a sage of the School of Economics, and writes a regular column for the Philippine Star set up by anti-Marcos journalists in 1986. Sicat wrote a 500-page hagiography of Virata published and financed by the UP.

Laya set up what would be one of the top accounting firms in the country, and has been chairman or board member of a dozen firms, including the Yap family's PhilTrust Bank, Ayala Land, Manila Water, and GMA Network.

The smartest of the Marcos technocrats has been Ongpin. While his colleagues have remained essentially highly-paid employees, he has become one of the country's richest tycoons, ranked 16th in 2017 by Forbes magazine, with a net worth of $1.2 billion.

Are these the kind of people who messed up our economy?

I covered the economy as a *Business Day* reporter from 1981 to 1987, and had so many interviews with Virata, Laya, Mapa, and Ongpin. No one ever complained that Marcos was intervening in economic policy, although Virata was very critical of Imelda Marcos' projects that required huge government funds, such as her human settlements program and the heart, lung and kidney medical centers. That, or he felt politically threatened by Imelda, who could take over after Marcos, instead of him, the designated Prime Minister.

Why the Marcos rule ended in economic conflagration, as in any phenomenon in this world, is a complicated story. The Yellow Cult's simplistic narrative that blamed everything bad that happened in that era to Marcos and wife Imelda's "greed" is mostly rubbish, intended to portray Cory Aquino and her anti-Marcos oligarchic allies as the saints and saviors of the country.

Seeing the big economic picture

I can give only the broad brushstrokes to explain what happened.

GDP average growth in the first nine years of martial law from 1972 to 1980 averaged 6 percent, reaching 9 percent in 1973 and 9 percent in 1976, a rate never reached again.

However, from 1981 to 1985 — amid the global recession, the spike in crude oil prices and the Philippine debt crisis — the average GDP growth rate became negative 1 percent because of the economy's unprecedented 7 percent contraction for each of the years 1984 and 1985.

It is those two years of recession that brought down the average annual GDP growth for the entire period of martial law to only 3.5 percent, the figure often cited by anti-Marcos writers as proof of the strongman's "economic mismanagement."

But the Philippines wasn't the only country on a "debt-driven" growth mode.

After the Arab countries wrested from the industrial nations their oil wells, they were awash with "petro-dollars" looking for some outlet.

Flushed with cash, US banks then rushed to push loans to Latin American and Asian countries, including the Philippines, in the 1970s.

The crisis unfolded when the Iran-Iraq war broke out in 1980, disrupting oil production, pushing prices up, and global interest rates shot through the roof.

Starting in October 1983, the Philippines couldn't afford to pay its foreign debt. Ninoy Aquino's assassination in August 1983 merely hastened, but was not really the main reason, for the country's debt default and economic recession.

As what happened in the same period for Argentina, Brazil, and Chile, the debt crisis meant that the country was isolated from the world economy. It was nearly in economic meltdown.

It was this economic crisis that was the basis for the widespread dissatisfaction with Marcos by 1985. With or without Cory Aquino, the strongman had reached the end of his rule.

According to an academic study, Virata believed to the very end of Marcos' rule that the country's economic downturn in 1983 was not due to corruption or cronyism but to three factors: negative balance of payments, accumulating debts and low returns on capital. (Teresa S. Encarnacion Tadem, 2012: *Virata: the trials and tribulations of a "chief technocrat,"* **Philippine Political Science Journal**, 33:1, 23-37.)

It is important for us as a nation to have an objective, accurate analysis of the Marcos era, especially its economic history if we are to develop our nation. It is worrying that some of our academics in the Ateneo and the UP have been easily mesmerized into believing the Yellow Cult's inaccurate, simplistic narrative of the Marcos era.

(March 3, 2016 and November 28, 2016)

Asia's strongmen: 1st row; Korea's Park Chung Hee, Taiwan's Chiang Kaishek and son Chiang Chingkuo; 2nd row: Singapore's Lee, Thailand's Kittikachorn, and Indonesia's Suharto; 3rd row, Marcos and Malaysia's Mahathir.

WHY DIDN'T DICTATORSHIP WORK FOR US?

EVERY FEBRUARY 25 SINCE 1986, in a kind of a ritual, government and the Yellow Media ask Filipinos to commemorate their purported day of deliverance from a dictatorship — the dawning, they say, from an era of darkness. The living heroes boast of their bravery during that time of revolution.

The narrative disseminated year after year is that the Philippines became poor because of the Marcos dictatorship, because of the greed of one man and his family, and his small cabal of cronies. Because the media since 1987 has been owned and run mostly by Marcos' enemies and by journalists he put out of work in 1972, that good-versus-evil narrative has stuck.

But reality has a way of catching up with our illusions, and after nearly three decades, most of the poor are still poor and Filipinos will die in the class they were born into.

We've been economically overtaken by most of our neighbors, all of which do not have divisive celebrations like the EDSA 1 holiday.

Most Asian countries have become richer than us, and war-ravaged, election-less Vietnam under the authoritarian rule of the Communist Party of Vietnam, will almost certainly overtake us in a few years' time.

What the apologists of the ruling class, especially its vanguard, the Order of the Yellow Ribbon, have tried to hide from us is this: Dictatorship in the Philippines was not an exception, but more the norm in the region. Nearly all Asian nations in the post-war period were under dictatorships, with many lasting even longer than Marcos' 13-year authoritarian rule.

This is the reality that should be an eye-opener for those who would be worshipping at the altar of democracy in those "People Power" celebrations this year. All of the Asian Economic Dragons, as well as the Tiger Cubs, depended a lot on authoritarian rule in order to become industrialized nations.

Generalissimo Chiang Kai Shek, and then his son Chiang Ching Kuo, ruled Taiwan with an iron fist from the day they fled to the island in 1947 from China after their Kuomintang forces were defeated by Mao Zedong's forces, to the time Taiwan embraced democracy in 1988.

Two strongmen ruled South Korea for nearly three decades: Syngman Rhee for 12 years until 1960, and General Park Chung Hee for 17 years (1962-1979).

Singapore's Lee Kuan Yew, whom many Filipinos idolize, ruled Singapore for 31 years. After a clever hiatus, during which time Go Chok Tong was prime minister, Lee's son Hsien Long took over the reins of government and has since been prime minister for 12 years now. Lee's People's Action Party as in the 1950s continues to control the press through Singapore Press Holdings.

Suharto and his cronies

Indonesia's Major General Suharto grabbed power in a bloody coup d'état in 1967, and stayed in power for 31 years. Marcos' cronies were amateurs compared with those of Suharto, whose closest crony Soedono Salim was given monopolies on cloves, flour, cement and even government bank deposits.

While most of Marcos' cronies are forgotten now, Suharto's top cronies, the so-called Gang of Four, set up First Pacific Co. Ltd in 1981, now one of the biggest regional conglomerates in Asia, which owns PLDT and Meralco, ironically controlled by Marcos' cronies during martial law.

Malaysia's Mahathir was in power for 22 years starting in 1981, and is still a formidable political force in his country, having effectively suppressed the leading opposition figure, Anwar Ibrahim, on charges, of all things, sodomy.

Field Marshal Thanom Kittikachorn ruled Thailand as military dictator from 1963 to 1973, until violent student protests forced him down from office.

The average length of strongman rule in these Asian countries was 23 years, Marcos' held on to power only for 13 years. Is there a case for claiming that strongman rule didn't work here, given that Marcos' strongman rule did not last as long as those in other countries did?

The reality stares us in the face: The Asian Economic Tigers grew to industrial status in one generation — such that the phenomenon has been called the Asian Economic Miracle — all under authoritarian rule, and not under democratic systems, as in the West.

Country	Strongman	Years in Power	No. of Years in Power	Average annual GDP growth during strongman rule
Taiwan	Chiangs	1947-1988	41	8.1
Malaysia	Mahathir	1981-2003	22	6.3
Singapore	Lee Kuan Yew	1959-1990	31	9.3
South Korea	Park Chung Hee	1962-1979	17	8.9
Indonesia	Suharto	1967-1998	31	7.2
Thailand	Kittikachorn	1963-1973	10	8.2
Philippines	Marcos	1972-1985	13	3.4 (5.5)*

*(*5.5% if the debt-crisis years of 1982-1985 are excluded)*

How Asia's strongmen fared.

Western academics, of course, with democracy as their quasi-religion, couldn't believe this. So they tried, instead, to attribute it to "Asian values," even Confucian culture that valued collective good rather than individualistic rights.

That's hogwash: strongman rule is strongman rule if there is no democratic election, in whatever cultural milieu it is operating.

So the tiger economies all grew under strongman rule. But for us it resulted in poverty, which we haven't been able to overcome after 27 years. Why?

Strongman rule not strong

One answer is that strongman rule in the Philippines, despite all the now prevalent Yellow narrative of a ruthless regime, wasn't really as strong nor as ruthless as it was in the Tiger Economies and in Southeast Asia.

Among numerous examples, Marcos retreated from his land reform program, beat back by the landlord class. Why, he couldn't even dismantle through agrarian reform Hacienda Luisita, owned by his arch-enemy, the Aquino-led Cojuangco clan. It took 40 years to do that, and by the Supreme Court in 2011 and at the cost of its head, Chief Justice Renato Corona.

More importantly, the main answer to this seeming riddle: The Philippine ruling class did what they have been doing throughout the country's history — that is, to screw the working classes, and to collaborate with and even exploit whoever controlled the political apparatus.

Except for a few property and retail tycoons who got the chance to exploit the surge in OFW remittances in the 1980s, it has been the same sugar and rice hacenderos; the Spanish-descended elite epitomized by the Ayalas; the Chinese-Filipino compradors such as the Ques, the Sys and the Gokongweis; and fake Filipino nationalists who grew through martial law and took advantage of it, who are still on top of the Philippine economic pyramid. Even Jollibee, set up in 1974, grew during martial law. Ayala Alabang for example became prime property only when Marcos built the "South Superhighway" in the 1970s, along with the "North Diversion Road."

The tiny faction of the elite that Marcos feuded with, the hacendero-descended elites such as the Lopezes, Osmeñas and Aquino-Cojuangcos, have more than recovered their wealth and power.

The debt crisis — when we couldn't pay off our foreign loans — from 1983 to 1985 actually explains the deep hole we are in. Because we were practically cut off from global trade at that time, our GDP contracted 14 percent in 1984 and 1985, really an unimaginable decrease in output that happens only in a war-ravaged economy.

There were a lot of reasons for this debt crisis, but one factor had been the fact that our elite from 1970 to 1981 brought out in a massive capital flight $3.1 billion. This is roughly one-third of the increase in the country's total external indebtedness.*

I believe the elites still regularly take out their money from the Philippines even today, instead of reinvesting it back into their supposed homeland.

Lack of nationalism

There is one explanation why our elite are so rapacious, in stark contrast to their counterparts in Southeast Asia. The ruling classes in the Asian Tigers had identified themselves with their nations, that is, they had a strong sense of nationalism.

They had to, as their very physical survival depended on their nations' economic growth. If South Korea, Taiwan, and Singapore hadn't quickly developed economically, these would have fallen under the Communist forces that threatened them, and their leaders, the elite, would have been executed, or at least their assets confiscated, as indeed happened in South Vietnam.

In short, the elites in these countries were under siege by the communist forces, and had no choice but to be nationalists, and develop their nations' economies. In the case of Indonesia and Thailand (because of their strong feudal states from centuries back, creating their unique cultures) their elites identify themselves strongly with the nation.

The Philippine ruling class, on the other hand, love to identify themselves with the country's colonizers. They identify themselves with Spain (where many of them originated) and the US, and in recent decades, with China.

For the Filipino elite, the Philippines is simply a market or a production site with cheap labor, and not really their homes. They simply cooperate or ingratiate themselves with whoever is the current leader, in order to further their business interests.

This kind of thinking, that nationalism is an unnecessary baggage, has even trickled down to the masses, so that many Filipinos even think somebody like Grace Poe-Llamanzares, who became an American citizen and renounced the Philippines, should be President.

Most of our elites, in fact, have their biggest mansions in London, Barcelona, Los Angeles and New York, and in recent years, in Shenzhen and Hong Kong. All their children study abroad, and have little cultural ties now to the country. Why, even their children no longer speak Pilipino, but English, and more recently, Mandarin. Pilipino is just the language they use to talk to their servants.

This is the reason why the Lopezes, Osmeñas, and the Aquino-led Cojuangcos have been propagating the Yellow Myth of Good-vs-Evil, with the elites supporting it, and even the Left believing it. It conceals the reality that through dictatorship and democracy, the elites continue to screw the masses.

(February 24, 2016)

---

* (From Dohner, Robert and Intal, Ponciano, **Debt Crisis and Adjustment in the Philippines in Developing Country Debt and the World Economy,** National Bureau of Economic Research, 1989.)

The Communist Insurgency

OUR ELITES LET THE LAST MAOISTS ON EARTH FLOURISH

THERE ARE SEVERAL unique features of our unlucky country that distinguish us from the rest of the rich and prosperous Southeast Asian nations, among them:

Our people have weak sense of nationalism both reflected in, and the result of the fact we are the biggest migrant nation in the region. This is due to myriad of factors: an exploitative Spanish- and Chinese-descended elite that does not really see itself as Filipino; a feeble state that is easily manipulated by the oligarchy; and a nation in inane awe of foreign capital that it allows foreigners to dominate telecoms and other public utilities even if the Constitution prohibits such.

The Philippines has another unique feature that a single administration could have corrected if only it had the political will. We have the longest standing communist insurgency, not only in Southeast Asia but also in the whole world. Last December, the Communist Party of the Philippines celebrated its 48th anniversary.

Other Southeast Asian nations were of course not immune to communist insurgencies, especially since China under Mao Zedong tried to foment Marxist revolution in the region in the late 1960s to 1970s in order to construct a wall of communist client states around it and keep out US hegemony.

However, all such countries that faced communist insurgencies have crushed them more than two decades ago — except the Philippines.

The most brutal was by Indonesia: Suharto's government from 1965 to 1966 physically wiped out Asia's biggest communist party after China's, in such a ferocious manner that about one million Indonesians of Chinese ethnicity were killed, not just by government troopers but by racist Javanese militias who labelled all Chinese as communists.

Malaysia and Singapore started to prosper only after their British colonial administrators, and then their independent governments, crushed the Malayan Communist Party, defeated by 1960. Thailand's communist insurgency lasted from 1965 to 1983, with the ruthless crushing of its militant student movement in the infamous Thammasat University massacre in 1976, largely unprotested by the world.

One insurgency defeated

The Philippines actually defeated one communist insurgency, the one led in the early 1950s by the pro-Soviet Partido Komunista ng Pilipinas that tried to mimic the Chinese model of developing an anti-Japanese army during World War II into a communist "People's Liberation Army".

Its Hukbo ng Bayan Laban sa Hapon became the Hukbo na Magpapalaya sa Bayan ("Huks"). The Huks were crushed by 1954 by a popular President, Ramon Magsaysay, assisted -- or led by the nose as some accounts would have it -- by the US Central Intelligence Agency.

It was the newer, pro-Chinese communist party of the last Maoists on this planet, which has led the longest-running communist insurgency, with its so-called New People's Army. That such a Maoist insurgency has raged for nearly five decades is astonishing, if you look at it.

Indeed, its strategy for capturing power — a people's army emerging out of a Red base in the hinterlands and then encircling the cities (as Mao did in the 1940s) — in this day and age is so out of touch with reality that it is as patently insane as believing that a Divine Messiah will take over the reins of the Philippine government because it is a devout Catholic nation.

The communists' declared main enemy, US imperialism, may not have been completely vanquished. But they have been arguably defeated though not by the communists. At the very least their hegemony has drastically diminished, as evidenced by the kicking out of all US military bases in the country and the passing of land reform laws.

There is no longer "US monopoly capital" dominating the economy, as Sison asserted in the 1970s, but an Indonesian monopoly capital, as it were, controlling telecoms and public utilities. On the Indonesian stranglehold of the telecom sector, however, the communists are strangely quiet.

China — which is the local communists' beacon of 'Mao Zedong Thought' and which even tried to give the NPA 10,000 M-14 rifles in 1971 to speed up the revolution — now has become the booming market of both ethnic Chinese and foreign capitalist billionaires.

To say that the communist insurgency persists because of Philippine poverty begs the question. Why aren't there surging communist insurgencies in the poorest nations on the planet, mostly in sub-Saharan

Africa like the Congo and Ethiopia?

Rather, the reasons for the emergence and persistence of the communist insurgency are an indictment of the Philippine elite.

The refusal of the strongman Marcos, supported by a faction of the Philippine elite, to step down when his regime was in decay, explains much of why the NPA expanded in the late 1970s until his fall in 1986. The Communist Party managed to portray itself as the only armed force capable of overthrowing a dictatorship. The efforts of Marcos' forces to defeat the NPA were spun as human rights abuses, thereby further demonizing it.

Marcos' arch-enemies

But it was Marcos' political enemies that nurtured the communist insurgency from its very inception in the late-1960s. Benigno S. Aquino, Jr. linked up the college English teacher Sison, then the head of the old PKP's tiny youth bureau, with the leaderless Huk commander Dante and his surviving gang of younger generation of Huks.

The Cojuangcos allegedly — and inarguably the Mao-era Chinese communists — financed heavily the new party and its military wing the NPA. The vast landholding that was Hacienda Luisita became the NPA's refuge, its de facto Red base. Their motive? To make governing difficult for President Marcos who was at that time gearing for a second term, and seemed to be succeeding.

Throughout martial law, it was the faction of the elite that was against Marcos that helped finance the NPA. Logging and mining companies of course did so not out of political motives, but out of sheer business opportunism. Provincial governors, such as those in the North, helped the NPA as long as it helped them defeat their political rivals.

President Corazon Aquino saw the communists as her allies against military mutineers, that one of her first orders when she assumed power in 1986 was to free all communist leaders, including Sison and Dante. Sison of course fled abroad to raise funds from Marxist organizations around the world, and to undertake global propaganda to propagate the party as a legitimate revolutionary quasi-state.

Even after a military-police faction fired upon leftist demonstrators that resulted in the infamous Mendiola massacre, the Cory government's implicit policy was to let the communists alone, and seek a peaceful settlement with them. Cory even ordered a new 1987 Constitution to be formulated that would allow the communists to get their representatives into Congress through the so-called party-list system, which gave them a larger platform for propagating their demands and for getting government funding.

All succeeding Presidents followed Cory's policy of appeasement. This was especially so in the case of her son, Benigno S. Aquino III, who even let communist fronts hound and prosecute military commanders such as General Jovito Palparan who tried to suppress the NPA in his field of jurisdiction.

There was of course an element of opportunism on the part of our presidents, even in the case of the general in charge of fighting the NPA during martial law, President Fidel Ramos. They wanted their terms to be without overt conflict, even as the insurgency covertly grew.

With the presidents of the Republic leaving the communists alone, with the elites even abetting them, is it then any wonder that their insurgency continues to thrive for the past 50 years?

The communist insurgency is a cancer all Philippine Presidents have allowed to grow. Other Southeast Asian nations battled them head-on and consequently extinguished them, removing a major block to their economic growth and political stability.

(February 8, 2017)

CPP-NPA'S BOTCHED PLAN TO IGNITE A CIVIL WAR

THE OLIGARCHS RESURRECTED by the EDSA revolt badly needed to demonize Marcos in order to propagate the myth that his overthrow was a national uprising against him, and not just a Metropolitan Manila episode backed by the US and triggered by a bungling coup attempt against him. They succeeded: they controlled media, the creator really of what the public thinks, and spread widely their version of history.

But that was 30 years ago, and the Yellow Cultists are no longer in power, and their big business allies don't really care about them and their narrative, and as usual have sought more powerful political patrons. Only ABS-CBN and to some extent the *Philippine Daily Inquirer* remain, as the latter's late editor herself had put it, as the "torchbearers" of the February 1986 toppling of Marcos that the media in the 1980s had glorified.

Now, one of the leaders that brought down Marcos, his defense secretary two years before and during the entire martial law period, Juan Ponce Enrile, perhaps wants to put the record straight in his retirement years. In a speech last month at the Methodist Protestants' Cosmopolitan Church in Manila, Enrile said:

"The most significant event that made President Marcos decide to declare martial law was the MV Karagatan incident in July 1972. It was the turning point.

"The MV Karagatan involved the infiltration of high powered rifles, ammunition, 40-millimeter rocket launchers, rocket projectiles, communications equipment, and other assorted war materials by the CPP-NPA-NDF [Communist Party, its New People's Army, and its disguise, the National Democratic Front] on the Pacific side of Isabela in Cagayan Valley.

"The CPP-NPA-NDF attempted a second effort — their MV Andrea project — but they failed. The MV Andrea sank in the West Philippine Sea on its way to the country."

Enrile, to the credit of his sharp memory, related many details on the episode, which bolsters his narrative's veracity, among them, that it was one Lieutenant Edgar Aglipay (who would become Philippine National Police chief 32 years later) who headed an eight-man Army team that intercepted and boarded the MV Karagatan and that Air Force fighter planes and even the Presidential Security Command soldiers were deployed to assist the Army platoon when it battled a bigger NPA force of 300 guerillas who were tasked to recover the arms.

Enrile pointed out that the Liberal Party then led by the fiery senator Benigno Aquino, Jr. claimed that the incident was a *"palabas"* (a show) with the Lopez-controlled Manila Chronicle, one of the biggest newspapers at that time, calling it a hoax.

Enrile said that after several days of fighting with government forces, the NPA retreated when they ran out of ammunition, with the military recovering 1,000 M14 rifles and 166,000 rounds of bullets and magazines for those arms, and 564 rounds for 40-millimeter rocket launchers.

Perhaps feeling like a statesman, Enrile, however, was totally silent about where the arms shipment came from.

Former communist cadres themselves who arranged for the shipment while they were in Beijing have disclosed that it came from China, more precisely its Communist Party intelligence department headed by Kang Sheng, under orders from Mao Zedong himself.

Enrile (in leather jacket) inspecting crates of Chinese-made M-14s captured after they were unloaded by an NPA platoon from MV Karagatan (right photo) anchored at Digoyo Point in Isabela.

Former ranking communists Mario Miclat (in his book **Secrets of the Eighteen Mansions: A Novel**) and Ricardo Malay (in an article on March 25, 2005 in the *Philippine Daily Inquirer*, where he was a copy editor) had disclosed in the minutest detail how their group, dispatched to China by Sison, organized with Chinese Communist Party intelligence operatives how the arms shipment would be undertaken.

That was the era when Mao Zedong didn't hide intention to export communist revolution throughout the world.

Enrile in his speech said:

"The MV Karagatan event affected President Marcos immensely. He wasted no time convening a military conference where he said: 'The Karagatan presents a new and serious dimension to the insurgency problem of the country. It means the subversive elements have succeeded to open a supply line to support their operations.'

"He asked the command conference to reassess all military plans. Ominously he added: 'I will not allow the problem to go out of control. I will nip it in the bud.' I never saw or heard President Marcos talk or act that way before. He was grave, firm, and resolute. On my way out of that command conference, the thought flashed in my mind that martial law was nigh.

"True enough, not long after, he convened another command conference. This time, he ordered the preparation of a plan for the declaration of martial law. No one in that command conference asked any questions or raised any objections."

Martial law was publicly announced on September 23, 1972, two months after the Karagatan incident. Perhaps Marcos would have declared it earlier if he had learned the scale of the Chinese Communist Party's project to send arms to the NPA.

This was inadvertently disclosed only in the past several years by arms traders and gun collectors who wanted to determine the quality of Chinese rifles, particularly an M14 clone called M305.

The M305 had become popular in America as a cheap, but reliable rifle, with the Chinese firm Norinco aggressively selling it. Norinco is a huge manufacturing company whose many products include rifles and pistols. It is said to be cloning Western products such as the Smith & Wesson and Colt guns, which are getting to be popular in our country because they cost a third of the American pistols.

A blog by an arms trader on this topic read:

"In the late 1960s, the Chinese government reverse-engineered the design for the US rifle M14 from weapons captured in Viet Nam. 100,000 M14 rifles and the necessary magazines and ammunition were produced by the Chinese for export, to arm rebels in other countries.

"These Chinese select fire M14 rifles were made to look just like captured American M14 rifles, including even the serial numbers. The rifles and ammunition were manufactured with US and British markings so as to avoid any connection to the People's Republic of China, and possibly to serve a role in disinformation (propaganda) campaigns for the planned uprising.

"The Communist Chinese government made two attempts to ship its 'select-fire' M14 rifles to the Philippines. The first attempt was largely unsuccessful and the second was a total failure. A source was recently shown the remainder of the approximately 100,000 Chinese-manufactured M14 rifles. The Chinese M14 rifles were packed in crates in one warehouse while the British-marked, Chinese-produced 7.62 x 51 mm NATO ammunition was stored in a separate warehouse."

China had built a factory to produce 100,000 rifles to arm the NPA, which, if it had enough revolutionaries to carry and use them, would have resulted in a bloody civil war in our country. The arms shipment plan was such a huge operation that, ironically, when China embraced capitalism, it jump-started its small-arms industry.

What Enrile did not disclose was that the arms shipments from China made up just one of Sison's two-pronged plan to foment revolution.

Sison in June 1971 confidently told the executive committee of the party central committee, his innermost core of followers, about the arms shipment from China, with Karagatan and Andrea only to be the first, intended to debug the supply line. "But even if we get the rifles, we don't have enough revolutionaries to carry them," he said.

"So, we have a plan to trigger another revolutionary flow like the First Quarter Storm," Sison said. As Miclat related it in his **Secrets** book, Sison explained what this was: the attack on the Liberal Party *miting de avance* at Plaza Miranda on August 21, 1971.

Miclat quoted Joma Sison as saying before the attack: "We will force Marcos to declare martial law... People will rise up in arms when he finally shows his fascist face."

That plan of course didn't quite work out. Instead of imposing martial law, Marcos simply suspended the writ of habeas corpus after the Plaza Miranda bombing.

While that made it easy for government to detain for days suspected subversives, the Supreme Court upheld its constitutionality, and Marcos used it only sparingly, arresting less than a dozen suspects, defeating Sison's expectation that Filipinos would rise up in arms when he "showed his fascist face".

Instead, what made Marcos decide to declare martial law was Sison and his operatives' bungling nearly a year later: the interception of the MV Karagatan arms shipment from China.

Enrile ended his speech as follows:

"If President Marcos did not declare martial law, what could or might have happened to the country? I am sure every one of us has an individual opinion about that."

Good question.

(March 31, 2017)

DARK SECRETS OF THE COMMUNIST PARTY

DR. MARIO MICLAT'S **Secrets of the Eighteen Mansions: A Novel** (Manila: Anvil Publishing, 2010) reveals in rich detail many of the covert factors that contributed to the growth of one of our country's biggest problems — the Communist Party of the Philippines.

The "18 mansions" of the title refer to the buildings in a secret compound in Beijing where the Chinese Communist Party in the 1960s and 1970s housed delegations of communist parties all over the world to facilitate its clandestine aid to their insurgencies.

Mansion No. 7 housed the living quarters and offices in Beijing of the delegation from the Communist Party of the Philippines (CPP) founded and led by Jose Ma. Sison, aka Amado Guerrero.

Miclat was a member of the CPP delegation who, with his family, lived and worked in that mansion starting in 1971. He returned to the Philippines in 1986, totally disillusioned with the party, which he says was a monster he "helped create, yet which devoured" him. He has since become an academic with a PhD and is at present dean of the Asian Center at the University of the Philippines.

Miclat's is not a fictional novel, but a personal and political memoir of his nearly two decades as one of Sison's earliest recruits, even living for two years in the leader's "underground" house as his editor and translator, and then as a cadre in the party cell in Beijing. Many of the persons in the book are identified by their real names; others are thinly veiled, while a few are named only by their aliases, probably in order for Miclat to write more freely or to spare these persons from embarrassment.

For instance, "Herz" was one of Sison's key operatives, who supervised the party's youth organizations in the crucial years of the early 1970s, the era of student power that led thousands of idealistic teenagers to communism, wrecked lives and, for many, death in some lopsided firefight.

Herz now lives a very comfortable bourgeois life in Canada, even as his Filipino community newspaper continues to rant against the Philippine government and paint the country black.

Herz's superior, "Goldie," who recruited Miclat to the party and who, he claims, ordered the killing of a suspected, but unlikely, military agent was Monico Atienza, head of the party's organization department during that period. After being comatose for months, Atienza died in 2007 after many years of living alone, despondent and destitute, on a meager UP assistant instructor's salary.

Sison, a womanizer

Secrets' secrets range from the personal to the political. For instance, the book claims that despite the rigors of running a revolution, Sison had the time to womanize, go on dates to nightclubs, and bear an illegitimate daughter.

In a scene straight out of a soap opera, Miclat and New People's Army chief "Kumander Dante" (Bernabe Buscayno) were shocked to see Sison's wife pound "at the leader's back with her fists even as she cried about her husband's indiscretion."

This might seem trivial today — after all, we had a President who boasted of his womanizing. But womanizing has been a capital offense in the "revolution" for dogmatic and practical reasons, punishable by death, or assignment to hazardous guerrilla frontlines.

After witnessing that conjugal spat, Dante "cried like a little boy," and between sobs asked Sison rhetorically: "How many good comrades have we condemned to die because of sexual opportunism?" I hope Dante will e-mail me to confirm or deny if this really happened.

What is not secret at all to those who have studied the insurgency, but which Miclat provides more details of, is that the Chinese government provided funds and arms to the CPP at its crucial embryonic stage. (A similar account was published in the *Philippine Daily Inquirer* on March 25, 2005 by Ricardo Malay, who had headed a CPP cell.)

A courier was even arrested in 1974 by the US Federal Bureau of Investigation for carrying undeclared $75,000 intended for the CPP as she was exiting from Canada where she got the funds from the Chinese Embassy there.

As regards arms shipments, Deng Xiaoping himself was so incensed over his Filipino comrades' incompetence. The first shipment on the MV Karagatan in 1971 was easily intercepted by the military and most of the 1,200 smuggled M14 rifles were thrown overboard.

In 1974, the MV Andrea, also financed by the Chinese, didn't even reach the Philippines as it ran aground on a sandbar, which was not unexpected as it was captained by a seasick-prone student activist who just got a crash course on seafaring.

Red plot: Plaza Miranda bombing

The most earth-shaking secret in this book involves the bombing of the Liberal Party rally at Plaza Miranda on August 21, 1971, the most crucial man-made event that formed the contours of our history since it happened.

Miclat asserts with total certitude that it was Sison's plot, and that he learned of this days after the bombing. He quotes Sison as saying before the attack: "We will force Marcos to declare martial law... People will rise up in arms when he finally shows his fascist face."

Two ranking comrades in Beijing knew of the attack beforehand. Miclat quotes "Peter," one of Sison's closest operatives, as telling him in October 1971: "Ninoy Aquino did not go to Plaza Miranda on the night of the bombing. Kumander Pusa phoned him."

That it was Sison's project has already been claimed by credible figures, such as the late Senator Jovito Salonga and journalist Gregg Jones in his book, **Red Revolution.** For Miclat, however, the attack seems to have left a deep wound in his heart. Before leaving for China two weeks before the bombing, he says he was asked to keep two grenades, which he was later convinced were the ones used in the carnage.

He could have dedicated his book to so many other people close to him. Instead he dedicates it "To an unidentified boy whose life was cut short by a terrorist bomb in Plaza Miranda, August 21, 1971."

(December 10, 2010 and November 29, 2017)

THE BANKRUPTCY OF SISON'S COMMUNIST PARTY

THE PHILIPPINE COMMUNIST MOVEMENT in the 1970s recruited not only the best and the brightest of the generation that came of age in that period, perhaps also one of the most patriotic, mostly in their teens and early twenties, yet who were willing to devote and even give up their lives to change this nation.

Many of them, such as my close friends and fellow Ateneans Ferdie Arceo and Billy Begg were sent by the Communist Party to rouse the masses to revolution in now forgotten hinterlands, without any military training at all and armed only with World War II carbines — and therefore easy picking not just for the military and police, but even local militias who thought they were bandits.

A sadder tragedy though was the torture and killing of at least a hundred communists at the hands of their own comrades in the 1980s, who believed the paranoia of their superiors that they were military spies and therefore must be executed.

But the bigger tragedy, in that it has and will affect millions of Filipinos of this and succeeding generations because the social and economic structure will remain unchallenged, is the following:

Even as the Philippines has one of the most exploitative class structures in Asia, and even as Marxist theory exposes the roots of this country's poverty, the Maoist mentality of the Communist Party of the Philippines (CPP) that could have been the vanguard in changing such a system has not changed a bit in five decades.

Thus, the communists have become irrelevant, politically and intellectually bankrupt. Its strategy for revolution, for its army to emerge from some Red base to encircle the cities to capture political power, as Mao Zedong did in the 1940s, is so out of touch with reality, a myth to give revolutionaries a false hope.

All such strategy has done is create political and economic instability for the country that has deterred foreign and local investments, thus creating more poverty in the country.

The CPP would have been relegated as a fringe leftist group, if not for its New People's Army. But its emergence and survival reflects not the correctness of its cause or its strategy, but the fact that there are pockets in this vast land (as in all poor countries) where because of the weakness of the physical and political infrastructure as well as government's armed forces, the Philippine state has not been able to assert its authority.

This also explains the persistence of other armed groups such as the Moro Islamic Liberation Front, the Abu Sayyaf, and other bandit groups in Mindanao.

The CPP's analysis of Philippine society and its "program for a people's democratic revolution" isn't even original, but a work of shameless plagiarism. After all, for all his pretense at being a theorist, Sison was merely an English instructor, with the totality of his knowledge drawn, not even from Marx or Lenin's works, but from Mao Ze Dong. He never advanced his education from his A.B. English, and his thinking therefore was never put under rigorous academic scrutiny.

Sison simply copied from Indonesian communist chief Aidit who copied from Mao the analysis that "imperialism, feudalism, and bureaucrat-capitalism" are the targets of the Revolution.

The party's analysis of Philippine society, the local communists' bible, remains founding chairman Jose Ma. Sison's **Philippine Society and Revolution** (PSR) first published in 1970, 46 years ago, now on its sixth printing.

Sison copied from a copier

Yet PSR is not even an original work. It copied the framework and even the words as well as phrases of Indonesian Communist Party leader Dipa Nusantara Aidit's **Indonesian Society, Indonesian Revolution,** written in 1957. Aidit in turn copied much from Mao Zedong's **Specific Characteristics of People's War**, written in 1948.

Sison got a copy of Aidit's book when he was sent to Indonesia in 1965 by the pro-Soviet Partido Komunista ng Pilipinas to observe its fraternal party's revolutionary struggle, which his party believed was on the brink of capturing power.

Sison barely escaped the massacre in 1965 by Suharto's forces of the Indonesian Communist Party, in which Aidit was killed, an episode in his life that traumatized him so much that he has never talked nor written about it.

The local communists haven't changed at all their analysis that the three evils of our society are "imperialism, feudalism, and bureaucrat-capitalism" — which Mao formulated to describe Chinese society before World War II.

Mao wrote in 1948 in his analysis of China: "The Chinese revolution at the present stage is in its character a revolution against imperialism, feudalism and bureaucrat-capitalism." Sison wrote in 1970 in his PSR for his analysis of the Philippines: "The central task of the Philippine revolution in the present stage is the overthrow of US imperialism, feudalism, and bureaucrat capitalism."

Aidit in 1957 wrote with regard to Indonesia: "When we say that the basic targets of the Indonesian revolution are imperialism and feudalism, this means that the principal enemies of the Indonesian people at this stage of the revolution are the big bourgeoisie of the imperialist countries and the landlord class at home."

Sison in 1970 wrote with regard to the Philippines: "The targets or enemies of the Philippine Revolution are US imperialism and its local lackeys which are the comprador big bourgeoisie, the landlord class and the bureaucrat capitalists."

It is astonishing for instance that Sisons's PSR even in its 2005 edition lists as top US firms, the so-called agents of imperialism, such companies that have long closed shop such as Atlas Consolidated, ESSO Philippines, Gulf Oil Corp., Standard Philippines Fruit Corp, and Bank of America.

Sison's outdated book has a tabulation of 10,400 landlords owning at least 50 hectares, when land reform laws since Marcos' martial law had already distributed nearly 90 percent of these lands to former tenants.

How can two generations of patriots devote and even give up their lives believing in a plagiarized work like Sison's PSR? Alas, that was a time without a World Wide Web, which now allows one to easily retrieve in a few clicks of the keyboard information and people's writings from nearly all parts of the globe.

What is also tragic is that Sison and his clique had ruthlessly suppressed and allegedly executed party leaders who questioned the PSR analysis and strategy, such as the fiery Popoy Lagman who organized and led the dreaded hit squad, the Alex Boncayao Brigade, and Romulo Kintanar who led the Davao City insurgency in the 1980s.

From their revolutionary praxis in these two urban areas, they advocated an urban-based "pol-mil" (political-military) model of revolution.

The party's dogmatism is even worse than that of the Catholic Church, which managed to absorb and adopt new ideas through the Age of Reason and the Age of Enlightenment, to make it more relevant to contemporary society, and thus more credible despite its basically superstitious beliefs.

Because it merely plagiarized Mao and Aidit's assessments of their countries, our communists have been totally incapable of understanding important Philippine developments, among them: the rapid expansion in the number of urban salaried workers as well as of overseas workers and the consequent drastic decrease of tenant farmers; the growth of the Philippine bureaucracy and the resulting worsening of both petty and big-time corruption that has sapped state funds; the replacement of US monopoly capital by those from other countries such as Japan and even Indonesia, in the case of public-utility magnate Anthoni Salim; the emergence in the country of a particularly rapacious form of capitalists, totally bereft of nationalism; and even the explosion of technology that has made this thing called the World Wide Web a more powerful a venue for protest than street demonstrations.

What an unlucky country. Even our communists who are supposed to topple a rapacious ruling class are so intellectually and politically bankrupt that they have become more of a minor nuisance to the elite, rather than a revolutionary force to reform our very backward and exploitative society.

(February 10, 2017)

REDS' DEMANDS WILL CAUSE ECONOMIC COLLAPSE

PRESIDENT DUTERTE'S DECISION TO end all peace talks with the Communist Party of the Philippines (CPP), its New People's Army and its dummy organization, the National Democratic Front, dismantles the illusion, propagated not just by the communists but also even by the president's negotiators, that the peace talks are proceeding well, and that peace is at hand.

Finally, it has taken a tough, no-nonsense president to call for an end to this now criminal organization, deluded that it can establish a one-party dictatorship in our country by killing our soldiers and police to submission. The communists' armed attacks against the Republic have been one of the biggest factors blocking our nation's prosperity.

Its ideologue and chief propagandist Jose Ma. Sison, now 78, has been in the Netherlands since 1987, or for 30 years, more than three times the nine years he spent in actual revolutionary practice in the Philippines. No wonder this demagogue and his followers are so totally out of touch with the situation in our country and the world, so as to preposterously demand a "coalition government," a 1940s Maoist idea during the Chinese revolution, that is, joint sharing of power with the Republic.

Ever since peace talks were undertaken 30 years ago, the communists have been making what are in reality impossible demands on government before they lay down their arms.

If Duterte or any other President agrees to the communists' demand, he will be impeached, since by doing so he is committing to the communists what isn't his to commit: for the independent Congress to repeal or pass numerous laws, according to the communists' wishes.

If by some miracle the government repeals the laws the communists want repealed, the result would be economic Armageddon for the country. This might be what the communists in reality want, since the country would be in such chaos as a result that it could grab power and establish its one-party dictatorship.

Delusional demands

Peruse some of the communists' delusional demands in its negotiations with government, and you will be shocked, and even angry over why

Duterte's negotiators haven't been revealing these to the public:

- The creation of a "new political authority" — a euphemism for the communists' joint control of government — which will be empowered to implement the agreed-upon economic and social reforms;
- The recognition of, and participation of the New People's Army and its front organizations, in the implementation of land reform in the rural areas;
- The total banning of all imports of agricultural and fish products;
- The repeal of the Comprehensive Agrarian Reform Law, Investors Lease Act, Agriculture and Fisheries Modernization Act, Fisheries Code, Mining Act, Indigenous People's Rights Act;
- The termination of all bilateral investment treaties and agreements, bilateral and regional free trade agreements, and agreements under the multilateral World Trade Organization;
- The "dismantling of import-dependent and export-oriented" companies, which now assemble computer chips and other information-technology products that make up 40 percent of our exports;
- The repeal of the law on the automatic appropriation for the public portion of the foreign debt service;
- Prohibition on the ejectment of squatters until after they are provided "with housing and utilities, employment or livelihood, and social services in the area of resettlement";
- Scrapping of the Electric Power Industry Reform Act;
- A ban on "advertisements and the airtime" that spread "colonial mentality, foreign worship, consumerism, and other similarly objectionable values";
- The abolition of value-added taxes and excise taxes on basic goods and services;
- The institution of capital controls "to promote financial stability" and stabilize the peso's international value; and,
- The cancellation of foreign debts that are "onerous or fraudulent".

Foolish government panel

These demands, and many others, are contained in the so-called Comprehensive Agreement on Social and Economic Reforms (Caser) that it had submitted to government negotiators, and which Sison and his negotiators keep babbling about as if Duterte could just very easily okay it.

The communists in the Caser are essentially demanding that government reverse nearly all of its economic reforms in the past several decades, as embodied in laws passed by more than a dozen Congresses.

It is astonishing that communists like Sison and CPP chairman Benito Tiamzon, isolated from the country in Holland or in our godforsaken jungles for decades, see themselves as expert economists who know how an economy should be developed.

If the Duterte government agrees to undertake just one of these demands, the result would be a deadly blow to the country's image of economic stability, which in turn would trigger such a total loss of confidence in our economy, resulting in massive capital flight.

Our negotiators and the communists, even as they have been blabbering continuously about the "Caser," have refused to release it to the public. I managed to get my copy only through my sources.

Our foolish panel has fallen for the communists' ploy to portray the Caser as the embodiment of their noble agenda to undertake reforms that would supposedly uplift the country's poor.

Secretary Jesus Dureza, the presidential adviser on the peace process, has even been trying to get government agencies to support the Caser, saying, "It will address the problems that lead to armed conflict — landlessness, poverty and inequality."

Haven't our negotiators been consulting with Duterte's economic managers to find out what they think of such provisions in the Caser such as the imposition of capital controls, and the scrapping of economic bilateral agreements? Or have they been spending too much time wining and dining with the communists, exchanging jokes with them in Norway and the Netherlands?

What is so shocking in the Caser is its Section 6 of Part VI: "This Agreement shall be binding upon the GRP and the NDFP and their respective successors. Any change in the form of the political structure, government and authority within the GRP shall not affect the validity and binding nature of this Agreement."

How can the communists demand that an agreement, which Duterte would sign, should be honored and implemented by all future presidents and by prime ministers, in case the country shifts to a parliamentary form of government?

What the communists are asking for is not what Duterte can give, nor even promise to give: for the Congress, which is an independent branch of government, to pass laws that would repeal what the communists don't like and enact laws they think would further the revolution.

Read the Caser, and if you've been a student of the communist movement or a member, as I had been, you will see that it is entirely based on the view that Communist Party founder Jose Sison presented in 1968, or nearly half a century ago — plagiarized from the writings of Mao Zedong and Indonesian communist chief Aidit — that the Philippines is a "semi-colonial and semi-feudal" country.

In fact, the Caser openly claims that in entering into the agreement, the NDF is guided by the **Guide for Establishing the People's Democratic Government** and the **Program for a People's Democratic Revolution of the Communist Party of the Philippines.** Both documents were made 49 years ago. For the communists, nothing at all has changed in the country's economy, and Sison's (or more accurately, Mao's) godlike vision is still applicable to our country in this day and age.

And here's what's also shocking. Sison, who wrote the Caser, demands that it be signed first before the communists agree to a ceasefire.

This is in the Caser's Section 3, Article VI: "The Parties agree that, irrespective of the course and outcome of the peace negotiations, the provisions of this Agreement that uphold the economic, social and cultural rights of the people shall remain in force and in effect."

What idiocy is this? The communists are demanding that the Caser be signed as one of the conditions for them to agree to a peace pact. Yet, they are saying that even if the peace talks fall through — say, if the NPA decides to launch a full-scale attack on government forces — this agreement will remain in force?

Yet still another shocking provision in the Caser, in its very last section: Section 7: "To enhance and strengthen the legal and moral force and effect of this Agreement, the representatives of the governments hosting the formal negotiations as well as those of the UN Secretary General, the UN Economic and Social Council and the UN Commission on

Human Rights shall sign this Agreement as witnesses upon the signing of the same by the negotiating panels of both Parties."

What lunacy is this? The communists in effect are demanding that the government treats the Caser as an agreement between two states, as witnessed by the United Nations!

For making such impossible and even absurd demands, I suspect Sison and these septuagenarian communists in Utrecht are getting senile, and enjoying themselves with the fantasy that they have won the revolution, and are now outlining what their "coalition government" would be doing.

Or, they are just so wily that the peace talks will give their NPA the opportunity to strengthen itself, with the publicity making it more frightening that it will be easier for them to extort more money — reputedly P1.5 billion annually — from helpless businesses and landlords in our rural hinterlands.

Meanwhile, Filipino soldiers, policemen, and civilians in the country are getting killed yearly by the NPA in their now irrelevant attempt at a revolution.

Our nation really has no choice but to crush this terrorist organization, which has been pulling the country down as much as the drug lords.

(November 27, 2017)

Gloria Macapagal-Arroyo

THE GMA YEARS: LOST OR A VERY GOOD DECADE?

APPOINTED ONLY TWO MONTHS AGO by President Benigno Aquino III as the chief of the National Economic and Development Authority, former UP School of Economics dean Arsenio Balisacan seems to have fast caught the yellow 'I-hate-Arroyo' bug that afflicts this administration.

In a speech, Balisacan even mimicked the Aquino propagandists' crass tack of using clichés in the asinine belief that catchy terms can substitute for facts and reason.

Balisacan labeled former President Gloria Macapagal-Arroyo's years from 2001 to 2010 as a "lost decade," because, he claimed, poverty was not reduced during the period. "You know what happened in the last decade? *Walang nangyari sa poverty talaga, flat lang,*" he said.

To refute Balisacan's claim, I'll just repeat what he himself wrote, together with four other economists, in a report for the Asian Development Bank in 2010 titled **Social Impact of the Global Financial Crisis in the Philippines.** That he didn't think he made mistakes in his conclusions in that article is reflected in the fact that he later wrote shorter versions of the study in various academic journals.

The Balisacan report was all praise for the reduction of poverty during Arroyo's term: "[Poverty] significantly decreased from 33 percent in 2006 to 29.7 percent in 2009. The growth of household incomes in 2007 and 2008 has favored the poor as their incomes have increased proportionately more than those of the richer households."

It even emphasized: "The decline of poverty in the rural areas is remarkable. It was decreasing at an annual rate of 3.7 percentage points between 2006 and 2008."

While Balisacan claimed in his speech last week that there was no poverty reduction during Arroyo's watch, his own study reported that it declined from 33 percent in 2006 to 29.7 percent in 2009 *(see next page table, reproduced in toto from the study).*

But not only that, the Balisacan study's important insight is that it was the global financial crisis that broke out in 2008, and was at its worst the next year, which was the main reason for the worsening of poverty from 2008 to 2009, to a 29.7-percent incidence. Because of this, the very wrong impression — which afflicted even the author

Year	GDP	GDP per capita	Inflation
1981-1990	1.8	-0.9	14.4
1991-2000	2.4	0.1	8.3
2001-2010	4.8	2.4	5.1

Figures are average annual growth rates.

	2006	2007	2008	2009	2009 if no Global Crisis
Poverty Incidence (%)	33.0	37.8	28.1	29.7	29.7
Magnitude (thousands)	28,734	28,177	25,412	27,361	27,361

of the study when he was appointed Neda chief — is that "nothing happened in reducing poverty" during Arroyo's term.

Using rigorous econometric models, the Balisacan study concluded that if not for the global financial crisis (considered worse than the Great Depression of the 1930s), the poverty incidence in 2009 would have been 27.7 percent and not 29.7 percent, or a huge two percentage points lower. Without the global economic crisis, there would not have been a 2-million increase in poor Filipinos.

The Balisacan study, in fact, extolled the Arroyo administration's moves that enabled the country to still post a 1.1-percent GDP growth, when most countries went into recession.

It noted that the Arroyo administration had a comprehensive response to the emerging global crisis, contained in the so-called "Economic Resiliency Plan" (ERP), which the then President ordered the Neda (at that time headed by Ralph Recto) to formulate and execute when the global crisis started to emerge in 2008.

The Balisacan study also explained: "With a total budget of P330 billion or an estimated 4 percent of GDP, the ERP aimed to stimulate the economy through tax cuts, increased government spending, and public-private sector projects." The increase in public infrastructure projects substantially boosted the GDP, since private economic activity — especially in exports, as the US market contracted — had slowed down."

According to Balisacan's calculations, because of the country's economic fundamentals, the GDP growth rate in 2008 (if the global crisis did not occur) wouldn't have been just 4.2 percent but 5.2 percent, and in 2009, not 1.1 percent but 4.9 percent.

Because of the economy's strengthening during Arroyo's watch (through such policies as the very unpopular expanded value-added tax law) and because of her appropriate response to the crisis, the economy bounced back immediately after the global financial storm with a remarkable 7.6-percent growth in 2010. This has made possible such things that you will hear Aquino crow over such as international credit-rating upgrades, low inflation rates, and robust government coffers.

Even with the lower GDP growth because of the global crisis, the annual average GDP growth during Balisacan's "lost decade" is 4.8 percent, much higher than those in the past two decades (see table below, based on World Bank data). In fact, the last decade had the highest annual growth in GDP per capita and the lowest inflation rate — two crucial economic measures that determine poverty incidence.

What "lost decade" is Aquino's top economist talking about? Just go by the hard data: It was a very good decade.

(July 19, 2012)

ARROYO, FARMERS VICTORIOUS OVER AQUINO HACIENDA

YOU'D HAVE TO VISIT Hacienda Luisita to realize how vast it is. It's been a symbol not only of elite rule in our country but also of their hypocrisy and powers of deceit. It's the biggest hacienda in the country, with a total area of 64.4 square kilometers — nearly as big as the cities of Manila and Makati combined.

The sugarcane fields as far as the eye can see were a marvel for me when I first visited the hacienda in 1970. It was troubling though to see emaciated sugar workers, their skin blackened by the hot Central Luzon sun, their shoulders nearly buckling under the weight of sugarcane poles, and after seeing such abject misery, to be personally served US steak from the nearby American Clark Air Base in the comfort an air-conditioned mansion. Class exploitation and class struggle are not ideas but realities in this hacienda.

Indeed, it was in this hacienda where the legendary guerrilla at that time, Kumander Dante, as a teenage cane-cutter named Bernabe Buscayno, took up arms against the ruling class. Yet it was ironic that it was also in the hacienda that an opposition figure named Benigno Aquino Jr. — who married into the Cojuangco clan that owned the plantation — brokered a historic meeting between Dante and Maoist demagogue Jose Maria Sison, which led to the organization of the New People's Army.

The hacienda until martial law would be the recruitment center, training camp, and refuge for the fledgling NPA, which Aquino calculated he could utilize in his fight against Marcos.

It wasn't Marcos who invented behest loans. The hacienda, together with the sugar refinery, was acquired from the Spanish firm Tabacalera in 1958 by the clan led by President Corazon Aquino's maternal grandfather Jose Cojuangco by way of a P12.9-million loan from the Government Service Insurance System, and also through a $2.1 million-loan from the Central Bank of the Philippines. The loan's condition though was that the hacienda's agricultural lands would be sold to its tenants at "reasonable" costs.

Because the Cojuangcos rejected the demands made several times

How big is HACIENDA LUISITA?

11 Barangays in Tarlac City, La Paz and Conception Town, Tarlac Province
6,453 Hectares

by the Central Bank and the Land Authority starting in 1967 to implement this condition, the government in 1980 filed a case in the Manila Regional Trial Court to compel them to do so. There are no tenants to distribute the land to, the Cojuangcos replied.

The case dragged on for five years until Judge Bernardo Pardo (years later the Comelec chairman and then Supreme Court justice) in December 1985 ruled that the hacienda's lands should be distributed to the farmers. "Persecution by the Marcos regime," the Cojuangco clan claimed, and ran to the Court of Appeals.

Two months later, the EDSA Revolution of February 1986 would save the hacienda for the Cojuangcos. In 1988 during President Cory's term, the Department of Agrarian Reform, the Central Bank of the Philippines, and the GSIS informed the Court of Appeals that they were no longer interested in pursuing the case to require the Cojuangcos to distribute the lands to the farmers. The Court ruled that the hacienda would instead fall under the provisions of President Aquino's "comprehensive agrarian reform program."

Fortunately for the Cojuangcos, that program provided for an option in which, instead of distributing the land, the landlord may issue the farmers papers called stock certificates, representing their supposed minority ownership of shares in the corporation the landlord sets up to own the hacienda.

This scheme made land reform such a farce that only 12 other much smaller haciendas dared use it. Cory though was the saint of Philippine democracy who could do no wrong, and the defiance by her clan's hacienda of the Constitution's land-reform mandate receded in the public mind. Starting in the 1990s, parts of the Hacienda would be transformed into a profitable modern complex with an industrial park, a business center, a shopping mall, two hotels, and a world-class golf course.

In November 2004, after the Hacienda Luisita massacre in which seven striking plantation workers were killed at the picket line — and seven others murdered one by one by assassins later — the DAR, under President Gloria Macapagal-Arroyo, accelerated its investigation over a complaint by the hacienda union that the stock distribution scheme was a farce.

In December 2005, upon recommendation of the DAR, the Presidential Agrarian Reform Council (a body Cory set up in 1987, made up of 15 Cabinet members and chaired by President Arroyo) ordered the hacienda's fake land reform ended, and for the land to be distributed to the farmer-workers.

"Persecution by the Arroyo regime," the Cojuangco clan complained.

This time around though, there was no People Power uprising to overthrow the administration that went against them so they could hold on to the hacienda. The Cojuangcos appealed to the Supreme Court. It is only six years later last week (November 22, 2011) that the Court upheld the Arroyo government's decision.

The Court's decision could mean the clan's bankruptcy. The Court not only ordered the Cojuangcos to immediately distribute 4,915 hectares to the haciendas' farmer-workers. It also ordered them to pay the farmer-workers P1.33 billion, the proceeds of the sale of hacienda lands that became the industrial and business parks. Agrarian reform laws will peg "just compensation" for the clan at 1989 levels, or just about P200 million. The Cojuangcos had demanded that the hacienda be priced at is 2006 market value, which calculates to at least P10 billion, excluding P3.5 billion interest from that year to 2011. Now I understand why they hated Chief Justice Renato Corona and Arroyo so much.

Arroyo's critics claim she went against the Cojuangcos to retaliate against Cory's participation in the July 2005 conspiracy to topple her. The counter-argument could be posed in a question: If Arroyo was overthrown in 2005, would the new DAR and a new Cabinet have ordered real land reform at the hacienda?

Now I understand why they would torment and put a former president in jail on the basis of the say-so of a lone witness implicated in the Maguindanao massacre. "Accountability" and "reckoning" have indeed taken a chilling meaning.

(November 30, 2011)

MASSACRE SUSPECT IS SOLE WITNESS AGAINST HER

A FORMER PRESIDENT of the republic is arrested, humiliated, and tormented on the sole basis of the very dubious claim of one man: Norie Unas.

He is Mindanao warlord Andal Ampatuan Sr.'s former underboss, of whom relatives of the 58 victims in the Maguindanao massacre claim was involved in the atrocity. Governor Esmael Mangudadatu, whose wife's and two sisters' bodies were abominably mutilated, said it was Unas who even deployed the tractor backhoe to dig the victims' mass grave.

Yet Justice Secretary Leila de Lima calls it "a triumph of justice," on the basis of the testimony of this massacre suspect.

"Drag her out of the hospital, crucify her now," the lynch mob, led by the communist-inspired Bayan Muna, shrieks. Cartoonists laugh hysterically as they caricature a seriously-ill person wearing a device that prevents her from being paralyzed for life, or who may even be dying.

Schadenfreude, the sadistic pleasure over the suffering of others, has now become the ethos of this Christian nation. Rage has eclipsed reason; a mob's frenzy has overcome decency.

The accuser Unas' allegations? After a dinner of over a hundred people in Malacañang in 2007, he claimed he overheard Gloria Macapagal-Arroyo order his boss Ampatuan Sr. to cheat for her senatorial candidates in the elections that year. He overheard her, despite the deafening din of a hundred people talking in an enclosed hall.

President Benigno Aquino III is asking us to believe that, already accused of cheating in the 2004 elections, Arroyo would order within hearing distance of many, a politician, who owed his rise to power in 1986 to Corazon Aquino, to commit a crime, and not even for her candidacy but for her senatorial candidates.

That's it. It is solely this massacre suspect's claim that is the sole "evidence" against Arroyo. No other witnesses, no other documents. The other "voluminous" documents, which the Pasay judge claims he read in a few hours, do not have anything to do with Arroyo.

With the plot to jail a former president undertaken on the second anniversary of the Maguindanao massacre and with the only witness against her, one of that abomination's planners, President Aquino is sending us a chilling, arrogant message: I can do whatever I want, as I have media behind me. I can even use the country's worst crime ever, the Maguindanao massacre, to jail Arroyo, and do it on the atrocity's anniversary.

This tragedy's alarming aspect is that the media have been so caught up in the frenzy that they have abdicated their role of reporting and analyzing the facts. That famous formulation of the media's sacred duty has been depraved to read: "Afflict the afflicted and comfort the comfortable."

Instead of protesting why Aquino's lone witness against Arroyo is a Maguindanao massacre suspect who will escape justice for his false testimony, the National Union of Journalists imposed a student-paper gimmickry of altering columnists' photos to have their eyes closed. Instead of looking like a morgue's mug shots, these unwittingly symbolize a media seeing no evil: that of Aquino spitting on the massacre victims' graves, just to jail Arroyo.

I will not have my eyes closed; this piece is my cry for justice for the 58 lives snuffed out two years ago, who are turning in their graves as their massacre is being immorally exploited for Aquino's conspiracy.

Facts are being casually thrown to the garbage bin. A veteran columnist recently wrote in this paper (*Philippine Daily Inquirer*) "Ampatuan Sr. and detained Comelec official Lintang Bedol ... said they were instructed by GMA to cheat in the 2007 polls."

That is utterly false. Despite pressures on him to back up Unas' claims, and despite his vulnerability as he is already in jail for the massacre, Ampatuan swore in writing that Unas is lying to his teeth. Bedol didn't say he was instructed by Arroyo to cheat. All he said is that Ampatuan told him so, which the former governor denies. Both are among the accused in the electoral fraud case to pressure them to testify falsely against Arroyo.

An editorial also in this paper stated that the "charges against Arroyo [are] in connection with the alleged rigging of the 2004 elections," the subtext being that she cheated to be president. The charges had nothing to do with the 2004 elections, but on the 2007 senatorial elections.

Aquino's officials for 15 months tried but failed to fabricate charges of 2004 electoral fraud. It was only in September that they hit upon this demonic scheme of convincing a suspect, whose name (Unas) is not commonly associated with the Maguindanao massacre, to testify falsely against Arroyo, in exchange for his exclusion among those accused for the atrocity.

Hundreds of articles have been written on Arroyo's arrest, on her medical condition, on the constitutional issues involved even on the kind of cell the former president would be put into. But there hasn't been a single print or broadcast article on the accuser who triggered all these events: Unas. Why did he suddenly volunteer to accuse Arroyo? Was he promised not to be included in the massacre case? Is he even alive? Or is he already dead, in which case he can never be cross-examined nor retract his accusations?

A French politician is accused of rape and in a few days media uncover the minutest details about the accuser, which helped expose her as an extortionist. In our case, a former president is arrested for an electoral crime and most media men, even a senior columnist, do not even know the name of the accuser.

I can express the darkness that has descended on this land now only in Yeats' chilling poem titled, quite aptly now, "The Second Coming":

Mere anarchy is loosed upon the world,
The blood-dimmed tide is loosed, and everywhere
The ceremony of innocence is drowned;
The best lack all conviction, while the worst
Are full of passionate intensity.

(November 21, 2011)

A PREPOSTEROUS PLUNDER CASE

MAD THAT GLORIA MACAPAGAL-ARROYO was freed on bail on a clearly trumped-up electoral sabotage case built entirely on the claim of a massacre suspect, President Benigno Aquino III pivoted: "But there is a case pending before the Sandiganbayan for plunder, and plunder is not bailable."

There you have it straight from the horse's mouth. This isn't about accountability, certainly not about justice. It's a President ruthlessly using all his resources he can wield, all the technicalities he can find just to jail his predecessor.

Read the charge sheet against Arroyo — really a prattle of sweeping accusations—and the only conclusion one can arrive at is: Never mind if the charges are obviously cooked up, the aim is to keep her in jail. Never mind even if the court acquits her, after many years the case is pending.

What's the "plunder" charge? That Arroyo and the directors of the Philippine Charity Sweepstakes Office (PCSO) from 2008 to 2010 "accumulated and/or acquired ill-gotten wealth in the amount of" P366 million.

Where did they get that P366-million figure? That's the total "confidential intelligence funds" from 2008 to 2010 reported in PCSO books, and used for such operations as countering sweepstakes scams and jueteng operations. A significant amount of this, according to former PCSO chair Manuel Morato, was used for paying the so-called "blood-money" that saved the lives of several overseas Filipino workers accused of homicide in certain Mideast countries.

Quite idiotically and appallingly, the Ombudsman Conchita Carpio-Morales alleges that all these confidential intelligence funds went into the pockets of the accused — without however even presenting a single instance of misuse of the funds, or an iota of evidence.

That allegation had already been proven totally wrong. The Commission on Audit (COA) chair during that period, Reynaldo Villar, officially informed the Ombudsman eight months ago when the case was filed there that the PCSO officials had submitted the required documents showing the funds' legitimate use, validated by the COA auditors.

However, in Ombudsman Morales' toadying and blind obedience to Aquino (and her officers' dimwittedness), they included COA chair Villar and senior auditor Nilda Plaras, who audited the PCSO funds, among those accused of plunder. That has shocked not only the COA but also the entire government bureaucracy.

No evidence was presented, no specific accusation was made that the two COA officials connived with Arroyo or the PCSO board for the issuance of the audit clearances. If they found nothing wrong in the use of the funds, the Ombudsman argued, they're therefore part of the plunder conspiracy.

That's a big blunder for this plunder charge as the Ombudsman is disputing the integrity of the COA, without even having her own auditors study the PCSO documents. Aquino and his Ombudsman have in effect declared that the audits of the COA — the sole, independent body vested by the Constitution with the authority to audit government funds — are worthless.

If the case against the PCSO officials is obviously baseless, that against Arroyo is utterly imbecilic.

She is accused of "raiding the public treasury" when what she did was merely to approve the request for the use of additional intelligence funds, which is authorized by law. Furthermore, it was the PCSO management, and not the former President, that undertook the actual disbursement and monitoring of all confidential intelligence funds.

She didn't even release the funds; neither did these pass her hands or the Office of the President, since the PCSO is an autonomous government corporation. If Ombudsman Morales' pea-brained argument is followed, then all the members of Congress who approve the government budget, as well as the budget secretary and department heads who actually disburse the moneys, would be liable either for graft or plunder in any case that is diverted to corruption by any official.

Moreover, what the Plunder Law requires is proof that the "ill-gotten" wealth (of at least P50 million) acquired through graft has ended up in the bank accounts of the accused.

Former President Joseph Estrada was convicted of plunder not just because former governor Chavit Singson and others testified that he had received part of the tobacco excise tax and jueteng protection money. He was convicted because the prosecution presented over two dozen bank officials such as Clarissa Ocampo who submitted to the court photocopies of over 100 cancelled checks in accounts where the ill-gotten wealth were deposited, and identified to be Estrada's, totaling P4.1 billion.

In contrast, the P366 million the Ombudsman is bandying about is not what Arroyo and the PCSO officials allegedly pocketed. These are simply the total intelligence funds reported in PCSO's books disbursed over three years. There is not even any specific allegation that Arroyo diverted any of these to her bank accounts, only that she approved such funds.

There are no Singsons or Ocampos, no bank documents, in this plunder charge. Quite hilariously, the main witnesses cited in the charge sheet are the complainants themselves, who are Aquino's on-call, rent-a-crusader operatives: communist party ally Akbayan's Risa Hontiveros and deputy customs commissioner Danilo Lim, both of whom are begging Aquino to be included in his senatorial slate next year.

Why are they witnesses? Because they watched on television the playing-to-the-gallery Senate hearings that investigated the PCSO last year. Their corroborative witness: Antonina Barros, head of the Senate's records and archives division.

Only this kind of deluded President could ever order the pursuit of this phony, preposterous plunder charge.

(August 1, 2012)

POSTSCRIPT:

The Supreme Court on July 19, 2016, by vote of 11 to 4, dismissed this plunder charge against Arroyo, ordering her freed after nearly five years of incarceration. Aquino-appointed justices Maria Lourdes Sereno Marivic Leonen, and Alfredo Caguioa as well as Antonio Carpio voted against the majority. The Court ruled that the Sandiganbayan that ordered her arrested and jailed "ignored the lack of evidence establishing" her innocence and that it "acted capriciously, gravely abusing its discretion."

Corona Impeachment

CORONA PH.D. QUESTIONED

UST 'breaks rules' for C

Red Cross

CJ keeping $12M in
banks–Ombudsma

AMLC unlocks Corona foreign currency accou

BALANCED NEWS, FEARLESS VIEWS

'Corona asse
worth ₱200

45 Corona assets eye

Philippine Daily Inquirer's screaming headlines against Corona during his trial. Each and every one of these, and about a dozen other allegations were proven false.

AQUINO'S ATTACK ON THE JUDICIARY

ON MAY 29, 2012, the Senate removed the Chief Justice of the Supreme Court, the head of the judicial branch of government that is co-equal with the executive and legislative branches, for failure to declare his dollar assets in his Statement of Assets and Liabilities and Net Worth (SALN), for which the simple and legal remedy was to correct the SALN entry.

Still, the Senate voted Corona guilty, but not because of the highest standards they felt the Chief Justice should meet. Rather, it was because of the lowest standards they felt they needed to comply with, that it was the wish of President Aquino to remove Corona from that post and they got rewarded for making his wish come true.

Rather than the evidence against Corona, it was the billions of pesos given the congressmen and senators in pork barrel funds and money through a new Aquino scheme called the Disbursement Acceleration Program (DAP), it would be disclosed later, that made them vote Corona guilty. The five months during which, we were regaled by then Senate President Juan Ponce Enrile, with his legal acumen and apparent impartiality was all for show.

The smokescreen that there wasn't any 30 pieces of silver, for the crucifixion of our Republican system of three co-equal branches of government was the campaign of vilification against Corona, the likes of which we really hadn't seen before, even if we include the demonization of President Gloria Macapagal-Arroyo.

The difference between the smear drive against Arroyo and Corona is that in the latter's case, state entities were used, from the Congress, the budget, the BIR, the Land Registration Bureau, the Ombudsman and even the central bank, which controls the Anti-Money Laundering Council (AMLC).

It was a pyrrhic victory for Aquino though. Removing Chief Justice Renato Corona took five months to undertake, with his target refusing to resign before the trial started. Aquino thought he would resign as easily as another Arroyo official he bullied into submission, Ombudsman Merceditas Gutierrez.

However, the impeachment, the vicious character assassination against Corona and the threat to remove another justice, Mariano del

Castillo, failed to intimidate the High Court to rule for Aquino in the case of his family's Hacienda Luisita.

On April 2012, at the height of the impeachment trial, the Court ruled with finality that the sugar hacienda had implemented a bogus land reform. It was ordered to distribute its vast estate to its farmer-workers, and for them to be compensated a tenth of the cost his appointee Lourdes Sereno, who replaced Corona, had propounded.

Even if Aquino had proven by some miracle to manage the country well after May 2012 — which he didn't — his attack on the Supreme Court, if only we had a patriotic and independent Congress and armed forces, should have been enough to remove him from power.

Never has a Philippine president schemed and mobilized illegally everything under his control as chief executive, to attack the head of an equal branch of government.

Bribery exposed

What kind of country have we become, that the bribery to convict Corona had been exposed, yet we have not as a nation moved to correct such injustice? We have swept this colossal scandal under the rug.

Philippine historians in the future will be astonished how Aquino was able to mobilize and mesmerize institutions, which theoretically, are our bastions of democracy, to attack Corona.

I've never seen such a vicious demonization campaign against an individual who stood his ground. Aquino gave a new meaning to that term "throw everything but the kitchen sink": he threw everything against the Chief Justice, from the petty to the cruel.

Corona's passion for learning represented by the PhD he earned from the University of Sto. Tomas, the oldest university in Asia, was distorted by a writer who claimed the university "bent rules" to accommodate him. It was the banner story by the country's biggest newspaper, simultaneously with a news website, whose ownership remains a mystery. That was a total hogwash.

I am astonished that those who were at the lead of this lynch mob still strut around as if nothing had happened. A megalomaniac blogger posted on her blog, details of what she alleged were Corona's bank accounts. When people ignored her post, she gave it to Liberal Party congressman Rey Umali, one of the prosecutors, who, after he leaked the illegal information, timidly told the Senate he got the data from a "small lady" whose name he forgot.

Another yellow operative congressman, Jorge Banal, fantastically claimed that information on Corona's accounts he got and gave the panel, was in an envelope he found at the gate of his residence. Harvey Keh of the Ateneo School of Government tried to get Senate President Juan Ponce Enrile to admit as evidence, these illegally acquired documents on Corona's bank accounts. The former martial law administrator rebuffed him and lectured him on the principles of fair play and the rule of law.

We would only know later what these bungling attempts to have illegal documents adopted by the impeachment court were all about.

The AMLC had already thrown our bank secrecy and privacy laws to the dustbin, and had given Aquino's operatives details of Corona's bank accounts even before the trial stared. Their only problem was how to distort and disclose it. Ombudsman Conchita Carpio-Morales showed them how.

With dramatic flair as she waived purportedly AMLC documents given to her, Morales claimed Corona had $12 million in his dollar accounts. Why, it was a Commission on Audit member, Heidi Mendoza, who analyzed the data and came up with that figure, she reported!

How could they think we are all stupid, or have never had bank transactions? Morales and Mendoza added up transactions over nine years, not Corona's balance. He had only $2 million, most of which he had accumulated as a private corporate lawyer in the 1980s. Count the debit and credit entries for each of your transactions in your bank book, and you'll find you're a millionaire.

Did Morales ever apologize for her colossal error? I cannot comprehend why Morales could have treated her former colleague in the Supreme Court as a common criminal, a money launderer. Aquino had even destroyed people's sense of decency.

They claimed Corona had P200 million in his accounts, which he couldn't have accumulated with his salary as chief justice. It turned out to be his savings when he was still a private lawyer, proceeds of sales of property that was part of the inheritance of his wife, and the savings of her daughters and son commingled with his account in order to command a higher interest rate.

It was lie after lie against Corona. Land Registration Authority head Eulalio Diaz II, an Aquino appointee, claimed his office's records show that Corona had 45 real estate properties. It turned out that most of these 45 properties were astonishingly not in Corona's name, in a namesake's name, or which the Chief Justice had long ago disposed of. How many properties did Corona actually own? Five.

Corona was reportedly hiding a property in California, an allegation leaked again by Aquino's operators to that dingbat blogger. It was bought dirt-cheap during the real estate crisis in the US in 2008, by Corona's daughter Charina, a physical therapist who worked two jobs to cough up the money for the mortgage. Aquino even used a Corona family squabble with his wife's relatives to portray him as an evil man. A 90-year old nun was virtually dragged out of the convent, so she could be interviewed and misquoted to say something bad about the Coronas.

Why do we allow such liars who besmirched not only a person's reputation, but also that of his entire family, to go unpunished?

There were eight articles of impeachment against Corona. Each was proven wrong by Corona's defense counsels that by April, the Liberal Party prosecutors sheepishly announced they will pursue only one article, that on Corona's SALN.

It was because they already had illegally acquired from the AMLC details of Corona's bank accounts, even if the matter of whether Corona's failure to declare his dollar accounts violated his oath of office was debatable. After all, we have a secrecy law on dollar bank deposits. And after all, the penalty for submitting an inaccurate SALN was to correct it within a year.

Aquino's double-cross

It would be more than a year later in September 2013 that Senator Jinggoy Estrada — when he had become Aquino's next target, together with Enrile and another senator, Bong Revilla — would rat on Aquino. Estrada was shocked and exasperated over the double-cross by Aquino, whose Justice Secretary subsequently got him jailed over the misuse of the pork barrel funds.

I endured the tediousness of watching Corona's televised trial for five months, and spent many hours studying the case, and asking legal experts for their analysis.

It turned out to be a waste of time. It was a charade, as much a moro-moro as congressman Rufus Rodriguez' months of hearings on the Bangsamoro Basic Law are now.

Estrada disclosed that administration operatives bribed him and the rest of those who voted Corona guilty, with pork barrel funds, and with money raised through the DAP.

Senator Bong Revilla even narrated how he was brought to Malacañang in a car driven by Mar Roxas himself to meet with Aquino, who asked him to vote Corona guilty. Also in the meeting was Budget Secretary Florencio Abad, who assured him his P100 million pork funds would be released if he cooperated.

Defense counselor Judd Roy had actually made the charge of bribery during the trial in early 2012, as Abad declared that "not a single centavo was released in PDAF funds before, during, and after the trial." The mainstream yellow media ignored Roy's bribery claims.

But data on DAP and other pork barrel releases were routinely posted on the DBM's website. This was the smoking gun that everyone else ignored. I collated these and reported the exact amounts in PDAF and DAP funds released immediately before, during, and after the impeachment trial. Estrada, Revilla, and Roy's bribery charges against Aquino were confirmed with solid data.

A nation is supposed to be built step by step as its institutions are strengthened each time it confronts a crisis. But what happened under Aquino is the opposite. His illegal and unconstitutional moves damaged the institutions of democracy — from the Supreme Court, to the Senate and Congress, the Press, and the entire bureaucracy under his control. All of these tyrannical acts happened just because he wanted to get more money for his Hacienda Luisita.

For starting a lynch mob against Chief Justice Corona, a good and decent man who suffered through lies and humiliations, Aquino will be judged by history as the worst ever president of this country.

(May 28, 2015)

IMPEACHMENT WAS ALL ABOUT HACIENDA LUISITA

'TIME DISCOVERS TRUTH.' This proverb by the Roman philosopher Seneca is useful in understanding, what the impeachment of Chief Justice Renato Corona was really all about. Consider the following historical timeline and be shocked at seeing, that the real motive for the removal of Corona, was the billions of pesos in compensation money that the Aquino-Cojuangco clan wanted to get for Hacienda Luisita.

Early 2010: Benigno Aquino III's rivals allege that the real reason he wants to be president, is to save his Cojuangco clan from utter bankruptcy, which would happen if the Supreme Court rules against the sham land reform at its vast Hacienda Luisita. Since Corazon Aquino's time and every administration thereafter, the Hacienda has escaped from being part of the Comprehensive Agrarian Reform Program.

May 12, 2010: President Gloria Macapagal-Arroyo surprises everyone, by appointing Renato Corona to replace Chief Justice Reynato Puno who retires May 17, 2010. That is a relief to most in the legal community, since President Aquino would have likely appointed instead Associate Justice Antonio Carpio, which would give the law firm he founded another administration, its third, under its sway. Aquino III is enraged by Arroyo's move.

June 30, 2010: Aquino sends the strongest message possible, that he wants Corona out by having Justice Conchita Carpio Morales swear him into office instead of the Chief Justice, breaking a tradition respected by all past presidents. (Morales is Antonio Carpio's cousin who was the only dissenter in the Court decision upholding Corona's appointment. Aquino would appoint her Ombudsman in July 2011 soon after she retired from the Supreme Court.)

June 2010: Aquino tells Corona that he has a chance to be his patron if he gets the Court to rule constitutional his "Truth Commission" — which it didn't, by a vote of 10-5, in December 2010.

July 2011: The Court rules the Cojuangcos' agrarian reform program in their plantation a sham, and orders it to distribute Hacienda Luisita to its farmers, and pay them P1.3 billion for lands they already sold. Aquino's sole appointee at that time, Lourdes Sereno, writes a kilometric dissenting opinion arguing for a land valuation that would amount to P10 billion, way above the P196 million the Court ruled.

August-September 2011: Aquino appoints two more justices to the Court, making it possible to reverse its July 2011 decision — but only if Corona capitulates along with Justice Mariano Castillo, whom Aquino's operatives were already pressuring to resign, with the threat of impeachment on grounds of plagiarism.

November 15, 2011: The Supreme Court issues an order, restraining the Justice Secretary from preventing without a court order, Gloria Arroyo's travel abroad for medical treatment. Aquino demonizes the former president and creates a platform to rationalize his wanting to take out Corona: he claimed that Arroyo would evade justice, that his anti-corruption crusade would fail, as long as Corona is the Chief Justice.

November 22, 2011: The Court affirms its July 2011 ruling, dismissing Sereno's argument for a P10-billion payment. Aquino was livid and his plotting against Corona continued.

December 12, 2011: While the Cojuangcos' appeal on the Hacienda Luisita decision was pending, and on orders from Aquino, the House of Representatives

> impeaches Corona, even if nearly all of the 188 complainant-representatives had not read the complaint. This was clearly a dictatorial move coming from an Aquino, whose family built their political reputations on being anti-dictatorship. The impeachment against Corona was clearly not based on evidence, but was intended merely as a peg for a media demonization of Corona to force him to resign. Indeed, the past months have seen a shameless "yellow" media being yoked to a sitting President's agenda.

The High Court's final ruling in April 2012 on the Hacienda Luisita case — eight against six — showed how crucial it was to take out Corona. If Corona had resigned, there would be only seven justices left defying Aquino, since his slot would be taken over by the President's appointee, and there would be a deadlock: seven against seven. However, Carpio would likely be appointed chief justice, a post he will invoke to lift his abstention from the case, to be the swing vote favoring Aquino's Hacienda.

> **March 2012:** Corona — to the Aquino camp's surprise — refuses to resign, and the impeachment against him all but collapses. The 45 properties the prosecutors and media screamed he owned prove to be blatant lies, manufactured by the Land Registration Authority head Eulalio Diaz (Aquino's buddy since his school days). The prosecution drops five of the eight articles of impeachment, realizing they would be dismissed if pursued. The claim that Corona protected Arroyo in the Supreme Court — Aquino's declared reason for wanting him out — is torn to pieces.

That Aquino's impeachment project was sputtering was proven by the fact that Ombudsman Morales was, in April, already preparing another complaint, which she publicly boasted she would ask the House of Representatives to file in December. The new charge, that Corona had unexplained wealth of over $12 million, turns out to be at best a colossal, devious deception and, at worst, an imbecilic ignorance of banks' reporting of their clients' transactions.

The charges against Corona, which were distorted to allegations of massive corruption, have drastically shrunk solely to the issue that he should have declared his dollar assets, no matter how small — and he did have such holdings after a 40-year law career — in his statement of assets, liabilities and net worth.

But really, is this what all the savage campaign against Corona and his family all about? Is this really what the Constitution meant when it provided that a public official may be impeached "for treason, bribery, graft and corruption, other high crimes, or betrayal of public trust"?

Would the senators convict Corona, knowing (or having even just the slightest suspicion) that this has been all about a President's plot to save his clan's wealth and to control all three branches of government? Will they be party to one of the most ruthless campaigns ever by a Philippine president, employing the vast apparatus of government and a subservient press, against one man who refuses to bend to his will?

(May 24, 2012)

PHILIPPINE DAILY

INQUIRER

BALANCED NEWS, FEARLESS VIE

SALN allows Ombudsman to secure documents

2 senators note 'missing' entries in Corona SALNs

CJ keeping $12M in 5 banks–Ombudsman

AMLC unlocks Corona foreign currency accounts

Jeepney fares, pan de sal price cut

PDI's front-page story on Carpio-Morales' deception

COLOSSAL DECEPTION ON CORONA'S ACCOUNTS

OMBUDSMAN CONCHITA CARPIO MORALES' allegation that Chief Justice Renato Corona had \$12 million in dollar accounts, will go down in Philippine history as one of the biggest and most deviously constructed deceptions ever foisted on the public.

Morales swallowed hook, line, and sinker the deeply flawed analysis of raw data made by Heidi Mendoza, whom President Aquino deep-selected to overtake five officer-levels, to become deputy commissioner of the Commission on Audit. Or perhaps she connived with Mendoza to invent this blackest of black propaganda.

Morales' allegations are based on two colossal errors. One involves confusing the meanings of "transactions" and "balances"; the other exploits laymen's ignorance of banking transactions and how these are documented.

The first error actually was deliberate, as Aquino's operatives still had a big problem when they got raw data from the secretariat of the Anti-Money Laundering Council (AMLC). These didn't report Corona's bank balances but merely transactions, whose average amount per transaction for deposits was only \$104,737, hardly eyebrow-raising. (The AMLC report, marked "For Intelligence Purpose Only," however, has no authorship and its entries have no source document, which opens the possibility of its tampering.)

Morales or Mendoza, therefore had to surreptitiously misrepresent "transactions" as "balances," to generate significant amounts. This was done by a conceptual sleight of hand.

Morales' PowerPoint presentation states: "The amounts appearing in the tabulation are not account balances but transaction balances." This was a devious invention of a term in order that the sum of transactions would be confused with "balances," so that Corona would appear to have huge bank accounts. Indeed, Morales would later on drop the "transaction" adjective, referring only to "aggregations," "balances," or "bank accounts."

Transactions are the withdrawals and deposits on your bank account over time. The net result of these, what's left, is your bank balance at a given time.

To illustrate, if I have P100,000 in my bank account and lend it out at a 5-percent interest rate for a month's use to six borrowers consecutively, my bank balance at the end of six months would be P130,000. This is the sum of my initial P100,000 plus the interest of P5,000 earned for each of the six lending transactions.

For Morales though, my bank account would be 10 times more: P1.33 million. This is her "transaction balance" for the 13 transactions — my initial deposit of P100,000 plus P600,00 (the sum of six withdrawals of P100,000 each when I lend it) plus P630,000 (the sum of six deposits of P105,000 each when I'm repaid).

This is exactly how Morales arrived at Corona's "$12 million dollar accounts." She and Mendoza summed up all of the transactions, rather than reporting the balances.

From this data, Morales claims that Corona's dollar accounts for 2004 "aggregate" to $1.1 million — the sum of all deposit transactions ($550,740) and withdrawal transactions ($550,000). She does this kind of computations for the nine years 2003 to 2011, and — voila! — Corona's bank accounts total $12 million. (Since we don't know what the initial deposit was, determining what Corona's balance was at end-2004 can only be a guess.)

Morales' second colossal error is based on ignorance (a pretended one) of banking transactions and how these are documented.

Morales and the prosecution panel claimed that the fact that Corona had 82 dollar accounts indicated that the Chief Justice was trying to hide his money and may even have engaged in money laundering. In her presentation, Morales was aghast at her "significant observations": "multiple accounts created for similar purpose!" "Circuitous fund movements!"[!] "Deposit and withdrawal made on the same day!" Bankers have been laughing at such display of banking illiteracy.

There are 82 accounts (in nine years), since Corona or his fund manager has been active in generating as much earnings from his funds through the usual money market placements, each of which are reported as different accounts.

For example, a 30-day placement amounting to $390,000 was made on April 4, reported in the AMLC data as another dollar account. The placement was terminated May 6, with $390,526 credited to Corona's account — earning $526 in a month's time. Mysterious deposits and withdrawals on the same day? These are either the usual overnight money market placements or documentation requirements on certain transactions.

So how much did Corona have in his bank accounts, and did he report this in his SALN? While only a guess, it would be the biggest and last of Corona's banking transactions reported: $687,433.

That dollar amount is worth P29.4 million now. But in 2001 when the exchange rate was P51 to the dollar, that was equivalent to P35 million. Doesn't that figure remind you of the P34.7 million payment by the Manila government for the Basa-Guidote property, which the Chief Justice's better-half, Cristina Corona, received and said she was holding in trust, and therefore was not their asset?

(May 17, 2012)

IMPEACHMENT CHARGES COLLAPSE

ANYONE WHO HAS ACTUALLY watched and listened to the 34 impeachment trial sessions, and therefore spared himself from the yellow filters of a partisan press, can only but conclude: The impeachment case against Chief Justice Renato Corona has all but collapsed.

This has become obvious even as his defense has just warmed up. President Aquino would have to exhaust his resources to bribe or threaten senator-judges, to undertake intellectual and ethical contortions to vote Corona guilty.

Consider the facts.

For starters: Recall that the House of Representatives in December, forwarded with much bravado to the Senate eight articles of impeachment — or allegations of eight instances of wrongdoing by Corona. On the 25th trial day, the prosecution sheepishly declared they had nothing else to present, and were no longer pursuing five of the eight allegations (articles 1,4, 5,6, and 8), giving no reason why.

The reason had become obvious though: these had been hurled merely as a propaganda barrage, that there were so many issues against Corona that he was better off resigning. They thought they could take out Corona just as easily as they removed former Ombudsman Merceditas Gutierrez who, after being demonized in the press, resigned a few days after the impeachment case was filed.

But the man fought back, and there were courageous people in the country rushing to his succor — the likes of the 83-year-old former associate justice Serafin Cuevas, veteran top-notch lawyers, and young, cultured defense spokespersons.

The prosecution had realized after two months of trial that Cuevas would be making mincemeat out of the five made-up charges, and therefore dropped them. Article 5 involved the Court decision for the creation of 16 cities and of Dinagat Island as a province, while 4 and 6 involved its resolutions, respectively, on Gutierrez's impeachment and the plagiarism case against an associate justice. But all these Court actions and others alleged in Article 1 were by the majority of the justices, and Corona's votes weren't even tiebreakers. Article 1 even claimed that Corona should be impeached because he accepted his appointment as chief justice!

Article 8 — the most preposterous — alleged that Corona "failed to account for the Judiciary Development Fund," the reporting systems for which have been unchanged since it was set up nearly three decades ago in 1984.

The trial now therefore involves only Articles 2, 3 and 7. Article 7 accuses Corona of protecting former President Gloria Macapagal-Arroyo, when the Court ordered the justice department to allow her to travel abroad. But Corona in that case, was just one of eight justices (against five) who voted in favor of Arroyo's petition to travel.

The prosecution presented Article 3 only with respect to the Court's rulings on the Philippine Airlines labor case, which however were also decisions agreed upon by the majority.

What the impeachers are in effect saying is that Corona should have always voted with the minority. If Corona had done that, he definitely should be removed — for being a nutcase.

The first part of Article 2 alleged that Corona "failed to disclose his statement of assets, liabilities, and net worth." But the Court issued a resolution two decades ago that justices (in order to shield them from harassment) must submit these documents only to the Court, and would have to get its permission to have these publicly disclosed.

The second part alleged that "tens of millions worth of assets and cash" were not declared in his SALNs.

The prosecution claimed that Corona had not disclosed 40 properties, with Land Registration Authority head Eulalio Diaz, Aquino's long-time buddy, submitting copies of titles he claimed were registered either under the Chief Justice's or his wife's names.

That has been proven to be such a big lie, that Senator Loren Legarda demanded that the prosecution should apologize for trying to fool the Senate and the public. Some 17 of the titles with the Coronas' names Diaz submitted already had the prominent "CANCELLED" marking, meaning they no longer were the owners.

Another 12 were not even in the Coronas' names, but were in his in-laws' namesakes' and children's who had the means to purchase the properties.

Seven Marikina properties were sold in 1990 to one Demetrio Vicente who credibly testified to that effect in court. Three were parking lots attached to the condominiums.

One title was part of a property Corona had declared. Undervalued? But Corona reported the valuation of his properties made by city assessors, which is used by most government officials, even by Aquino who reported his upscale Quezon City home at its assessor's valuation of P3 million.

And the moneys Corona had in his bank accounts but was not reported in his SALN?

President Aquino's minions obviously were able to illegally access his bank accounts, and probably jumped up and down in joy when they discovered that it had over P40 million or so — much more than what he reported in his SALNs.

But last week, it was shown that Mrs. Cristina Corona had received (in trust for the corporate owner) P35 million for the payment of a land sold to the city of Manila, which she had deposited in her husband's bank.

"So it turns out that it is not (Corona's) money, but that of the company. So, it was only proper that he did not include it (in his SALN)," Senator Miriam Santiago concluded.

Why did they ever undertake this vicious but foolhardy campaign to crush the Chief Justice?

"Truth overcomes deceit," the Buddhist Dhammapada said more than 2,000 years ago. The deceit is that Corona should be taken out for corruption. The truth is that Aquino clan can get P10 billion for Hacienda Luisita, only if Corona is removed.

(March 29, 2012)

Benigno Simeon Cojuangco Aquino

THE WORST PRESIDENT EVER

PRESIDENT BENIGNO S. AQUINO III will go down in history as the country's worst President ever.

This President damaged the very institutions of our Republic, and that puts the Philippines a decade back in building a modern, prosperous nation-state that uplifts the welfare of all its citizens.

To better understand this, keep in mind that in the last two centuries, the method or discipline of rational inquiry (or simply the scientific method) has subjected and demystified in many cases, nearly all phenomena under the sun, both natural and those created by humanity.

In the last two decades especially, one question that has been placed under close scrutiny, has been why certain nations on earth have become prosperous and why others haven't. While there are still opposing schools of thought to answer this question, there has remarkably been some convergence in the various analyses.

One consensus is that what plays a crucial role in a nation's growth (or impoverishment) has been this thing we call "institutions."

Noted political scientist Francis Fukuyama in his 2011 book, **Political Order and Political Decay: From the Industrial Revolution to the Globalization of Democracy,** in fact, analyzed the strengthening and weakening of different nations in the world within the framework of how their institutions have grown or not, or have become inappropriate for their stages of development.

That kind of framework is centuries ahead of that prevailing mode of analysis you read in sophomoric blogs, and even in juvenile opinion columns, which agonize with a neurotic kind of self-immolation, on "what's wrong with the Filipino character," or what bad habits this group of people has that allow them to get stuck in a lousy nation with a lousy leadership.

"Institutions are stable, valued recurring patterns of behavior that persist beyond the tenure of individual leaders," Fukuyama explained in his book. "They are in essence, persistent rules that shape, limit and channel human behavior."

Abstract as that may seem to be, we would very easily understand what sort of institution manifests such examples. For instance, post-Qaddafi Libya's problems following the US-led military intervention in 2011 were triggered by the lack of basic institutions, notably a state.

Fukuyama added that until there is a "single source of authority that exercises a legitimate monopoly of force in that country, there will be no citizen security or the conditions for individuals to flourish."

On the other hand, the political scientist noted the US has long-standing and powerful institutions, but they have been subject to political decay.

Using the author's analysis, the Aquino regime has resulted in our political decay.

Fukuyama explains that there are three sets of institutions, whose strength or weakness have determined which nations are prosperous and strong, and which are not.

The first institution is the State, which he defines, as most political scientists do, as the institution that "possesses a monopoly of legitimate coercion and exercises that power over a defined territory."

Prosperous countries have a modern state, the administration of which "does not consist of the ruler's family and friends; rather recruitment to administrative positions is based on impersonal criteria as merit, education, or technical knowledge."

The raison d'être of modern states, of course, is to provide the necessary public goods and maintain order, which only it can do as it has the resources, through taxes and the bureaucracy, and the legal right and power to do so.

'Student government'

It is obviously in this context that former senator Joker Arroyo's jest, that Aquino has an amateurish "student-council" government, is in actuality an insightful criticism.

In the five years he has been in office, the Aquino administration couldn't even make the MRT-3 trains run on time and efficiently. In five years, even if the Congress had given it the funds, the Aquino state could not modernize the military and instead, has all this time been stuck in allegations of corruption in the purchase of military equipment. Despite Aquino's boast in 2011 that the country would be exporting rice soon, we are still importing one million tons of rice yearly.

The antithesis of the modern state is the "patrimonial" state, considered a "personal property of the ruler, and state administration is essentially an extension of the ruler's household," Fukuyama explained.

The second institution is the Rule of Law, or rules that are binding on the most politically powerful actors in a given society. Fukuyama makes a distinction that reminds us of what has been called Aquino's "selective justice":

"Rule of law should be distinguished from what is sometimes referred to as 'rule by law'," which he explains as "commands issued by the ruler but not binding on the ruler himself" or his allies.

Three opposition senators are jailed for alleged involvement in the pork barrel scam. Aquino's allies, though, were exempt from any such investigation.

The third institution, in Fukuyama's framework, is Democratic Accountability. Its mechanisms include the Supreme Court and its lower courts and Congress, both of which are separate and independent and which act as checks to the ruler, i.e., the executive branch. Another important mechanism is made up of free and fraud-free elections.

Fukuyama, though, emphasizes how the three institutions all have to exist at the same time. He even uses the Philippines as an example of how things can go wrong if one institution is missing:

"(The Philippines) democratized before it had a modern state and has, therefore, experienced substantial amounts of patronage and clientelism."

Fukuyama is quite categorical, asserting that the least developed parts of the world today are those that lacked these institutions or had only weak versions of these. "Many of the problems of developing countries are by-products of the fact that they have weak and ineffective states," he emphasized.

I would think that the many cases of how Aquino has damaged all three institutions have already crossed the reader's mind. Among the most prominent cases, by no means a complete listing, are as follows.

Judicial branch decapitated

Aquino damaged severely the Philippine state's most important institution, the Constitutional separation of the three branches of government.

The executive headed by Aquino bribed the legislative branch to decapitate the judicial branch, with its head replaced by a known ally of the President. That really was this regime's defining moment. With

Chief Justice Renato Corona out of the way, he thought his clan could get a much bigger land reform compensation for Hacienda Luisita.

There were eight counts of impeachment against Corona. All were proven wrong in the trial, yet he was still removed by the Senate for his failure to disclose his dollar accounts — which was not among the eight counts.

It would only be unearthed later that each of the 20 senators who found him guilty had received during, and right after the trial, hundreds of millions of pesos in pork barrel from the so-called Disbursement Acceleration Program funds, Aquino's scheme for using state funds not authorized by Congress in its annual budget act.

Aquino appointed as associate justice and then chief justice a mediocre legal academic, with little actual practice of law, whose main qualification was that she was the President's college buddy, and that she allegedly prepared his family's Supreme Court brief to get better compensation for their Hacienda Luisita's expropriation.

He appointed another inexperienced academic to the High Court, Marvic Leonen, just because he negotiated an agreement with the Moro Islamic Liberation Front (MILF) that was so favorable to the insurgent group, but inimical to the Philippine Republic.

Aquino damaged the Supreme Court, which has had decades of tradition that its members must have proven themselves to be legal luminaries both in practice and theory. Thrown to the dustbin in the appointment of the Court's members, is a modern state's practice of appointing to government positions, as Fukuyama explained, "those based on impersonal criteria as merit, education, or technical knowledge."

Even the chief of the Philippine National Police, a crucial position, was chosen not because of his qualifications but because he was Aquino's close-in security, his bodyguard, during his mother's term. Aquino pulled out of retirement general Voltaire Gazmin to be his Defense Secretary. His qualification? He headed his mother's presidential guards.

Aquino even corrupted a bastion of democracy, the Fourth Estate, by recruiting a major newspaper and an Internet-only news outfit as his propaganda tools in his campaigns against Corona, leading opposition senators Juan Ponce Enrile, Jinggoy Estrada, and Ramon Revilla, and more recently Vice President Jejomar Binay, just because he is the frontrunner in the 2016 elections.

Rubber-stamp Congress

The institutions of democratic accountability had been all but wrecked with Congress, bribed by Aquino with pork barrel funds, becoming his personal rubber stamp.

An example of this was Aquino's decision to file the case against China questioning its nine-dash line — a move that would weaken the country's diplomatic relations with the superpower for the next four to five years until the case is resolved. His lawyers filed the case at the Permanent Court of Arbitration at The Hague on January 21, 2013.

At the same time, Aquino ordered both houses of Congress to issue a resolution supporting it. The resolution was filed and approved on the same day on January 22, with no discussion in either the Senate or the House of Representatives.

One would have to be very gullible not to believe that Aquino bullied former Ombudsman Mercedes Gutierrez to resign, so she would be replaced by Conchita Carpio-Morales, who had become his political assassin, even against vice-president Binay.

The many cases the Ombudsman filed against Aquino's enemies will likely be dismissed sooner or later, as these were rushed to meet political deadlines or had no basis in the first place. The Office of the Ombudsman as the anti-graft institution has thus been weakened, probably for a decade, or until it proves it is not a tool of the sitting President.

Aquino damaged the institution called the Rule of Law in so many instances, two of the most important:

He ordered his police general, Alan Purisima, to head the Mamasapano operations against international terrorists even if the police general, his former close-in security, was suspended at the time by law for a graft investigation. Aquino hasn't been made accountable for such violation of the law.

He threw to the dustbin the General Appropriations Laws from 2011 to 2013, by hijacking funds authorized by those laws, for a fake Disbursement Acceleration Program. The Supreme Court ruled he violated the Constitution. He hasn't been made accountable for that at all.

Even the Bangko Sentral ng Pilipinas (BSP), one of our few institutions that showed world-class operating standards, had been prostituted by Aquino.

The confidential bank accounts, first of Chief Justice Corona, and then of Vice President Binay and his family, were released — without a court order — to the Ombudsman by the Anti-Money Laundering Council, which the BSP governor headed. It was the Ombudsman's distorted report of these accounts that shifted public opinion against Corona, that was the smokescreen for the Senate to find him guilty.

Aquino hasn't even been able to lead the state in undertaking one of its basic functions, which is to provide services to the citizens of this country. His officials have made a mess of the MRT-3, that it has become a daily torture for hundreds of thousands of commuters in Metropolitan Manila.

His incompetence and that of his government, has reached a criminal level in their failure to implement an effective rescue-and-relief operation for the hundreds of thousands of victims of the Yolanda super-typhoon.

He has also failed in his duty to keep intact, the territory of the Philippine nation state when he bungled the negotiations over the Scarborough Shoal crisis, so that in the end we lost it forever to the Chinese.

Forget all those figures Aquino rattled off in his annual State of the Nation Addresses, which he usually distorts to paint a rosy, false picture of his regime.

He won't dare boast that he has strengthened the institutions of the Philippine Republic, which is actually the most important task of a President, but which is really beyond his exiguous intellect.

(July 27, 2015)

THE COJUANGCOS WANTED P10B FOR HACIENDA LUISITA

WHEN PRESIDENT BENIGNO AQUINO III was asked for his reaction to the Supreme Court's decision ordering Hacienda Luisita to be turned over to its farmers, he didn't bother to applaud this epic victory for social justice. He instead replied quickly: "But there is also just compensation for the landowners."

That was a slip of the tongue. If the presently embattled high court knuckles under and rules for his kinsmen, "just compensation" would be a staggering P10 billion windfall for one of the country's most powerful elites.

The Court in its November 22, 2011 decision, stipulated that "just compensation" for the Hacienda's lands to be distributed to farmers will be determined based on its value in 1989, when it undertook its fraudulent land reform that instead gave its tenants shares of stocks in Hacienda Luisita, Inc. That's P40,000 per hectare, which the Cojuangcos used to determine the farmers' "stocks" in its sham land reform undertaken that year. "Just compensation" for the 4,335 hectares would therefore total P173 million.

When the nation's attention was on the impeachment against Chief Justice Renato Corona that was rammed through Congress December 12, the Cojuangcos' law firm Belo, Gozon, Elma, Parel, Asuncion on December 16 filed a "Motion to Clarify and Reconsider" the Court's resolution.

The motion argued that using the land's 1989 valuation is wrong, and that its 2006 market price (when the agrarian reform department ordered the Cojuangcos to undertake a real agrarian from) must instead be used. That's 17 years later, during which economic growth made a Luisita Industrial Park with adjacent malls and posh residential areas so profitable, that property prices in the area went through the roof.

From being a remote sugar plantation like from some Gabriel Garcia Marquez novel, the Hacienda has developed into an industrial-commercial area that by 2006, its land prices had little semblance to its 1989 levels. (In 2009, former President Gloria Macapagal-Arroyo's Subic-Clark-Tarlac Expressway project built an artery to the Hacienda that made it so accessible from Manila. With a land area as big as Manila and Makati combined, the Hacienda could even rival the Clark Freeport Zone.)

Under the agrarian reform department's formula for computing "just compensation" in which the Hacienda's lands will be valued, one element includes 90 percent of the price of "comparable sales."

There are "comparable sales" made after 1989 that the Cojuangcos themselves cleverly made. One was the 1997-1998 sales by Hacienda Luisita Inc. to its wholly-owned subsidiary Luisita Realty Corp. of 200 hectares for P500 million. The other is the 1998 sale to another subsidiary, Centennary Holdings, of 300 hectares for P750 million.

The value of Hacienda lands based on these sales: P2.5 million per hectare. To use the DAR's formula, 90 percent of this will be P2.25 million per hectare (the other element in the formula, an addition, is 10 percent of market value per tax declaration).

2006 not 1989 reckoning

The cost of the 4,335 hectares, using 2006 as reckoning year when the land price was P2.25 million per hectare, as the Cojuangcos are demanding, would be P9.75 billion.

But the Cojuangcos are even asking for more — why not if they have a scion for a president? Their motion pointed out: "The landowner must be compensated with interest for the time that lapsed before actual payment."

That means interest must be paid on the P9.75 billion cost of land up to the time of actual payment. At a minimum 6-percent interest rate, that totals P580 million annually from 2006 to whenever they are paid the P9.57 billion. If government pays them at the end of 2012, the total interest to be paid to the Cojuangcos on top of the P9.75 billion would be P3.5 billion.

It's a humongous amount the President's clan wants to be paid for the Hacienda lands: P9.8 billion (excluding interest) to P13 billion (including interests). Those figures are bigger than the government's 2012 P6-billion budget for agrarian reform or the P7 billion for housing.

It won't be the Hacienda's farmers who would pay the P10 billion, per agrarian reform's principle of affordability. It would be us taxpayers.

Aquino, hands-off on the Hacienda case? Highly unlikely. It was his first appointee to the Court, Ma. Lourdes Sereno, who prepared a mountain of arguments for the Cojuangcos' demand for a 2006 date of reckoning. Her dissenting opinion in the Court's July 5, 2011 decision was an angry treatise arguing for a 2006 reckoning.

Her 19,000-word dissenting opinion in the November resolution even pointed to where the government can get the huge funds (PAGCOR and PCSO, among other sources) to pay the P10 billion. Sereno in fact saved the Cojuangcos' lawyers a lot of work, as they extensively quoted her arguments in their motion.

Aquino's two other appointees, Bienvenido Reyes and Estela Perlas-Bernabe, have also proven to be deserving of their appointments: both also asked for a 2006 pricing.

Note the recent impeachment move against another justice, Mariano del Castillo, do a bit of arithmetic, and the objective of Aquino's assault against the Court would be crystal clear.

Justice Lucas Bersamin changed his vote in July and in the November resolution also asked for a 2006 pricing, making it four justices pushing for the Cojuangcos' wish, as against 10 (Justice Antonio Carpio abstained). But if Corona and Del Castillo are taken out, that would mean (since Aquino would appoint two replacements) six pro-Cojuangco justices versus eight. That's just two justices short for the Court to order a P10-billion payment for the Cojuangcos.

That's really what the impeachment of Corona was all about: a last resort move to bludgeon the Supreme Court to reverse its November decision.

(February 8, 2012)

COMMUTERS SUFFER DAILY DUE TO THE MRT-3 GRAFT

IF WORKING-CLASS FILIPINOS had a capacity for quick mobilization to protest the injustice done to them without the help of the elites, there would have already been street actions by now on the scale of the EDSA 1 and 2 revolts, this time against President Benigno S. Aquino III and his officials in charge of the Metro Rail Transit-3.

The corruption allegedly involving the maintenance of MRT-3, is graft of the kind that has caused the daily suffering of hundreds of thousands of commuters in Metro Manila: queuing for hours to get a ride in its jam-packed trains, risking life and limb with the regular occurrence of accidents and derailments.

Before Aquino hoodwinked Filipinos with his *tuwid na daan* rhetoric, even those with cars would use the MRT-3 for its speed and convenience. But now that they have to line up and wait for hours just to catch a train, many have had no choice but to use their cars again — contributing to the horrendous traffic along EDSA.

Why do MRT-3 trains keep breaking down that the train system needs to be shut down for hours at times; why do the trains stop in the middle of the tracks, and why are the trains derailed and jump off the tracks?

Why are there fewer trains now compared with the previous years such that its carrying capacity has decreased, causing the long queues of commuters at the stations?

Why were there no such incidents and queues before, from 2000 to 2011?

The reason is quite simple, and I was astonished when I learned its details, shocked at why we Filipinos allow such anomalies that torture the working class daily, and outraged that mainstream media hasn't gone to town against this scandal.

The reason involves the P1.2 billion — so far — in maintenance contracts given by the Department of Transportation and Communications (DOTC) starting October 2012 to two firms that appear to have close ties with President Aquino's political allies.

These outfits (first PH Trams and then APT-Global) turned out either to be bumbling amateurs in light-rail vehicle maintenance, or decided to skimp on the necessary spare parts to keep the trains running efficiently.

They didn't import and stockpile the high-quality spare parts needed for the light-rail vehicles and the replacements for the tracks. Parts were, instead, cannibalized from the other cars that were put out of operation, so that only 50 out of the 73 cars operating in 2011 are running now.

One evidence of this is a September 4, 2014 report to the DOTC official in charge of the MRT-3, Renato San Jose, which read:

"When Global-APT JV assumed as (sic) the Temporary Maintenance Provider of MRT 2 on 4 September 2013, there were twenty-nine pieces of Stock Rails replacement. Since then, the said number has gone down to two and a half (2.5) pieces. Furthermore, the latest Rail Replacement Summary as of 06 August revealed that in at least two instances, Global APT JV has used old rails instead of new ones."

Six months' inventory

This is one reason why the trains' speed has had to be slowed down: parts of the track had worn out and should have been replaced but hadn't because there were no replacement rails. The result: fewer trains have been running, requiring commuters to queue for hours to ride the jam-packed, not to mention, dangerous trains.

Capital costs are huge for a train maintenance operator since the spare parts needed have to be ordered in advance, because of the minimum six-months' time for these to be manufactured and shipped to the country from abroad.

Light-rail system parts aren't exactly items one could buy at the hardware store or ordered online. They are made of high-grade, precision steel, which mostly only the original builder can provide, and on a "per-order" basis.

A unit of the giant manufacturing Japanese firm Sumitomo that built MRT-3 with Mitsubishi Corp. in the late 1990s, when it maintained the system until September 2012, had a six-months' inventory of the usual parts needed to be replaced.

There is a second reason why the MRT trains' speed had to be reduced. Its signaling system — its computerized, sensor-based network that manages railway traffic in order to prevent trains from colliding — had been built more than a decade ago by a unit of the Canadian aircraft manufacturer, Bombardier Inc. The firm informed the DOTC in 2010 that the system had to be upgraded, as there were no longer parts for it since it had become outdated.

The upgrade would have cost P185 million and included in the maintenance contract. It wasn't. Why? Was it too big a cost that would eat into the contractors' profits?

Bombardier engineers who were initially hired by PH Trams to maintain the signaling system, reportedly left in a huff in 2013 when they stopped receiving their due fees.

The result: There's an inadequate signaling system that train operators have resorted to a manual method, using "walkie-talkies' bought from Ace or True Value, to report their positions, a process that requires much slower train speeds.

Out of the total cost for maintaining the MRT in the past ten years, 60 percent was used for buying spare parts for the cars and rail tracks, as well as for maintaining the computerized signaling system, while the remaining 40 percent was for management and labor costs.

These means that if the two maintenance operators who got the P1.2 billion contract from the DOTC had not purchased the parts needed for the trains' maintenance, they could have easily pocketed the 60 percent that should have been used for their parts inventory, which means a huge P742 million income. The Senate committee that has been investigating the MRT problems should subpoena these firms' books.

What makes this kind of corruption so outrageous is that the grafters were as dumb as they were so arrogant. They thought they could make money by taking over the contract of a world-class, experienced engineering firm that built and had maintained the system for a decade, and that they didn't need to import the high-grade precision-engineered spare parts for the trains.

I can just imagine what a top DOTC and Liberal Party official told his accomplices: *"Pukpok lang naman ang mga kailangan sa mga bakal na gulong at riles na iyan, hindi na kailangang mag-import tayo ng spare parts kaya malaki ang kita natin. Magagaling naman ang mga Pinoy na mekaniko."* [A little pounding is all that's needed on the steel wheels and the rails. We don't really need to import the spare parts, so we're going to make a killing on this. And Filipinos are good mechanics.]

Because of such arrogant stupidity and insatiable greed of Aquino's people, hundreds of thousands of Filipino commuters have been suffering every day going to and from their workplaces.

(October 6, 2014)

HE AXED ARROYO'S KEY FLOOD CONTROL PROJECT

PRESIDENT BENIGNO AQUINO III axed in November 2010, one of the country's most ambitious flood-control projects that was scheduled to start that year. If he had not cancelled that milestone undertaking, it would have been completed last month [July 2012], and would have significantly mitigated the disastrous flooding of recent weeks.

The venture was the Laguna Lake Rehabilitation Project, which, as part of its plan to save the lake, would have dredged it of 4.6 million cubic meters of silt and waste so it could contain more floodwaters. The project would have also involved the deepening of the critical 7-kilometer Napindan Channel in Taytay, so that it could better and more quickly draw floodwaters away from the metropolis to the lake.

Costing P18.7 billion, the project was to be undertaken by the 150-year-old Belgian dredging firm Baagerwerken Decloedt En Zoon (BDZ) and financed by a loan from the BNP Paribas Fortis bank, with Brussels providing a P7-billion grant — the biggest development aid it would have given the country ever.

"A much deeper Laguna de Bay would relieve residents of Metro Manila, Rizal and Laguna of the flooding that happened at the height of [Tropical Storm] 'Ondoy' and [Typhoon] 'Pepeng'," Laguna Governor Jorge Ejercito, an ardent supporter of the project, summed up in September 2010 the aim of the planned massive dredging.

Why did Aquino cancel such a crucial project? Because of his irrational, apoplectic bias that everything his predecessor did or planned was corrupt. Just a few months after he assumed office, Aquino claimed that the project was a "midnight," corrupt deal during President Gloria Macapagal-Arroyo's administration.

"They have been trumpeting that corruption tainted the project," Governor Ejercito said angrily in 2010. "But where is their evidence? Just to find fault in the past administration, Laguna residents will be at the receiving end of their vengeful politics."

To this day, Aquino has not presented an iota of evidence, or even any specific charge of corruption, in the project.

Then Belgian Prime Minister Yves Leterme himself vouched for the project's integrity, and even submitted to Aquino an independent engineering firm's evaluation of the project. "As I understand from the report of this expert, which is enclosed, the project can be an undeniable improvement for the Metro Manila area and alleviate flooding, improve local transport infrastructure and increase water capacity," Leterme wrote in a letter to Aquino in March 2011.

Leterme, now deputy secretary general of the Organization for Economic Development and Cooperation, appealed to Aquino to allow the Belgian contractor to respond to the allegations against the project. Aquino rebuffed Leterme.

Instead, Aquino ramped up his opprobrium against the project, saying as recently as last week that the project was a "big joke" since it would "just dump silt to be recovered to another portion of the lake." (In his memorandum canceling the project, though, Aquino gave no explanation for his action.)

That is an utter lie. The project very clearly specified that the dredged material would be deposited in designated sites off Taytay-Angono and San Pedro, which in fact would become reclaimed land where waste-water treatment facilities would be built.

Seven government departments, agencies, and interdepartmental bodies evaluated the project for three years, and endorsed it for immediate implementation in 2010. Bangko Sentral ng Pilipinas Governor Amando Tetangco Jr. said in his approval of the project's foreign funding: "Its purpose is to improve the Lake's capacity as a catch basin to reduce flooding in nearby towns and cities."

Aquino's Justice Secretary Leila de Lima, in her August 2010 legal opinion, found nothing wrong with it: "The project cannot be construed as a midnight deal since it is covered by official development assistance from the Belgian government." The Laguna Lake Development Authority general manager whom Aquino appointed supported it — and was fired for that.

Fish pen operators in the lake, environmentalist NGOs, and most of the political leadership of towns around Laguna de Bay passionately pushed for the undertaking, as it would stop the lake's environmental deterioration and lead to the transformation of the lakeshore into a modern area with fish ports, ferry terminals, and marina complexes.

Other than Aquino and Senator Franklin Drilon who claimed that "dredging is a rich source of corruption," the main opposition to the project came from Pamalakaya, the communists' agitprop group for fishermen's issues — a member of Communist Party founder Jose Ma. Sison's International League of Peoples' Struggle.

The cancellation of this crucial flood-control project will go down in Philippine history as one of the country's most tragic, most shameful episode in which more than a billion pesos in taxpayers' money were wasted, and hundreds of thousands of flooded Filipinos put in misery because of Aquino's malicious vindictiveness.

(August 15, 2012)

POSTSCRIPT:

The World Bank's International Center for the Settlement of Investment Disputes (ICSID) on January 23, 2017 ordered the Philippines to pay the Belgian dredging firm BDZ about P1 billion. This represented the amount of investment the company had already put into the project, plus interest costs, after Aquino scuttled the project in November 2010. The Philippine government spent about P400 million in lawyers' fees.

FAKE ANTI-GRAFT CAMPAIGN

EVERY ONCE IN a while, especially on slow news days, Bureau of Internal Revenue (BIR) chief Kim Henares would appear in a televised press conference announcing the filing of charges against an unknown taxpayer (a Greenbelt bar, a beauty parlor, a Valenzuela factory) or against a prominent personality (actor Zoren Legaspi, former Chief Justice Renato Corona, and even national boxing hero Manny Pacquiao).

A similar ritual has ensued at the Bureau of Customs especially during the time of Customs Commissioner Ruffy Biazon when he would open container vans in front of media cameras, and show all those supposedly smuggled goods. Flanked by his subordinates, he would announce the filing of smuggling charges. The Finance Department in a similar manner would issue press releases regularly, saying that its Revenue Integrity Protection Service has proven again a case of unexplained wealth against a finance official.

And like a broken record, President Benigno Aquino III in every State of the Nation Address would claim that he is winning his fight against corruption. He would ad nauseam cite the charges against former president Gloria Macapagal-Arroyo (conveniently forgetting how one by one the charges had been dismissed), and his latest boast of course would be the incarceration of the three pork-barrel senators Enrile, Revilla, and Estrada.

This he would say is his biggest legacy to the nation. But this is all a fraud.

At its best — if you are a yellow believer and want to assume that Aquino did not deliberately lie to the Filipino people — this shows the idiocy and ineptness of Aquino and his cabinet.

What are the facts behind this "anti-corruption" hype? How many of the tax evaders, smugglers, and corrupt officials the Aquino administration has gone after have been actually convicted?

Zero. Zilch. Not one. After four years of shouting *"Kung walang korap, walang mahirap."* Even a Department of Finance report in February 2013 revealed that only 6 percent of the BIR's tax evasion cases had reached the courts.

It is the same sad story as the one I had written* about Ombudsman Conchita Carpio-Morales and the cases her office has been filing since 2010. Aquino's anti-graft campaign is all smoke and mirrors.

Take the BIR's tax evasion cases.

Based on the BIR's "Profile of RATE Cases" (referring to its Run After Tax Evaders program), it "filed" 132 cases against tax evaders from 2010 to 2012, and another 95 (based on its press releases) in the past two years. Interestingly, 13 out of the 31 filed in 2014 involved the cases against former chief justice Renato Corona, his wife, and daughter.

Out of these 231 cases that the BIR filed under Aquino's watch, how many did it win, how many tax evaders did it get to pay their right taxes, and send to jail under our "stiff" tax laws?

None. Not a single tax evader.

HOW MANY TAX EVADERS CONVICTED BY AQUINO ADMINISTRATION?

YEAR	Charges filed by BIR	Dismissed by Courts or by DOJ	For Resolution of Court decision	Still being processed by BIR or DOJ	TAX EVADERS CON-VICTED
2010	23	6	12	5	0
2011	60	11	46	3	0
2012	49	1	20	28	0
2013	64	0		64	0
2014	31	0		31	0
TOTAL CASES 2010-2014	227	18	78	131	0

Source: BIR and DOF documents, press releases

Zero: No tax evader charged since 2010 has been convicted.

Most cases are still being heard at the Court of Tax Appeals (CTA), which is hearing cases filed as far back as 1995. And those cases filed since 2010 that it had already decided on, the CTA's decision was a mere dismissal.

According to the BIR's own report, out of the 132 cases filed from 2010 to 2012, 16 percent were dismissed either by the CTA or by the BIR itself after its own review, while 78 or 70 percent are still "For Resolution."

Amazingly, there were still 36 out of the 132 cases filed in 2010-2012 cases that were either still with the BIR undertaking "preliminary investigation," or awaiting assignment of a lawyer to handle the case. Most of the cases the BIR "filed" in 2013 and 2014 are still being investigated at the level of the BIR or by the Department of Justice (DOJ).

There were three notable exceptions in which the tax evasion cases moved swiftly from the BIR to the DOJ to the CTA.

These were the cases against Social Security System chairman during President Arroyo's term Romulo Neri, against Chief Justice Corona whom Arroyo appointed, former First Gentleman Miguel Arroyo's lawyer Jesus Ṣantos, and comic-strip creator and scriptwriter Carlo Caparas, whom Arroyo gave a National Artist Award. The cases against the latter two, however, were swiftly dismissed by the CTA. Tax cases as a tool for persecuting political enemies? Of course, it's way too obvious.

The BIR also joined the mob against pork queen Janet Napoles by filing a tax evasion case against Napoles and her husband. The DOJ, already busy with its own plunder cases against the couple, will of course have to handle the case. On the basis of Facebook posts of her inside a limousine and in a posh New York apartment, the BIR also filed tax cases against the Napoles daughter.

Of course, the tax court since 2010 had convicted accused tax evaders, which BIR head Henares has been boasting about. But these were all cases filed in the last decade, mostly when former President Arroyo first launched the BIR's Run After Tax Evaders' program, which Aquino has been falsely claiming as his own program.

For instance, the most celebrated case recently decided by the court involved actress Judy Ann Santos, whom the court convicted as guilty of tax evasion in January 16 last year. But that case was filed eight years ago in 2005, during President Arroyo's watch. (Santos was acquitted of the criminal charge, but ordered to pay P3.4 million plus a 20 percent interest from 2008.)

Another case, about which this BIR had been boasting, was the case of "beauty doctor" Joel Mendez who runs a chain of dermatological clinics, and was charged for not filing income taxes from 2001 to 2003. But the case was filed nine years ago, and the decision a rather strange one: he was sentenced to two years' imprisonment, although ordered to pay a fine of only P20,000. *Dura lex, sed lex* ("The law is hard, but it is the law") indeed but probably only if you don't get good lawyers.

The reality is that the campaign against tax evasion is seriously blocked by the weakness of our justice system, and Aquino has done nothing to strengthen the capacity of our courts to hear these cases.

There are only nine justices in three divisions in the Court of Tax Appeals. Their pending cases every year have been increasing to the 900 this year. (Quite strangely though, the cases the BIR files are almost all against this contractor or other small businessmen, an actor or a merchant in the provinces. There's not a single case against oligarchs or any of the Top 500 Taxpayers — one can almost say the BIR is 'protective' of the country's elite.)

It is not the court's fault alone. The BIR has no prosecutorial body, but is required to get the Justice Department to file tax evasion cases at the CTA. But the DOJ has been involved in so many cases, most of them obviously politically motivated.

Most of its lawyers are also bogged down by the pork barrel scam cases, which would tie them down for years.

DOJ lawyers, I was told, have been complaining that cases are being filed at the department have very little documentation from the BIR. "They've been looking good in the press in announcing tax evasion cases. But we are the ones given the huge work," one DOJ lawyer. "Worse, we're the ones blamed if the case is dismissed, when those rich BIR officials did sloppy jobs," one source said.

This could be the reason — or another more pecuniary reason — why several CTA cases I've pored through were dismissed on the following rather strange grounds:

"For failure of the prosecutor to comply, despite notice… requiring her to submit to this Court the original or certified true copies of the duly signed approval for criminal prosecution of the accused on all other records in her possession… the case is hereby DISMISSED." (Duly capitalized in the original.)

This means the prosecutor simply abandoned the case, and didn't even appear during the hearing.

Two other cases I've read were dismissed for the following intriguing reason:

"For failure of prosecutor to comply… with the Resolution requiring her to submit to this Court the original or certified true copies of the written authority from the Commissioner of Internal Revenue to file the case and the records of the preliminary investigation, the case is hereby DISMISSED." (Duly capitalized in the original.)

Such cases could be explained only by the following reasons:

1. The prosecutor felt the BIR case handed over to her (or him) was too stupid that he or she didn't want to waste time on it. Refusing the Court's order to submit certain documents was the easiest way to relieve her of that stupid case.
2. He or she was paid off by the accused not to submit the documents the Court asked for so the case would be dismissed.
3. Especially in the second case, it was all "press release" by the BIR head: she never really authorized that the case be brought to the court.

Do you still wonder why Aquino has moved heaven and earth to put the three senators in jail? That's the only thing he is holding on to claim that he has won victories against corruption. In reality, it's a fake campaign.

(June 20, 2014)

* Tiglao, Rigoberto D. "Morales: All bark, no bite," *Manila Times,* June 16, 2014)

HE NEVER BOUGHT OR SOLD A PORSCHE

REMEMBER THE PORSCHE 911 Carrera that former President Benigno Aquino III, just months into his presidency, claimed he bought for P5 million, and that he used the money he got when he sold his BMW?

Remember how because of the furor over such display of opulence, he claimed he sold it six months later for exactly the same price?

Remember how I had bet in my column of March 18, 2014 that Aquino would never let a Freedom of Information (FOI) Act pass — even if it was one of his campaign promises in 2010 — as long as he was President, or the press would demand that he disclose the deeds of sale and LTO registrations for his purchase and sale of his BMW?

Six years in power, and different versions of FOI bills filed, the Congress that Aquino controlled (so tightly he ordered the removal of Chief Justice Renato Corona, and it was done in just five months) never did pass such a bill.

His successor, President Duterte, however, simply signed an executive order requiring government agencies to release any information they have, subject to certain restrictions such as national security and people's right to privacy under the Constitution.

So, I thought I would invoke Duterte's order to find out how serious it was. I went straight to, that is, wrote LTO head Edgar Galvante — a former police general known for his integrity and efficiency — and asked for the deeds of sale and registration papers of the Porsche Aquino had bought and sold.

Galvante's reply and that of his staff: LTO records, which are in a computerized database, do not show Aquino having a Porsche 911, nor a BMW he said he sold to buy the new sports car.

LTO records show that the only cars under his name are a 2003 Toyota Land Cruiser he registered in June 30, 2003 and a 2016 Ford Explorer registered June 15, 2016, two weeks before he stepped down as President.

I wondered, maybe the LTO database would no longer report somebody as an owner of a car if he had sold it later. The LTO staff replied: "It will be recorded on our database if Mr. Aquino transferred the ownership of vehicles under his name."

The only possible conclusion from the LTO report: Aquino lied. He never bought a Porsche nor did he sell it. It was a gift from a Chinese-Filipino tycoon, as had been the rumors during that time.

If that were the case, Aquino violated the Anti-Graft and Corrupt Practices law, which deems criminal the acceptance by a government official of such an expensive gift.

The law defines such a gift as those from a person "other than a member of the public officer's immediate family, in behalf of himself or of any member of his family or relative within the fourth civil degree, either by consanguinity or affinity, even on the occasion of a family celebration or national festivity like Christmas, if the value of the gift is under the circumstances manifestly excessive."

Aquino could easily prove that he did buy and sell a Porsche. He can just release to the public copies of the LTO registrations of his Porsche, and, please, the deeds of sale. I'm still suspicious that it was a gift to him by a Chinese-Filipino tycoon whose business boomed during his regime.

That tycoons would be so bold as to give a President such expensive gifts was demonstrated recently by President Duterte's disclosure that he was given a Mercedes-Benz. Duterte, however, ordered the luxury car impounded at the Presidential Security Group headquarters until it could be sold, with the proceeds going to government.

Duterte said he is happy with the 1988 pickup he has been using ever since he became mayor of Davao City.

What a different President this is from the one before, who loved pontificating about the 'straight path' but whose actions tell us otherwise.

(March 15, 2017)

THE YOLANDA FIASCO

A YEAR AFTER THE disaster wrought by super-typhoon Yolanda, the biggest boo-boo of President Aquino's top officials tasked to deal with the catastrophe remained unexposed, or at least not given the appropriate media reportage. If our senators are so fond of investigation, this is one issue they should probe — after all, the archipelago, again and again, will be hit by supertyphoons, and our nation can't afford this yellow type of blunder.

This gigantic slip-up is, in fact, a microcosm of everything that's wrong with the Aquino administration, other than its corruption: its arrogance and amateurishness.

Here's what happened:

Told in Manila on the eve of the disaster that Super Typhoon Yolanda would be hitting Central Visayas on November 8, 2014, Interior and Local Government Mar Roxas and Defense Secretary Voltaire Gazmin, who also heads the National Disaster and Risk Management Center (the command and control center for disaster management), rushed to Tacloban to oversee the evacuation, as well as the rescue and relief operations.

The two arrived at 5 p.m. on November 7 and after a press conference at the airport, they called and presided over a meeting of more than two dozen local officials, including the city mayor, Alfred Romualdez, for preparations for the typhoon.

Guess what kind of official Roxas and Gazmin failed to bring with them from Manila, or require the local counterparts to attend the meeting? The weather forecasters of the Philippine Atmospheric Geophysical and Astronomical Services Administration (PAGASA).

Worse, neither of the two nor their staff was in contact with PAGASA forecasters. It was like an army marching into battle without an intelligence staff, unmindful of where the enemy was situated.

(PAGASA actually has a regional official for Central Visayas and had five field stations in Samar and Leyte. A PAGASA weather forecaster, Salvacion Avestruz, was killed in the onslaught of the typhoon as she manned a weather station.)

In a video of that meeting, Roxas obviously didn't realize how the weather forecast was critical to their work. He asked in the meeting if there was a PAGASA representative among the more than two dozen local officials present, and when the question was met with total silence,

Big Mistake: Roxas at the meeting in Tacloban 8 p.m., the evening before Yolanda struck — not at noon as he announced it would, but at 5 a.m.

he just moved on to another topic without giving an order to get the weather forecaster.

Big boo-boo

Roxas and Voltaire's biggest mistake — which actually nearly cost their lives — was that they were totally out of touch with PAGASA and weren't updated on the movement of the typhoon. In that meeting (video grab above), Roxas said: "We still have 10 o'clock tomorrow morning to evacuate these people."

It is a mystery, or another demonstration of confusion at the top rungs of government, why Aquino claimed in his 6 p.m. televised speech on November 7, during which he boasted that his government has made all the necessary preparations to respond to the typhoon, that it would hit central Visayas that midnight. *"Inaasahan pong tatama si Yolanda sa mga probinsya ng Samar at Leyte simula mamayang hatinggabi,"* he said.

On the other hand, Roxas' "10 a.m." November 8 deadline was based on PAGASA's Severe Weather Bulletin issued 11 a.m. November 7, which said that Yolanda's landfall would be at noon November 8.

However, PAGASA would issue several other bulletins in the course of the day, when its stations detected that the typhoon's speed had increased. In its 9 p.m. November 7 bulletin, PAGASA warned that Signal No. 4 denoting winds of more than 185 kilometers per hour would cover Samar and Leyte and many other areas "in at least 12 hours," which means by 5 a.m. the next day.

Its bulletin issued 2 a.m. was more categorical: the typhoon would make landfall on Eastern Samar at 5 a.m.

Roxas and Gazmin made a horrific mistake that would cost thousands of lives. They expected the typhoon to hit at noon; it hit at 5 a.m. City and provincial officials relied on the national government officials' information.

Everyone went to bed after that meeting, perhaps thinking that nothing else was going to happen until the morning. Using a military analogy: because Roxas and his people lacked an intelligence group (in this case, the PAGASA meteorologists) to give them timely and accurate information, they were ambushed… and wiped out.

Two sources claimed that Roxas and Gazmin, after a round of brandy, retired before midnight and slept soundly. By daybreak the typhoon would strike, and after the storm surge hit their hotel, their terrified aides nearly broke down their door to wake them up. Both nearly drowned, as did one local-based security man who was assigned to them.

Gazmin lost his insulin kit for diabetes, and had to be rushed back to Manila through Cebu on the first helicopter available for his life-saving shots. They lost even their satellite phones, which made them incommunicado until after noon of November 8. After Yolanda left by 10 a.m., Roxas and Gazmin were walking like dazed zombies on Tacloban's streets along with the rest of the victims, escaping from the horrors towards the airport.

No wonder, when he recovered from his shock, Roxas was in the foulest of moods, and demanded that the mayor turn over the city to him in a meeting two days later. Why? "Because you are a Romualdez, and the President is an Aquino," he barked at the city mayor in a meeting several days later. That arrangement would have been his last remaining chance of proving his leadership in a crisis.

It would be kind to describe what had happened to Roxas and Gazmin with those famous two lines from the poet Robert Burns: *"The best-laid plans of mice and men / Often go awry."*

But really, it was more a case of hubris combined with ineptitude. Roxas was perhaps hoping for a heroic saga to demonstrate his qualities as a leader, a savior of the poor, which would have boosted his ratings and lifted him to the presidency.

Instead, it became a horrific nightmare for Roxas that nearly cost his life, and an episode demonstrating one more time the Aquino government's ineptness and lack of leadership during one of the worst tragedies to hit the nation.

No wonder Aquino was also in a foul mood during a meeting with Tacloban officials and citizens that he snapped at a businessman worried over looting: *"Buhay ka pa naman, di ba?"* ("Stop whining. After all, you're still alive, aren't you?")

And through the year, the bumbling and incompetence would continue in the relief and rehabilitation work. Can you believe this, Aquino would only approve the plan for rehabilitation 11 months after the supertyphoon hit. How clueless can you get?

(November 7, 2014)

DID HE CODDLE AND PROTECT DRUG LORDS?

I CERTAINLY WOULD THINK SO, either because of his sheer incompetence, or outright complicity.

That's the only conclusion one would get after the police all over the country, following incoming President Rodrigo Duterte's announced priority, have arrested or killed more than 200 drug lords and dealers in just a few weeks.

All of a sudden — with hundreds of self-admitted, small-time dealers and users even surrendering to authorities, fearing they would be victims of summary executions — the nation has been awakened to the reality that our drug problem, which really afflicts mostly the poor, indeed has reached horrific proportions. So much so that many sectors of this purportedly Catholic nation are now reviving the call for the death penalty.

Such scale of the illegal drug and crime menace couldn't have emerged overnight. I can only conclude that President Benigno Aquino III allowed it to grow during his six years in office. He had hundreds of millions of pesos in confidential funds and the Presidential Anti-Organized Crime Commission (headed by his executive secretary, Paquito Ochoa), yet he did little to fight the drug lords.

Aquino did not make fighting the proliferation of illegal drugs, or for that matter combating crime in general, his priority. Instead, his declared priority was to fight "corruption." I put that in quotation marks because his fight against corruption targeted only the opposition, and not grafters in his administration. He refused to touch allies involved in blatant cases that affected the lives of millions of Filipinos, such as the corruption in MRT-3 and the botched contract to provide the Land Transportation Office with car plates.

I've reviewed all of Aquino's six State of the Nation Addresses (SONAs), and it is shocking that in all of these, he had not even mentioned that we have a serious illegal drug problem, as if he were deliberately concealing its existence.

In Aquino's first (2010), second (2011), and last (2015) SONAs, there was absolutely no reference at all to the fact that we have a huge illegal drug problem in the country. The word "drugs" is not even mentioned at all in these SONAs.

Aquino mentions the drug problem in his 2012 address, but only once, and as if he had already defeated it. He said then: "He shares the same fate as the more than ten thousand individuals arrested by the PDEA in 2011 for charges relating to illegal drugs."

But the President's statement really was strange, since by "he," Aquino was referring to one Raymond Dominguez, who was arrested for carnapping charges, as well as an unnamed suspect in the Makati bus bombing in 2011. The suspect, a member of the police's Special Action Force, was acquitted of all charges in 2015.

There is a similar dismissive tone in his single reference to drugs in his 2014 SONA: "I will leave you to your conscience — if you feel any remorse for your fellowmen who have become addicted to the illegal drugs you have helped to smuggle in, or for the farmers who are being deprived of fair profit from doing honest work."

Not Aquino's priority

Why would the police and other drug enforcement agencies combat drug lords, if that is not the priority of their commander-in-chief? Since the boss doesn't think it's a problem, wouldn't the police just resign themselves to coddling the drug lords who provide them with "monthly allowances?"

To illustrate it, an analogy could be: you hire a new pest control expert and he reports, after examining your house, that it is badly infested with termites and mice. He even shows you a colony of such vermin beneath your living room. Then you recall that your previous pest-control guy had been telling you that you have a pest-free residence, and that he's doing his job, impressing even your neighbors.

There has also been no mention at all of the worsening crime situation in two of such presidential reports. Aquino made only a single, passing reference to this scourge, which Duterte, before he even formally steps into the presidency, has made into the top priority together with his anti-drug campaign.

In his 2012 SONA, Aquino claimed he had overcome the country's crime problem: "Crime volume continues to decline across the country. In 2009, over 500,000 crimes were recorded — this year, we have cut that number by more than half, to 246,958. Moreover, 2010's recorded 2,200 cases of carnapping have likewise been reduced by half — to 966 cases this 2011."

I nearly fell off my seat when in his 2014 SONA, he cited as an example — his sole example — of his administration's success against "lawless elements:" "We apprehended the chairman of the CPP and secretary general of the NPA this March. Normality and order are now returning to the 31 provinces previously troubled by the NPA."

In his 2015 SONA, he made it appear he had totally defeated the crime problem in the country: "We studied how criminals operate and strategically deployed our policemen. This is how we have caught the "big fish" gang leaders, dismantled syndicates, and lowered crime rates across the nation." What a President, so totally out of touch with reality!

This is, of course, one of the big reasons why Duterte became so popular in the last elections, so much so that Aquino's Liberal Party decided to throw their presidential candidate Manuel Roxas under the bus and instead focused their operations behind their vice presidential candidate, Leni Robredo.

Duterte's was even a single-issue candidacy that he would defeat illegal drug and crime lords who, Aquino either protected or coddled because of his incompetence. Duterte's victory (getting nearly twice the votes over Aquino proxy Roxas) demonstrated that he was right in his priorities, and he knew that Filipino voters wanted a strong leader who would eradicate criminality.

Only those ensconced in their gated exclusive village, including many top members of the Yellow Cult, couldn't see the worsening problem of crime and illegal drugs.

Aquino, of course, isn't the only one to blame for the Filipinos' misery amid the terrible breakdown of law and order in the country. He had two alter egos, whose responsibility was supposed to make him, or force him to see reality. If he didn't, these two simply failed to do the jobs they have vowed to carry out.

I am referring to Aquino's Interior and Local Government secretary, Roxas, and his Justice secretary, Leila de Lima, who didn't perform their jobs well.

From the day he assumed that post, which put the Philippine National Police under his supervision, Roxas' mind and efforts had been focused on how he could use his department's resources for his presidential campaign.

De Lima, on the other hand, not wanting to risk her plans for Aquino to include her in his senatorial slate, acted as his very loyal attack dog against the opposition.

What has taken much of De Lima's time and resources the past year? Her efforts to put former president Gloria Arroyo in jail, and to incarcerate through the PDAF or pork barrel issues the opposition, especially its leaders, senators Juan Ponce Enrile, Jinggoy Estrada and Ramon "Bong" Revilla. Right under her nose, the Bilibid National Prison had become the headquarters of the drug lords in this country, embarrassing us before the whole world.

With so many poor Filipinos brutally killed, raped, and robbed by criminals under this incompetent or complicit Aquino regime over the past six years, reading a columnist in this paper singing paeans to Aquino, "that he did wonders to the economy and to the country before the international community" — just makes me sick.

(June 29, 2016)

SMUGGLING OUT OF CONTROL

WHILE PRESIDENT BENIGNO AQUINO III and his Bureau of Customs, have moronically focused on opening the *balikbayan boxes* of Overseas Filipino Workers in order to squeeze more revenues, smuggling by big-time traders has exploded to unprecedented levels under his regime.

Nearly one-fourth of imports into the country in the last five years have been unreported and untaxed, totaling $94 billion — for an astronomical P4 trillion. That's more than four times the estimated smuggled value of just $21 billion from 2005 to 2009.

The Aquino government lost revenues from duties and value-added taxes on these smuggled goods in the last five years, totaling P760 billion, as a result of the massive collusion between importers and the Bureau of Customs, the likes of which had never been seen in the country's post-war history.

To give you an idea of the magnitude of those P760 billion foregone revenues, that could have doubled the budget of the public works department to start the building of two MRT-type of mass transport systems, to solve the horrendous traffic problem in the metropolis. Alternatively, it could have doubled the education department's budget so that the poor can have a totally free education.

Aquino's failure to curb corruption is one of his biggest sins against the nation, which remarkably he has been able to keep largely unnoticed from media.

These figures I cited are based on data from the International Monetary Fund's Direction of Trade Statistics, which allows us to compare exports to the country as reported by the exporting country, and the Philippines' imports, as reported by the Bureau of Customs, to come up with an estimate in the value of smuggled goods.

The discrepancies in the two sets of figures may in part be due to reporting errors, for instance due to different reporting times. However, especially when the discrepancies involve significant amounts and when a time-series is available, the methodology approximates the magnitude of smuggling in a country. The methodology has been routinely used by international trade economists and multilateral lending institutions.

The validity of the method is such that the import figures for other

(Graph based on accompanying table)

countries known to be relatively free of smuggling — such as Europe and Saudi Arabia — do not show such massive discrepancies.

The accompanying table and chart show, that the estimated value of goods smuggled into the country jumped as soon as Aquino took office. It rocketed from $8 billion in 2009 or just 15 percent of the imports as reported by the exporting countries, to a massive $26 billion in 2014, more than a fourth of the actual imports.

"It's the biggest open secret in Manila," a veteran broker put it. "Biggest as I've never seen such blatant smuggling ever in my 30 years

SMUGGLING ESTIMATES (US$ B)				
YEAR	Imports according to PHL BOC	Imports according to exporting countries*	Discrepancy (Smuggling estimates)	% smuggled of imports, according to reporting countries
2005	47.4	47.4	-0.1	-0.1
2006	51.5	52.7	1.2	2.2
2007	55.5	59.8	4.3	7.2
2008	60.4	67.8	7.4	10.9
2009	45.9	53.8	7.9	14.7
2010	60.2	71.8	11.6	16.1
2011	60.2	80.5	14.3	17.8
2012	67.9	87.4	19.6	22.4
2013	68.0	90.4	22.3	24.7
2014	71.0	97.6	26.6	27.3
TOTAL 2010-2014	**333.2**	**427.6**	**94.4**	**22.1**

Source: IMF, Direction of Trade Statistics
** Discounted 10% for freight and insurance cost*

in this business. Open because we brokers all know it and how to do it. And secret, as this government has managed to keep it under the public radar, what is really their biggest racket."

The broker added: "Just go to Divisoria or any mall, or any supermarket, and you won't have a doubt at all that smuggling has been so rampant under this administration. It's been institutionalized."

"I don't mind, of course," he quipped with a smile. "A Johnny Walker Black 1-liter costs $55 (P2,400 at P44 to $1) in places I've visited abroad. Here a popular supermarket sells it for just a bit less than P1,000."

(August 26, 2015)

NOTE:

The estimates on smuggling are based on data from the International Monetary Fund's (IMF) Direction of Trade Statistics (DOTS), which starting 2015 were made available by the IMF without charge, and can be accessed through their website.

The DOTS provides two sets of data. The first set has the value of exports to the Philippines, as reported, for example, by China. The second set of data has the value of imports from China as reported by the Philippines.

To compare the two sets of data, economists use various formulas, the simplest of which involves reducing the export value by 10 percent to account for the cost of freight, insurance and other shipment costs.

The difference between the exports of China, less freight and insurance and other costs, and the Philippine reports of its imports from that country represents the estimates of smuggled, i.e., unreported goods.

The foregone revenues are computed as follows:

First, the import duty is applied on the value of estimated value of smuggled goods, converted into Philippine pesos. I used a very low 6 percent duty, which is the average weighted duty on all imports of the country.

The value of the shipment plus the duty is then used to compute the 12 percent value added tax, which is actually the bigger cost for imports now even as the country has been lowering its duties to comply with the WTO and ASEAN commitments.

(November 12, 2012, and August 25, 2015)

THE PORK BARREL REGIME

IF THERE'S A SINGLE THING that should convince you, dear reader, how much of a rapacious wolf disguised in sheep's clothing President Aquino's administration has been, it is the pork-barrel issue.

For 2016, Aquino's last year in office and an election year, the pork barrel funds he got the Congress to approve amounted to P24.7 billion, disguised as financing for "Bottom-up Budgeting" (BUB) projects.

It's the same old pork barrel with a different name, though, which the Supreme Court had defined as "government spending meant for localized projects and secured solely or primarily to bring money to a representative's district."

What that definition though doesn't include is that, it is a President's sophisticated form of bribing a legislator to get his support for his administration and/or its projects. At best he would claim to his constituents (especially the voters in the next election cycle) that he is bringing home the bacon, and they should therefore reelect him (or his wife, or his son). At worse, he can extract illegal commissions from the contractors of projects financed by his pork barrel.

From 2011, the first year for which the Aquino administration formulated the national budget up to 2016, the pork-barrel funds he had the largesse to distribute totaled P145 billion, the largest ever such type funds under the control of a president. (This pork-barrel kitty was called the Priority Assistance Development Fund from 2011 to 2013 and BUB funds from 2014 to 2016).

The pork-barrel for this year, an election year, is the biggest such kind of fund ever in our entire history.

Obviously this election year is intended to bribe local government officials to support the candidacy of Aquino's bet, the lackluster Manuel A. Roxas II. That money will, together with other funds lodged in the Interior and Local Government department, make up the largest vote-buying kitty this nation will have ever seen.

It was Aquino's mother, Corazon, who in 1990 created that sort of fund and called it the Countrywide Development Fund, amounting to P2.3 billion. It became her means of buying the political support of local government officials to counter the coup attempts mounted against her.

More than two decades later, her son Benigno would allocate an

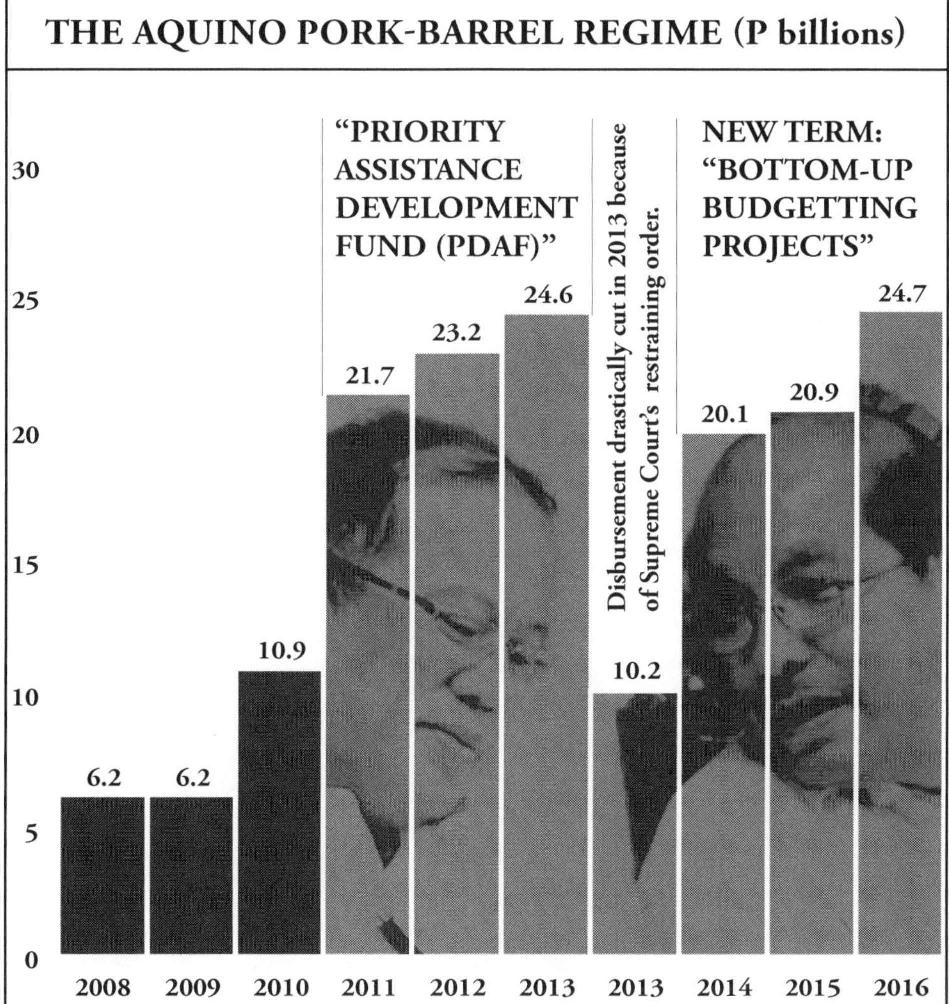

average of P21 billion yearly in pork barrel funds in his six years in power, to secure enough Congress votes to do his bidding and stifle the opposition.

With it, and with another form of pork barrel on a bigger scale for senators — called the Disbursement Acceleration Program (DAP) fund amounting to P157 billion — Aquino was able to assault the Supreme Court and remove Chief Justice Renato Corona from office, in a desperate attempt by the Aquino clan to squeeze billions of pesos in compensation for its Hacienda Luisita.

The power of the pork barrel continues to work as Aquino wields it: maintaining his hold on Congress so much so that he has escaped congressional scrutiny and impeachment for such utter failures in governance such as the Mamasapano massacre and the MRT-3 scandals.

It was the pork barrel funds that made Congress such a docile body, as to kiss Aquino's feet even as he threw in jail the leaders of the opposition, Senators Juan Ponce Enrile, Jinggoy Estrada and Ramon "Bong" Revilla.

For instance, why wouldn't one Eastern Samar representative lick Aquino's boots, given that under former President Gloria Arroyo, his district got only P30 million yearly in pork-barrel money, but in 2015 he got P290 million and will be getting P342 million this year?

It is not an exaggeration to call Aquino's six years in power as the "pork barrel regime" that mouths righteous slogans. Pork barrel under the administrations of Fidel Ramos, Joseph Estrada and Gloria Macapagal-Arroyo averaged just P5 billion yearly. Under Aquino, pork barrel funds have averaged P24 billion yearly, for a total of P145 billion during his six-year term.

Bribe money

Very few legislative bodies in the world now have pork barrel schemes, as it is, first of all, indisputably a bribery scheme that eats into the integrity of legislators, making them beholden to the head of state, and therefore, undermining the republican system of checks and balances.

Secondly, it dissipates government funds, which should more appropriately be used for projects that require huge amounts of funds beyond the capacity of local governments, and which only the national government can amass. For instance, P24.7 billion this year will be used for 14,324 very small projects such as potable wells, birthing facilities, goat production and preservation of historical landmarks, which are the responsibility of local governments.

The P24.7 billion, instead, could be used as equity to raise P100 billion more for the national government to build a subway or another railway, that could alleviate the worsening traffic in the capital or build an entirely new airport — which could ultimately boost the economy and consequently benefit the country's poor. But the rationale for pork barrel funds isn't economics but politics, a way for a President to bribe Congress.

We, as a nation, continue to complain that we have weak infrastructure because we don't have the money to fund their rehabilitation or construct new ones. That's not really true. We have the money, but we dissipate its use.

A truly reformist government would have scrapped the pork barrel system, using the outrage over the (Janet) Napoles scam as an opportunity to do so. Aquino even expanded it, claiming that it has made the budget "responsive to the needs of the Filipino people." That's utter hogwash: "responsive to congressmen's demands" is more accurate. Aquino's legacy would be a pork barrel scheme his successors are likely to find difficult to scrap.

It is not his success in fighting corruption, nor his "good governance" that explains Aquino's wide political support in Congress. It is the money — taxpayers' money — that he has been distributing every year to our very opportunistic congressmen.

Ironically, Aquino ramped up pork barrel spending when that kind of government expenditures was exposed the past two years as so vulnerable to large-scale corruption, with legislators not just pocketing a percentage of the funds, but stealing everything by utilizing non-existent NGOs and falsifying documents. That is what is now known as the infamous Janet Napoles scandal, named after the alleged mastermind of one part of the grand pork barrel scheme that has outraged the nation. Yet Aquino has acted as if there had been no such earth-shaking corruption exposé.

Aquino has demonstrated his lack of respect for the rule of law by continuing pork barrel allocations, even increasing them, after the Supreme Court ruled it unconstitutional in 2013.

Aquino and Abad simply gave it a new name, "Bottom-up Budgeting" projects, and created the illusion that the legislators had no role in choosing the projects to be funded. The two, however, simply made it a pencil-pushing exercise, by having each congressman submit the projects he wants for his district that are contained in the list of BUB projects — 14,324 projects for 2016 — before the budget is passed into law.

This is to go around the Supreme Court decision that ruled the pork barrel system as unconstitutional since the Constitution gives only the executive branch, and not the legislative, the authority to implement a government project.

However, the BUB projects are not listed with such details as, for instance, where exactly a deep well would be built, which gives the local congressman the covert power to choose the specific location and, therefore, have a say in its implementation.

The spirit of the Supreme Court decision declaring pork barrel illegal is contained in the definition given for it: "An appropriation of government spending meant for localized projects and secured solely or primarily to bring money to a representative's district."

BUB projects obviously fit that description. But no one has brought a case before the Supreme Court questioning why Aquino has defied its ruling.

Such is what our country has become.

(January 4, 2016)

DAP: THE BIGGEST HIJACKING OF GOVERNMENT FUNDS EVER

FORMER PRESIDENT Benigno Aquino III and his budget secretary Florencio Abad's Disbursement Acceleration Program (DAP), involving P157 billion of taxpayers' money was their biggest hijacking of government funds. Through this scheme, they usurped the exclusive power of Congress to determine how taxpayers' money are to be used as detailed in the annual Appropriations Acts.

Aquino and Abad instead ignored these laws and imperiously declared funds allocated by the budget laws of 2011 and 2012 to various agencies, even several state corporations, as "savings," and accumulated this into a fund they cloaked with the term DAP, and used entirely at their discretion.

Abad thought that he was clever in discovering that they could allocate funds as they wished through the technicality of declaring certain money allocated by the budget laws as "savings." He thought they could get away with it, as long as nobody investigated the DAP.

However, it clearly violated budget regulations that specify that "savings" can be declared only by year-end and can be used only by the same agency. Aquino and Abad declared "savings" either early or in the middle of the two years, and transferred funds from one agency (even state firms) to another.

To disguise the scheme, the fund was purportedly intended to speed up utilization of government funds, which had slowed down during Aquino's first year in office. Thus, it was called the *Disbursement Acceleration* Program, whose aim, they claimed was to stimulate the economy by releasing more quickly government funds into the system.

The World Bank however would later debunk that excuse by pointing out in its December 2012 report that DAP represented "a mere realignment of funds", and its magnitude compared to the size of the entire economy was "miniscule" as to have no effect in stimulating it.

Indeed, the DAP was actually contrived by Aquino and Abad to pursue their agenda that had nothing to do with stimulating the economy.

First, it financed Aquino's plot to enrich his Cojuangco clan when it had to surrender Hacienda Luisita under agrarian reform. Second, the DAP money were was used for programs intended to maintain their Liberal Party's hold on the country after he stepped down from office in 2016.

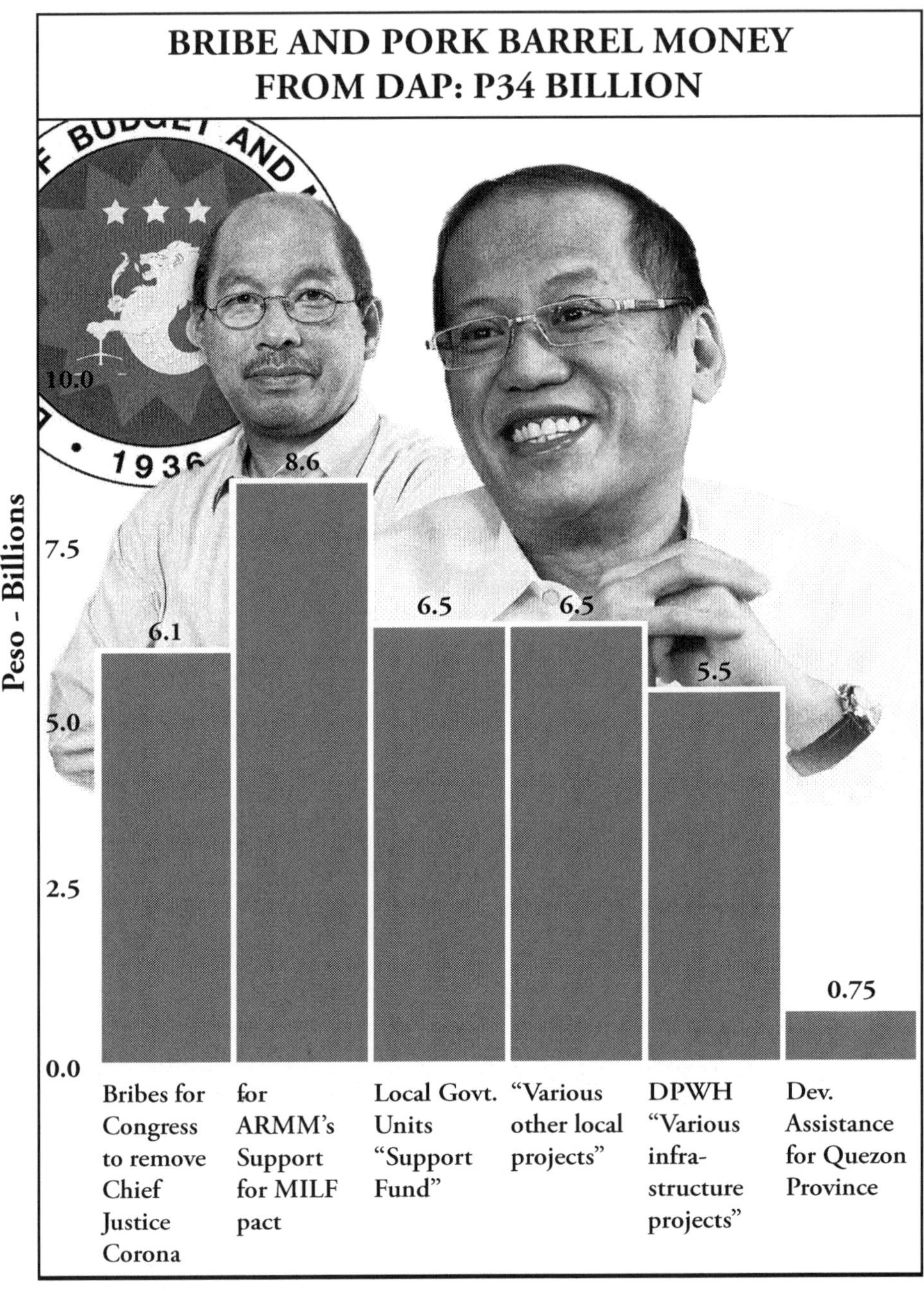

The origin really of this DAP scheme involves the saga of Hacienda Luisita, owned since the late 1950s by Aquino's Cojuangco clan. That sugar-producing and milling estate was that family's main source of wealth, and was the biggest such hacienda in the country with an area 64 square kilometers — nearly as big as the cities of Manila and Makati combined.

In July 2011, President Aquino had told his key inner circle that by hook or by crook, then Supreme Court Chief Justice Renato Corona must be removed. He claimed that the appointee of former president Gloria Macapagal-Arroyo would impede his anti-corruption campaign.

However, Aquino's real reason was that he and his Cojuangco clan had become desperate to reverse the Supreme Court decision issued that month. The ruling voided the fake land reform in 1989 undertaken by Hacienda Luisita, and the Court ordered the hacienda lands to be distributed to its farmers.

The Cojuangcos, according to the Supreme Court decision, should be given only the just compensation of P173 million, or Hacienda Luisita's 1989 value when they undertook their fake land reform program. The landlord clan wanted at least P10 billion, its market value 17 years later, in 2006.

Aquino's appointee to the Supreme Court, the very inexperienced classmate of his, Lourdes Sereno, couldn't convince the Court to increase the payment to the clan from P173 million to P10 billion. I was told then that Sereno herself told Aquino, that there was no way for her to sway the Court if Corona remained as chief justice.

He had to be removed, and that could be done only through impeachment.

The problem obviously is that Congress would have to be bribed for that to happen, in the *modus operandi* of pork barrel allocations, but the existing source for such, the Priority Development Assistance Fund, wasn't enough to push the legislators to undertake such an unprecedented action, even if Aquino and Congress more than tripled the pork barrel fund from P7 billion in 2010 to P22 billion in 2011.

Funds for the DAP was invented to be the source of the secret slush fund, for the Congress to remove Corona.

Some P5 billion were used to bribe the House of Representatives, through huge allocations for projects they determined, for them to quickly (two days before the 2011 Christmas break) pass the articles of impeachment against Corona.

Then P1.1 billion of DAP funds were used, also using in the genre of pork barrel allocations, to bribe the Senate to convict Corona with a weak impeachment charge: his non-inclusion in his statement of assets and liabilities of his dollar accounts, which after all are covered by bank secrecy laws.

The DAP funds handed out to the Senators, as exposed even by those who received it, notably Senators Jinggoy Estrada and Bong Revilla, were released in P50 million and P100 million tranches for the senators' chosen projects, immediately before and after the May 29, 2012 impeachment vote.

Aquino also used P14 billion of DAP funds to build up support for his Yellow Party candidates in the 2013 elections, by channeling these funds to projects in their bastions.

These funds were released two months before the 2013 elections, and even included P2 billion in infrastructure funds to Aquino's home province of Tarlac, one of the most overbuilt provinces in the country.

Some P10 billion, according to Budget department documents, were given to the Autonomous Region of Muslim Mindanao and its leaders to bribe them to support Aquino's peace pact with the Moro Islamic Liberation Front, which he thought would win him the Nobel Peace Prize.

Shocked in the 2010 elections by Vice President Jejomar Binay's unexpected strength among local government leaders, Aquino and Abad used the DAP funds to build up the Liberal Party base among local governments.

It allocated P6.5 billion from the DAP funds for what is essentially a pork barrel scheme, cloaked as LGU (Local Government Unit) Support Fund for local governments, down to the municipal level,

Aquino and Abad cleverly allocated DAP funds to other seemingly productive uses, to conceal its main intention of bribing Congress to remove Corona.

Among these were the P750 million "Development Assistance to the Province of Quezon," P750 million; P100 million "Relocation sites for informal settlers along Iloilo River and its tributaries"; P2.8 billion for the "Mindanao Rural Development Project," P919 million; P1.8 billion to the Cordillera People's Liberation Army and the Moro National Liberation Front ostensibly for the training in livelihood projects of their surrendering guerillas; and P2 billion to the Department of Social Welfare and Development for such projects as day-care centers and its "supplementary feeding projects".

Nobody knew anything about the DAP, until Senator Jinggoy Estrada in September 2012 exposed it and claimed that senators were each given P50 to P100 million for voting in favor of the impeachment of Chief Justice Corona. Abad reacted that nothing was wrong it with, that it was part of the then unheard-of DAP.

Over two dozen private citizens and organizations filed in 2013 a case at the Supreme Court to declare it unconstitutional. By a vote of 13, the Court did rule that its main features violated the Constitution, namely: the creation of savings prior to the end of the fiscal year and the withdrawal of these funds for implementing agencies; the transfers of the savings from one branch of government to another; and the allotment of funds for projects, activities, and programs not provided for in the General Appropriations Acts.

(This piece is based on over a dozen columns I had written since the DAP was exposed in 2012, mainly from columns published in October 31, 2013, June 30, 2014, July 4, 2014 and March 10, 2017.)

POSTSCRIPT:

To the utter dismay of many, Ombudsman Conchita Carpio Morales in 2017 cleared Aquino of any wrongdoing over the DAP, and slapped Abad with a ridiculous fine of three months' salary, finding him guilty only of "Simple Misconduct" for "Usurpation of Legislative Powers."

Aquino wasn't indicted, said Morales, because the alleged crime was committed when he was President and therefore he was immune from prosecution.

However, a month before her term ended, Morales reversed herself and indicted Aquino in June 2018 for usurpation of legislative powers when he undertook his DAP scheme. It was still seen as a mere slap on the wrist as the possible crime of technical malversation was ignored, according to legal experts.

Even then, the Ombudsman's press release noted that penalty for the crime Aquino was charged with is *prision correccional*, or imprisonment from six months to six years.

Aquino meets twice with drug company officials that sold the P3.5 billion of the defective deadly anti-dengue vaccine.

THE P3.5B DENGVAXIA DEAL

WAS THERE CORRUPTION on a massive scale, with former President Aquino III earning hundreds of millions of pesos in dirty money from his administration's purchase of Sanofi's dengue vaccine Dengvaxia?

If indeed it was a case of corruption, it would be among the biggest ever for a single corrupt deal, as just 10 percent of the P3.5 billion cost of the one million dosages of the vaccine purchased — without any bidding and through secret negotiations — is P350 million.

It could have likely been more, considering that Sanofi-Pasteur's $70 million sale to the Aquino administration gave it the much needed financial and advertising boost for a vaccine it had developed at a cost of $1.8 billion, yet which it could sell only $20 million worth in the entire world, in two years of aggressive marketing.

But more than the magnitude of dirty money involved, this case of graft, if proven as such, would be the most abominable: The health and lives of 730,000 Filipino children were put at risk, just to rush the vaccine's purchase before a new government would come to power.

President Duterte must leave no stone unturned to determine the answer to this question, if he is to be true to his promise to rid the country of corruption, and to get justice for 730,000 children.

He will be met by stiff resistance by the Yellow Cult. Already, the most expensive PR campaign ever has been contracted and launched to use media for a massive cover-up of this ignominy. Just check the articles and opinion columns of the newspaper still in the Yellow Cult's control.

I don't think arriving at the truth will be so difficult: Aquino's Health Secretary Janette Garin, who is from one of the most powerful political clans in Iloilo, would likely throw her former boss under the bus to save her own skin.

You, dear Reader, decide for yourself if Aquino got graft money or not from his dengue vaccination program. I will just narrate the facts.

Intense interest

First, it was Aquino himself who demonstrated intense, inexplicable interest in the Dengvaxia mass vaccination program, when he had hardly any interest in health issues in the past. He gave direct orders to Garin to undertake the program and buy the vaccines from Sanofi, despite appeals by the medical community to wait for the World Health Organization's recommendation.

Aquino also had to order Budget Secretary Florencio Abad to find ways to fund the P3.5-billion cost of the vaccines, as this wasn't covered in the 2015 or 2016 budgets set by Congress. I wrote this in my column last Wednesday, and neither Aquino nor Garin have denied this claim.

Second, Aquino was in an extraordinary rush to purchase Sanofi's Dengvaxia, quite obviously so the vaccination program could be undertaken before he stepped down from office on June 30.

Those familiar with the anatomy of corruption in any country would recognize such rushed purchases as a red flag pointing to graft. The speed at which the purchase was undertaken looked puzzling until one sees it as a 'graft project':

- December 2, 2015: Aquino met with Sanofi officials in Paris — the second time he did so — and as the meeting adjourned, he ordered Garin to rush the order to purchase the vaccines.
- December 22: The Food and Drug Administration, headed by Garin approved the use of Sanofi's Dengvaxia. It normally takes two years for the FDA to give its approval for new drugs, longer for risky vaccines since these are essentially weakened forms of the virus introduced to the body, in the hope it will develop its own immunity.
- December 29: The Budget department's authorization (SARO) for the purchase of the P3.5 billion vaccines was issued.
- January 2016: Garin (who had replaced Enrique Ona at the Department of Health in January 2015) announces that the mass vaccination program would be undertaken starting in February.
- March: The Education department and the Interior and Local Government department issued their memoranda on their personnel's participation in the program.
- April: The mass injection of 733,000 fourth-grade students with the Dengvaxia begins.

Never before has such a major government program, a health program at that, with a risky new vaccine, been undertaken in the span of just a few months.

So despicable

Aquino's sprint for his administration to buy the Dengvaxia vaccine is so despicable considering that the UN's World Health Organization in July 2015 had withheld recommendation on its mass use. It told the world that its Strategic Advisory Group of Experts (SAGE) on immunization was still evaluating the evidence and would only "likely" submit its findings on the use of the vaccine to the body in April 2016.

But for Aquino that obviously would be too late to purchase the vaccine, and the WHO had not really committed to the April date. Indeed, it was only in July 2016, that the WHO issued its recommendations based on the studies of the SAGE.

The WHO said Dengvaxia must be used only in areas where at least 50 percent of the population were infected with the dengue virus. It emphasized that it should not be injected into those who have not had the disease. If this was done, dengue would be more severe than it normally is, even leading to death, when the vaccinated person gets the disease.

Because of the dangers of Dengvaxia, only the Philippines in the entire world has undertaken a government-sponsored mass vaccination program using the drug on such a scale, with the aim to cover a million children.

There was no plague-like outbreak of dengue at the time (or ever), with the disease only ranked as the ninth most prevalent disease in the country. The only urgency was perhaps the fact that the national elections were coming up in a few months time, and Aquino had to yield his seat to the next president. Most everyone, too, including media would be distracted by the heat of the political contest.

But still, why couldn't Aquino just wait for the WHO recommendations? For hundreds of millions of reasons?

Laws violated

Third, Aquino violated government laws and regulations when the Health department purchased the P3.5 billion Sanofi vaccine, thereby risking being charged and imprisoned.

There wasn't any public call to suppliers to submit their bids for the vaccine. It was a non-Sanofi firm Zuellig that was licensed to sell Dengvaxia in the country, although it isn't clear if the French firm coursed the vaccine it sold to the government through this company.

The purchase of the vaccine wasn't in the Health department's budget for 2015 or in 2016, and was therefore unauthorized by Congress, the body that determines how taxpayers' money may be used.

The funds were hijacked from the 2016 budget for "miscellaneous personnel benefit funds," created for the compensation of newly hired government employees. But this is illegal, as the Supreme Court categorically ruled such fund juggling unconstitutional in the case involving the Disbursement Acceleration Program controversy.

Do you think Aquino would risk going to prison in order to protect Filipino children from dengue, using a vaccine that the WHO had not approved? Known to have a deficit of empathy (shown for instance in his behavior in the aftermath of the Mamasapano massacre), it is hard to believe that he broke all these laws just so he could protect children from dengue.

Fourth, the process for the P3.5 billion Dengvaxia purchase was shrouded in secrecy, with the talks between government and Sanofi on the price for the vaccine never made public. This is another red flag for a purchase involving pay-offs to government officials.

The only report I have been able to find on this, was a January 4, 2016 article in GMA News that quoted Garin as saying that Aquino got a 34 percent discount when he met with an unidentified Sanofi executive in Paris.

Really? Or was Garin confused, that the 34 percent figure was actually the commission?

Sanofi reports in its website that it does not make public the Dengvaxia's price, claiming that this is subject to negotiations with buyers. That of course gives so much flexibility for under-the-table pay-offs.

There are indications that the Dengvaxia vaccine bought was overpriced. The purchase order for Dengvaxia was for 1 million dosages at a cost of P3 billion, which means P3,000 per dosage. The Brazilian government reported that it bought its Dengvaxia at $37 per dosage, or P1,871. An Indian company though has put out an advertisement that prices its Dengvaxia at the equivalent of P9 per dose.

Fifth, Sanofi has been linked to corruption cases before. A German court in 2013 convicted two former Sanofi staff of bribery and slapped the French drug maker with a $39 million fine for making pay-offs to get more buyers for its drugs. The company's officials were also alleged to have given pay-offs to doctors in China, Kenya, and East African countries from 2007 to 2012.

Indeed, "big pharma" has had a reputation for corrupting local governments for its requirements that the renowned spy-thriller novelist John le Carré wrote a novel (**"The Constant Gardener,"** which was made into a 2005 movie) in which a drug company bribed Kenyan officials to test secretly its tuberculosis drug, called "Dypraxa," on a village that got many of its residents killed. The Aquino administration's health department essentially agreed in 2011 to have 3,500 children become guinea pigs for Dengvaxia.

Was Aquino so desperate to make big money in the "last two minutes" of his regime that he risked the health and lives of 730,000 Filipino children? The only other explanation is that he was just utterly stupid, and that he was played by France's Sanofi-Pasteur.

(December 8, 2017)

SUCH A SHAMELESS, SOCIOPATHIC LIAR

FORMER PRESIDENT Benigno Aquino III demonstrated how much of a shameless, sociopathic liar he is at the hearings of three Congress committees on the Dengvaxia debacle.

He claimed that he undertook the mass vaccination using the defective Dengvaxia vaccine since 1 million Filipinos get sick of dengue annually, and boasted that he "cannot allow this to happen."

That is a total lie. Health department figures show that in the past 10 years the incidence of dengue has never exceeded 200,000 annually, with 131,827 cases in 2017. Dengue is not among the top 10 prevalent diseases in the country or among the top 10 causes of deaths in most years.

The most prevalent diseases in the country are those affecting the lungs. About 2 million Filipinos get sick of respiratory infection, pneumonia, and bronchitis; 345,000 of hypertension; 326,551 of diarrhea; and, 272,000 of influenza.

Deaths due to dengue has averaged less than a thousand per year (731 in 2017) in contrast to the 140,000 deaths due to heart and vascular diseases, 36,000 to pneumonia, 25,000 to tuberculosis, and 20,000 to diabetes.

Why would Aquino lie about the incidence of dengue, to exaggerate it?

In order to justify why he and Janette Garin — a politician who became Aquino's health secretary in his last year in office — chose dengue as the disease to focus on, and to allocate P3.5 billion for it, even violating budget laws in his last year in office. In fact, never has there been a program of such cost for a single year targeted to alleviate a particular disease.

And why did they do this? The only rational answer is this: None of the country's most prevalent diseases and causes of mortality involved a new drug or vaccine offered solely by a single firm, as the French company Sanofi did in the case of its Dengvaxia, so far the only such vaccine claimed to prevent dengue.

No prevalent disease in the country has ever involved a single, huge firm such as Sanofi — alleged to have been involved in cases of bribery in other countries — that was getting desperate to sell its Dengvaxia quickly to recover the $1.5 billion it had spent in developing the vaccine.

It had expected to sell $200 million worth of Dengvaxia since 2015. It has reported only $63.6 million sales of Dengvaxia so far.

The confirmed P3 billion the Aquino government paid for the 1 million doses it bought was worth $58 million, or 92 percent of Sanofi's Dengvaxia sales.

Yet the incompetent congressmen who undertook the hearings on the issue the other day still did not suspect that Aquino and his cabal earned a single corrupt dollar out of this deal? None of them interrogated Aquino on this.

Sanofi was also racing against time as other entities, including Japan's biggest pharmaceutical firm Takeda Pharmaceuticals and the mammoth Merck & Co., were reportedly in the last stages of trials for their own anti-dengue vaccines. Even US military institutions, the Walter Reed Army Institute of Research and the Naval Medical Research Center, were rushing to develop a vaccine against dengue in order to protect their soldiers in future wars in the jungles of the Third World. Aquino was manna from heaven for Sanofi.

Aquino again showed how much of an inveterate liar he is, or alternatively such an extremely criminally negligent president, when he claimed that he would have stopped the Dengvaxia program if he had known about its downside, which he said was revealed by Sanofi only in November 2017.

No consultations on safety

Aquino ordered a mass vaccination program that would inject live (albeit purportedly weakened) dengue viruses into 1 million children — the new Dengvaxia vaccine — and he relied solely on the seller Sanofi's assurances that it was safe, and he didn't consult any third party on its safety.

Aquino in fact ordered the purchase of Dengvaxia months before the Food and Drug Administration approved it in a span of a month (during the holiday-filled month of December) and after the Philippine Pharmaceutical Council was pressured to okay it for government purchase.

Aquino lied that only Sanofi could check on Dengvaxia's safety and efficacy, and that its defects were disclosed only in November 2017.

The World Health Organization in 2015, months before the December purchase order for Dengvaxia was issued, announced in its website that its group of experts would issue its evaluation of the vaccine's effectivity and risks only the next year, in May 2016.

Aquino ignored the WHO position, and had the health department undertake the vaccination program in April 2016. In a Senate hearing two months ago, he claimed that if he had not ordered the Dengvaxia, it would have taken at least a year for a new administration to undertake the vaccination program, or it might even decide not to.

What a liar. The real reason is most probably that he saw it as a huge financial opportunity he would miss if he didn't act swiftly before his term ended, never mind if he risked the health of a million children.

Unfortunately, the members of the House of Representative's three committees that undertook the investigation mostly demonstrated how incompetent they are in ferreting out the truth in this controversy, or were so awed by the former president they let him run circles around them. The communist-party representative Isagani Zarate proved that he can only argue in slogans.

I understand President Duterte's distancing himself from the controversy since as he put it, "it is not his style" to go after a now largely powerless predecessor, as Aquino had done with such ruthlessness against former President Gloria Arroyo.

I hope though that he gets around to realizing that this is the worst case of corruption in our nation ever, since for money, they put at risk the life and health of more than 800,000 children, injected with a defective medicine that would make them contract a severe, potentially fatal case of dengue if they had never contracted it before. Have you heard of such a similar contemptible case of corruption ever, anywhere in the world?

It is Duterte's sworn duty to first to uphold justice, and second to prosecute the guilty in this case in order to set a precedent that would end corruption in this country.

(February 28, 2018)

AQUINO AND THE YELLOWS' ABOMINATION

MARIA LOURDES SERENO as the Chief Justice of the Supreme Court has been former President Aquino III and his Cojuangco clan's abomination, one of their worst insults to, and the most injurious damage they inflicted on, the Republic, the judiciary, and the legal profession.

She should be removed from the Supreme Court swiftly and decisively in order to restore the dignity of the Supreme Court and the integrity of the Republic's institutions.

Her appointment as head of the high tribunal has been a glaring, shameful anomaly in our Republic that has been crying out to be corrected. After Sereno, people just shrugged off Aquino's appointment of two other justices with as little merit as she.

Our republican system stands on the pillars of the principle of the rule of law and the Constitution. It is the Supreme Court that has the main task among the three branches of government for defending and strengthening these foundations.

Yet Aquino appointed in 2012 to head the Supreme Court a mediocre legal academic who had never even seen the insides of a Philippine courtroom. By any standard or stretch of imagination, she doesn't have the qualifications to be Chief Justice of the Supreme Court or even associate justice — or even judge of a municipal trial court.

25 allegations

Even worse, according to the twenty-five allegations filed in Congress for which she is allegedly liable for impeachment, she has had a penchant for trampling to the ground the rules and procedures of the high court, for acting as a despot and refusing to consult with her colleagues, and lying through her teeth to them.

Sereno quarreled with her colleagues. She ignored them in the administration of the justice system. She ordered for her personal use, without court approval, a bullet-proof Toyota Land Cruiser worth P8 million; she falsified court documents to cover up orders she alone made; and she traveled first-class and stayed in five-star hotels, charged to the court, against government rules. She also shamelessly asked

Muntinlupa judges not to issue arrest warrants against former justice secretary and suspected drug-coddler Sen. Leila de Lima.

Such behavior isn't really surprising. Her sole claim to being a successful lawyer was when her mentor, the 77-year-old retired Justice Florentino Feliciano, took her in as his legal researcher in the NAIA Terminal 3 case brought against the Republic by the German contractor Fraport before the International Center for the Settlement of Investment Disputes.

For that, she earned a whopping P37 million in fees, an astronomical amount, which constituted the biggest earnings of her entire career that she admitted allowed her to buy her house and several cars. Those fees, paid by us taxpayers, were ruled to have been "excessive and illegal" by the Mandaluyong regional trial court.

But one would probably call subsequent events a case of poetic justice, or karma. Among the allegations in the impeachment complaint against her is that she didn't declare that P37 million income in her statement of assets, liabilities, and net worth (SALN). That allegation has been bolstered by the report of the University of the Philippines, to which she should have submitted her SALNs, that it anomalously doesn't have these documents which should have contained her declarations of her P37 million earnings.

Why did Aquino do such a stupid thing to foist such an abomination that is Sereno on our nation?

Aquino placed Sereno in the high court a *month* after he assumed office. Her assigned role was to convince the members of the Supreme Court to agree to at least P5 billion compensation for Hacienda Luisita's Cojuangco owners. A majority of the justices ignored Sereno's kilometric arguments that made her seem like the Cojuangcos' lawyer. The court in its November 2011 decision, ruled that the Cojuangcos should be paid only P196 million.

The next month, impeachment charges were filed on the most flimsy charges against the then Chief Justice Renato Corona who championed the government's position, apparently to browbeat him and the court into complying with the Cojuangco clan's wishes.

After Corona was removed, Aquino appointed Sereno as Chief Justice in 2012 in the stupid hope that with that post she could reverse the court's November 2011 decision. The majority of the justices stood their ground though, affirming the court's Hacienda Luisita decision with finality.

It was Aquino and the Yellow Cult's in-your-face insult to the nation and to the country's legal profession, its supreme demonstration that it could do whatever it wanted. A principled person, or one with the nation's interest foremost, or one who doesn't have delusions of her worth, would have declined Aquino's appointment, content that she had defied all odds to be in the Supreme Court already.

If this case had happened elsewhere — and it hasn't — there would have been a revolution.

That there is no outrage against Sereno is another illustration of the power of media in this country. The Yellow-controlled media of that period which helped lynch Chief Justice Corona, were so servile to Aquino that it raised his appointee Sereno's image to a pedestal that bordered on the absurd.

For instance, the *Philippine Daily Inquirer*, Aquino's main propaganda arm at the time, had her appointment as its banner headline: "Excellent Choice." It gushed over Sereno as "The Chosen One" and that Aquino's appointment of her was a "bold tradition-breaking choice." Her utter deficit in qualifications was buried by hosannas that she was the first female Chief Justice of the country, and the second youngest.

Yet even with Aquino no longer in power, Sereno has been getting sympathetic coverage from the mainstream press.

Retired Justice Arturo Brion in his *Manila Bulletin* column pointed this out: "The chief justice has been all over the media in an apparent multi-media blitz. I saw her twice on TV last week and the news media are writing about her. (That an active campaign is under way is obvious from the similarly written articles in several newspapers.) 'Legal experts' openly theorize in their columns that the impeachment complaint should be dismissed."

I would think that such media support is due to the that fact she is the Yellows' sole hope of having a believer in one of the four highest posts in the Republic for another 13 years. Aged 57 now, Sereno, if she doesn't resign or isn't kicked out, will be required to step down only in 2030.

With that kind of potential advantage, I would think the Yellows with the billions of pesos they amassed in corruption in the past regime, could throw hundreds of millions for her legal defense and for media.

(December 1, 2017)

A MORALITY TALE

IT'S DISGUSTING at the same time astonishing, that the Yellows and clerics-turned-professional-agitators have rushed to defend the fallen chief justice-pretender Maria Lourdes Sereno, portraying her as a victim of injustice.

If they would just drop their Yellow blinders, they will see Sereno's rise and fall as a morality tale that should teach us the value of holding on tightly to our moral compass, and to always keep our egos under control.

Sereno would have remained an obscure legal academic if the late Supreme Court Justice Florentino Feliciano had not — inexplicably — taken her under his wing, and if President Benigno Aquino III did not have a need for his own hand-picked operator in the Supreme Court, to carry out his Cojuangco clan's game plan to get P10 billion in government compensation for Hacienda Luisita.*

Appointed to the Supreme Court right after Aquino became president and while the high tribunal was deliberating on his clan's P10-billion claim for compensation for putting Hacienda Luisita's under agrarian reform, Sereno in 2010 was the youngest justice named to the post since 1945.

With the barest of qualifications — she hadn't even seen the inside of a courtroom — to even deserve being a junior justice in the highest court of the land, Sereno's appointment was as if she had won the biggest prize ever in the lotto. She should have been content with her incredible luck.

Appointed at 50 years old, she would have had ahead of her 20 years as associate justice (until she reached the mandatory age of 70). That was certainly enough time to learn the ropes from her seniors in the court, to make up for her lack of experience.

Hubris and delusion

But it got into her head, and she seemed to really believe that it was not Aquino who put her in the post but God himself. "The whole world is witness that this appointment is God's will … Only God put me in this position," she declared in her first flag-raising ceremony as chief justice at the court grounds. Perhaps she thought that it was the deity who had struck out of the running then Justice Secretary Leila de Lima, reportedly Aquino's initial choice.

When Chief Justice Renato Corona was unjustly taken out on Aquino's orders, she applied to replace him, apparently after getting inside information that De Lima might not make it because of the pending cases filed against her.

That was hubris of the highest order.

She knew she wouldn't even be able to comply with what should have been a minor requirement for the post, the submission of statements of assets, liabilities and net worth (SALN). But in her ambition to be Chief Justice at 52, and the first female at that, she threw to the dustbin her moral compass, and would later lie that she had submitted her SALNs, and that it was the University of the Philippines' fault that it lost her files.

She lost track of the ethical or moral standards, to even mind that Aquino would overpower the Judicial and Bar Council, for it to ignore her failure to comply with the SALN requirements. (In order to ensure that the JBC did his bidding, Aquino even appointed to the council his deputy executive secretary Michael Frederick Musngi, a move former President Fidel Ramos himself pointed out in an e-mailed letter to the JBC was "patently unconstitutional.")

But I doubt now if she ever really had a moral compass. If she had moral values, or even just had some concern for taxpayers' money, would she in conscience have accepted the P22 million in fees from government for merely being the legal researcher from 2003 to 2009 of Justice Feliciano in the PIATCO arbitration case, which the Court of Appeals has ruled was illegally given to her? Her morals could even be found to be much worse, if the BIR concludes after its ongoing investigation that she had not paid the correct taxes on the huge fees that she received.

If she had a moral compass, she could have on her own (as three applicants to the Chief Justice post did) withdrawn her bid to be appointed to the position. If she had done that, she would have been left alone and perhaps just a decade later could have, by sheer seniority, become chief justice.

Big lessons

But her hubris and her delusion that God wanted her to be Chief Justice got the better of her.

For this, she might just face instant impoverishment if the government files a case for her to return her PIATCO fees, jail for not paying the correct taxes, and even disbarment as she could be found to have violated the lawyers' Code of Ethics.

There are big lessons from the Sereno episode for us. Your patron won't be in power forever, so be careful about complying not only with the written rules but also the unwritten ones. Assume a job you are really qualified for, and not one that you got because of your, as Filipinos put it, "connect." Don't even think of joining government if you have skeletons in your closet, even the smallest ones such as your laziness in filing your SALNs.

Justice Teresita de Castro tried to impart the lessons of the Sereno episode to a new generation of lawyers, when she said in her speech a few weeks ago before the 2017 Philippine bar passers, obviously referring Aquino's fake chief justice:

"Yes, you will encounter people who might be promoted ahead of you because of a carefully cultivated glittering persona and a talent for self-promotion or credit-grabbing, not things of substantial accomplishment. They believe their own hype or lose humility. When they attain a position of authority without real effort, they tend to be blinded by power and intoxicated by the perks and privileges attached to the position. You will see it many times in your career that those who rise too fast fall just as quickly."

I would say the simplest lesson from this Sereno episode involves that ancient adage: *"Whom the Gods wish to destroy, they first make mad."* An interpretation of that is, whom the gods will destroy, they first swell the head.

(June 13, 2018)

---

* Sereno's arguments, later contained in the dissenting opinion she wrote against the court's ruling, was virtually the Cojuangcos' entire petition, which asked that they be paid for the hacienda's 4,335-hectare land at 2006 prices, of P2.5 million per hectare.

That converts to P9.75 billion. Plus interest, which Sereno argued was justified, of P3 billion by 2011. The Cojuangcos would have had a windfall of nearly P13 billion — which certainly explains the crucial role of Aquino's handpicked justice.

The court however ruled that the valuation should be made based on 1989 prices, or when the hacienda undertook its fake land reform, by which its tenants became "stockholders" of Hacienda Luisita, Inc. It valued its lands at P40,000 per hectare to compute how much stocks would be given to its tenants-turned-shareholders. That would amount to only P173 million, which was the compensation the Court decided on.

The Mamasapano Massacre

THE WORST CRIME EVER

THE OMBUDSMAN the other day filed a graft case against former President Benigno Aquino III for, in her words, "utilizing the services" (for the police operation in Mamasapano, Maguindanao, in January 2015 that led to the massacre of 44 police commandos) of Philippine National Police chief Alan Purisima when he was under suspension at the time.

What a clever way for Aquino to escape justice.

The Ombudsman's charge is like, if ever, US authorities charging the New York terrorist who mowed eight people to death using a rented truck, solely with the charge of reckless driving.

As relatives of the Special Action Force (SAF) troopers who were killed have pointed out — and are planning to ask the Supreme Court to order the Ombudsman to do — Aquino should be charged with 44 counts of criminal imprudence resulting in homicide.

There has got to be some graver offense in our laws to charge Aquino with over the Mamasapano tragedy.

Aquino's failure — or refusal — to prevent the massacre of our elite troops in Mamasapano by Muslim rebels could even be the worst crime ever committed by a Philippine President.

Aquino had been told early that morning that troops of the police's Special Action Force (SAF) tasked with terminating an international terrorist were pinned down, and that its commander Getulio Napeñas, was pleading for his troops to be rescued. Yet Aquino did nothing the whole day.

Only at dusk

He called for a "command conference" of his security officials to deal with the crisis only at dusk. Army troops with air support were ordered — nobody even knows by whom — to act only towards sundown, when the 44 SAF soldiers had already been killed by Muslim rebel snipers, with some of the wounded shot at point-blank range.

This is not speculation, but facts that nobody has disputed. These had been established by testimony in Senate hearings a month after the tragedy, by several officials who were with the President throughout that tragic day.

Aquino himself claimed in an impromptu speech before a SAF gathering two days later that, *"Maaga pa lang, tuloy-tuloy na ang mga ulat na natatanggap namin."* (Since early morning, the reports had been coming in continuously.)

In the transcript Purisima submitted to the Senate hearing, Aquino learned of the progress of the operation he had ordered at 7:36 a.m., and that the troops were trapped before 11:36 a.m.

Aquino didn't do anything that entire day, and pretended that nothing was happening as he went around Zamboanga City with his officials, including Interior Secretary Mar Roxas and Defense Secretary Voltaire Gazmin.

The scenario that he had worked out was that on the pretext of being in Zamboanga City that day to inspect buildings damaged by a bombing two days before, he would rush to Cotabato City, the nearest city to Mamasapano and an hour by helicopter, to congratulate the SAF troopers for their capture of the global terrorists in Mamasapano, and to boast how he himself was on top of the operation. Instead, his glorious scenario turned out to be a horror for our troops.

Two explanations

There are two explanations for why Aquino abandoned his troops to the wolves, to be slaughtered, as it were.

One is that, given reports of psychological instability and of his penchant for burying his head in the sand in the face of crisis, he simply panicked when he realized that the scenario that was in his mind was turning into a nightmare, and he was paralyzed into inaction.

He also realized the consequences of being blamed for the massacre of 44 commandos, and prosecuted for having given the authority as overall commander for the operations to his long-time buddy Purisima — his bodyguard during the entire term of his mother, from 1986 to 1992 — even if Purisima had been suspended at the time by the Ombudsman over corruption charges, and therefore had no authority at all to direct police operations.

A second explanation, which President Duterte himself has advanced, is that he was allegedly told by Teresita Quintos-Deles, his chief negotiator with rebel groups, including the secessionist Moro Islamic Liberation Front, not to order the military's air assets from bombing the Muslim rebel positions as the battle raged, as this would endanger the peace talks with the MILF.

While Deles has denied she ever told Aquino to order his troops to stand down, the reports have been persistent that indeed she did so. Deles had allegedly convinced Aquino that he, together with his negotiators, had a good chance of being awarded the Nobel Peace Prize if they finalize the peace pact with the MILF. (Incredible as this notion may initially seem to be, it has credence given the fact that Colombia President Juan Manuel Santos got the Nobel in 2016, for his peace pact with the leftist rebel group, the Revolutionary Armed Forces of Colombia, known as FARC, that had been waging a guerrilla war for 50 years.)

Dante Ang, the chairman emeritus of the *Manila Times*, had reported in an article published September 6, 2015, that based on accounts of his sources, police and army reinforcements were on the way to rescue the SAF troopers, and their commander asked Aquino for his final approval. Aquino, however, replied: "Negative. Negative. Stand down."

Abomination

Whichever explanation is accurate, Aquino's failure or refusal to order the military he commanded to rescue the SAF troops who had been pinned down since early morning is an abomination to the military and the nation.

Past presidents have been accused of corruption, on such a massive scale even. But Aquino is the only President who abandoned his troops, so that they were brutally massacred.

The Congress he controlled — with the Senate headed by Liberal Party pillar Franklin Drilon and the House of Representatives by Feliciano Belmonte, Jr. — share Aquino's shame and crime, as even in this controversy that involved the massacre of the Republic's troops, it chose to conspire in the cover-up of the worst crime by a Philippine president ever.

For the sake of the nation's integrity, President Duterte with the help of Congress should find ways to get Aquino pay for this crime. We cannot allow an ingenious scheme that only pretends to bring him to justice to succeed.

(November 10, 2017)

AMERICANS CARED MORE ABOUT SAVING SAF THAN AQUINO

THE SENATE REPORT on the Mamasapano massacre revealed one of its saddest chapters, narrated in one of its executive (read: secret) sessions.

Special Action Forces were radioing for help as they were trapped, and real-time video by American drones showed the actual battle that Muslim snipers were killing them one by one with their caliber-50 Barrett rifles.

It was most probably midday, five hours after Philippine National Police (PNP) officers, not only those on the ground but even PNP acting chief Leonardo Espina, had asked Major General Edmundo Pangilinan, commander of the 6th Infantry Division, for artillery to fend off the Muslim forces.

According to the Senate Committee report there were six Americans at the command post, probably civilian contractors under the US military's payroll:

"One of the Americans (at the tactical command post) ordered Pangilinan to fire the artillery. However, Pangilinan refused and told him, 'Do not dictate to me what to do. I am the commander here.' " Appearing even proud of his remark, Pangilinan confirmed he said that in a Congress hearing the other day to confirm his promotion to top major-general rank.

I don't think the American gave an "order," or he wouldn't have any business in that kind of clandestine affair.

Most probably, he was viewing in real time provided by their drones that the SAF troops were trapped and would be soon massacred. Probably, nobody else in the tactical command post had the guts to emphasize to the general that without the artillery, the commandos were goners. Probably, the American got to be friends with the SAF commandos, based on reports that Americans had trained them.

So most probably, and considering how informal — and emotional — Americans could get, he got mad, and maybe one of them even raised his voice to Pangilinan and told him: "Can you fire your f——ng artillery now, general, or those soldiers will be f——ng massacred!"

And how did Pangilinan respond? Not with a rational reply that the artillery didn't have precise coordinates and may hit civilians.

Instead, his reply was so petty and egoistic: "Do not dictate to me what to do. I am the commander here." Pangilinan was more concerned about his bruised ego, that he was being "dictated to," than about saving the lives of the SAF troopers.

Was it because Pangilinan didn't want to appear to be "dictated to" and to assert his position of authority, so that he ordered the artillery to fire three white phosphorus markers, only at 5:48 p.m.—10 hours after he was first requested to do so by PNP officers at 8 a.m.? But that was actually hours after the 44 had been killed, with the Muslim insurgents even having the time to be able to approach the wounded, shoot them in the head and rob them even of their personal belongings.

Indeed, the Senate committee's report that six Americans were at the operation's tactical command post providing real-time monitoring (with the use of their drones and high GPS systems) belies Pangilinan's excuse, which he gave in the hearing.

He had claimed that he didn't want the artillery fired, since without precise information, they risked hitting the SAF or even civilians. But the US monitoring systems at the command post were the most technologically advanced in the world, that coordinates could be precisely established, and had been, in fact, given.

He even claimed that he had not deployed "forward observers," i.e., personnel watching where the first rounds would land so as to adjust the next firing, because the PNP had not coordinated with his troops. But the US drones, in effect, meant a limitless number of "forward observers."

There's another instance in which the Americans seemed to care more for the lives of the SAF than those of Aquino and his generals. Even as the battle was still ongoing, they sent at least one helicopter to evacuate the wounded. The Western Command had six helicopters based in Cotabato City. Why weren't they deployed? There was no request, Aquino's generals replied.

Did the thought cross Aquino's mind that fateful day while he was pretending nothing serious was happening, as he toured Zamboanga City to ask the helicopters hovering above the city for his security to, instead, be deployed to rescue the SAF in Mamasapano? Not a chance.

There could only be three reasons why Aquino's generals dragged their feet on saving the police commandos:

One, it was petty jealousy, and even inter-service rivalry. The Laguna-based SAF would be praised for having killed a notorious international terrorist in Maguindanao, where the Army's 6th Infantry Division was based and should have had a vast intelligence network to know that the terrorist lived there, apparently for years.

Since the SAF didn't want to share the credit, and didn't coordinate with them on the operation, they were left to fend for themselves, until the generals realized the casualties would become too high that they moved to rescue and fire the artillery to save the 84th SAF company, after the 44th SAC had been decimated.

Two, the generals were in cahoots with the insurgents, especially with the MILF. While this may be a cruel accusation, I was told way back in 1996 by my MILF informants: "Don't you notice that nearly every general gets to be assigned in Maguindanao before he retires? They amass their retirement money here, since we buy our arms and ammo from them."

And third, the most likely reason, which is why suspended police chief Alan Purisima (Aquino's commander of the operations) claimed his boss's last text message was at 10:16 a.m., and why Chief of Staff Gregorio Catapang and his generals refused to submit their cell phones to the PNP Board of Inquiry: Their commander-in-chief told them to stand down, or his peace plan with the MILF would be derailed.

This is not just dereliction of duty, not just betrayal of public trust. This is criminal, deliberate negligence that resulted in the deaths of 44 of our elite troops.

(March 20, 2015)

DID SMART HAVE THE SMOKING GUN?

THE INDONESIAN-Japanese venture Smart Communications has proof, or at least the smoking gun, for President Benigno S. Aquino's "stand-down order" to the military, telling them not to save the police commandos who got trapped in Mamasapano, Maguindanao in its operation January 2015 to terminate international terrorist Zulkifli Abdhir aka "Marwan" and two of his collaborators.

As part of his sworn testimony to the Senate hearing last month, former Police Chief Alan Purisima, Aquino's bosom buddy whom he illegally ordered to supervise the operation, submitted a transcript of what he claimed was the exchange of SMS messages between him and Aquino on that fateful day. (Aquino's designation of Purisima was illegal, as he was suspended from his post at that time on charges of graft.)

His first message was at 5:45 a.m., which in a self-congratulatory tone reported that Marwan was killed, the mission successful, although the body was left behind. Purisima sent seven more text messages, his last at 6:20 p.m.

Aquino replied when he woke up, at 7:36 a.m., not to ask how the SAF troopers were but only as follows: "Why was it (Marwan's body) left behind? The other two targets?" (Aquino's second question reflected his intimate knowledge of the operation, as he knew more than what the public had been told that there were only two targets, Marwan and his associate Basit Usman. Only when this transcript of SMS messages was submitted by Purisima and inquiries made why Aquino referred to two targets did the government disclose there was a third target, who got away — another Malaysian bomb expert, Amin Baco.)

But according to Purisima's testimony, Aquino's last message was at 10:16 a.m.

This is impossible. Aquino couldn't have abruptly ended his communication with Purisima at 10:16 a.m. This even contradicts Aquino's statement in his impromptu speech before the SAF on January 31 that "he was receiving reports the whole day" on the ongoing firefight.

The most crucial hours of the firefight were around midday, when the SAF 55th company commandos — ironically the "blocking force"

— were being overrun and massacred.

That was the life-or-death period when Purisima could have told Aquino how desperate the situation of the SAF troopers was, and when Aquino, the commander-in-chief, should have issued his crucial orders to save them.

Testimonies at the Senate and, more recently, at the House of Representatives yesterday bolster this newspaper's February 5 report that President Aquino ordered his troops to "stand down" for the sake of his peace talks with the Moro Islamic Liberation Front (MILF), whose forces attacked and killed the SAF troopers.

As SAF officers' testimonies revealed yesterday, how could veteran army generals invoke the "peace talks" as their reason for withholding artillery fire they knew could save the lives of their comrades-in-arms, if they were not just following the President's orders?

Based on the testimonies of Aquino's officials in the Senate, only Purisima was reporting to him, except for a single message Interior and Local Government Secretary Mar Roxas sent to him early morning, to which the President replied with an obviously dismissive, "Thank you."

Or perhaps Armed Forces of the Philippines (AFP) Chief of Staff Gregorio Catapang was actually briefing him the whole day, which means the general was lying, committing perjury in his testimonies at the Senate as he stated he didn't have cellphone communications with the President that day.

Purisima is obviously taking the Senate and us for fools by testifying that Aquino's last message was at 10:16 a.m. He is covering up for his bosom friend.

Why did he delete Aquino's messages after that early hour of the daylong crisis?

Because Aquino's messages would have indisputably shown that he ordered his forces to stand down, as army actions to save the SAF troops could have endangered his peace talks. The messages would most probably show that he told Purisima that he had spoken with peace adviser Teresita Deles, who assured him that the MILF had issued a ceasefire order to its troops.

This reminds us of the infamous 18-minute gap in the 79-minute conversation between US President Richard Nixon and his chief of staff, Bob Haldeman, which had obviously been deleted deliberately as it would have shown his complicity in the Watergate break-in cover-up. (At least Nixon agreed to submit the tapes to Congress. In our case, our Congress has been too timid to ask Aquino to surrender his cellphone.)

But modern technology could come to our rescue so the truth would come out, even if Aquino and Purisima refuse to submit their cellphones for investigation.

Smart Communications, operator of the cellphones Aquino and Purisima used, has confirmed that it stores the logs — but not the messages — of SMS sent through its system.

These would show whether or not there were other SMS messages exchanged between the cellphones of Aquino and Purisima, or between the President and his other officials that day. It would be a smoking gun if the logs showed there were other SMS exchanges between the two that Purisima did not include in his affidavit.

Why hasn't Smart complied with the Senate's request for it to submit these logs?

I do hope Smart Communications would be patriotic enough to submit to Congress the SMS records of Aquino and Purisima — and even of Gen. Gregorio Catapang and his field commanders — so the truth can be established, which is important for strengthening our rule of law.*

What am I talking about asking Smart to be patriotic?

It is a foreign-owned firm. A 100-percent subsidiary of Philippine Long Distance Telephone Co., Smart, therefore, is 46 percent owned by foreign firms, with the next biggest single stockholding bloc of only 8 percent being owned by Filipino John Gokongwei. About 26 percent is owned by the First Pacific Co. Ltd of Hong Kong, of which, 45 percent is held by Indonesian Anthoni Salim, son of former Indonesian strongman Suharto's biggest crony, the late Sudono. The other 20 percent is held by the Japanese giant NTT, which is in charge of the firm's technology. (Its chairman, Manuel V. Pangilinan, only has 0.11 percent)

Foreigners control a strategic, near-monopoly communications firm that provides crucial telecom services for the battles fought by our military. Foreigners now hold information that would determine indisputably whether this President, deliberately or not, allowed 44 of our elite troopers to be massacred?

The Mamasapano tragedy is another confirmation of the doctrine of most Asian countries: That the telecom sector is so strategic, and could involve matters of state that it should be controlled by nationals and even by the state.

What a pathetic and unpatriotic country we've become.

(April 10, 2015)

* Smart had not denied that there were text messages between Aquino and Purisima after the 10:16 AM message the latter disclosed in his testimony.

Territorial Dispute

Pag-Asa Island in the Spratlys.

Philippine marines announcing our sovereignty through a makeshift sign. Undated, but definitively in the 1970s. Photo from retired Navy Capt. Domingo Tucay, who was in the expedition ordered by Marcos to lay claim to seven islands in the Spratlys.

WE OWE MARCOS OUR SPRATLY TERRITORIES

MAKE NO MISTAKE ABOUT IT. The Spratly islands dispute could get messy. In March 1987, a clash between Chinese and Vietnamese warships in the disputed island group resulted in both sides losing a vessel, and 120 Vietnamese soldiers killed. A year later, Chinese ships sank three Vietnamese vessels in Fiery Cross Reef with 74 sailors dead. The United States just watched, of course.

Before President Aquino's three spokespersons go on another flag-waving, saber-rattling tack, they should take very seriously Senate President Juan Ponce Enrile's advice: "Don't agitate China."

"What they are doing is posturing, but when things go really bad, I'm sure they will be the first to run. These subalterns are very talkative," Enrile angrily said.

Enrile knows what he is talking about: he was there at the inception of this geopolitical flashpoint.

There is a bit of irony, in that Aquino is melodramatically vowing to defend a territory that became part of our country, largely through the efforts of his family's arch-enemy: former president Ferdinand Marcos.

Whether a legacy or a curse, without Marcos and his martial rule, we wouldn't be involved in the Spratlys issue.

The story begins with Tomas Cloma, a courageous seafaring adventurer from Batangas, who was in the fishing business. Partly because of his search for rich fishing waters and partly because of his venturesome personality, Cloma with several of his fishing boats wandered into the Spratly islands in 1956, with his crew of over 40 men going ashore at the group's biggest island.

As the islands were not in any standard maps then, Cloma issued a "Proclamation to the Whole World," that announced the creation of a new state he called "The Free Territory of Freedomland," made up of most of the island group. While no nation recognized it, he persisted in asserting "sovereignty" over the area despite his obvious difficulties in occupying it. About 380 kilometers from Palawan, it was totally inaccessible in the monsoon season.

Martial law changed a lot of things. In 1974, Cloma turned over all claims to the islands under a "Deed of Assignment and Waiver of Rights" to the Marcos government for one peso.

Then in 1978, basing his claim on Cloma's discovery of the islands, Marcos formally annexed the archipelago and made it a municipality of Palawan through Presidential Decree No. 1596.

Marcos certainly knew his international law, especially that part which in effect says that occupation is ownership. Right after Marcos got Cloma's "deed of assignment," the Armed Forces of the Philippines under Defense Secretary Enrile quickly and covertly transformed the group's biggest but uninhabited island into a fortification and named it "Pag-Asa Island."

A heavily armed battalion of Marines was stationed there, and a 1.3-kilometer runway was constructed, making it easily accessible from Manila. Marcos even had it populated with over 200 civilians. It was the first and probably the last time our country added a new area to our territory, beyond what the Spanish turned over to the US when they left in 1898.

The incontrovertible truth is that without Marcos — and his authoritarian powers — we would not have any island, atoll, or reef in the Spratlys.

Marcos' action angered the Chinese so much that it made moves that would profoundly affect our history. As Malaysia helped the Moro National Liberation Front in order to retaliate against Marcos' attempt to re-incorporate Sabah into the Philippines, China sent finances and arms (the latter, unsuccessfully though) to Jose Ma. Sison's Communist Party of the Philippines, in the hope that Marcos would be toppled for his "aggression" in the Spratlys.

China and Vietnam claim the Spratlys on grounds that these have been theirs even before the Philippines was born as a sovereign state. The Chinese point to documents (as far back as the Han dynasty in 110 AD) that arguably referred to the area as part of the Middle Kingdom, where Chinese warships and fishermen sought refuge in storms. Vietnam says that the islands it claims were already part of the 17th century Nguyen dynasty's kingdom.

After all the debate though, "Might is Right" and its corollary "Occupation is Ownership" have been the supreme principles in the Spratly islands, as these have always been in controversies over nations' territories.

China violently evicted the Vietnamese from the Paracel Islands in 1974, and subsequent attempts at incursions by the Vietnamese were met with force. Pag-Asa is a Philippine municipality because of its occupation by our Marines starting 1974, possible only in a martial law situation. The Chinese especially resented that, as they claim we managed to occupy Pag-Asa, only because it was weak and distracted during the chaotic "Cultural Revolution" that ended only in 1976.

But with China resurgent in the 1990s, and since we practically had a zero naval force, we would just sit idly by while China built, starting in 1995, military structures on atolls in Mischief Reef in the Spratlys.

An understanding of how we got to have territory in the Spratlys, should emphasize the need to go on a different tack, other than that juvenile "just-try-crossing-my-line" dare of the Aquino administration. A shooting war in the Spratlys certainly isn't like a video war game Aquino is fond of playing, in which after a lost "battle" one can just walk away for a smoke in the garden.

(June 22, 2011)

AQUINO AND DEL ROSARIO LOST US PANATAG

DUE TO THEIR BUNGLING, President Benigno Aquino III and his foreign secretary Alberto del Rosario lost a territory of the country, specifically Scarborough Shoal, which is also known as Panatag Shoal or its Spanish-era name, *Bajo de Masinloc.*

Aquino's losing such valuable territory due to ineptitude should be a case for impeachment, if not for his tight grip on yellow media.

China now controls Scarborough Shoal, because of Aquino's juvenile belligerency and also because of his irresponsible appointment of Senator Antonio Trillanes IV, as his personal envoy to China to deal with the crisis.

One of the first things incoming President Duterte should ask Congress to do is to undertake a formal investigation of how that happened, and whether Aquino should be criminally charged for losing Philippine territory.

If they find out that there aren't laws in place penalizing a President's stupidity, such investigation would at least clarify how on earth the country's excellent, decades-long relationship with China was quickly reversed in a span of two years by Aquino.

Here are the indisputable facts, and neither Malacañang nor the foreign affairs department had disputed these when I first published them in May and June 2015.

Some background: Although China and the Philippines have each been laying claim on Scarborough Shoal, there had never been an attempt from either the Chinese or Filipino forces to permanently station their troops there. Fishermen from both countries have acted as though there were no dispute, fished around and in the area, and routinely used its lagoon as a refuge from storms.

This "peaceful coexistence" of sorts changed suddenly in April 2012.

> **April 10, 2012:** Sailors from a Philippine Navy surveillance ship board eight Chinese fishing vessels anchored in the shoal's lagoon. They try to arrest the Chinese fishermen for illegal fishing and "harvesting endangered marine species." However, two China Maritime Surveillance (CMS) ships come to their rescue

and prevent the arrests in circumstances that are unclear.

April 11, 2012: Itching to try his new second-hand warship from the US, President Aquino orders the frigate BRP Gregorio del Pilar (a refurbished cutter from the US Coast Guard) to confront the Chinese at Panatag Shoal. "What is important is we take care of our sovereignty. We cannot give [Scarborough Shoal] away and we cannot depend on others but ourselves," Aquino blustered.

April 12, 2012: Three CMS ships enter the shoal, bringing with them a flotilla of 31 Chinese fishing boats and 50 dinghies. The number of CMS vessels in the days that follow increases to 10. BRP Gregorio del Pilar suddenly leaves the area. According to Navy Flag Officer in Command Alexander Pama, it needed "to replenish fuel and food provisions" in its base in La Union.

That was a lame excuse. Aquino was actually told by Washington that sending a naval warship was a stupid move, as it made the Philippines appear as the aggressor. While CMS vessels have been practically China's muscle in enforcing its claims in the South China Sea, these are officially civilian, part of its Ministry of Transport's Maritime Safety Administration.

Aquino may have even played into China's hands as the Asian power claimed to the whole world that the Philippines militarized the dispute by sending a "warship," even though the vessel was a hand-me-down from the US Coast Guard. China, therefore, felt it had the right to retaliate and occupy the shoal.

When BRP Gregorio del Pilar left, Aquino ordered a vessel of our Bureau of Fisheries and Aquatic Resources (BFAR) and two Coast Guard vessels to remain near the entrance to the shoal's lagoon.

In a casual talk with President Aquino and Executive Secretary Ochoa in his regular visits to Malacañang, Senator Antonio Trillanes IV claimed he had high-level contacts within the Chinese government. Aquino told him to go to China and talk with his contacts to resolve the standoff.

It is still unexplained by Aquino why he would trust Trillanes and not his Foreign Affairs secretary, Albert del Rosario, when the latter is known as rabidly anti-Chinese and pro-American.

June 2, 2012: After his trip to China to talk with his "contacts" — "of Politburo rank," he told me — Trillanes told Aquino that the Chinese agreed on a simultaneous withdrawal of the Chinese ships and the Philippine vessels. "PNoy directed me to work on the sequential withdrawal of government ships inside the shoal," Trillanes wrote in his aide-memoire on the crisis, which was later made available to me.

June 4: "PNoy called me to inform me that our BFAR vessel has already left the shoal but China reneged on the agreement of simultaneous withdrawal of their ships, so two of them [were] still inside the shoal," Trillanes wrote.

June 10: Aquino orders the remaining two Coast Guard vessels to leave the area. The Chinese didn't. They haven't left the area to this day.

'Backchannel talks'

In his aide memoire on his "Backchannel Talks" made available to me, Trillanes put the blame squarely on del Rosario:

"I asked him who agreed with what, since I was just hammering out the details of the sequential withdrawal because the mouth of the shoal was too narrow for a simultaneous withdrawal. The President told me that Sec. del Rosario told him about the agreement reached in Washington," Trillanes wrote.

"This time I asked PNoy: 'If the agreement was simultaneous withdrawal, why did we leave first?' PNoy responded to this effect: "Kaya nga sinabihan ko si Albert kung bakit niya pinalabas yung BFAR na hindi ko nalalaman." ("That's why I asked Albert [del Rosario] why he ordered the BFAR vessels to leave without my permission.")

Since that time no Filipino ship or fishing vessel has been able to enter the shoal, now occupied by CMS vessels and Chinese fishing boats. The Chinese imposed a 15-nautical mile restriction perimeter around the shoal, and prevents any vessel from going into the shoal's lagoon.

Chinese strategists must have rolled on the ground laughing at Aquino. They brilliantly manipulated Trillanes and their US contacts, to fool Aquino that they would withdraw their ships from Scarborough if we did. They didn't.

US officials have expressed concern that because a geological survey ship has been going around the shoal, China intends to build an artificial island on which a fully armed garrison could be built there, just like it has done in several shoals and atolls.

That's how bad things can get with a stupid yet arrogant President, who listens to the counsel of a megalomaniac senator. Now I understand why Foreign Affairs Secretary Alberto del Rosario wanted to strangle Trillanes during a Cabinet meeting, and why the latter alleges the former provoked the Chinese aggression.

Aquino during the entire crisis didn't even seek the counsel of his Cabinet, and decided solely on Trillanes' advice. Obviously, both were so utterly ignorant of the operative law in the South China dispute, and for most territorial disputes: "Occupation is ownership."

Even American generals closely monitoring the Spratly territorial disputes must have pulled their hair in utter dismay at how their puppet Aquino dropped the ball.

A November 2014 report of the Center for Naval Analyses — a private think-tank for the US military — entitled "The South China Sea: Assessing US Policy and Options for the Future" pointed out matter-of-factly that in the past 40 years, China has been able to take other nations' territory only in two instances.

The first was in 1974 when Chinese troops and vessels fought South Vietnamese forces on the Paracel islands, resulting in 53 Vietnamese soldiers killed and dozens wounded. One Vietnamese warship was sunk and three others damaged. Chinese forces have since occupied the area.

The second territory acquired by China was Scarborough Shoal, though in this case, because of a bungling President, no single shot was fired:

"From its perspective, China resolved the sovereignty dispute with the Philippines over Scarborough Shoal in 2012 when it established control over the shoal. Again, it is unlikely to relinquish it. The government of the Philippines is in no position to even begin to contemplate the use of force to recover Scarborough, and the United States is not going to become involved in any attempt to expel the Chinese."

If we cannot jail this idiot for losing our territory, at least we must shame him and put his stupidity on record, and in the history books.

(May 25, 2016)

FOREIGN SECRETARY ADMITS HE WAS HOODWINKED INTO GIVING UP PANATAG

HURT BY DEFENSE SECRETARY Delfin Lorenzana's remarks that "President Aquino mismanaged the Philippine sea dispute with China," former Foreign Secretary Alberto del Rosario blabbered too much in order to hit back.

In an article posted at the website of the pompously named "Stratbase Albert Del Rosario Institute for Strategic and International Studies"* — which the billionaire appears to have bankrolled — del Rosario admitted what he and his boss Aquino had hidden from the nation since 2012: the country lost Panatag (Scarborough) Shoal, just 124 nautical miles off Zambales, because of their huge blunder.

In his article, del Rosario wrote: "During the impasse at Scarborough Shoal with China, we were approached by the US, an honest broker, for both China and the Philippines to agree to a simultaneous withdrawal of ships from the shoal. We therefore agreed. At the appointed time, we withdrew, whereas China did not — in violation of our agreement."

Del Rosario's statement, though, is flawed. Neither the US nor China has admitted that there was such an agreement; only talks for such an agreement. Indeed, if there was such an agreement, would the "honest broker" US not have raised a ruckus that China reneged on an agreement it brokered?

Del Rosario's statement in his article is in sharp contrast to what he said on June 16, 2012, quoted in nearly all media that day two weeks after our ships left the shoal June 3: "Citing bad weather, President Aquino has ordered home two Philippine ships engaged in a stand-off with China over Scarborough Shoal."

Until his piece was posted in his website, del Rosario had not himself claimed that there was an agreement with China for a simultaneous withdrawal of each country's vessels from Panatag.

Senator Antonio Trillanes IV, appointed as backchannel envoy in that crisis, claimed there was no such agreement yet when Del Rosario, and not Aquino, ordered the vessels out.

Both in an interview with Trillanes with me in 2015, and in his aide-memoire "Backchannel Talks" that he gave me, the senator claimed it was Del Rosario who was responsible for the boo-boo, with Aquino himself blaming his foreign secretary.

"PNoy called me to inform me that our two BFAR (Bureau of Fisheries and Aquatic Resources) vessels already left the shoal but China reneged on the agreement of simultaneous withdrawal of their ships, so two of them [were] still inside the shoal," Trillanes wrote in his aide memoire.

"I asked him who agreed with what, since I was just hammering out the details of the sequential withdrawal because the mouth of the shoal was too narrow for a simultaneous withdrawal. The President told me that Sec. del Rosario told him about the agreement reached in Washington," Trillanes wrote.

Trillanes continued: "This time I asked PNoy: 'If the agreement was simultaneous withdrawal, why did we leave first?' PNoy responded to this effect: *'Kaya nga sinabihan ko si Albert kung bakit niya pinalabas yung BFAR na hindi ko nalalaman.'* (That's why I asked Albert [del Rosario] why he ordered the BFAR vessels to leave without my permission.)"

What really happened

Based on accounts of very credible sources, what actually transpired was as follows:

Fu Ying, China's vice minister of foreign affairs in charge of Asia (who had been ambassador here from 1998 to 2000) met June 1 in Washington with Kurt Campbell, US assistant secretary of state for East Asian and Pacific affairs, to discuss Aquino and Del Rosario's request for the Americans to intervene — even militarily, my sources claimed — in the Scarborough Shoal crisis.

Campbell relayed President Obama's position that the US cannot intervene in the dispute, and instead suggested a simultaneous withdrawal of vessels from Panatag Shoal (also known as *Bajo de Masinloc*) to de-escalate the tension.

The Chinese official told Campbell that she would relay the suggestion to her superiors in Beijing. However, for some unexplained reason, the then US Ambassador to Manila Harry Thomas that very day told Del Rosario that China had already agreed to a simultaneous withdrawal.

Del Rosario immediately ordered, in the middle of the night, the BFAR and Coast Guard vessels to pull out, leaving the Chinese in complete control of the shoal. Aquino would only find out about the pull-out when he woke up — late, as per usual — the following morning. With our vessels leaving what we claim as our territory, we've lost it, forever, as it were.

Neither the US, China, President Aquino, or anybody else at the foreign affairs department (except Del Rosario's protégé, then Ambassador to the US Jose Cuisia) has confirmed that there was such an agreement.

It is Del Rosario and Del Rosario alone, who continues to claim that China agreed with the Philippines on a simultaneous withdrawal, as brokered by the "US, an honest broker."

Did Campbell really tell their ambassador Thomas, to tell Del Rosario that the Chinese agreed to withdraw from the shoal? Or did Thomas misinterpret his superior's communication?

But diplomats are trained to get exactly what their headquarters ask them to relay to a host country. If unsure, an ambassador would request a written memorandum, especially on such an important episode as a stand-off in disputed seas that could even lead to a shooting war.

Or did the 73-year old Del Rosario hear what he wanted to hear, as the stand-off had lasted for seven weeks, and he was crumbling under the tension?

Another interpretation would be that, unwilling to intervene, the US tricked the Aquino government into abandoning the shoal, in order to push the Philippines to file a case against China in an international body as a propaganda tack against the Asian superpower.

Indeed, the Aquino government's suit against China was not just over the Philippines' territorial disputes with it but over the superpower's sweeping claim over the South China Sea, particularly its so-called "nine-dash line." China asserts in its maps that this crudely sketched tongue-shaped line, even if undefined in terms of geographical coordinates, demarcates its territory in the South China Sea.

Del Rosario's bungling of the Panatag issue is important as it explains his public detestation of China, as this conceals the fact that China didn't really just grab the shoal from us. He and Aquino let go of it, making the Aquino presidency the first administration to lose Philippine territory it already had control of.

Because of his personal hurt over being hoodwinked — both by China and by the US — into losing the Panatag Shoal for the Philippines, Del Rosario has been relentless in his and his stable of salaried academics' advocacy that our government adopt an aggressive anti-China stance.

Unfortunately for us, with the billions of pesos he's amassed as one of the top executives of the Indonesian tycoon Anthoni Salim (other than Manuel V. Pangilinan, he is the only other Filipino director in the Hong Kong based First Pacific Co. Ltd.), Del Rosario can bankroll the anti-Chinese propaganda through the "institute" he named after himself. They would even have a vast media empire to disseminate such propaganda: the newspaper *Philippine Star* and the Channel 5 network owned by the Indonesian Salim via Pangilinan.

What a country. A gang of big businessmen and executives are trying to control our most important foreign policy stance, led by Del Rosario who has a personal beef against China. And government doesn't have its own independent think-tank. This is the kind of thing Congress should be investigating.

If not for President Duterte's independent intellect and strength of character, the Philippines would have been steered by Del Rosario, his big business gang, Fidel Ramos' ideologue Jose Almonte, and Justice Antonio Carpio toward a disastrous, belligerent course against the inarguable superpower in Asia.

(June 18 and 20, 2018)

NOTES:

Del Rosario is chairman of both Stratbase and Stratbase ADRi. ADRi's co-chairman is Manuel V. Pangilinan, chief executive officer of First Pacific Co. Ltd., PLDT, and other huge firms in the Philippines that Indonesian tycoon Salim controls. Other tycoons in this outfit's board of trustees are Cory Aquino's nephew Antonio Cojuangco and Philip Romualdez, the husband of *Philippine Daily Inquirer* president Alexandra Prieto.

Stratbase reports that it is the Philippine partner of Bower Group, an American research and lobby group based in Washington, D.C. The head of Bower's Korea operations was a former CIA analyst and deputy intelligence officer in the US National Security Council.

ADRi's publication Spark is an anti-Duterte brochure, with the institute's academic pretensions shed off by sweeping statements such as the President "shielding China from global criticism" and the economy under him confronting a "perfect storm."

PHILIPPINE *Sunday* INQUIRER

PH ships leave Panatag

'Butchoy' forces end to standoff with China

IT LOOKS like stormy weather may break the standoff between the Philippines and China.

Arab TV reporter not 'missing,' says Sulu gov

Filtered By: News

Aquino orders pullout of PHL ships from Panatag Shoal due to bad weather

Published June 18, 2012

President Benigno Aquino has ordered all Philippine vessels in Panatag (Scarborough) Shoal to pull out from the area due to bad weather, a foreign affairs official said.

ABS-CBN NEWS

China pulls out boats from Scarborough

By Pia Lee-Brago, The Philippine Star

Total lies: Our ships had left two weeks earlier, ordered by Del Rosario without Aquino's authorizations, according to Trillanes.

THEY HID THEIR LOSS OF PANATAG FROM THE NATION

IT'S A CLICHÉ FOR SURE, but I can't help using it in disgust over the episode: "Only in the Philippines." Indeed, where else could a nation's loss of its territory be hidden for so long by its President, with the help of a media that claims to be independent?

The inept Aquino government on June 3, 2012 gave up Panatag Shoal (*Bajo de Masinloc* or Scarborough Shoal) to the Chinese, yet managed to keep it under wraps, so that the truth came out only in trickles over several years. So much so that many Filipinos, even knowledgeable ones, are unaware of that enormous loss, and how it happened, to this day.

This episode is also an indictment of how media, especially the most powerful newspaper at that time, the *Philippine Daily Inquirer*, betrayed the nation by wittingly or unwittingly hiding that loss of Philippine territory which was the result of President Benigno Aquino III and his foreign secretary Alberto del Rosario's bungling.

Chinese and Philippine government vessels had been on a stand-off for seven weeks in May and April 2012 in Panatag Shoal, with each party's vessels refusing to move. On June 3 though, del Rosario without Aquino's permission, ordered our three ships to leave the area. The Chinese never left the shoal; that's how we lost Panatag.

Del Rosario, a corporate executive-turned-foreign-affairs-secretary, obviously didn't do his homework on this most crucial foreign-affairs issue.

In 1975, the Vietnamese had fooled our troops who had been holding Southwest Cay (also in the Spratlys) since 1968, to leave for a party in a nearby island that Vietnam occupied. They returned the next morning to find that the Vietnamese had occupied their island, barring them from landing on it. The Vietnamese of course never left it and even built fortifications on it.

But in that case, it was low-ranking soldiers probably bored out of their wits in a so faraway island, who were fooled and lost our territory; in this case it was our foreign secretary.

The spokesman of China's foreign ministry Li Weimin issued

a statement on Sunday, June 4, 2012: "The remaining Philippine vessel finally left the lagoon on June 3." The spokesman even arrogantly warned the Philippines: "China does not hope to see any more provocative behavior that hurts China's interest," referring to what it called "Huangyan incident" when starting "April 10, Philippine warships* harassed Chinese fishermen."

It was Senator Antonio Trillanes IV who disclosed that Del Rosario had ordered the Philippine vessels to leave. Either Del Rosario was so gullible that he believed then US Ambassador Harry Thomas' communication to him that the US got China to agree to a simultaneous withdrawal of both countries' ships.

Or, as Trillanes alleged, Del Rosario simply wanted the rift between China and the Philippines to worsen. The senator explained that he was still working out with the Chinese details of the simultaneous withdrawal when he was told, to his shock, that the Filipino vessels had already left.

Del Rosario would later claim that the Chinese reneged on its agreement for a simultaneous withdrawal, although even the US has not confirmed that China had agreed to withdraw. He kept on referring to a stand-off over Panatag, never saying that the Chinese control it after our vessels were ordered out.

Yellow media hid the truth

The *Philippine Daily Inquirer* had a banner story on June 16, two weeks after China took control of the shoal after Del Rosario ordered our vessels out: "PH ships leave Panatag." The banner story's drophead read: "'Butchoy' forces end to stand-off with China," referring to a typhoon with international code name "Guchol."

The article quoted Del Rosario: "Citing bad weather, President Aquino has ordered home two Philippine ships engaged in a stand-off with China over Scarborough Shoal."

That was a total fabrication. Typhoon "Butchoy" never even entered the Philippine mainland, and had moved to the opposite side of Luzon. And even if it had battered Panatag, its lagoon had been for centuries a refuge for even small fishing vessels to shield themselves from the roughest seas. It was a lie disseminated by almost all print and broadcast media on June 16:

• GMA News: "Aquino orders pullout of PHL ships from Panatag Shoal due to bad weather"

• Rappler.com: "PH pulls out ships from Scarborough due to bad weather"

• *Philippine Star:* "President Aquino ordered two Philippine ships to pull out of Panatag (Scarborough) Shoal due to bad weather Friday night."

• ABS-CBN News' report though was a bigger fabrication: "China pulls out boats from Scarborough."

ABC-CBN's lede paragraph read: "Following a similar move by the Philippines, China pulled out its fishing boats from Panatag (Scarborough) Shoal last Sunday due to 'inclement' weather." Chinese vessels, of course, had remained in the shoal in the lagoon, and leaving only when replacements arrive.

The much bigger smokescreen that Aquino and Del Rosario employed to conceal their culpability for the loss of Panatag, was the case it filed against China at the Permanent Court of Arbitration, for violating the United Nations Convention on the Law of the Sea.

Even as the PCA's "award" cannot be enforced, and it didn't rule on who owns Panatag as well as other disputed areas in the Spratlys, the case had portrayed Aquino and Del Rosario as boldly fighting for Philippine territory, thus concealing the fact that they lost Philippine territory because of their ineptness.

Trillanes' disclosure

To be honest, I myself for two years had been fooled that we hadn't lost Panatag and that we were still struggling with China over it, although I had written a column* during the stand-off explaining that it was Aquino who triggered the crisis when he sent our biggest warship in the area.

It is ironic that it was in an interview in November 2014 with Trillanes, in which he alleged del Rosario's culpability for the loss which he claimed was deliberate, that I realized that our government stupidly lost Panatag to the Chinese.

To this day, it has been only specialized articles on the South China Sea by foreigners that we are told unequivocally that the Aquino administration lost Panatag in 2012. A recent one was an article in a book (**Examining the South China Sea Disputes: Papers from the Fifth Annual CSIS South China Sea Conference**) which narrated:

"In the Scarborough Shoal incident of 2012, China's Fisheries Law Enforcement Command (FLEC) prevented the arrest of Chinese fishers by a Philippine coast guard cutter... The FLEC ships moved between the Philippine cutter and the fishing ships, beginning a standoff that ended when Manila withdrew its cutter and other vessels, and China occupied Scarborough Shoal."

A report of the Center for Naval Analyses, a think tank for the US military, explained the implications of such occupation:

"China resolved the sovereignty dispute with the Philippines over Scarborough Shoal in 2012 when it established control over the shoal. Again, it is unlikely to relinquish it. The government of the Philippines is in no position to even begin to contemplate the use of force to recover Scarborough, and the United States is not going to become involved in any attempt to expel the Chinese."

(June 25, 2018)

THE CORRECT SOUTH CHINA SEA POLICY

THE OPPOSITION'S ALLEGATION that President Duterte has been kowtowing to China on our territorial disputes is unadulterated hogwash, so grossly ignorant of what sovereignty in the South China Sea entails.

After four administrations that just whined to the world over our claims in the South China Sea, as President Aquino III most especially did, President Duterte, without much fanfare, ordered in April last year the most rational and realistic approach to defend our claims in the South China Sea:

Duterte directed our military to fortify the islands and reefs that we have occupied in the Spratlys, which we call the Kalayaan Island Group (KIG). This is what Taiwan, Vietnam, China and Malaysia have been doing in the past two decades on the islands and reefs they occupy.

Although under-reported by local media, Duterte's announcement was big news abroad.

The *South China Morning Post's* headline was: "Duterte orders troops to occupy and fortify Philippine-held islands in South China Sea." The announcement was the Wall Street Journal's banner story for its Asia section: "Rodrigo Duterte Orders Fortification of All Philippine-Held South China Sea Islands" with its drophead: "Philippine armed forces told to occupy all islands, reefs and shoals the country controls in the disputed waters."

The *Philippine Daily Inquirer*, known for its anti-Duterte stance, reported on April 7, 2017: "Duterte said Thursday he had ordered the military to occupy and fortify all Philippine-held islands in the disputed South China Sea to assert the country's claims amid what he says was a race to control territory in the area."

"We tried to be friends with everybody but we have to maintain our jurisdiction now, at least the areas under our control," he said during a visit to a military camp in western Palawan province. Duterte said he ordered the armed forces to occupy and place Philippine flags on all islands, reefs and shoals controlled by the Philippines.

"There are about nine or 10 islands there, we have to fortify," he said. "I must build bunkers there or houses and provisions for habitation."

I have not been able to confirm if the Armed Forces of the Philippines has fully complied with its commander-in-chief's orders. It is possible though that our government has diplomatically chosen not to brag about our program to fortify what we occupy in the KIG. Or perhaps Duterte is still unable to raise the billions of pesos needed to defend our territories.

However, credit is due to the *Manila Times* for its exclusive reporting in its banner story on Sunday, for an article* in the Washington-based Asia Maritime Transparency Initiative of the Center for Strategic and International Studies, that read: "The Philippines has begun long-delayed repairs to its crumbling runway at Thitu, or Pag-asa, island, the largest of its nine outposts in the Spratly Islands."

The Center pointed out: "Philippine defense officials in April 2017 announced that they would be upgrading facilities at the country's occupied islands and reefs, but little work was apparent until now. In addition to the runway repairs, a comparison of recent imagery with photos from February 2017 shows minor upgrades to facilities on Thitu and three other outposts in the last year."

That Duterte's move to fortify our islands is the only correct policy in the South China Sea is incontrovertible, considering the following facts.

Whatever the legal basis of claims over islands and other features in the South China Sea by Vietnam, China, Taiwan, the Philippines and Malaysia, the unwritten rule in the territorial disputes is that "possession is 9/10th of the law," with the qualification that a claimant country cannot forcibly take an island already occupied by another.

And to strengthen possession, claimant country "A" in the South China Sea has to build up the island it holds so that it would require so much violence for claimant "B" to wrest control. If B will resort to such violent act, it is certain to be condemned by the entire world.

Taiwan's Taiping

This principle is most clearly demonstrated in Malaysia's occupation of Swallow Reef (which it calls Pulau Layang-Layang) in the Spratlys, which China and Vietnam claim. Merely on the basis of its own unilateral assertion that the reef is on its continental shelf, and close to its mainland, Malaysia sent a company of its elite Special Forces to occupy it in 1983.

Malaysia in a few years turned Swallow Reef, also claimed by Vietnam and China, which it seized in 1983, into an "exotic scuba resort."

In subsequent years, Malaysia rushed to build what it calls the Layang Airport with two hangars, a radar station, an air traffic control tower, watchtowers, a jetty, a marine research facility, and just in the past few years, a five-star hotel. It has gradually gained a reputation as a top-of-the-line scuba diving resort, with its official website giving no hint at all that it is in the disputed Spratlys.

All international law experts have concluded that Malaysia has no basis to claim it, yet it has been the only disputed feature in the Spratlys visited by the head of the occupying state, Prime Minister Abdullah Badawi, in 2009.

The largest island in the South China Sea, Taiping island, or Itu Aba, is occupied by Taiwan. When a Philippine firm in 1952 tried to mine sulphur there, the Kuomintang-ruled "Republic of China" sent its troops to evict the miners and built a Marine garrison there. It constructed an airport in 2007, capable of accommodating military planes, a port that could berth navy destroyers, and four-storey bunkers.

Have you heard of any news or opinion article claiming that the Taiwanese should be evicted from Taiping island? The Permanent Court of Arbitration that favored the Philippines ruled in 2016 that Taiping is not an island but just a "rock." That of course has been totally ignored by the world.

While the West' attention has been focused on China's land-reclamation activities to turn the atolls and reefs it controls into islands, Vietnam, the biggest property holder in the South China Sea in terms of hectarage of its holdings, has been fortifying its islands in the past decade. Reuters in April 2016 reported that Hanoi "had moved rocket launchers to five bases in the Spratly islands within range of China's newly built airstrips."

The reason why China's moves in the South China Seas has gained more attention, and been condemned is that since it doesn't have a single island it occupies in the region, it instead reclaimed land starting in the 1990s on its atolls and reefs, and then built airstrips and fortifications on these.

We got our territories in the Spratlys because, much like Malaysia did in the case of Swallow Reef and the Taiwanese with Itu Aba, we just grabbed them and gave them Filipino names. It was President Marcos who in 1974 boldly took hold of 10 islands and reefs which call now the Kalayaan islands, the biggest feature of which is Pag-Asa, claiming — falsely — that no country owned them (*terra nullius*).

Kalayaan Island Group

He could do this because China at the time was in chaos and militarily weak because of Mao's "Great Proletarian Cultural Revolution." Vietnam, on the other hand, was divided and was embroiled in civil war in which the US backed, and even fought for, the South against the North.

Marcos calculated that the US certainly won't allow the North or the South to try to kick us out of the KIG — as South Vietnam did in 1974 in the case of the Chinese-controlled Paracel — what with the American military bases in the country at the time playing a crucial role in the Vietnamese war and in the Cold War as a whole.

To implement the "occupation-is-ownership" principle, Marcos deployed a company of heavily-armed Marines on Pag-Asa island, and built an airstrip (the first such to be built in the whole of the South China Sea) that could accommodate C-130 transport planes. That sent the message to the world that he could deploy troops there quickly to defend the island. He made Pag-Asa a municipality of Palawan, which even has its annual contrived elections for its local officials.

What did the four administrations after Marcos do to strengthen our occupation of the Kalayaan Island Group?

Nothing. Absolutely nothing.

President Fidel Ramos in 1995 had foreign and local media fly on Vietnam-era helicopters over Mischief Reef to draw the world's attention to the small fortifications on stilts that China had built there. The photos were splashed all over the world's media. But did the world do anything?

Nothing. Even with billions of pesos raised through the sale of Fort Bonifacio, Ramos himself did nothing to fortify Pag-Asa island..

Purportedly to deter the Chinese from occupying Ayungin Reef near Mischief, President Estrada in 1999 ordered a World War 2 vintage ship to be grounded there, manned by a platoon of Marines, to serve as our outpost. That was the most that we did to fortify what we claim in the Spratlys.

Fourteen years later, the *New York Times* magazine would publish an article melodramatically titled, "A Game of Shark and Minnow", replete with photos, narrating the pathetic situation of a platoon of marines manning that rusting ship grounded at Ayungin. The Philippines was portrayed as *kaawa-awa*, a poor defenseless country for the world to rally around it to block "Chinese militarization" of the Spratlys.

Did the world help us fortify our islands and reefs? Of course not.

As a smokescreen for his bungling that lost us Scarborough Shoal (which we call Panatag), President Benigno Aquino filed a suit at the Hague-based Permanent Court of Arbitration to order the Chinese to hand back the shoal to us and to rule Kalayaan as ours. The PCA did rule that China's nine-dash-line did not have any basis in international law, and that Scarborough was within our exclusive economic zone, but it didn't rule on what country owns the KIG.

Did we get back Panatag? Nope. A better use of the over P600 million spent for our PCA suit would have been to repair the airstrip at Pag-Asa, or even just the Marine barracks that have been falling apart to be inhabitable.

From 2010 to 2013, Aquino had P220 billion in funds at his discretion to use for almost any purpose — P63 billion as Priority Development Assistance Fund, or PDAF, and P157 billion in Disbursement Acceleration Program funds. He even used P2 billion of this for infrastructure in his Tarlac home province and P10 billion to bribe Muslim-dominated areas to support his Bangsamoro Basic Law bill.

Did he use a single centavo of this P220 billion to fortify our islands and reefs in the Spratlys?

No. Not a single centavo. The only thing Aquino did, other than losing our Panatag Shoal to the Chinese, was to rename part of the South China Sea nearest us as the West Philippine Sea, which he hadn't even asked the United Nations to recognize.

While our Pag-Asa airstrip during the Aquino regime had become nearly unusable, its length shortened as its ends were being reclaimed by the ocean, its barracks dilapidated, and the marine detachment there armed only with handguns and rifles. And all the while Aquino kept crying to the world complaining that China has been transforming the reefs it occupies into fortifications.

At least in the case of our foreign policy on our territorial claims, change has definitely come under Duterte.

(June 1, 2018)

* See the full article at https://amti.csis.org/philippines-launches-spratly-repairs

AQUINO, DEL ROSARIO BEGGED US TO USE ITS MILITARY IN PANATAG STAND-OFF

IF NOT FOR THE US leaders' pragmatism and cool-headedness, President Benigno Aquino III and his foreign secretary Albert del Rosario could have dragged the US into a war with China over the South China Sea territorial dispute. This conflict could have even led to a nuclear war between the two superpowers — and all of this, just because Aquino and del Rosario wanted to cover up their bungling of the Scarborough Shoal crisis.

On April 2012, Chinese civilian-government and fishing vessels went to their fishermen's succor at Scarborough Shoal (*Bajo de Masinloc* or Panatag Shoal) when the Philippine Coast Guard and Bureau of Aquatic Resources accosted them for alleged illegal fishing. Aquino ordered to the shoal the Navy's biggest warship, acquired only a year earlier, the BRP Gregorio del Pilar to board the fishermen's vessels to take them in.

That was a big boo-boo. China pounced on Aquino's blunder by loudly protesting that the Philippines had "militarized" the dispute, and that "Philippine warships" were detaining its helpless fishermen.

Cleverly, China did not respond by sending its own warships, even as several of its modern frigates were on alert stand-by just over the horizon. It instead undertook a sea-borne version of people power by having over 60 Chinese fishermen's vessels —escorted by some six civilian government vessels — to the shoal. The Chinese and Filipinos vessels were then locked in a stand-off that lasted for about six weeks from late April to May 2012, with each party aware that whoever blinks, or withdraws from the shoal, will lose it — forever, as it were.

Diplomatic sources here and abroad disclosed that Aquino and del Rosario begged the US to intervene in the conflict, by sending US warships to the area in order to send the message to China that it would defend the Philippine vessels if attacked.

Del Rosario and defense secretary Voltaire Gazmin rushed to Washington, D.C. on April 30, as the crisis that started on April 10 seemed to go against the Philippines, to meet with US Secretary of State Hillary Clinton and Defense Secretary Leon Panetta. Del Rosario invoked Clinton's statements a year earlier, that the US would stand by its 1951 Mutual Defense Treaty, that requires it to defend the Philippines in case of attack by any foreign power on its military forces.

Del Rosario even issued an official statement on May 9, 2012, a few days after his meeting with Clinton, in which he declared that "US officials have publicly declared four times that it would honor the 1951 Mutual Defense Treaty, that obliges American troops to help defend the Philippines if it comes under attack."

The US embassy in reaction to del Rosario's claim, issued a statement saying that Clinton in their meeting did say that "the United States reaffirms our commitments and obligations under the Mutual Defense Treaty." Clinton however, in several statements instead emphasized, that the "US does not take a position in territorial disputes between two countries."

Clinton and even the US defense secretary did not respond to del Rosario's demand for a categorical US commitment, that it would come to the Philippines' defense in case a shooting war breaks out in the Scarborough crisis.

We were blissfully oblivious of the Scarborough stand-off when it was happening, with the Yellow newspapers here successfully toning down the crisis, helped by the fact that the burning issue of the day was Aquino's project to take down Chief Justice Renato Corona.

There was, however, a clear danger of war breaking out, as Aquino's mishandling of the Scarborough crisis — reported in China as his deployment of "Philippine warships" against helpless Chinese fishermen — had stoked Chinese nationalist sentiment. "The leadership of the Communist Party of China would have even fallen if they appeared to be soft on the Philippines," a diplomat said.

The Chinese of course got wind of del Rosario's pleading for US military intervention, and escalated its rhetoric.

Belligerent editorials

As has been its practice of sending its messages to the world, "editorials" of China's state-run newspapers were practically calling for war against the Philippines over Scarborough. On April 22, 2012, the editorial of state-owned Global Times urged the Chinese government to engage the Philippines in a small-scale war to end the stalemate once and for all. It stated that "once war erupts, China must take resolute action and deliver a clear message to the outside world that it does not want a war, but definitely has no fear of it."

On May 9, the People's Liberation Army Daily ran a toughly worded editorial saying that China would not tolerate any violation of Chinese sovereignty on Scarborough Shoal. According to the editorial, "Not only will the Chinese government not agree, nor will the Chinese people, and the Chinese Army will disagree even more." The flurry of threatening editorials from the PLA newspaper underscored its well-known hardline stance when it comes to territorial disputes.

Unreported in the country were media reports from Taiwan and Japan, that alleged that China's South Sea Fleet had forward-deployed a landing ship flotilla and a naval task force consisting of destroyers and amphibious ships in waters off the Philippines. There were also reports that China had already ordered two submarines to stand by at international waters off Scarborough Shoal.

US officials, however, rebuffed del Rosario and Gazmin's pleadings. Clinton and Panetta were worried that the two Philippine officials kept pressing them to give a categorical answer to their question: Will the US military come to the Philippines' rescue if one of their vessels is attacked by the Chinese?

That worried the US that Aquino might order his vessels to provoke the Chinese at Scarborough Shoal, in order to get the Americans into the fray, which could have thrown the situation completely out of control, to lead into a full-blown war between two nuclear powers.

That concern bolsters a narrative I had discussed in my column last Friday, that it was the US that hoodwinked del Rosario and Aquino into believing that there was an agreement brokered by the Americans for the Chinese, to simultaneously withdraw with the Filipino vessels from Scarborough's lagoon.

There wasn't an agreement, but merely a proposal for such, and del Rosario naively ordered our vessels out of Scarborough on June 3.

Aquino meets Obama

When del Rosario realized the colossal blunder he made when he ordered the Philippine ships to leave the lagoon, which practically turned over Scarborough to the Chinese, he asked Aquino to request an urgent meeting with then President Barack Obama for a last-resort move to convince the Americans to intervene. Obama reportedly told Aquino in so many words in their meeting on June 8: "We can't and won't go to war over this. Just file a case in court, and we'll help you."

Aquino of course obeyed Obama. His government filed an arbitration suit invoking the law of the seas at the Permanent Court of Arbitration in Hague, with a Washington D.C. firm Foley Hoag LLP, and a special team of American lawyers recommended by the State Department handling everything. The work of then Solicitor General Florin Hilbay and his staff was limited to photocopying the US lawyers' documents.

The US also cleverly took advantage of the crisis to advance their interest. In the long discussions with their US counterparts in which del Rosario and Gazmin begged for US military intervention, US defense secretary Panetta pointed out that even if the US intervenes militarily, the logistical problem is that with the closure of US military bases in the country in 1991, the American military would find it difficult to supply its ships in the South China Sea. The US officials in effect told Aquino and his officials: "Next time you come running to us begging for our help, you should find a way for our troops to have a logistical base in your country."

After that, Aquino rushed the passing of the so-called "Enhanced Defense Cooperation Agreement", that allows the US to rotate troops into the country for extended stays and to operate facilities, and stock up war materiel on Philippine military bases. That was one of the most important of his priority bills that Aquino asked Congress to enact.

(August 6, 2018)

SUIT VS CHINA A US MACHINATION

WHATEVER THE RESULTS of the Permanent Arbitral Court deliberations on the Philippine suit against China, which would be known after this column had been submitted, I can't shrug off the suspicion that the US deftly played with President Aquino's administration to file the case. For good or for bad.

Here are the facts, you decide:

1. With Aquino just a year in office, the US rushes to turn over to the Philippine Navy its refurbished Hamilton-class cutter that had been a fast-patrol vessel of its Coast Guard. The cutter, renamed the BRP Gregorio del Pilar, was commissioned by the US Navy in December 2011.

2. Throughout 2011, Aquino's rhetoric against Chinese alleged intrusions into waters that are within our exclusive economic zone was rising. He even made the foolish boast that "he will protect Recto Bank as if it were Recto Avenue." (As if we could send battalions to Recto Bank as easily as we can to a Manila area.) The US was also starting to criticize more stridently China's reclamation of submerged atolls to transform them into artificial islands.

3. On April 10, 2012, operatives of the Bureau of Fisheries and Aquatic Resources (BFAR), together with armed Coast Guard men, board eight Chinese fishing vessels anchored on the shoal's lagoon. They try to arrest the Chinese fishermen for illegal fishing and "harvesting endangered marine species." Two China Maritime Surveillance (CMS) ships — civilian vessels — come to their rescue, however, and prevent the arrests. It is a mystery why the Navy decided to inspect the Chinese fishing vessels: the shoal's lagoon has for decades been used both by Chinese and Filipino small fishermen.

Aquino orders on the same day the BRP Gregorio del Pilar to proceed to the shoal.

4. Three other CMS ships enter the shoal, bringing with them a flotilla of 31 Chinese fishing boats and 50 dinghies. The number of CMS vessels in the days that follow increases to 10. It was a standoff, as our warship with the much-smaller Coast Guard vessels and those of the CMS vessels faced each other threateningly in the lagoon, both refusing to leave what each party considered its sovereign territory.

5. A few days later, the BRP Gregorio del Pilar — unexpectedly — leaves the area, according to Navy Flag Officer in Command Alexander Pama, "to replenish fuel and food provisions" in its base in La Union. The Philippine Coast Guard and BFAR vessels remain.

That was a lame excuse. Aquino realized sending a warship was a stupid move as it made the Philippines appear as the aggressor.

6. Aquino orders Senator Antonio Trillanes IV to undertake backdoor negotiations to resolve the standoff. Foreign Affairs Secretary Albert del Rosario, known to be very close to US authorities since his stint as Philippine Ambassador to the US for nearly eight years, does his own thing, which is to ask the Americans for help.

7. On June 7, 2012, Aquino orders the Coast Guard and BFAR vessels to leave the lagoon. The Chinese don't, and would then physically block any kind of vessel, whether those of small Filipino fishermen or of the Coast Guard and BFAR ships, to even approach the shoal.

Stupid and incompetent

Aquino tells Trillanes that he ordered the ships out of Scarborough Shoal, as Del Rosario was told by the US that the Chinese had agreed to withdraw their vessels simultaneously with our ships. Trillanes was incredulous, telling Aquino that he was just in the midst of negotiations with the Chinese.

It was such a colossal boo-boo for us, a lesson never, never again to elect a stupid incompetent to head the nation. The Chinese were probably rolling in the ground laughing, as Aquino gave them the excuse to take over Scarborough by sending a warship, which technically was a military move, only to withdraw it two days later, giving them total physical control of the territory.

The rule of the game in the Spratlys dispute, after the last violent takeover of the Paracel Islands by the Chinese from the Vietnamese in 1974, is that an area is yours, as long as you don't take it by force. Thus we lost Pugad Island in 1975, which we had occupied since 1968, when the Vietnamese lured the Filipino garrison to an overnight birthday party in the nearby Parola Island. When they returned the next day, the Vietnamese were on the beach there, with their guns and mortars aimed at the approaching Filipino troops, and yelling at them to go away.

Now any Filipino vessel even of those of small fishermen approaching Scarborough Shoal is told to go away.

Embarrassed and livid, Aquino would tell the nation there was no other alternative but to file a case in an international venue, which turned out to be the Permanent Arbitral Court, against the Chinese takeover of Scarborough.

While you're at it, the US probably told Aquino, expand your suit, so you would have us and other Western powers backing you, to include that crazy nine-dash-line the Chinese claimed within which was Chinese territory. A team of American lawyers had been to the Palace to help draft the Philippine case.

Would Aquino have sent to Scarborough the other rusting Navy vessels, if he didn't have the recently-donated BRP Gregorio del Pilar from the Americans? Would another less "American-boy" foreign affairs secretary (Del Rosario was our ambassador to the US from 2001-2006), have been more skeptical of the US information? How did Trillanes, known since his coup-attempt days as having high-level contacts with US intelligence, get into the picture?

Brilliant. The US has refused to ratify the UNCLOS (United Nations Convention on the Law of the Sea) so it can't file a suit invoking that international agreement. It doesn't even have a territorial claim in the entire South China Sea, and therefore no business there. Its involvement in the region is totally based on its sheer super-power status.

Malaysia, Brunei Darussalam, Taiwan and Vietnam — the claimants in the Spratly Islands — of course hadn't moved nor will ever move publicly against China, much less file a case against it, as they calculate they are better off with an unsullied friendship with China.

The Chinese fought with the Vietnamese in 1974 over the Paracel Islands, killing over 52 Vietnamese Marines, and sinking two of their ships. Despite this, Vietnam isn't publicly cheering the Philippines. This is wise since they know they badly need China's trade and official aid at this stage of their development.

The Philippines was, as it has always been, America's reliable lackey in the region. Perhaps it would be good for the world if we win the case, with China pressured by international public opinion to stop its militarization of the South China Sea.

There will certainly be a nationalist euphoria over our victory for a few months, and you can expect Aquino to go out of his cocoon to claim credit for it. I doubt, however, if that victory will really benefit us, and we're left with an angry, superpower as our neighbor. Will we recover Scarborough Shoal with a favorable court decision? Ask the Marines.

(July 12, 2016)

Nationalism

ONE MAJOR FACTOR FOR ASIAN TIGERS' GROWTH

FORMER US AMBASSADOR Philip Goldberg unsurprisingly described President Duterte's alleged frame of mind as "old-fashioned nationalism," in effect lecturing the country that we should instead open our doors totally to foreign investors, and just trust that the market will work out to our advantage.

However, it is historical fact that the so-called Asian Tigers — the now highly developed economies of Hong Kong, Singapore, South Korea and Taiwan — grew starting in the 1960s because their leaders were economic nationalists, pragmatists without dogmas, without illusions that free markets alone would magically lead to the most efficient allocation of resources.

In contrast, economic nationalism in our country has been inanely caricatured as involving solely what were alleged to be disastrous "import-substitution" policies that were in place in the 1960s, protecting local industrialists, i.e. the elite, from foreign competition.

However, all the Asian Tigers did employ such protectionist policies, and in fact, so did almost all industrialized countries before their economic takeoffs in the 19th century. What they did, which we failed to do, was to shift to export-oriented industrialization when the local market could no longer absorb the products of the import-substitution industries.

The governments of the Asian tigers nurtured their export-oriented industries as well as strategic industries such as telecoms — through such means as preferential credit, subsidies hidden or overt, and lower tariffs for their inputs, to enhance their competitiveness in the world markets.*

In Japan, there was such close cooperation between the designated "champion firms" and government, particularly the Ministry of Trade and Industry, that the system was dubbed Japan, Inc. This was how the country miraculously achieved economic growth after its devastation in World War II. The engine of Japan's growth was its *keiretsus*, and for South Korea, its *chaebols*. Both were conglomerates assisted by their governments, on the condition that they focused on key industries regarded by state planners as vital to stimulating economic growth.

We have had no such *keiretsus* and *chaebols*, although the strongman Marcos in the late 1970s thought he could develop firms controlled by his cronies as such.

Our conglomerates operate as though there was no state at all, except perhaps in terms of bribing bureaucrats when needed, or betting on certain candidates during national elections. State officials operate as though there were no conglomerates at all, except to get bribes or campaign funds from them.

Stranglehold of neoliberalism

Without such a framework for growth that the national economy should be directed through state intervention (as Japan, South Korea, Taiwan and China did), the ownership, whether foreign or local, of public utilities especially telecoms, becomes unimportant. That has been one of our biggest weaknesses, one that has hobbled us since the era when the American GTE was the telecom monopoly. Today, what we have is a monopoly of the industry owned overwhelmingly by foreigners.

"The developmental history of a nation is in its government's hands," pointed out a very lucid and readable book** on how the Asian tigers developed and why other Southeast Asian countries, including the Philippines, failed to follow the same path. That idea, really, is the essence of economic nationalism, in contrast to neoliberalism.

Neoclassical economics ideologue Villegas and lobby groups such as the Foundation for Economic Freedom, lobbying for the lifting of restrictions on foreign capital in public utilities have been claiming that we should emulate industrialized countries in adopting current liberal policy on foreign capital.

What they do not mention, though, is that in the period when these countries were still developing, they put restrictions on foreign capital in their strategic industries. They lifted these only when their state firms or those owned by their nationals, were strong enough to withstand the impact of new competition amid the entry of foreign corporations. ***

Nearly all industrialized countries, when they were still struggling during their developmental stages, had state-owned firms operating their power systems to have better control at ensuring the most efficient supply for their citizens and their nascent industries.

They realized that the power sector was too important to turn over to private firms, no matter how efficient they may be at management. This is because the prime directive of private companies is profit generation and the distribution of money to stockholders, NOT public service or low rates of electricity.

Only when the industrialized countries had fully developed, and their companies had become among the world's strongest and biggest, did they begin to privatize the power sectors and opened them up to foreign competition, but even then only on a limited scale.

Why the restrictions? Such sectors involve limited national, and natural resources. In the case of telecoms, this is the radio spectrum for cellular telephony and a captive market that is the nation's population.

These sectors possess natural-monopoly features that must be reserved for citizens since these involve rent profits, part of which the state must appropriate for the welfare of its own people. These are public utility firms, which by definition must serve public welfare as their paramount objective, rather than the generation of dividends.

The country certainly needs foreign investment, why not? But not in public utility firms, and the framers of our Constitution must have realized this that they decided to put the 40 percent cap on foreign investment in public utilities, as well as land ownership — laws which have not been followed because of our weak legal and regulatory systems.

Nationalism vanishing

Nationalism is vanishing in our country, despite its resurgence in both the academe and policymakers in the rest of the world. The growth of the Asian Tigers and the emergence of China as an economic superpower constitute incontrovertible evidence that economic nationalism, rather than laissez-faire economics, result in nations' economic growth.

The nation's youth have also been brainwashed into seeing themselves as "citizens of the world," a cockamamie belief that in today's world there are no more nations, that economic nationalism is the evil that generates poverty in the country.

This erroneous thinking has even gained ground in the country in recent decades, what with economists such as Dr. Villegas propounding it, exemplified in his July 25, 2015 column with the preposterous title, *"Nationalist industrialization hurts the poor."*

Hasn't he heard at all of industrialized countries like Japan, South Korea and Taiwan, which became rich through nationalist industrialization policies? (A recent, popular account of the economic growth of these countries on the basis of nationalist industrialization was done by Joe Studwell, **How Asia Works: Success and Failure in the World's Most**

Dynamic Region, Grove Press: 2013.)

Cronyism, corruption, and regulatory capture — in various forms, levels of government, and degrees — have been pervasive in our country, weakening the state so much that its efficiency and efficacy in serving not just a class but the entire nation and in redistributing assets have been drastically diminished.

The saddest phenomenon in our country is that the elite have lost the sense that they belong to a nation, which is not just a market. This has trickled down to the rest of this society so that many Filipinos have also lost their sense of nationalism, so that few care that our telecom industry is under foreigners' control and that our government regulatory bodies have allowed them to trample upon our Constitution.

Economic nationalism is the worldview that we are not just consumers or producers in an each-to-his-own market, but members of a nation — in this age, the most important community a human can be a member of — organized for the welfare of all its members, and that the state has the duty, and all the resources and tools to do so.

The decline of nationalism since the 1990s, so obvious in our country today, is actually rooted in the fact that we have jettisoned economic nationalism as a plan of action, as the spell of neoliberalism and globalization descended on the country.

We have remained poor despite EDSA 1, and through four Presidents, because we have not embraced the kind of economic nationalism that made the Asian Tigers the highly developed countries they are now.

Should we wonder why the GDP per capita growth rate of Vietnam — one of the most nationalistic countries in the world — averaged 5 percent from 2000 to 2015, significantly higher than our 3 percent?

(December 30, 2016)

---

* A very detailed account of this, using the case studies of Taiwan and the Philippines' textile, semiconductor, and plywood export industries, is in Kuo, Cheng-Tian and Kuo Cheng-Tian's **Global Competitiveness and Industrial Growth in Taiwan and the Philippines**, University of Pittsburgh, 1995.)

** Studwell, Joe. **How Asia Works: Success and Failure in the World's Most Dynamic Region.** New York: Grove Press, 2013.

*** Chang, Ha-Joon. **Kicking Away the Ladder: Development Strategy in Historical Perspective.** 1st ed. Anthem Press, 2002.

REVIVING ECONOMIC NATIONALISM

THE MOVE TO LIFT the limits on foreign ownership of telecom firms by amending the Constitution, has been framed in the propaganda spin based on two false arguments repeated over and over again, in the Hitlerian fashion of the "Big Lie."

Essentially, these claims deny the historical fact that it was economic nationalism, not globalization nor foreign capital which helped bring most developed countries, including those in Asia, to their prosperous status today.

The first argument is that the constitutional restrictions on foreign capital in public utilities, are one of the main reasons why foreign direct investments (FDIs) in the country are smaller than those in many other ASEAN countries. The second is that a major reason for our economic quagmire, is that FDIs have been small. Both claims are utter nonsense, and are based not on empirical evidence, but on ideological beliefs.

On the first claim, it is not the restrictions on foreign investment that explain why inflow has been low. Foreign capital are now the biggest shareholders in the telecom and power industries. How could that be if there were restrictions? The fact is that Indonesian and Singaporean capital, in collaboration with the local elite and government agencies, have de facto removed the constitutional restrictions through legal maneuvers.

Poor and inefficient business conditions; the lack of physical and technological infrastructure; expensive electricity; a limited and run-down highway network; an inefficient port system, and corruption are the real principal factors that hamper the flow of investments into the country. (See among other numerous studies* on this topic, the World Bank's "Ease of Doing Business" annual reports.)

Our small FDI stock compared with that of our neighbors is also the result of a unique set of events in the 1980s.

The 1989-91 coup attempts against the Philippine government, together with the kidnapping of a Mitsui executive here in 1987 scared off foreign investors, at a crucial time when Japanese investments inundated Asia like a tsunami as part of Japan's thrust to internationalize their manufacturing sectors.

Those events took place after the so-called "Plaza Accord" of 1985 led to a massive appreciation of the yen relative to the dollar and other world currencies. From an annual average of $3 billion from 1970-1980, Japanese investments abroad swelled 10 times to $31 billion from 1986 to 1992.

Because the Philippines was perceived as unsafe due both to the many coup attempts and the kidnappings, Japanese investors skipped the country and, instead, went to Malaysia, Thailand, and Indonesia.

Our FDI stock stood at $2.8 billion in 1986, bigger than Thailand's $2.3 billion. By 1992, though, Thailand's FDI level grew six times to $12.3 billion, mostly due to the massive inflow of Japanese investment, while the Philippines recorded only $4 billion.

Malaysia (with its assembly operations for the electronics industry) and Indonesia (for its natural resources such as tin and oil) caught much of the wave of Japanese investment during that period, so that Malaysia's FDI stock nearly tripled from $6 billion in 1986 to $17 billion in 1992, while FDI in Indonesia doubled from $6 billion to $12 billion, according to UNCTAD statistics.

None of the FDI flows in that period found their way into telecoms and other public utilities in our neighboring countries, because foreign investment in such industries were curtailed either through explicit regulations or bureaucratic hurdles. Instead, FDIs in these countries were encouraged and supported into export-oriented and high-tech industries, and not into public utility monopolies.

The second claim in the propaganda over FDIs, is the belief that such capital inflows are necessary for the economic development of any capital-deficient country such as the Philippines.

However, a growing body of studies since the 1980s has debunked such a view. The fact is that FDI inflows in the Asian Tiger economies, as well as in Japan and China, increased *only* when they started taking off on their high-growth path, not before, as transnational companies were quick to take advantage of low wage rates and expanding markets.

FDIs were not the fuel behind the Asian Tigers' growth. Foreign investors simply piggy-backed on economic growth in the region in its early stages, achieved through a national pragmatic plan that disregarded laissez-faire dogmas.

In fact, Asian Tigers, at the start of their growth in the 1960s (except for Hong Kong and Singapore, which are anomalies since they are tiny entrepôts) also imposed strict restrictions on foreign investments, and shepherded those that came in into specific industries they calculated would stimulate economic growth. These were mainly heavy industries (especially in the cases of Japan and Korea) and export-oriented manufacturing enterprises (as those in Malaysia and Taiwan).

The Philippines, since after World War II up to the mid-1970s, absolutely had no restrictions on investments or on imports from the biggest economy and capital-exporter at that period, the United States. This was because we had that grossly misnamed "Parity Amendment" to the 1935 Constitution which gave US businesses until 1974 the same rights and privileges as local capitalists.

Did such policy of free-flow of American capital result in huge US investments here? Did US foreign capital boost our economic growth? No, they did not.

'Brownfield' projects

While it remains debatable whether FDIs may even have a negative impact on a country due to the massive profit remittances and crowding of the local credit market involved, what is not disputed is that FDIs should not get into "brownfield" projects (the acquisition of existing companies and facilities) but "greenfield" enterprises, or new industries into which local capital has been hesitant to go.

Salim's control of Philippine Long Distance Telephone Co., obviously, was into a very "brown" industry, an acquisition of a decades-old telecom firm.

One of the main arguments for foreign investment is that the country does not have sufficient capital to fund its economic expansion. However, several studies using data from different countries have disputed this, as foreign companies either tap the local credit markets, or use their assets in the host country as collateral for loans from the world financial markets.

This argument citing lack of capital does not stand in the face of facts.

The power distribution monopoly Meralco, for instance, was acquired by the Indonesian magnate Anthoni Salim not through new money coming in from Hong Kong or from one of his many British Virgin Islands-registered companies, but mainly through the finances of PLDT's pension fund (which the Indonesian controlled since 1998) which he deployed and through capital raised through the stock market.

Foreigners' dominant shares in PLDT, Meralco, and Globe, have in fact contributed to substantial capital outflow from the country in the form of dividends. From 2000 to 2015 these profits have totaled $10 billion, the equivalent of the country's historical net foreign investment inflows for seven years, except that in this case these went out of the country.

A response posted so many times in the comments section of my columns on Salim's control of our public utility firms goes as follows: "I don't care who runs PDLT or Globe, as long as I get efficient, cheap service."

That's a certainly a valid view for an ordinary consumer. But it is a very short-term view, because down the road the consumer will suffer the consequences of a foreign-dominated telecom industry. Among these consequences are the foreign firms' capital outflows that contribute to overall economic underdevelopment and the government's surrendering of this strategic industry, which is actually a tool for economic growth.

Foreigners' monopoly of our telecom industry in fact has already made Philippine cellphone service one of the most expensive in Asia, and broadband speed here among the lowest.

That perspective would also be irresponsible for the country's leaders to take, given their task of not only running an efficient government but laying down the groundwork, including the necessary infrastructure, for sustainable development for decades, even a century to come.

Telecom firms provide essential public services, and the state has the duty to assure its citizens that these are efficiently provided at the least cost — without the profit margins usually exacted by ordinary enterprises — and in the same way government provides such public services as police security, along with water and electricity supply.

Telecoms essential to growth

The telecommunications industry is essential to economic growth, as much as roads and bridges are, because the efficient transmittal of information makes markets and production more efficient, besides the fact it reduces transaction costs. Efficient transmission of information improves productivity. Thus, telecoms directly and indirectly contribute to a country's economic growth.

The poor state of our telecoms industry contributed to the host of factors that explain our weak economic growth rates in the 1980s and 1990s. This is reflected in the marginal increase in the number of fixed-lines per 100 inhabitants in the Philippines from 0.7 in 1975 to 1.0 in 1992, according to World Bank data.

This is in contrast to the increases in Malaysia and Thailand, which rose in the same period from 1.4 to 10.9, and from 0.5 to 3.1, respectively. That, undoubtedly, was a factor that discouraged foreign investments in our case.

Most states in the world have realized, logically, that the telecom sector is too crucial to be left alone to private corporations, whose prime directive, after all, is not to deliver efficient services but to generate profit for their small group of stockholders.

Most countries in the world and all Asian countries (as well as most Scandinavian countries), therefore, have state agencies or their citizens' corporations, and not foreign entities, running their telecom sector.

Moreover, the Asian Tigers regarded telecoms not just as a sector that must provide efficient service to their people; they consciously developed the industry and its support sectors, nurturing the mostly state-owned telecom companies to make them global industry and technology leaders that they are now.

Take the case of Japan. The totally state-owned (until 1985) Nippon Telephone and Telegraph (NTT) is now the third largest telecom company in the world and a global technology leader. In South Korea, the state-owned Korean cellular phone firms have helped make Samsung and LG Electronics among the biggest cellphone manufacturers in the world.

It was only as recent as the 1980s that mature economies with developed, state-owned telecom operators started to inject competition into their telecom markets, partly by privatizing the sector, or opening up the state firms to minority private investors and operating them as independent corporations.

Japan's NTT, for instance, was privatized in 1985 but only to the extent that state ownership, by law, was not reduced to less than one-third of the company's equity.

In contrast to almost all Asian countries, the Philippines never considered telecoms as a sector that needed to be nurtured and developed by the state as a sector crucial for economic growth.

"The Philippines is an exception to the statist model of Asian telecommunications. Ownership and control of nationwide telecommunications have been in the private sector from the era of American colonialism to the present," a comprehensive study of the Asian telecommunications industry said.

It had not occurred to Philippine governments that the telecom sector is such a crucial public utility, that the industry cannot be left alone in the hands of the private sector.

(December 26, 2016)

---

* Among such studies:

1. Carkovic, Maria V, and Ross Levine. **Does Foreign Direct Investment Accelerate Economic Growth?** University of Minnesota, Department of Finance, Working Paper, 2002.
2. Eichengreen, Barry. **Capital Account Liberalization: What Do Cross Country Studies Tell Us?** The World Bank Economic Review 15, No. 3, 2001: 341-365.
3. Pereira, Luiz Carlos Bresser. **Globalization and Competition: Why Some Emergent Countries Succeed While Others Fall Behind.** Cambridge, New York: Cambridge University Press, 2010.
4. Rui Moura and Rosa Forte. **The Effects of Foreign Direct Investment on the Host Country's Economic Growth – Theory and Empirical Evidence.** FEP Working Papers, November 2010.
5. Action Aid. **Where Does it Hurt? The Impact of the Financial Crisis on Developing Economies.** 2009.
6. Rodrik, D. & Subramaniam, A. **Why Did Financial Liberalization Disappoint?** IMF Staff Papers, International Monetary Fund, Washington, DC., 2008.

DEATH, NATIONALISM, CHINA

THE DEATH OF A LOVED ONE or a friend — two friends Michael Marasigan and Roy Sinfuego passed away recently — always reminds one how fleeting life is.

Brief it is, but life is a magical moment, a miracle in the universe's 14 billion years of existence in which a species called *Homo sapiens* has evolved that it is now able to reflect on himself and on the world.

Most of us celebrate that brief span with our loved ones, making sure (usually simultaneous with satisfying our own needs) they have all the necessities to enjoy life, and not suffer it. Occasionally, we move out of that circle, with acts of kindness to those outside it: handing out coins to the ragamuffin who taps on your windshield; giving an unexpected end-year bonus to your household help; donating money to help victims of floods or the Marawi crisis.

But with the realization that life is such a miracle, shouldn't we devote at least a significant part of our lives to help our fellow human beings (not just those within our circle) to enjoy it too, instead of living it in misery?

Many well-off people actually do, or think they do. They believe their companies give jobs to people who would otherwise be out of work or underpaid; they give scholarships to the poor; or fund charitable organizations. Communists struggling to overthrow an exploitative state think they help by working in non-governmental organizations, while the devoted Catholics think they are actually helping by praying for the poor.

In this age we live in, though, the most efficient way to help as many people in the shortest period of time is to help make the State under which one is a member of by birth or choice, as strong and efficient as possible. This is so that the State can supervise the nation it has the authority to control and thus its economic structure is able to lift the majority of its citizens from poverty.

Think about it. When a Filipino moves out of the country to migrate to the US, Canada, or any other developed country, he gets to live a much better life, on average, and even develops his talents to the full.

That's a cliché of course, but we forget that the US or Canada are that way because their early citizens had built, often at a high cost to themselves and their families, the political and economic structures that have made their nations great. Thus most of the people living in these developed countries would have the necessities of life as well as the means and opportunities to be a successful individual.

After all, it is a nation's government that is the apparatus of institutions and practices that order and regulate society, and appropriate and distribute the resources of a nation. It is in this age the most important organization that determines whether humans live in happiness or misery. That is why we revere or hate presidents so much, since they head the organization, the State or Government, that has had the most impact on people's lives.

This hasn't always been the case. The supreme role of a nation-state over humans emerged only in the last 300 years or so of humankind's million-year history. In the past, what determined people's lives were the leadership of a tribe or band of tribes, later of kingdoms (and the character of their kings), of empires that conquered tribes, and even of the Catholic Church and the Islamic Caliphates.

The realization that the nation-state is the most important organization that determines whether a human being lives in happiness or misery is called nationalism.

The term or even the notion of it has been denigrated, even caricatured by the term "nativism" here and abroad, by the global capitalist elites, whose businesses have gone not just beyond their own nations, but depend on removing the boundaries of nations. They have even spread the lie that it is them — "foreign investments" — that is the biggest factor for a nation's growth.

In our country, nationalism has been all but killed by the elites, who after all look at the Philippines not as their country (they see themselves as Spanish, Americans, or "globalists", but not Filipinos), but only as a lucrative market or production site.

Contrast this with the Japanese, Thai, or South Korean capitalists' nationalism, and you will realize how bad our situation is. Our elites have dived into the idea of "globalization": most of them have mansions in New York, California, and even London, which they consider as their real homes. The most famous executive in our country, much admired for his corporate successes, is Manuel V. Pangilinan. Yet he works for foreigners: the lucrative conglomerate he manages has given a billion dollars in profits to its main owners, the Indonesian Anthoni Salim and rich American investors.

All these points would be just theoretical if not for recent developments: the emergence as an economic powerhouse of China, one of the world's most nationalist countries.

China's 'modern miracle'

According to the World Bank, China lifted out of extreme poverty (those living on $1.90 per day, roughly P96 per day) 800 million of its citizens from 1988 to 2013. The most important factor for China's growth is that it had a strong state that adopted whatever policy, absent the dogmas, that would grow the economy and lift its people out of poverty.

That 800 million lifted out of poverty is equivalent to the population of eight Philippines. How many poor Filipinos have managed to crawl out of poverty after the EDSA Revolution? Just 20 million, although the net increase, according to World Bank data, is just 2.5 million because of our population growth, which has bred more poor people.

"China's progress accounted for more than three-quarters of global poverty reduction and is the reason why the world reached the UN millennium development goal of halving extreme poverty," an article in the UK-based newspaper *The Guardian* pointed out.

China's poverty reduction was even seen by several scholars as a "modern miracle" as never in humankind's history, have so many people been lifted out of poverty, in such a short span of time as three decades.

Indeed, humanity has been in such misery for most of its existence that it is a dogma for major religions. A Christian after-life heaven wouldn't have had traction if most people were happy alive. Islam views life as so miserable that one should pass through it as fast as possible, which indeed jihadists do. Buddhism says there are ways to eject from the cycle of (miserable) life.

Isn't it mind-boggling that 800 million Chinese souls in just 25 years — less than the time span between our EDSA revolution and today — were lifted out of poverty, so that they and their descendants will be able to celebrate life? Wouldn't it have given those responsible for that feat all the meaning in life? Shouldn't we emulate them?

Between collecting Porsches and helping get out of poverty 10 million Filipinos, which would include their hundreds of millions of descendants in the future, shouldn't the latter give you the bigger thrill?

(August 16, 2017)

INDEPENDENCE: TO BE 'RUN LIKE HELL BY FILIPINOS'?

"I PREFER A GOVERNMENT run like hell by Filipinos to a government run like heaven by Americans." That's the famous statement by the Philippines' second president Manuel Quezon, quoted in so many emotional speeches extolling nationalism.

I'm sure some smart aleck would post in his Facebook page: "Careful what you wish for. We have a government run like hell."

But Quezon's affirmation does challenge your rational mind. With one life to live, or one family to raise, why on earth would you want to live in hell?

Quezon's is a view obviously not shared by the 15 million Filipinos who migrated abroad (the bulk to the colonizing country Quezon referred to) or by workers overseas who are spending their entire working lives there. Another 15 million probably want to live abroad, and have just been thwarted in doing so.

And these aren't — except for the first wave of migrants to Hawaii and Alaska in the early 1900s— from the poor. They're from the lower and middle classes, and the rich, or else they wouldn't even be able to afford the visa fees, plane fares, and other migration or deployment fees.

More than half of my batchmates at the Ateneo de Manila high school and college (who are mostly from the upper class) also didn't prefer a government run like hell by Filipinos, and have migrated to the US and Canada, many straight from college.

Even many of the best and brightest of my generation of journalists are now working abroad. Take a moment to think: how many of your college classmates or office mates in you first job are abroad?

Most of our upper class now have permanent resident status in, or are citizens of the US, Canada, Spain, and Australia and many of the second and third generation of our elite have spent much of their youth abroad in secondary schools and college, that they can't speak straight Pilipino, just, "yaya Tagalog".

History nearly made a cruel joke, and would have ridiculed Quezon if presidential candidate in 2004 Fernando Poe, Jr. (Ronald Allan Kelley Poe), with a Spanish father and an American mother, had become president. With Estrada actually running an FPJ presidency, would we have had a government run like hell by an American (or Spaniard?).

His adopted daughter, now Senator Grace Poe, spent nearly all of her working life in the US as a naturalized American citizen. She had rejected the Philippines in her Naturalization Oath of Allegiance ("I hereby declare, on oath, that I absolutely and entirely renounce and abjure all allegiance and fidelity to any foreign prince, potentate, state, or sovereignty, of whom or which I have heretofore been a subject or citizen….") and yet now she wants to become president of the country she had renounced.

Quezon expounded on why he prefers "a government of Filipinos run like hell".

"The Philippines of yesterday are consecrated by the sacrifices of lives and treasure of your patriots, martyrs, and soldiers . . . The Philippines of tomorrow will be the country of plenty, of happiness, and of freedom; A Philippines that is a mistress of her own destiny, holding in her hand the torch of freedom and democracy."

"A republic of virtuous and righteous men and women all working together for a better world than the one we have at present," Quezon described his vision of the then future Republic.

That sent shivers down my spine. Quezon uttered those inspiring statements in 1920, nearly a century ago. Today, instead of a republican utopia, we have a dystopia, one of the poorest nations in Asia now, a republic of the corrupt, the inept, and the hypocrite.

Fate seems to be mocking us that this year's Independence Day celebration coincides with the indictment and arrest of three senators representing two generations, with many more legislators charged with the same crime, which reminds us of how deep we have sunk as a nation.

And we have a President running away from it, pretending to lead the Independence Day celebrations in Naga, but simply obviously afraid of the mass demonstrations scheduled on Independence Day, June 12, in Luneta in the capital city, the symbol of our independence.

But rather than cursing ourselves, that the Filipino character is just so flawed, consider a different framework explaining the nature of societies and nations.

Society is a class-divided one, consisting of those owning the means of production, the ruling class, who by virtue of that ownership claims ownership of the entire output, and those who don't.

The means of production were predominantly land before, which evolved into capital, e.g., our landlord class created by the Spanish and the Americans evolving into today's finance and industry magnates.

The rest, those who don't own land or capital, are the exploited, whose shares in production are determined not by what is fair but what the ruling class wills.

Nation-states are not really associations or communities of equal citizens, a notion the ruling class has brainwashed all its members to believe. Rather, nations are creations of the ruling classes of a particular territory, just as a medieval baron would block off a vast tract of land as his fiefdom.

The notion of a nation has indeed been a very powerful and even necessary fiction for the ruling classes.

In pre-modern society, it was religion that put the exploited in its place, so that they'd never dreamed of breaking their chains — Christianity in Europe and in its colonized territories, Sons-of-Heaven kinds of crap as in Japan and China. Never mind if your land was confiscated to make up a friar estate, never mind if the colonizer demands you turn over to it half of your crops as taxes. After all, you are part of a bigger entity, the Kingdom of God.

In modern society, the opium is membership in and fealty to the nation. Never mind if you are a landless farm worker, a mall saleslady given only a three-month contract so the magnate can evade mandatory workers' benefits, or an unemployed factory worker with a family to feed. After all you are part of a bigger entity: the nation.

In rich nations, the ruling classes at least managed to make their economies so productive as to enlarge the incomes of the working classes. (The recent best seller, **Capital in the 21st Century** by Thomas Pikkety however argues on a mountain of data that this wasn't because of capitalists' largesse but the result of political factors and forces, which the ruling class even tried to block.)

The premise of Quezon's view was wrong. His nationalism was based on the assumption that the government will be run by ordinary Filipinos, for the welfare of ordinary Filipinos. It hasn't been that way. It has been from the beginning, a government by the elite, of the elite, and for the elite.

(June 11, 2014)

WHEN WILL WE HAVE 'PHILIPPINES FIRST'?

WHILE THE NEW US President Donald Trump is arguably a demagogic megalomaniac, he demonstrated a streak of genius, or a deep insight into his countrymen's feelings, that made him win, when he made his campaign battle cries "America First" and "We will make America great again."

While some have pointed out the anti-Semitic, KKK origins of the "America First" slogan, still, these are essentially calls for the revival of nationalism. This vision has been denigrated, even here, by those who delude themselves into thinking that the nation has ceased to be the most important organization in this era for anyone to be a member of.

Contrast Trump's slogans which contain the word "America" to Hillary Clinton's "Together, Stronger," or Obama's "Yes We Can," which do not refer to the United States as a nation, and which can be adopted by any English-speaking political candidate anywhere in the world.

It is not fuzzy entities like "The Globe" or "World Markets" that determine whether a human being will live his life in misery or in comfort. Rather, it is the nation where he is a member of or where he lives, and how its members from the past to the present have built in a particular territory a community (with a unique name), with the institutions to ensure the prosperity of its members, and to prevent one tiny group from getting richer by exploiting the majority.

Indeed, nationalism in the past decade has been resurgent almost everywhere in the globe — except in the Philippines — given the economic rise of China and Russia, Great Britain's decision to leave the European Union, and the emergence of nationalist parties all over the world. Narendra Modi, the leader of the second most populous country in the world, India, won by a landslide because of his nationalist rhetoric.

A prescient 2014 article in the prestigious globalist magazine The Economist, said: "In recent years, any writer who predicted that nationalism was the wave of the future would have been regarded as eccentric — at best. All the most powerful forces in business, technology and finance seemed to be pushing towards deeper international integration… In 2015, however, it will become increasingly clear that nationalism is back. From Europe to Asia to America, politicians who base their appeal on the idea that they are standing up for their own countries will grow in power and influence."

The least nationalistic

Nationalism is the belief and practice that the nation and nothing else, not the clan, not the company, not the Church nor a fantasy Kumbaya world-where-we-are-all-brothers-and-sisters is the primary organization that determines a human being's welfare, so that one must have loyalty to it and devote some part of one's life to strengthening.

We are one of the few nations in the world, and the only country in Asia that is the least nationalistic, and this is really our core problem.

There are two major factors why our Asian neighbors are fiercely nationalist. One is their monarchic feudal histories in which kings strove by every means to develop a strong sense of community among their subjects, since this was essential for their rule. This is the case in China, Japan, Thailand, and Indonesia.

The other factor was the very serious threat of their communities' survival, as happened with South Korea (nearly conquered by the China-backed North Korea), Vietnam, Taiwan, and even Singapore, after the tiny island state separated from the Federation of Malaya.

The Philippine community has never experienced these two factors.

Pre-colonial "Philippines" was a collection of tiny kingdoms, and the kind of community the Spanish imposed was an ecclesiastical one, that is, we were a community because all of us, conqueror and conquered, were members of the Kingdom of God. That in fact is still the biggest delusion of Filipinos, that they are primarily members of their clan and the Kingdom of God, rather than of the nation.

The US never of course bothered to create a nation out of us, as we were merely something like Hawaii and Guam to be exploited for its unique agricultural products (coconut and sugarcane), and as a base to conquer China.

Being under the wing of the US, there never was a threat to our existence as a community, except during the Japanese occupation of course, which only weakened our nationalism, as it was General Douglas McArthur and his troops who saved us.

Threats to the survival of nations historically have been one of the most important factors for their prosperity for a simple reason.

With the existence of their communities threatened, their elites commit to making their communities prosper, or else these would be taken over by an external force, which would likely also exterminate them. Because of this, the elites even sacrifice their profit rates and refrain from horrendous levels of exploitation of the working class of that community, lest they rebel and weaken the nation.

In Asia, this is obvious in the case of Taiwan, whose ruling class was the Kuomintang that fled China after their defeat in the civil war with the communists, and their island refuge has continuously been under threat of invasion by China. This was obviously also the case with Japan that could have been obliterated by the US with their nukes. This was obviously the case with South Korea, threatened by the communist North.

Another major factor that has weakened our nationalism has been the massive migration of our people to the US and their prosperity there, which has the effect of probably half our population pining to be American citizens, and despising their homeland. The ruling class routinely send their children to schools abroad, whose world views become American, and thus see their country as a sorry, smelly place, but one where they can get profits from.

It is the State which plays a crucial role in developing and strengthening nationalism, and not even brilliant individual heroes like Rizal, simply because only government has the massive resources to change people's minds.

We are again so unfortunate that the last President to raise the flag of nationalism was the strongman Ferdinand Marcos. Remember his slogan "We will make this nation great again!" which preceded Trump's by five decades?

His attempt to junk the name of our colonizer's King as the country's name and instead have it called Maharlika, which means noble? His building of edifices like the Philippine International Convention Center and the Folk Arts Theater to foster pride in the nation? His project for a multi-volume history of the Philippines titled Tadhana, to project the idea that our nation has a great destiny?

How unlucky we are, really. Marcos' rule ended in an economic crisis, not entirely his fault, and the takeover of an elite group that is totally lacking in any sense of nationalism. Marcos was demonized by the victors, along with everything he espoused, including nationalism.

Yellow Cult

Corazon Aquino's devotion was to her clan and the Yellow Cult she founded, not to the nation, and her worldview was that we were destined to forever live under America's wing. Her symbol was a yellow ribbon derived from an American song, which she made the constant reminder to the nation of her husband Ninoy Aquino's assassination.

Her successor, Fidel Ramos, not only was imbued with the American way of thinking, perhaps brainwashed into him during his West Point days. He embraced the neoliberal ideology of a globalism in which free markets were more important than nationalism. No wonder really, as the globalist Thatcher and Reagan were the gurus of his era. It was Thatcherism and Reaganomics' failure to lift the welfare of the working classes however that led eventually to the resurgence of nationalism.

Ramos' mantra-vision for the nation was "deregulation, liberalization, and privatization." As a result, we have the lowest tariff rates in Asia, and even in the world, that even Thai fish sauce (patis) and foreign-owned brand of bread (Gardenia, owned by an Indonesian conglomerate) have dominated the local markets, and even soap and toothpaste manufacturers have left the country.

Ramos threw a local elite family, the Antonio Cojuangcos, out of PLDT, which right after he left office was acquired by an Indonesian tycoon. The telecom monopoly was dismantled, but a duopoly emerged, controlled by foreigners. The state-owned MWSS providing water services was sold to firms, one of which was controlled, again, by the Indonesian tycoon. The Ramos government got P50 billion from the sale of a vast military camp that is now a business district worth a trillion pesos. The modernization of the military, the motive for the sale, was never achieved.

The drunkard and corrupt president after Ramos, Joseph Estrada, despite his nationalist pretensions, helped the Indonesian tycoon Anthoni Salim take over PLDT in a very shady operation.

Sadly, the regime of President Gloria Arroyo, a nationalist, for various reasons not her fault, became too stormy for any resurgence of nationalism. Her successor, Benigno Aquino III, never once wore on his chest the flag, the symbol of nationalism. Instead of the nation's progress, Aquino's overarching ambition was for the Yellow Cult to remain in power forever.

Such is a very abbreviated history of how nationalism has all but broken down in our time, that no President could have thought of, or dared to have a slogan like "Philippines First".

When will we ever hear the cry "Philippines First"? Maybe President Rodrigo Duterte is already espousing it, in his own way. But he should shout it louder and clearer. We desperately need it.

(January 23, 2017)

Rodrigo
Roa
Duterte

DOGMAS DUTERTE DEMOLISHED

THE YEAR 2017 will be remembered as the year a mayor from Mindanao, who surprisingly became President, demolished long-held national political and cultural dogmas and myths, whose persistence has been a formidable obstacle to our growth as a nation — and yet he continued to be immensely popular.

First, Duterte demolished the dogma that a Philippine president and the Republic should consider the United States as its big white brother, that its national interests are our national interests. In our post-war history, Cory Aquino and her anointed, the West Point-trained Fidel Ramos, and her son Benigno III, were totally subservient to the US, while the other presidents just paid lip service to the policy of undertaking an independent foreign policy.

In a period when the US maneuvered geopolitically and pressured Asian countries to isolate China for its alleged aggressiveness in the South China Sea, Duterte drew the country closer to the emerging Asian superpower, not just diplomatically but in terms of economic relationship.

He has managed to change Filipinos' centuries-old anti-Chinese bias, with the nation now looking at China as its main trade partner and the funder for its much-needed infrastructure projects.

Part of the love-America dogma was that no president would remain popular, and would become ripe for overthrow if he crossed the US overlords. The reasoning was that (in sharp contrast to our neighbors) probably nearly all of the middle and upper-class Filipinos have relatives who migrated to the US or its sister country, Canada. Most of the masses on the other hand still dream of migrating to that land of milk and honey.

Duterte broke that myth, with his popularity even surging to a record 69 percent of Filipinos (based on the latest December polls) satisfied with his rule, a rise from his 65 percent grade when he assumed office in June 2016.

Second, Duterte broke the dogma that was the Spanish colonizers' main tool for occupying a country which allowed them to deploy only a minimal military force: That the Catholic Church was God's representative on earth, and rulers and the ruled must do what it says.

Until I shed the notion when I became a Marxist in my teens, I still believed a family myth my father told me, that our clan became impoverished because a great-grandfather told a local friar to his face, after the cleric got his laundrywoman pregnant: *"Putangina mong pari ka!"*

Well, it wasn't just a lowly provincial friar that Duterte cursed, even if it was in jest. It was the Pope himself, the very representative of Jesus Christ on earth. And unlike the reason why my great-grandfather cursed the friar, Duterte cursed the beloved Pope Francis for the traffic he caused during his visit that made Duterte spend five hours in his car.

Because of that mortal sin against the Pope, the local Catholic Church has secretly labelled Duterte as the Anti-Christ and mobilized all but its archangels to rouse public opinion to overthrow him, using as its cause célèbre the "extrajudicial executions" issue in his war against drugs. Its two institutions for brainwashing our youth — the Ateneo de Manila and De La Salle universities — became the think-tanks for raining fire and brimstone on Duterte.

Duterte obviously has survived the Church's war against Duterte. The Church's field marshal for this war, Archbishop Socrates Villegas (who saw Duterte as the Marcos that he, the new Cardinal Sin, would topple) is drifting to political oblivion and has even lost his main post as president of the Catholic Bishops Conference of the Philippines. I can't even remember the last press release of the moralistic churchgoers' group, the pretentiously named National Transformation Council. Its last posting on its official Facebook page was an article last month lifted from some crappy website about Duterte telling NDF consultants to surrender.

Third, Duterte has shattered the dogma that no Philippine president would get elected to the post, and survive for long without — or resist the bribery of — the oligarchy. His two main rivals to the presidency were heavily bankrolled by national oligarchs, competing for which of their factions would get their puppet to win. Duterte had only Davao-level rich businessmen to finance his campaign.

And his camp even exposed and prosecuted the illegality of the source of the wealth of a Davao billionaire who supported him in the elections.

Duterte in 2017 collected the unpaid taxes of Mighty Corp., the country's second biggest cigarette manufacturer that had grown through all of the past post-war presidents. Think of "10 percent" of the taxes collected — P30 billion — and one would get a realistic idea of the billions of reasons why this tobacco oligarch survived all of the past presidencies. Think in the same way about the P6 billion the Duterte administration collected in unpaid navigational fees from Philippine Airlines, owned by once-powerful oligarch Lucio Tan.

Fourth, Duterte destroyed the dogma of the invincibility of the *Philippine Daily Inquirer,* which had claimed to be the torchbearer of the spirit of the People Power Revolution. No president since 1986 dared cross the paper. Duterte went for the jugular: He pursued the illegal hold of the newspaper's owners, the Rufino-Prieto family over the Mile Long property in the lucrative commercial district of Makati, kicking the clan out of the area last September, and is pursuing the collection of P1.8 billion in unpaid rentals.

Fifth, Duterte eviscerated the myth that the Yellow Cult has been God's gift of governance to the Philippines. That sorry myth has remarkably persisted that even somebody whose job is to study governance in the country, one Richard Heydarian — who boasts in his biodata that he is a regular contributor to Centre for Strategic and International Studies, the Council on Foreign Relations, and a dozen other US media outfits — idolizes the cult's leader Benigno Aquino III to this day.

In his recent 100-page "book" released late last year, Heydarian wrote: "Aquino was arguably the best president in recent memory… As popular as Aquino was at home he was even a bigger celebrity outside, especially to the global media-business complex. Under his watch, the Philippines [transformed] from a developing country into a full-fledged emerging market."

Heydarian is a sloppy scholar but a prolific writer who impresses foreign editors who know little about the Philippines by quoting other scholarly works at the rate of one every two paragraphs. However, his gall in continuing to idolize Aquino indicates how persistent the Yellow myth is.

By simply ignoring the Aquinos, allowing what they detested most, which was to allow former president Ferdinand Marcos' burial at the National Heroes Cemetery, and governing the Philippines in way that highlighted Aquino III's do-nothing, care-about-nothing rule, Duterte has started to bury this myth of the Yellow Cult that US State Department operators created in 1986 and has nurtured since.

The Yellow Cult's excrements, such as the Mamasapano massacre, the Dengvaxia debacle, the hijacking of government funds, have floated to the surface for the public to be aghast over.

This list of dogmas and myths that Duterte destroyed is certainly incomplete. But with his demolition of just those five that have obstructed the Philippines' growth as a nation, I have become optimistic about our country's future.

(January 3, 2018)

ICONOCLASTIC PRESIDENT

DUTERTE AS PRESIDENT is emerging as a historic break from our past. He is by attitude, maybe even class origin and pronouncements, a drastic departure from his predecessors.

There had been Presidents who came from the lower middle-class (Ramon Magsaysay and Diosdado Macapagal) but who never really challenged the ruling class, either by their statements or actions. President Joseph Estrada pretended to be for the masses, but turned out to be the best example of our lumpen-proletariat politicos.

The past president Benigno Aquino III was inarguably the last — I hope — representative of the landlord elite, whom history will judge as one who had been obsessed with, and had done everything (including assaulting the Supreme Court itself and removing its Chief Justice) to preserve his clan's Hacienda Luisita, the epitome of that vanishing class' means of accumulating wealth.

Duterte is nearly Aquino's antithesis, from the middle-class, yes, but hardly living in the ensconced world of the elite, which could explain his derision of the elite and the Philippine oligarchy.

Duterte recently demonstrated his disdain for the oligarchy when he revealed that ABS-CBN chairman Eugenio "Gabby" Lopez III tried to bribe him, to help its subsidiary Sky Cable enter the Davao City market. He hasn't denied reports that he replied to the main executive of that public utility owned by an Indonesian conglomerate: "Simply recall that you are just a puppet of the foreign-based Salim Group, while I am the chosen President of the Republic of the Philippines!"

The new President is also appearing to be an iconoclast, to use that word in the broader sense of a person ruthlessly upending traditions and institutions, cherished by certain sections of society. He vociferously criticized the Catholic Church for "hypocrisy" when it censured his campaign statements that showed his apparent disregard for human life, even if these [involved] suspected criminals, in his anti-crime campaign.

Both traits of the President — an anti-oligarch stance and an iconoclasm — are what this nation needs, so damaged as it has been by the ruling-class elite and by medieval beliefs the Church has irresponsibly allowed to prosper. But these are not enough.

I hope that he evolves from his iconoclasm and his simple, folksy disdain for the oligarchy, as well as from his commonsensical priorities

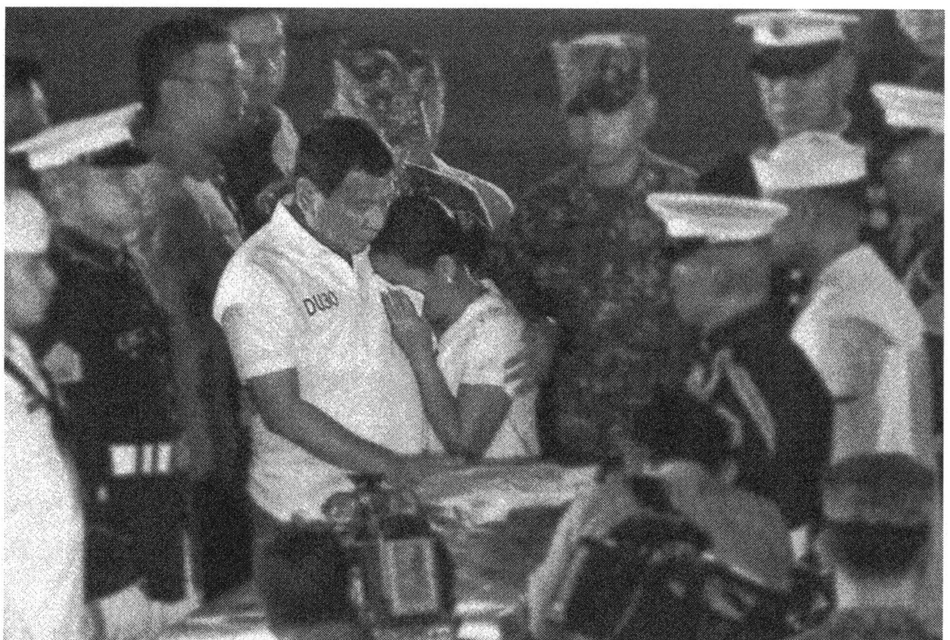

Duterte consoles the wife of a Marine slain in the Marawi fighting, June 11, 2017.

of combating crime and the illegal drug trade, into a leader with a more comprehensive understanding of what ails the Philippines.

He indicated in his inaugural speech yesterday that corruption, crime and illegal drugs don't make up the root of our national quagmire. He said these arise only from a more basic problem: the lack of respect for government and its institutions.

This is correct, yet it raises another question: Why is there such a lack of respect for government?

I submit that there are three reasons:

First, the government has become mostly a tool of the elite, even foreign magnates, exemplified by the fact that an Indonesian-owned, Hong Kong-based company and a Singaporean firm have been allowed to gain control over such strategic public utilities as telecom and power distribution, as I have exposed in numerous articles on PLDT, Globe, and Meralco — in violation of our basic law, the Constitution.

This was possible only because of what political scientists call "regulatory capture," or the elite's capability to put regulatory bodies under their control. Few even know who heads the National Telecommunications

Commission, with whom the telcos seem to be happy. Why shouldn't they be happy if they are not really being regulated?

A part of government that is not a tool of the elite, on the other hand, has become a moneymaking machine for a political-bureaucratic subclass, which the Left erroneously has labeled "bureaucrat-capitalism." Most mayors, congressmen and senators spend a lot of money to win their posts, perhaps partly to feed their egos, but also to tap into the bureaucracy's money-generating machine. We know this phenomenon simply as corruption.

Second, land, capital, and education have been unequally distributed, with the elite having almost a monopoly of these. To understand how important they are, know that they are simply "assets" in different forms, and those who own these assets, therefore, get most of the resulting output — they and their progeny get richer and richer.

We have to find ways to drastically change our grossly inequitable distribution of assets through such means as a radical change in our tax system (the path taken by Scandinavian countries for income distribution), an earthshaking change in the banking system to provide small entrepreneurs access to capital, or a massive scholarship program for a huge sector of the poor to allow them to get not just any education but the best education possible.

And third, Filipinos have lost their sense that all of us are in the same boat called the nation-state, and that our fates are intertwined because we are all in this boat.

We call this understanding, nationalism, which not a few young Filipinos even mock now as "xenophobia." It has become even chic for many young Filipinos to see themselves as "global citizens," which is an oxymoron really, as being a citizen presupposes a nation-state of which one is a member.

There are many reasons for such a decline in nationalism, the most important of which is that unlike the elites of Thailand, China, or Singapore, our elites see themselves as "global citizens" living in the US or Spain or even China now, and seeing the Philippines only as a market or a production site, or as a country they enjoy criticizing from their suburban homes abroad. They no longer really feel — as elites elsewhere do — that their fates are bound with the people of this country.

During the past regime, the symbol always pinned on the chest of the President of the Republic, Aquino III, has been a Yellow Ribbon, the symbol not of this nation but of his clan and its fanatic followers.

Whether we like it or not, it is really the economic elite in any nation that has the resources to mold its people's sense of nationalism. If they don't, it requires heroic struggle by the middle-class, or its intellectuals, to develop their people's nationalism.

As above, as it turned out, so below. The OFW phenomenon has made a big part of our lower middle-class really nationless. Blaming Marcos, and then disappointed that a post-Marcos era changed nothing, has resulted in a massive brain and talent drain from the country, including its best doctors, nurses, engineers, scientists, and even journalists.

If the Philippines isn't really their nation, why should they respect its State?

Only when President Duterte starts correcting these three basic problems of our country can we then say that he has moved from being just iconoclastic to being a revolutionary.

I entered adulthood by joining a movement that professed to be revolutionary, that it would solve these root problems of our country by overthrowing the bourgeois form of government. That movement failed miserably, with its leaders, ironically, even becoming citizens or permanent residents of the world's most advanced capitalist nations they had been condemning.

I hope I see in my lifetime our country moving toward solving these three basic problems.

At least this nation-state's symbol, the Philippine flag, yesterday appeared pinned on the chest of the new President, Duterte.

(June 30, 2016 and July 3, 2017)

AT LAST, WE'RE NO LONGER THE US LACKEY IN ASIA

THE BIG MESSAGE the Philippines sent to the world during its hosting of the 2017 Summit of the Association of Southeast Asian Nations (ASEAN) was as historic as can be in terms of our foreign policy:

We are no longer the Americans' lackey in this part of the world, not its proxy in the ASEAN, which the US secretly founded as the Asian equivalent of the North Atlantic Treaty Organization (NATO) to counter communist China.

Perhaps this owes much to the fact that President Duterte's background is so much in contrast to his predecessors.

Unlike Cory Aquino, he does not owe his rise to power and his hold over it to American political and military might (remember the Phantom jets flying over Manila to challenge the RAM rebels, as requested by Cory?). Unlike Fidel Ramos, who was after all Cory's male clone, Duterte was not brainwashed in an American military school.

In the case of Benigno Aquino III, he was all too happy to relinquish all thinking on foreign policy to the most Americanized, and most pro-American foreign secretary this country ever had, the Indonesian magnate Anthoni Salim's long-time board director Albert del Rosario.

How could Del Rosario not have been pro-American, when other than Salim himself, the biggest stockholders of First Pacific Co., Ltd. — the mother firm of his huge public utility conglomerate in the country — are US billionaires? His six years as Philippine ambassador to the US most probably deepened his love for America such that he pushed for the very unwise filing of a case against China in an international arbitral court.

Surprisingly for somebody who's spent most of his political life in the frontier provincial city that is Davao, Duterte himself is molding our foreign policy to the more realistic worldview in which the US is not our master. Sadly, most of our top foreign affairs officials are so pro-American. Who would blame them when except for the fiercely nationalistic Blas Ople, our foreign policy since our independence simply followed what the US told us to follow?

Only a Duterte could snub the Americans and declare to the world that his big foreign policy pivot is towards the People's Republic of

China, the economic and political rival of the US in the Asian region.

Duterte has even drawn the country closer to Russia and its president Vladimir Putin. The last time any Philippine President even gave some thought to Russia was in the mid-1970s when Marcos experimented with getting the country out of the claws of the US imperial eagle by pretending to get close to the Americans' enemies.

It's just been a year since Aquino and his pro-American Yellow Cult were in paroxysms of joy in getting the Permanent Court of Arbitration in the Netherlands to rule that China's historic claims to areas in the South China Sea cannot be in excess of claimant countries, such as the Philippines' exclusive economic zones set by the United Nations Convention on the Law of the Seas (UNCLOS).

But reality has quickly set in. The arbitral ruling means nothing. No state, not the United Nations, no coalition of countries would enforce it, not even the US. After all, China and the US don't even entirely recognize UNCLOS, and how logical is an arbitration in which one of the parties, China, had refused to be arbitrated?

The ruling actually even sets for us a dangerous precedent: What if Vietnam filed a case in the same arbitral court to claim Pag-asa island, our biggest property in the South China Sea which Marcos only claimed in 1974 and asked his troops to occupy — and we lost?

The biggest beneficiary of the arbitral ruling has been the US. It could not justify by any stretch of reasoning to deploy its mighty blue-water navy to patrol the South China Sea. Now the arbitral ruling gives it some flimsy reason invoking its self-appointed role as the global policeman to enforce international law. The US and its lackeys have portrayed China as an arrogant superpower disregarding international law and militarizing the South China Sea.

Prodded by the US, the past administration's tack was to get the ASEAN to condemn China for not complying with the arbitral ruling. But to do so didn't even cross Duterte's mind in this ASEAN summit. Rightly so.

Del Rosario had embarrassed the nation when he tried to force the ASEAN Foreign Ministers' meeting, in August 2016, just a month after the arbitral ruling came out, to issue a statement against China. When it didn't, Del Rosario came very close to claiming that the Cambodian host was China's puppet.

Why should the ASEAN ask China to comply with the ruling when only four out of its 10 members — the Philippines, Vietnam, Malaysia and Brunei — have claims to it, and the rest of its six members, especially its poorest members like Laos and Myanmar, are wooing China for investments and aid? There's a vivid Filipino term for that: *Nandadamay.*

Malaysia and Brunei don't even seem to be interested anymore in the dispute in the South China Sea. Malaysia after all is happy that it has transformed its Layang-Layang island into a tourism site, and calculates that the rest of the dozen shoals and islets there aren't worth antagonizing China, its biggest trading partner and foreign investor. Why would tiny Brunei with a population less than a fourth of the city of Manila antagonize a country of one billion people?

The timing of Duterte's pivot to China couldn't be better.

It is only in recent years that China has indisputably emerged as an economic and military power, and the dire prognostications that its hundreds of millions of its poor in its inner territory will slow down its growth have not occurred. World Bank economists are applauding what they see as China's miracle, that from 1988 to 2013, it has lifted out of extreme poverty (those living on $1.90 per day, or roughly P96 per day) 800 million of its citizens from 1988 to 2013.

Duterte had quickly warmed up to this Asian superpower, and China seems to have put the controversial arbitration decision we won behind it — as indeed most of the world has. Proof of this is that China pledged during Duterte's state visit $9 billion in low-interest or soft loans for our infrastructure projects. Total Chinese economic assistance promised by Chinese President Xi Jinping to Duterte is estimated at $24 billion.

Now, the other economic superpower in Asia, Japan, which also has serious territorial disputes with China, can't be outdone in wooing the Philippines. It rushed to extend to the country a similar magnitude of soft loans.

Even Russia has extended trade and military support to us, a country probably most of its citizens don't even know where we are on the map.

Indeed there are huge, material benefits in not being a US puppet.

(May 1, 2017)

EVEN WITH EJK ALLEGATIONS, MASSIVE SUPPORT FOR THE WAR VS DRUGS

THERE IS MASSIVE approval for President Duterte's war against illegal drugs, a level of support that has never occurred for any other major government initiative ever. This is despite Filipinos' perception that the campaign has involved "extrajudicial killings" (EJKs), or executions by the police of those suspected to be involved in illegal drugs — even before they are arrested and brought before the courts.

A harsh, even terrible reality that may be, but that is the national consensus, going by opinion polls.

Eighty-eight percent of Filipinos support it, according to the September 2016 poll of PulseAsia, while for Social Weather Stations, 77 percent. The person almost solely responsible for launching that war, executing it, and therefore identified with it, President Duterte, has approval ratings of 80 percent (PulseAsia) and trust ratings of 73 percent (Social Weather Stations).

The polls also provide evidence that there indeed has been a nationwide anti-drug campaign (in contrast to it being just a Public Relations operation) and that it was largely successful.

According to PulseAsia, 77 percent of its respondents reported that there were anti-illegal drug operations by the police in their barangays, and 95 percent claimed there were arrests, injured, surrenderees, and killed. Some 71 percent of Filipinos, according to the SWS, have concluded that the number of drug addicts in their locality has been reduced.

There has been such immense backing for the war against illegal drugs and for Duterte despite the fact that the Yellows and the Catholic Church have worked overtime to demonize it on grounds that the "extrajudicial killings" that occurred in the course of this campaign are unconscionable.

Two of the biggest broadsheets, the *Philippine Daily Inquirer* and the *Philippine Star*, the two TV networks ABS-CBN and GMA7, and the foreign-funded Rappler website have been especially relentless in portraying Metro Manila as having been turned into a killing field of the innocents.

The PCIJ, purportedly devoted to investigative journalism, hurriedly published a supposed children's book — a children's book, for god's sake — on an alleged victim of EJK the teenager Kian de los Santos, obviously in hopes of raising outrage against the war against drugs.

Fabricated figures

Three months after Duterte assumed power and immediately launched his anti-drug campaign, the Rappler website in September fabricated a figure — 7,080 —that it claimed was the total number of EJKs. This exaggerated figure naturally horrified the West, as was the intent.

Worse, the anti-Duterte propagandists then erroneously extrapolated that invented number of EJKs, so that they claimed that by March there were 14,000 EJKs, a figure reported even by a colleague in his column in this newspaper.

With the Yellows' efforts, I suspect especially with the help of a former Filipino who married a millionaire and is now based in New York, mainstream US and European media almost turned the alleged EJKs into their crusade to expose.

Rappler's sister company the US-based news website "The Intercept" called Duterte a killer whom President Trump shouldn't even have talked to over the phone; the Filipina female dean of a Columbia University journalism unit melodramatically labeled this presidency as "drenched in blood."

Yet based on both the Pulse Asia and SWS surveys, Filipinos have decided to tell these former Filipinos, local and foreign media, the Catholic Church, and the Yellow Cult: Go to hell, we support Duterte.

Significant is the finding that 73 percent of the citizenry, according to PulseAsia, believe that EJKs have occurred in the course of the war against drugs. The SWS even claimed (in a June survey) that 73 percent are "worried that they or someone they know" would be victims of EJKs.

If you think about it, it is rather astonishing. Most Filipinos are supportive of Duterte's war against illegal drugs, yet they believe it has resulted in extrajudicial killings, and are even worried that they would be victims? How do we explain this?

Highfalutin jargon

One explanation is that most Filipinos do not really understand the meaning of the term extrajudicial killing, defined in most legal dictionaries as "the killing of a person by governmental authorities without the sanction of any judicial proceeding."

It is highfalutin jargon that I don't think most Filipinos being surveyed can wrap their minds around. This is especially because we no longer even have "judicial killings," i.e., capital punishment meted out by a court. The term we used during martial law was simply "summary executions," which evoked ruthlessness and arbitrariness.

Do you think a respondent of the SWS in an urban slum would have understood its question: *"Gaano po kayo nangangamba na kayo o sino mang kilala niyo ay maging biktima ng "extrajudicial killing or EJK"?* For all we know, the SWS respondent would have heard only "killing," and sure enough he would say he'd be worried or else he'd think, he's challenging the fates.

If the term extrajudicial killing wasn't really understood by the pollsters' respondents, then their reports on Filipinos' awareness of — and worry over EJKs — are therefore useless.

The second explanation though would bring us to a hard reality: Filipinos have been so fed up with the proliferation of illegal drugs, how it has made the streets so unsafe, how it has made men so crazy as to do horrible things as rape and murder, how it has ruined families, how its main victims are the poor, that they support the executions of suspected drug dealers by the police.

Anyone who really knows the situation in our urban slums, or our rural hinterlands would know that Filipinos are so convinced that our legal processes aren't working, that if the police stick to the judicial process, the war against illegal drugs will never be won.

In the subdivision where I live, the security personnel a few years back were so worried that several resigned and vanished when they learned that two drug pushers that they had caught and turned over to the police were freed on bail, and had threatened to get back at them.

I know, I know. There would be that storm of arguments, "the end cannot justify the means"; "we cannot give up on our humanity"; and the classic line "that would make us uncivilized."

I wish somebody could give us a workable, real solution, not just some abstract motherhood statements about human rights. After all, we are talking about the future of 100 million Filipinos and their millions of descendants. Or perhaps, based on those polls, there is already a national consensus: they support this war against illegal drugs.

(October 20, 2016)

FIVE LEADERSHIP LESSONS

THE NORMALLY ANTI-DUTERTE newspaper, the *Philippine Daily Inquirer* reported the other day, to my utter surprise a positive article about the President, albeit with a backhanded compliment: "President Rodrigo Duterte may be doing something right as eight in every 10 adult Filipinos across the country and socioeconomic classes trust him and approve of his performance, according to the results of a recent Pulse Asia survey."

Also a few days ago, the Social Weather Stations released a survey that showed 94 percent of adult Filipino said they are happy with life in general, a record high. Levels of a people's happiness often reflect their satisfaction with their main leader, i.e., the President (or Prime Minister) since one determinant of happiness is the absence of worries over where one lives.

What could explain Duterte's popularity, which our politicians and those who aspire to be our leaders could emulate? What would be, in that particular genre of lists, the leadership lessons from Duterte?

I think the following:

1. Be yourself. Don't pretend to be somebody else.

The one thing about Duterte even his vociferous critics can't deny is his authenticity, his what-you-see-is-what-you-get character, which explains why he seems to have a foul mouth.

Having been a full-time journalist through five presidents, I can assert that every one of them tried to be somebody they were really not. Even President Estrada pretended to be one with the masses, even if that was really only his movie persona.

The worst pretender of course was the spoiled brat Benigno Aquino III. One could sense the hacendero performing whenever he talked in his formalistic Tagalog in front of the public. His sidekick, Mar Roxas (he of the elite Araneta family) shouting and cursing "putang-ina" (your mother is a whore) in a rally was a pathetic attempt to be somebody else.

In a recent talk with columnists, Duterte hinted why he couldn't pretend to be somebody else: "I'm too old to change my paradigm as a mayor to a paradigm of a president." Maybe the use of the term "paradigm" is inexact (unless understood to mean one's world view), but what he's essentially saying is that he's too old to pretend to be somebody else.

If as a politician you think the masses wouldn't like your real self, so that you have to pretend, then find a different career. You'll just be wasting your precious time and your billions of pesos trying to project a different persona from what you are. People will see through you.

2. It's not important what you say, but what you do.

Duterte seems to enjoy shocking people in his speeches and doesn't care if the hoity-toity elites are aghast at his curses and invectives.

Because of this, he would have easily been the most unpopular president in just his first year in office. But the people see that he's doing exactly what he promised to do — waging war against illegal drugs that was a scourge kept hidden under the rug especially by his predecessor, fighting corruption, building infrastructure, and leading the country away from its vassalage to America.

This isn't in most leadership-lessons lists. Britain's Churchill led his people in war by his eloquence while the communist supremo Jose Ma. Sison led revolutionaries totally by slogans. As early as ancient Greece, its philosopher Plato saw politicians as essentially demagogues. Duterte is in a class all his own.

3. Focus on one crusade at a time, but let your subordinates pursue their advocacies.

Duterte's current indisputable "branding" is as the President who will end once and for all the plague of illegal drugs, though the heavens may fall as it were, i.e., even if Western media and global institutions condemn him for allegedly trampling on human rights.

That has been his focus, with the war on illegal drugs halfway won, "on a scale of one to 10, we're at six now," he says. That he will demolish the illegal drug industry has been the single message the masses clearly hear, and they're happy with it.

But in the meantime, his other Cabinet secretaries are doing what they are supposed to do: Finance Secretary Carlos Dominguez is undertaking a difficult tax reform program; Speaker Pantaleon Alvarez has made the House of Representatives a smooth-running factory of needed laws and an investigator of the powerful's crimes; Public Works Secretary Mark Villar is implementing the "Build, Build, Build" infrastructure program; Environment and Natural Resources Secretary Roy Cimatu is cleaning up the cesspools created by greedy resort operators in once-pristine areas.

4. Defy and challenge the powers-that-be. The real power is people's support.

The default condition of most societies, which make up the obstacle for a country's growth, are its ruling elites that defend the status quo. Reforms would be a walk in the park, if there were no powers-that-be that block these.

Duterte has challenged not only the worst of the economic elites who have evaded taxes and refused to pay rent for prime government property they have held since Marcos' time. He has gone after the Philippine elite's weapons: the Catholic Church and the once most-powerful Yellow media tandem, the *Philippine Daily Inquirer* and ABS-CBN Network.

After all, the Catholic Church had functioned as a tool for dominant classes to rule. Just a few centuries after its emergence, Catholicism became the state religion of the most powerful empire at that time, the Roman Empire and after that, by the colony-seeking European states, which told the masses that the emperors and kings were God's representatives on earth.

The Spanish crown was able to rule their most distant colony the Philippine islands for four centuries not really through soldiers, but through the superstitious fears fostered by the friars among the *indios*.

That media tandem on the other hand openly declared they were weapons of the Yellow Cult. Since February 1986 they have been the vanguard not of the *masa*, but of the Philippine elite.

Duterte has also defied the United States, which has through its local lackeys, determined our foreign policy that supported its hegemony in the world.

Much of Duterte's popularity is because Filipinos sense that he is rebelling against the ruling elites that have controlled this nation since its birth.

I'm not sure though that he sees and intends to curb the shameful yet hidden dominance of a foreign magnate, the Indonesian tycoon Anthoni Salim over our public utilities, infrastructure, and even media — industries supposedly reserved to Filipinos yet through which the foreign magnate and American investors have been getting billions of dollars in profits, swiftly moved out of the country, instead of being reinvested here.

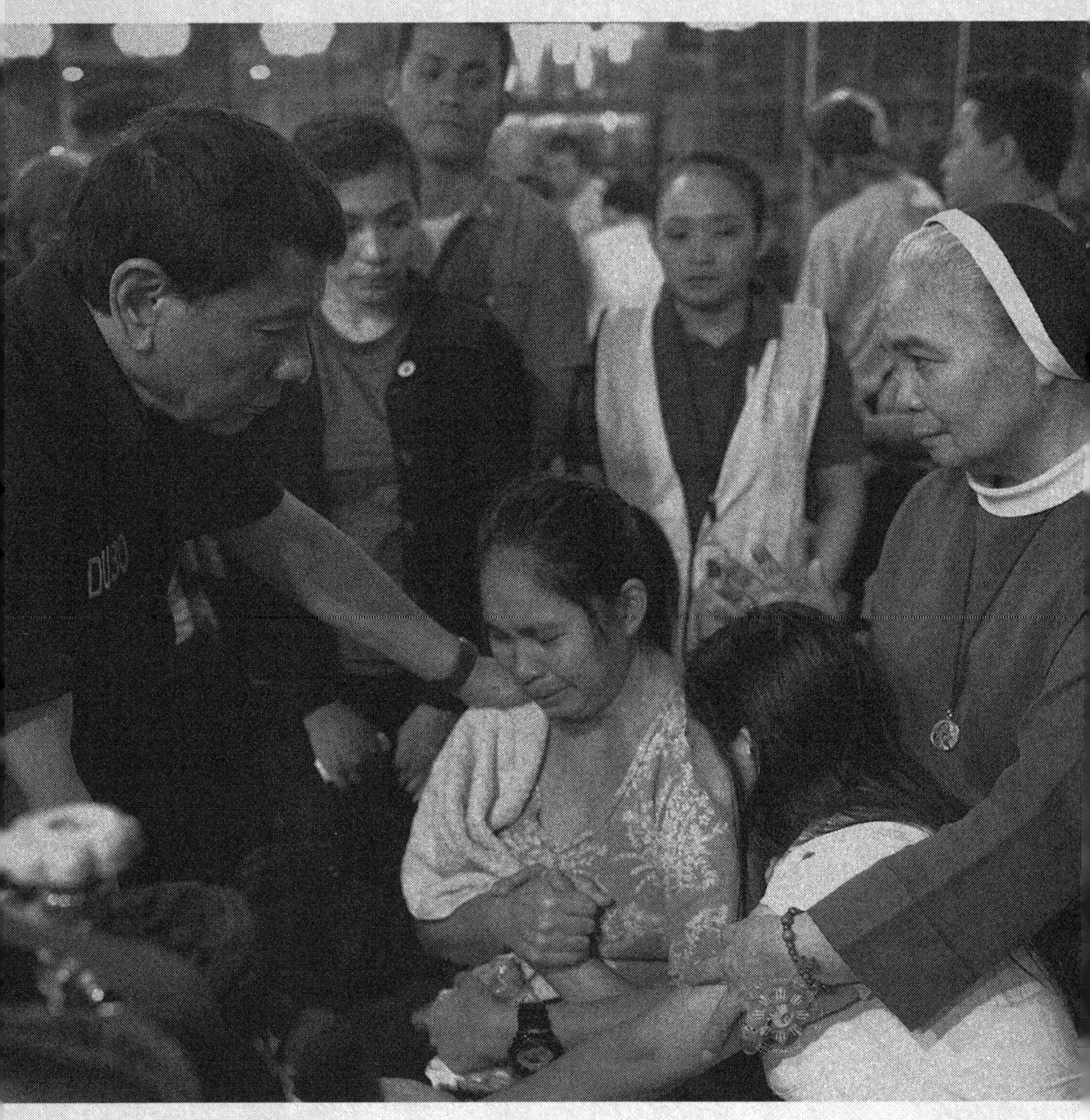

Duterte emphatizes witih victims of a fire.

5. Lastly, have a strong sense of empathy, and express it.

What all our past presidents have had, or pretended to have, was sympathy, which the dictionary defines as "feelings of pity and sorrow for someone else's misfortune." Empathy is not sympathy: it is the "ability to understand and share the feelings of another."

Empathy is what Duterte expresses as he embraces the widow of a marine killed in action, or shakes the hand of a wounded in a military hospital, often with misty eyes. An example of pretentious sympathy is Aquino III in a wake, where the camera even catches him guffawing at something that suddenly crossed his mind.

Human beings, psychologists say, have an innate capacity to sense empathy. After all, evolutionary scientists claim that this was a virtue for a tribe's survival. Its members' failure to sense strangers' deceit would have meant their extermination.

Or perhaps nations are still merely bigger versions of a family, and Filipinos especially do not see their Presidents as merely chief executive officers or managers of the nation. In their hearts, they yearn for a leader who reminds them of their father or mother, who will guide them even as he understands their concerns.

According to some neuropsychologists, there is a physical basis for some persons who lack empathy: they don't have the so-called mirror neurons, which have been found to be deficient in some individuals diagnosed as autistic.

My colleague Francisco Tatad in one column had described former president Aquino III when he was interviewed by CNN a few days after supertyphoon Yolanda struck: "Aquino looked completely detached, uninvolved, unfeeling, unaffected by the incredible human tragedy that has covered the world with grief and pain."

That describes exactly the absence of empathy. So if you detect in yourself such weakness in empathy — which seem to be the character of all Yellow leaders — spare the nation and yourself from suffering. Don't run for President. Be content being a senator, a congressman, or a Cabinet official.

(March 26, 2018)

DUTERTE'S ANTI-CHURCH STANCE: IT'S ABOUT TIME

IT'S ABOUT TIME that somebody of national stature had the balls to criticize the Catholic Church, as President-elect Rodrigo Duterte has done.

While the Church has failed to instill its prime teaching about the value of human life among its members, it has been extremely successful in serving the Philippine oligarchy since the Spanish era, allowing them to sleep soundly at night with the thought that with their huge donations and display of obeisance to the Church, they have VIP entrance passes to the Kingdom of Heaven in the next life.

Indeed, the Church for most Filipinos is really the Deity's embassy in this land, where the masses apply for visas to the Kingdom of Heaven.

The Catholic Church's history has been in service of conquerors. *Las Islas de las Filipinas* had not been as attractive as Mexico, Peru, and other Latin American countries for the Spanish crown to send troops to, and expend its dwindling funds.

The colony had become notorious for its typhoons, as a 17th century priest described it: "These occur very often and we suffer so much, that even after experiencing them, it is difficult to believe these can happen." And the most important disincentive for a full-blown Spanish colonization, gold — the main reason why the conquistadores and adventurers invaded Latin America — could not be found here.

There wasn't even the weakest rumor of an El Dorado, the City of Gold, and agricultural exploitation through the *encomienda* system wasn't too profitable (before the advent of the sugar industry). The Spanish Crown naturally found it difficult to justify the deployment of troops in this god-forsaken colony, and only the most adventurous (or desperate) such as the Basques dared to travel to this furthest outpost of the Empire.

Less than 2,000 troops

One estimate is that at the height of the Spanish rule in the mid-18th century, there were fewer than 5,000 Spaniards (half of whom were clergy) all over the archipelago and less than 2,000 troops were concentrated in Manila. Such a small military presence here was the reason why Spain couldn't really wage war to conquer the Muslims in the South, and why Filipino revolutionaries could have easily defeated them if the US had not intervened.

So how did Spain manage to control the *indio* population with such small military presence? First was through the co-optation of the ruling elites, who were given the nice title of *gobernadorcillos*.

And second, Spanish rule was so easily imposed because the Catholic Church and its missionaries managed to convert the *indios* with their unsophisticated tribal, mostly animistic religions into Christianity, and to convince them their obeisance to the Spanish Crown was a requirement of the faith.

Why were the *indios* so easily converted? As was the case all over the world where the West colonized the native population, they thought the Spaniards' superior technology, with their armor and muskets, as well as the unbelievable huge galleons that arrived in Manila, was an indication of Christianity's superiority. Or perhaps, the friars' promise of a wonderful, magical place that awaited them when they die was more attractive than the *indios'* vague notions of an afterlife in their animistic tribal religions.

It was also during this time that the various Catholic orders were competing among each other to proselytize in the Philippines, to convert enough *indios* or forcibly recruit them to join them in proselytizing people in what was then known to be the largest pagan nation that needed to be brought to Christ: China.

What stood as a very fitting symbol for what the Church really was in that period were the Spanish-era churches. Visit one church and you'd wonder: Why are they so massive, and built like fortresses?

One reason they were made that way was to convince the church-going natives who lived in nipa huts that such gargantuan structures were inhabited by divine beings, i.e., Jesus Christ, (the Goddess) Virgin Mary, and the other lesser gods, the saints.

Churches as fortresses

The other reason is that those churches were, in fact, built as fortresses or the "keep", which refers to the strongest part of a castle that acts as a final refuge. Such Hispanic churches' doors were huge and nearly impregnable; the windows were placed so high up on the walls, like in those in European medieval castles.

They were essentially military installations run by the clergy and the Spanish guardia civil. The faithful would escape to take shelter in them in the early periods of Spanish colonization when Muslim pirates would occasionally raid the towns. It was also the keep for the Spaniards and their local lackeys to escape into, in cases of the *indios'* revolt.

One thing about these churches that hasn't been studied in detail: How were they built? Were the *indios* and their families forced to provide manual labor upon pain of death? The strength of these churches has also been due to the fact that egg whites were mixed with lime to create the strong mortar that has lasted for a century. How many natives were deprived of their protein requirements because the Spanish required them to surrender so many eggs?

Think about it. In the 18th and 19th centuries, when the exploitive hacendero and landlord, as well as political bossism systems were at their height in the entire archipelago, and when the oligarchs started to entrench themselves here, had the Catholic Church as an institution spoken against such exploitation? Has it ever been at the forefront of social reform movements?

The Church's power over the Filipino mind has been such that other than the University of the Philippines, its educational institutions such as the Ateneo de Manila, De La Salle University and the University of Santo Tomas, have been molding the minds of the elite for decades — teaching them the most sophisticated ways to justify their classes' exploitation of the peasants and working class. It is certainly not coincidental that the Ateneo has been one of biggest fans of the hacendero-cacique rule of Benigno Aquino III.

Of course, there were a few brave priests, such as Fr. Jose Decena, who in the early 1970s exposed the horrors of the sacada system in Negros sugar plantations. There were also those converted into the Latin American type of liberation theology who were easily recruited into the Communist Party, such as Duterte's adviser Jun Evasco and the NDF's chief negotiator, Luis Jalandoni.

But on the whole, the Catholic hierarchy, together with parish priests and the elites, made up a single ruling class as they did in medieval Europe. The Church helped justify and even conceal the landlord class's exploitation of the peasants, and kept them in tow with threats of fire and brimstone if they challenged the status quo. The landlord class, on the other hand, donated lands and gold to the Church, and provided it with its armed protection.

In our history, there has only been one major critique of the Church that electrified the nation: that by Rizal through his novels **Noli Me Tangere** and **El Filibusterismo.** Since then, there has neither been a writer nor a leader who ever dared to cross the Church as defiantly as Rizal did. If Duterte's tirades against the Church are authentic, I'm certainly all for him in that struggle.

(May 27, 2016)

OOPS, HIS CRITICS ARE PORTRAYING HIM AS THE NEW RIZAL

THE CLERICS AND would-be champions of the Catholic Church who are having fits of apoplexy, over President Duterte's remarks about the Judeo-Christian deity in the Book of Genesis, better control themselves.

In their harangue against Duterte for insulting their God, they are putting this President on the same level as our national hero, Jose Rizal. Duterte's critics wouldn't want that, would they?

After all, Rizal and now Duterte are the only Filipinos of national stature who did not mince words in attacking the Catholic Church, with our national hero in fact making a name for himself through his compelling and vivid novels against it, which inspired the Philippine Revolution against Spain.

Consider the column in this newspaper the other day ("Will excommunication and exorcism help?) of Duterte's Torquemada*, Francisco Tatad. In that kilometric piece with details nobody cares about, Tatad, because of Duterte's blasphemy, "urges the appropriate ecclesiastical authorities… to study deeply and promptly and firmly act" on whether the President of the Republic should be excommunicated or — hold on to your rosaries — be exorcised.

What other well-known Filipino was threatened with excommunication? Jose Rizal, for his first novel **Noli Me Tangere.** Rizal himself disclosed this in his June 8, 1988 letter to one Protestant Pastor Karl Ullmer, who had become his friend during his stay in Heidelberg: "I have left my country on account of my book. The Filipino public welcomed **Noli Me Tangere** very heartily; the edition is entirely exhausted. The Governor General summoned me and asked me for a copy of it. The friars were most excited. They wanted to persecute me, but they did not know how to get me. The Archbishop threatened to excommunicate me."

Indeed, why wouldn't the Catholic Church in the Philippines at the height of its power during the Spanish colonial period not want — as it succeeded in doing — Rizal not just to be excommunicated, but executed for writing two best-selling novels that not only exposed the abuses of its friars but also questioned Catholic dogma? After all, the Spanish Church had a tradition of executing thousands of "heretics," by burning them at the stake after torture, condemned by its infamous Grand Inquisition organized by the Dominican cleric Tomás de Torquemada.

Nobody remembers the name of any Spanish military-man character in the Noli. Most Filipinos remember Padre Damaso the very hateful villain of Noli who fathered Maria Clara after raping her mother. Did the friars so hate Rizal because he was the first to put in words what probably was so well known during that period, that the friars were sex fiends?

Considering the total hold of the Church at that time on Filipinos' minds, Duterte's remarks about the Church and the God of the Genesis myth compared to Rizal's novels are just harmless, friendly teasing during a round of drinks.

If Rizal were reincarnated in our time and place, he would have thrown not *p***ng inas*, but *hijo de p***s* and cabrones not just against the Catholic Church but the new religious swindlers calling themselves evangelists — or brazenly in the case of Apollo Quiboloy as the Anointed Son of God. He would be furious that more than a century after the Church got him killed, that same Church is still in control of most Filipinos' minds, and is the pillar of an oligarchy-ruled society.

Rizal's **Noli Me Tangere** and **El Filibusterismo** were very persuasive tracts against the Church. They were made more powerful and popular because they were in the form of unputdownable novels.

Don't take it from me, but from the de facto head of the Catholic Church in the Philippines then, Cardinal Rufino Santos who issued in 1956 a **Statement of the Philippine Catholic Hierarchy on the Novels of Dr. Jose Rizal,** published in all broadsheets, that urged Congress not to pass a bill that required Rizal's novels to be read in college. (The bill was passed as Republic Act 1425 or the Rizal Law.)

Just a small part of Santos' lengthy letter reads:

"In these two novels we find passages against Catholic dogma and morals where repeated attacks are made against the Catholic religion in general, against the possibility of miracles, against the doctrine of Purgatory, against the Sacrament of Baptism, against Confession, Communion, Holy Mass, against the doctrine of Indulgences, Church prayers, the Catechism of Christian Doctrine, sermons, sacramentals and books of piety. There are even passages casting doubts on or covering with confusion God's omnipotence, the existence of hell, the mystery of the Most Blessed Trinity, and the two natures of Christ.

"Similarly, we find passages which disparage divine worship, especially the veneration of images and relics, devotion to the Blessed Virgin and the Saints, the use of scapulars, cords and habits, the praying of rosaries, novenas, ejaculations and indulgenced prayers. Even vocal prayers are included, such as the Our Father, the Hail Mary, the Doxology, the Act of Contrition, and the Angelus, Mass ceremonies, baptismal and exequial rites, worship of the Cross, the use of holy water and candles, processions, bells and even the Sacred Sunday obligations do not escape scorn."

How many Catholic beliefs did Duterte lambast? Just two by my count, the doctrine of original sin and the story that it was Eve who got Adam to eat the forbidden fruit.

The Spanish colonial government in fact cared little for Rizal's novels. It was the Catholic Church in the Philippines, through the most militant clerical order of that period, the Dominicans, who asked for Rizal's head.

They submitted a report to the governor-general on August 30, 1887 declaring: "The work **Noli Me Tangere** has been found heretical, impious and scandalous from the religious perspective, anti-patriotic and subversive from the political point of view, injurious to the Spanish government and its proceedings in the islands."

The Dominican pressure on the governor-general eventually led to Rizal's execution by firing squad, on the trumped-up (and false) charges of his involvement in the secret revolutionary group, the Katipunan. (Have these clerics ever apologised for framing and having executed our national hero?)

Duterte is so very lucky he didn't live during Rizal's time, or that Tatad isn't a high official in a dictatorship, or he'd be facing a firing squad by now.

Isn't it ironic — or a case of poetic justice — that a nation still mesmerized by medieval Catholicism has for its national hero one who vehemently criticized that religion?

As Rizal's novels inspired a nationalist Revolution, I hope Duterte's words inspire a similar, but perhaps a subtle but more earth-shaking revolution: against the oligarchy that the Church has primarily served.

(June 30, 2018)

* Tomás de Torquemada was a Spanish priest who was appointed as Grand Inquisitor by King Ferdinand and Queen Isabel in 1483 during the Spanish Inquisition. He became notorious for his cruelty, and under his leadership of the Inquisition thousands of alleged heretics were burned alive, tortured, or mutilated.

DUTERTE SHOWS POLITICAL WILL IN TAKING ON BORACAY'S ELITE

BORACAY'S ELITE lording it over the island shouldn't take lightly President Duterte's threat to close it down if they don't reverse the degradation of the island into a cesspool.

It is the state which has ownership of this once paradisiacal island. It therefore may decide just to take over the whole island.

Boracay is a classic case of a weak Philippine state losing control of land it is the supreme sovereign of, and allowing it to be ravaged by uncaring local and foreign capitalists.

Although scandalously ignored to this day, the 15-member Supreme Court under then Chief Justice Renato Puno unanimously ruled in October 2008 (G.R. No. 167707) that there is no legal basis for private individuals to claim ownership of any property in the island. (To his credit, even Justice Antonio Tirol Carpio, a member of the Tirol clan that is the biggest single landowner in the island concurred with the decision written by Associate Justice Ruben Reyes.)

There hasn't even been a move to ask the court to reconsider its decision. Many of the big resort owners who thought they owned their lands — like Orlando Sacay who was one of those who filed the Court case — have left the island after the decision, or have moved to what they think is the next paradise beach, Coron in Palawan.

"The island is State property," the high court ruled. It explained that for a land to be "alienable," or subject to private ownership, the state must declare it as such.

In the case of Boracay, the court pointed out, "no such proclamation, executive order, administrative action, report, statute, or certification was presented to the Supreme Court. The records are bereft of evidence showing that, prior to 2006, the portions of Boracay occupied by private claimants were subject of a government proclamation that the land is alienable and disposable."

The court was not unaware of the implications of its decision, and noted: "The Court is aware that millions of pesos have been invested for the development of Boracay Island, making it a byword in the local and international tourism industry. The Court also notes that for a number of years, thousands of people have called the island their home."

Law should prevail

However, it declared: "While the Court commiserates with private claimants' plight, we are bound to apply the law strictly and judiciously. This is the law and it should prevail. *Ito ang batas at ito ang dapat umiral.*" ("This is the law and this should be followed.")

The Court did note though that claimants "may look into other modes of applying for original registration of title, such as by homestead or sales patent, subject to the conditions imposed by law." However, not a single Boracay "claimant" — the term the Court used to refer to people who claim to be landowners in Boracay — has attempted to apply for such modes of ownership.

The Supreme Court also noted that "more realistically, Congress may enact a law to entitle private claimants to acquire title to their occupied lots or to exempt them from certain requirements under the present land laws."

There has been no such law passed in Congress, although bills were filed for such purposes in each Congress since 2008.

I don't think Boracay's land claimants should hope that Congress will pass such a bill during Duterte's presidency.

The latest such bill on Boracay's land titling was filed only last month by Magdalo party-list Representative Gary Alejano, a vicious critic of the Duterte administration who had filed together with his boss Senator Antonio Trillanes IV, a crime-against-humanity suit against this president and his other officials at the International Criminal Court. I don't have any information why on earth Alejano filed this bill, whether it is another financial project or whether he is an "Aklanon."

It is astonishing how private individuals got to claim to be landowners of Boracay, and how businessmen, which include foreigners, have set up establishments there that have through the years ruined the island, many of which have even dumped their human waste straight to the sea.

There have been rumors that a member of one of the biggest "land claimants" in the late 1980s had managed to control the Aklan Registrar of Deeds, which explains the clan's huge holdings.

President Marcos in 1978 through Proclamation 1801 had declared it— as well as two dozen other areas — as tourist zones and marine reserves under the administration of the Philippine Tourism Authority. Marcos' proclamation precluded the titling of lands in Boracay, although his buddy Fred Elizalde (a media magnate who owns DZRH) as well as about a dozen families that include that of Justice Carpio's got to own vast lands in the island.

The Marcos proclamation had a very categorical statement: "No development projects or construction for any purposes shall be introduced within the zones without prior approval of the President of the Philippines upon recommendation of the Philippine Tourism Authority."

Do you think such humongous projects on a small, environmentally-fragile island such as Fil-Estate's Fairways and Bluewater golf course set up during Fidel Ramos' term, Shangri-la Hotel and Discovery Suites during Aquino's, and the Elizaldes' D'Mall and D'Talipapa were approved by presidents at that time?

Such is the power of our elites to ignore a presidential proclamation and a Supreme Court decision.

Unclassified land

The Republic through various administrations took the official stance that Boracay was an unclassified land, and therefore its lands cannot be put under private ownership unless a President first "alienates" such lands from the public domain. This view was upheld in the Supreme Court decision.

As a result, most of the Boracay land-claimants' "proof of ownership" had been through their tax declarations — receipts that they paid the property taxes — in the hope that in the future these would prove their right to have titles.

President Gloria Macapagal-Arroyo took a major step in allowing land-claimants in the island to secure legal titles and at the same time to protect the island from further degradation. She issued in 2006 Proclamation 1064 that classified 40 percent of Boracay's 1,028 hectares as "reserved forest land" (which cannot be privately owned) and 60 percent as "agricultural land," which can be titled. The proclamation provided detailed geographic coordinates of the forest and agricultural lands.

The 60-40 distribution makes me suspect that Arroyo simply wanted to ensure that at least 40 percent of the island will be protected forestland, regardless of whether such areas were or are still forests.

I am quite sure, having visited the areas in the 1980s, that the locations of Fairways and Bluewater golf course and Shangri-la were thick forests.

It was in fact after Fairways was constructed that a breath-taking, unusual sight every sunset in Boracay vanished — the flight of thousands of bats away from the island forests towards their nocturnal haunts in the mainland. There were so many of them then they looked like thick black clouds. The loss of the bats signaled the start of Boracay's environmental degradation.

Arroyo's proclamation had a political blowback. It hardened the Western Visayas elite, where most of the land claimants are from, as a Yellow bastion, led by Mar Roxas.

But practically nothing was done to implement the proclamation. Because Aklan was Yellow territory, Aquino when he assumed power in 2010 allegedly gave the order to his environment and natural resources department, the entity in charge of implementing Arroyo's proclamation, to forget it was ever signed.

As result, 12 years after Arroyo's Proclamation was issued, the DENR hasn't even undertaken a cadastral survey to determine which of the Boracay lands are part of the reserve forest lands and which ones are agricultural, based on the coordinates it provided.

Solving the Boracay quagmire will be extremely difficult, as it has been left untouched for decades, putting it at the mercy of unrestrained capitalism.

Duterte would face enormous political pressure to just do what his predecessor Aquino did, which was to do nothing. But if the President will address the issue, and boldly uphold the Supreme Court decision, his success will be a precedent in preserving our national treasures that succeeding generations of Filipinos have a right to.

Isn't it so shameful that an island so well known in the world for its beauty that we have been so proud of it, is controlled and run by people, both local and foreign, who ignore our nation's rule of law?

Isn't it so scandalous that they are defying the Supreme Court' s unanimous decision, and the High Court doesn't even seem to mind?

(February 21, 2018)

POSTSCRIPT:

On April 4, Duterte announced the closure of Boracay to tourism for six months starting April 26. He ordered the department of the environment and natural resources to first enforce strictly environmental regulations, and close establishments that have violated these or any other municipal or national laws. He also ordered the department to finish the island's cadastral survey to determine the legal status of plots claimed to be privately owned.

HOW THE YELLOWS DEMONIZE DUTERTE ON THE WORLD STAGE

COMMISSION ON HUMAN RIGHTS chair Jose Luis "Chito" Gascon, who was the Liberal Party's director-general, is one of our highest-paid state government officials. We taxpayers give him P3 million a year, which puts him among the one-half of one percent of Filipinos, including those in the private sector, making at least that much.

Yet he shamelessly paints the blackest picture of the country and of President Duterte, spewing brazen lies in international forums to portray the country as one in which "tens of thousands of Filipinos are being murdered by our government," and that those opposing the president are persecuted.

I nearly fell off my seat when in a speech at the so-called Oslo Freedom Forum in New York (run by the Human Rights Watch based there), he claimed that the Duterte administration had forced Ombudsman Conchita Carpio Morales to resign. (The speech was melodramatically titled "Death and the Democratic Deficit in Duterte's Drug War," so cheaply using alliteration in the hope that it sticks in his audience's mind.)

Morales forced to resign? What?

Morales was still in office when Gascon made his speech on May 29. If he doesn't believe me he could call her up now to check if she's still there. She in fact, for some reason, has recently been in a frenzy of activity, ordering charges to be filed against officials of the past regime for corruption — including President Benigno Aquino, but on a very minor charge.

I cannot believe Gascon doesn't know that Morales is stepping down on July 26 because her seven-year term, mandated by the Constitution, ends on that date.

Duterte's communications people should be put on high alert. If the Supreme Court as Presidential Electoral Tribunal rules, as I am convinced they would, that Vice President Leni Robredo cheated her way to the post and should be ousted, Gascon will shriek to the world that Duterte removed her from the nation's second most powerful post.

Devious tack

Gascon put out that shameless canard about Morales as part of his devious tack to portray Duterte as not just your ordinary authoritarian but a cowardly misogynist picking on "strong independent women who oppose him."

Gascon also twisted the case of Aquino's justice secretary and now senator Leila de Lima, who he claims was "arrested and put in jail," as if armed men one night just barged into her home and took her to a military camp.

Of course, Gascon omitted the crucial facts: that De Lima has been charged for colluding with drug lords, allowing them to use the national prison as their command center, and receiving hundreds of millions of pesos in bribe money.

Not just one but three charges were filed by various entities, including the private-sector Volunteers Against Crime and Corruption, in three branches of the Regional Trial Court of Muntinlupa (where the penitentiary is). The court ordered her arrest and detention. Of course, Gascon didn't mention the fact that the highest court of the land, the Supreme Court, ruled en banc that de Lima's arrest and detention was legal.

Third in Gascon's list of women allegedly persecuted by Duterte is Lourdes Sereno, who he claimed the "authoritarian removed from office." Of course Gascon failed to mention that it was her colleagues in the Supreme Court who decided that Sereno was a fake chief justice, since she failed to meet the minimum requirements for the post — including that for psychological health — and must be removed in accordance with the law.

Last in Gascon's list of "women persecuted by Gascon" is Maria Ressa, editor of the online news outfit Rappler who he claims was "de-registered and facing tax evasion." Of course Gascon didn't mention that it was the firm that set up Rappler, of which Ressa is just one of the minority shareholders, which was "de-registered" by the Securities and Exchange Commission for violating the Constitution by taking in foreign funds.

Moreover, despite Gascon's claim that we have an authoritarian regime, Rappler is still operating, having appealed its case to the Court of Appeals. Rappler earned about P150 million in the sale of its shares to American entities. Is Gascon saying the Bureau of Internal Revenue shouldn't investigate that for tax evasion?

Gascon's lies about these so-called "persecuted women" are just for starters. He also claimed in his speech that the International Criminal Court has started an investigation "into the tens of thousands of people that have been murdered by our government in its war against drugs."

Tens of thousands of Filipinos? I have in several columns indisputably refuted grave exaggerations on casualties in the war against drugs started by Rappler, and disseminated by other anti-Duterte groups. The figure reported by an auditing group of the Philippine National Police is that 4,000 were killed by police in operations against "drug personalities" because they fought back, since Duterte started his campaign up to June this year.

The PNP report indeed pointed out that there was an additional 2,734 homicides that it is investigating as drug-related, but to conclude that this was perpetrated by the police and not by drug pushers and drug lords themselves is so grossly unfair.

Gascon claimed that the "ICC is investigating the killings" to give credence to his allegation of "tens of thousands of Filipinos murdered."

But this again is another lie. The ICC's Chief Prosecutor Fatou Bensouda merely initiated a "preliminary examination" — a routine chore it does whenever it receives a complaint. As explained by former Chief Justice Artemio Panganiban, who had been very supportive of the Yellow Regime, Bensouda (probably in two years) will have to get the approval of a higher body called the Pre-Trial Chamber to undertake the kind of investigation Gascon is claiming.

What is so despicable about Gascon's presentation is that he so cheaply appeals to the emotions of his gullible foreign audience. For instance, he uses as his background an enormous video projection of the artsy photo of pedicab driver Michael Siaron's dead body cradled in the arms of his partner in a Pietà-like pose. The *Philippine Daily Inquirer* (PDI) photo published in July 2016 became a viral poster by anti-Duterte groups to portray the president as a merciless killer.

However, after more than a year of police investigation it was conclusively proven in October 2017 that Siaron wasn't killed by police or anti-drug vigilantes but by drug-ring criminals, with the gunman Nesty Santiago identified without a shadow of a doubt.

Neither the *Inquirer* nor any other anti-Duterte group, not even the Commission on Human Rights, contested that police conclusion. The PDI claimed that it never really alleged that he was killed by the police.

It is impossible for Gascon not to have known about this as he mobilized a lot of his staff to investigate the case. Yet sickeningly, he presents this photo to tug at his Western audience's hearts so they'd believe that Duterte is a ruthless killer.

CHR: Demolition crew

Gascon as a citizen is of course entitled to his own opinions, even if these are intended to damage Duterte's legitimacy. This is in line with the Yellows and Liberal Party's hope that at best, the president would be forced out of office (as they tried unsuccessfully to do in the case of President Gloria Arroyo) or at worse, be so unpopular that the opposition would win the next presidential elections (as what happened when Arroyo's candidate lost in 2010).

But Gascon heads a government body, the Commission on Human Rights, designed by the Constitution to be independent from politics so it could be a credible and effective check against the state's abuses. The CHR has turned out to be another of the many institutions Aquino had damaged, turning it into a demolition crew against Duterte.

Aquino appointed Gascon, as well as its four other members who each get government salaries of P2.5 million, in June 2015, and who therefore will step down only in 2022. Other than Gascon, two of them are die-hard Yellow cadres: Roberto Cadiz, who was a private prosecutor (persecutor?) in the trial of Chief Justice Renato Corona, whom Aquino moved heaven and earth to boot out, and Leah Armamento, a former justice undersecretary who was de Lima's right-hand woman.

This country can't have another four years with Gascon using taxpayers' money to malign this nation.

If he is convinced that Duterte has committed human rights abuses, he should focus on the work of investigating these and filing charges in court, against at least the actual perpetrators so he would be in effect disarming him from undertaking further alleged crimes.

Gascon can't use his government post and our money for the Yellow strategy that worked in the case of Marcos, which is to get the US to help topple Duterte by painting him as an authoritarian and a human-rights abuser. He should be ashamed to use taxpayers' money to advance the Yellows' agenda.

Gascon should be impeached for betrayal of the public trust and the high crime of spreading lies against the country. There is a special place in hell for such a hypocrite and a liar who very falsely portrays us as a nation of cowards refusing to oppose an abusive dictatorship, with only him and his Yellow Cultists as the brave heroes doing so.

(July 13, 2018)

DOWNSIDE OF 'GLOBALIZATION': BRAIN AND BRAWN DRAIN

I WAS PLEASANTLY SURPRISED when President Duterte, for most of his working life a city mayor in Mindanao demonstrated a grasp of such a complex issue — globalization.

At the Asia Pacific Economic Cooperation (APEC) CEO Summit in Vietnam last week, after his speech, a British journalist at the press conference asked him about his views on the "rise in anti-globalization feelings in some countries."

That journalist obviously wasn't too familiar with the Philippines. Here, globalization, or the dismantling of nations' borders to allow untrammeled flow of capital, commodities, and even people, is strongly believed in and embraced almost on the same level as Catholicism.

Not a few millennials even think that it is chic to declare that they are only secondarily Filipinos, and mainly "global citizens" — an oxymoron as citizenship implies a single nation-state. Even the concept of a Filipina beauty (with the trend of having winners who are daughters of a Filipina mother and a Caucasian father) has been "globalized," so have our basketball and volleyball teams with their top players being foreign imports.

The dogmatic belief in globalization is due to several factors, among them: our colonial history, especially the American occupation during which we were brainwashed to believe that we were Asia's "brown Americans"; the fact that the education of our elites have been in the US, where the ideology of globalization — also called the Washington Consensus — was imbued on them; and the massive migration, permanent or temporary, of lower-middle-class to upper-class Filipinos to the US and elsewhere.

Duterte seemed to have either studied the issue or saw its actual impact on ordinary people and was bold enough to tell the APEC CEO Summit of the downsides of globalization.

Damaged economies

Duterte started his reply: "Globalization, to a certain extent has really damaged poor economies. Globalization by itself is the deprivation of some, those who have been called 'left behind.' There has be to some remedial measures."

Duterte zeroed in on one clear, very negative impact of globalization, for decades known in our country as the phenomenon of "brain drain."

Duterte explained: "The best of our young minds, Filipinos — the summa cum laudes, the valedictorians — upon graduation, they go somewhere else, most of them to America. So, they are there, they are in Silicon Valley or New York and they tend to gather in places where there is already an economy that is thriving, and leaving behind a country getting bereft of talent."

We have been underestimating the effect of our country's brain drain, as globalization has accelerated not just the free flow of capital and goods, but of our educated elite. It is a myth that it has been our poor who have mostly migrated abroad. It is rather the lower middle class to the upper class, including even the crème de la crème. Half of my Ateneo batch in high school and college have migrated to the US and Canada.

I was shocked a few years ago that even an old colleague of mine who had been one of our top investigative journalists abandoned her country to live a New Yorker's life — teaching Americans journalism in a top-notch (and expensive) university. And she was relatively well-off, one whom I had thought was imbued with the nationalism of the 1970s and 1980s, now all but vanishing.

Her case would be like a tuberculosis doctor educated in state-subsidized University of the Philippines and trained at the Philippine General Hospital who, after becoming a very skilled doctor, migrates to New York to practice cosmetic surgery there.

How better would the state of journalism in our country have been — and therefore of our democracy — if she chose to remain in her country? Now she's totally been brainwashed in US neoliberal ideology that she writes biased articles in US publications on the Duterte administration, in one case even using wrong data, as many other journalists who have moved to the US have done.

Human capital

The economic history of the world has one major lesson: Human capital (people's talents, intelligence, and skills) is one of the biggest factors for growth. A very backward territory like Australia and New

Zealand swiftly became developed nations in a few decades essentially because of the migration there of the British, who of course brought with them centuries of civilization that allow the blossoming of a human's talents and skills. The same phenomenon with tiny Israel, which is even a nuclear power, in that case migration of mainly European Jews.

A rigorous economic study in Taiwan using actual industrial data concluded that "human capital accounts for 46 percent of output growth in the manufacturing industry." A more recent study in Spain had similar results, emphasizing that economic growth is best accelerated by people with higher education.

Japan and Korea in the 1950s and 1960s and China in the 1980s sent hundreds of their youth to the US and Europe for studies in engineering, mathematics, and business — most of whom returned to help in the economic growth of their countries. How many Filipinos go to the US to study and never come back, and instead move to global economic centers? How many UP-educated doctors have left the country, many reportedly even agreeing to be nurses instead so they could more easily get jobs?

Duterte even pointed out that our problem isn't only "brain drain" but what has been called "brawn drain."

"The Philippines is having a boom in real estate but developers are having difficulties finding the workers and that leaves us behind in terms of how long it would take to complete a project," he said. "They have to scrape the bottom to find who can work to build houses. These are the effects of globalization."

Brain- and brawn-drain has certainly become a problem that has been colossally underestimated, and I hope Duterte walks the talk on this. Businesses, whether foreign or Filipino, would see no use for massive infrastructure if they are unable to find the skilled workers and intelligent staff to man their companies.

The need to replace millions of educated and skilled Filipinos who have migrated abroad, facilitated by globalization, has become more urgent, even as our educational system has deteriorated. The irony, if you can call it that, as I found out during my ambassadorial stint in Greece, is that a significant number of our domestic workers abroad were school teachers.

(November 17, 2017)

WHAT EXPLAINS HIS POPULARITY: BRAVERY

HUMANITY FOR MOST of its 250,000 years as a species lived in tribes or collections of tribes, in constant struggle against other tribes, or predators. We haven't really changed. We still choose and admire leaders who demonstrate that particular quality: bravery. After all, we want a leader who'd fight for us, don't we?

It is not really wisdom we most seek of leaders, but bravery. The wise King Solomon is overshadowed by far by his father King David who was so audacious to take on Goliath, while the Arthurian legends relegated wisdom merely as the function of an adviser, Merlin.

Churchhill's "blood, toil, tears and sweat" defiance of the Nazis, Mao's legendary Long March to escape the encircling Kuomintang forces, Ho Chi Minh's inconceivable fight against two superpowers, are few examples of audacious leaders. In our case, it is difficult for us now to appreciate the boldness of Bonifacio and Aguinaldo in defying not only the superpower of that age, Spain, but also its representative here in the country the Catholic Church.

Ramon Magsaysay was our most popular President not because he was the "man of the masses" which was a slogan his American PR handlers concocted; he was admired by Filipinos as the fearless Huk fighter.

Marcos certainly didn't project himself as from the masses. He had popular support in the early years of his rule, because of his audacity in imposing martial law to defeat the "forces of the Right and the Left". We even admired the landlord-class Corazon Aquino, the housewife, for her grit in going against a dictator, and assuming the presidency.

Duterte obviously isn't in the same league as such leaders — so far. But in just a year in office he has demonstrated the audacity we admire of these leaders.

This explains much of his tremendous popularity and political support. His 78 percent "satisfaction" (net +66), according to the Social Weather Station survey, is the highest since Aquino, for a President in his or her first year of office. PulseAsia's "approval" rating was higher, at 84 percent.

I suspect Duterte's support is higher. The voting to extend martial law in Mindanao to the end of the year, as Duterte asked for, reflects

ARMY

his huge political support. While the extension of martial law is a very debatable issue really, 94 percent of the 259 members of the House of Representatives voted for it, not really because they believed it would be good for the country, but because they trusted Duterte who told them it would be good for the country. Only 14 were against it, members of the party-list parties that are fronts of the Communist Party. Talk of fringe groups.

I would bet that if there is a survey on what quality Filipinos most admire of Duterte, what would overwhelmingly emerge isn't "incorruptibility", "wisdom in governance," or even "sympathy for the masses." It would be "matapang," brave. His sigil, the fighting fist, is so appropriate to Duterte's image among the masses.

While the hoity-toity elites and the Yellow Cult were aghast at Duterte's curses against the US, the Catholic Church, the oligarchs, and the drug lords, the Filipino masses interpreted this more as challenging these entities to a fight, as curses usually are used when uttered in the streets.

Indeed, there never has been a President to lock horns with the Catholic Church, one of the pillars of oligarchic rule in the country, even exposing to the masses what only a few have known: its nearly systemic sexual depredations against the youth under its care, and its vast wealth that remain untaxed to this day.

There has never been a President to challenge the mighty "we-set-the-nation's-agenda" *Philippine Daily Inquirer* and the ABS-CBN television network for their elite bias and for their having been the propaganda vehicle for the Yellow Cult since 1986.

There has never been a President to expose the power of oligarchs that has been very bad for the country, and to move — so far — at least against one such oligarch, the powerful magnate Antonio Floirendo. And to think that Floirendo was one of his biggest campaign financiers.

There has never been a President to go against the US, exposing its continuing hold on our foreign policy since our independence, and to even, in defiance, move the country closer to its rival superpower, China.

And of course, there has never been a President to wage an all-out war on the illegal drug industry, which his predecessors had ignored that our country was on the brink of being transformed into a narco-state. Duterte had such a tenacity in this war that he defied the Western media and NGOs' screams of human-rights violations. The West was shocked over such Duterte threats as feeding the fish in Manila Bay with the corpses of drug lords. Filipinos saw it as the bravest of words coming from a President.

Any other President would have buckled under the campaign of the *New York Times* and brown Americans in the US, to paint the country as one where the blood of innocents run through the streets every night.

The Marawi crisis, because it has lasted for more than a month now and has created so much destruction, would have drawn so much criticism under any other President, that he would have lost his political base. In Duterte's case, his PulseAsia approval rating even rose from 78 percent in March to 82 percent, while in the SWS satisfaction ratings, it rose from 75 percent to 78 percent.

Why? A major reason: Two weeks after the terrorists occupied Marawi, Duterte announced that he planned to go there to be "one with his troops."

Although he would get to Marawi only a month later — purportedly because the military found it too risky for the Commander in Chief as it would have required redeploying troops away from the front lines— it did send the message that this is a President unafraid to be with his troops in battle.

Duterte's announcement reminded Filipinos that his predecessor Aquino was gallivanting in Cotabato City pretending nothing was happening, while 44 of our elite SAF troops were massacred one by one in Mamasapano, Maguindanao, just a 30-minute helicopter ride away.

Bravery, of course, has its limits. For the sake of our country, Duterte needs, perhaps desperately, to find his Merlin or Merlins.

(July 24, 2017)

Strong Republic

ALL ASIAN TIGERS AND TIGER CUBS GREW UNDER STRONGMAN RULE

THE RECENT *Time* magazine article "Era of the Strongman" — which included President Duterte as among the strongmen who've risen in recent years, together with Russian President Putin — has a very questionable assumption underlying it: that strongmen are bad for countries and people. The reality though is more complex.

This bias of US media isn't surprising. Russia was ripe for the picking by the US and the West when the USSR was dissolved, and a weak (or drunken?) leader Boris Yeltsin was at its helm.

It was only when the strongman Putin emerged that his nation broke the West's encirclement of Russia (even literally as the US came to control many of the former Soviet republics).

Russia is now claiming its position as a superpower in a multi-polar world. Why, it could even have played a crucial role in electing the current US President, if the US media is to be believed.

What the *Time* article, nor most Filipino intellectuals, even its supposedly objective economists, do not say is this: All of the Asian "economic dragons," as well as the "tiger economies" grew to be industrialized nations under the authoritarian rule of strongmen.

The biggest, incontrovertible proof of this idea is of course modern China, ruled by "Paramount Leader" Deng Xiaoping for 11 years from 1978 to 1989.

Deng steered the country of over 1 billion and its Communist Party of 30 million at that time to embrace "socialism with Chinese characteristics." That was really a euphemism for capitalism guided and directed by the party in order to grow the economy fast and to benefit the masses.

China has really been from Deng's time to this day under strongman rule, with smooth transitions to power from Deng to the present leader President Xi Jinping. China two months ago even lifted term limits for its president, which potentially allows Xi to rule the way strongmen rule: without term limits.

Is strongman rule bad? China lifted out of extreme poverty (those living on $1.90 per day, roughly P96 per day) 800 million of its citizens from 1988 to 2013. Was getting 800 million souls out of the hell of poverty bad?

Generalissimo Chiang Kai-shek, and then his son Chiang Ching-kuo, ruled Taiwan with an iron fist from the day they fled to the island from China in 1947 after their Kuomintang forces were defeated by Mao Zedong's forces, to the time Taiwan embraced democracy in 1988.

Two strongmen ruled South Korea for nearly three decades, Syngman Rhee for 12 years until 1960, and Gen. Park Chung-Hee for 17 years (1962-1979).

Singapore's Lee Kuan Yew, whom so many Filipinos seem to idolize, ruled Singapore for 31 years. After a clever hiatus, during which Go Chok Tong was prime minister, Lee's son Hsien Long took the reins of government and has since been prime minister for 12 years now. Lee's People's Action Party, as in the 1950s, continues to control the press through Singapore Press Holdings.

What Lee's fans never note is that Singapore has been under so much dictatorship that its press has never been "free" to this day, with print, broadcast, and new media mostly run by state-owned firms like Singapore Press Holdings and Temasek Holdings.

Correspondents of critical foreign outfits have been routinely expelled, sued and their publications banned. I should know. The *Far Eastern Economic Review* where I worked was banned in Singapore for more than a decade, losing that lucrative market. Even I couldn't visit Singapore as a tourist as it banned all our staff, even the lowliest janitor, from entering the island state. Lee lifted the embargo on our magazine only after our British editor was fired, and replaced with an appeasing young American lawyer.

Suharto and his cronies

Indonesia's Major General Suharto grabbed power in a bloody coup d'état in 1967, and stayed in power for 31 years. Marcos' cronies were amateurs compared with those of Suharto, whose closest crony Soedono Salim was given monopolies on cloves, flour, cement and even government bank deposits.

While most of Marcos' cronies are forgotten now, Suharto's top cronies, the so-called Gang of Four, set up First Pacific Co., Ltd in 1981, now one of the biggest regional conglomerates in Asia.

It's ironic that the Yellow Cult is still mad about Marcos and his cronies who are long gone, and yet ignore the fact that Suharto's cronies are lording it over the Philippine corporate world. First Pacific led by Soedono's son Anthoni is the majority owner of key strategic utilities in the country, Meralco and PLDT, in contravention of the Constitution.

Malaysia's Mahathir was in power for 22 years starting in 1981, and is still a formidable political force in his country, having effectively suppressed the leading opposition figure, Anwar Ibrahim, on charges, of all things, of sodomy. (In a surprise move, the hitherto retired Mahathir ran in the May 2018 elections and won, becoming the world's oldest elected leader at 92 years old.)

Field Marshal Thanom Kittikachorn ruled Thailand as military dictator from 1963 to 1973, until violent student protests forced him out of office.

The average length of strongman rule in these Asian countries was 23 years; Marcos' held on to power only for 13 years. Is there a case for claiming that strongman rule didn't work here, since Marcos' strongman rule did not last as long as those in other countries did?

How Asia's strongmen fared

The reality stares us in the face: The Asian economic dragons and tigers grew to industrial status in one generation, all under authoritarian rule, and not under democratic systems, as in the West. But for us it resulted in poverty, which we haven't been able to overcome after 27 years. Why?

Two short answers. Marcos from the start really wasn't too strong a strongman, because he maintained the nation's legal framework. There wasn't even the extermination of our insurgencies on a ruthless level as occurred under Indonesia's Suharto and South Korea's Park Chung-hee.

And secondly, whatever degree of strongman rule he had imposed became weak when he lifted martial law, even if only on an official basis, in 1981, and diffused his power to the three competing factions at the time: that of his wife Imelda with his cousin, General Fabian Ver; Defense Minister Juan Ponce Enrile with the Philippine Constabulary Chief Fidel Ramos; and the technocrats under the World Bank-International Monetary Fund's aegis led by Finance Minister Cesar Virata.

The weakening of his strongman rule was even paralleled by the weakening of his body. His kidneys started to fail in 1982 that he had to undergo a transplant of his two kidneys in 1984.

It is not just coincidental that the Philippine economy surged at an average of 6 percent under Marcos' strongman rule 1972-1980, and then tumbled when he became a weak ruler, from 1981's 3.4 percent GDP growth rate to a recession in the two years of 1984 and 1985.

(May 7, 2018)

A STRONG REPUBLIC ESSENTIAL TO OUR DEVELOPMENT

EVEN IF SHORT-LIVED — crushed by the United States after 15 months — the first Philippine Republic was the first republican state to be established in Asia and Africa, which arguably inspired other colonized peoples in the world. It was an assembly in 1899 in Malolos town, which declared in the country's first constitution: "The political association of all Filipinos constitutes a nation, whose state shall be known as the Philippine Republic."

The Philippine Republic is not just the institution that is the state, with its government apparatus. Nor it is just the nation, the community of people with generally common descent, history, language, and culture living in a clearly defined territory. The Philippine Republic is both: an indivisible entity called the "nation-state". The 1987 constitution itself merges the two concepts of nation and state in its Section 1, Article II: "The Philippines [i.e., the nation] is a democratic, republican state."

The Philippine Republic consists of the state as an institution *and* Filipino citizens as a community. The nation-state is essentially a territorial-based corporation, with its citizens as shareholders, with its regularly elected board of directors (i.e., the President and the Congress mainly), and the different 'corporate' departments corresponding to its government.

The big difference is that the nation-state is the only corporation that defines the rules to be complied with not only for its members but also for other corporations in its defined territory, and using force if necessary to have its way.

Another big difference: this particular "corporation", since it became independent in 1946, has determined and will determine the fates of millions of Filipinos in the past, now, and in the future.

The two elements of the nation-state interact to create either a virtuous, or a vicious cycle. A weak nation creates a weak state, and a weak state continues to make for a weak nation.

One insightful and useful definition of a nation-state was that by the renowned scholar Benedict Anderson, that it is an "imagined community."[1]

The opening of the convention that first defined the Philippine Republic: the Malolos convention 1898-1899.

One Filipino citizen will never meet each and every other Filipino. There will never be a stockholders' meeting in some hotel ballroom for that corporation we call the Philippine Republic. But still, there is that community called the Philippines a Filipino citizen identifies himself as a member of, even without direct interaction with all of his co-members.

Calling it an "imagined community" doesn't mean that it isn't real or false. It emphasizes the difficulty of strengthening a nation. The community of a nation is unlike a family or an office where one directly interacts with all, or at least most, of its members so that it's easy to feel a sense of community. Yet it is the intensity of that image of a national community in the people's minds — even felt in their hearts — that determines their nation's strength.

Handicapped Filipinos

But history has handicapped Filipinos in imagining a community. The Spanish and American colonizers obstructed Filipinos' conceptualizing of the nation as a community that bonds them one way or another, whether they like it or not, to a common destiny.

Before Spanish colonization in 16th century, populating the archipelago were scattered, independent barangays, or groups of fifty to a hundred families. There was no imagined community. There were only small, directly-perceived communities of groups of families.

There was after all no compulsion to organize people on a scale bigger than the extended clan. Circa 1600, the archipelago called the Philippines today had a population of only 900,000. Compare that to Japan's 22 million, India's 135 million, China's 150 million, Java's 4 million, and Burma's 3 million. Such dense populations prompted the organization of kingdom-states with the God-King/Emperor as the organizing principle, as early as, in Japan's case, the 8th century.

However, despite the growth of the population to 4 million by 1850, a sense of national community (even as a subjugated community) was stunted by Spanish colonialism. The main factor for this was that, in contrast to the colonization of Latin America, Spanish colonial rule was dominantly through the Catholic parish friars.

The community, which the friars forced Filipinos to "imagine", was not a national entity, not even an earthly one. It was a religious community, the parish as a flock of God through the Holy Roman Catholic Church.

After the family, Filipinos' sense of belonging was, and continue to this day to be for many, in the "flock" with the Spanish friar as "shepherd". As the historian Reynaldo Ileto put it, the community most Filipinos at that time believed they were living in was foremost the religious realm: "The Spanish priest was the equivalent of the God-King elsewhere in Southeast Asia."[2]

That notion of being members almost solely of religious flocks, rather than of a national community was inculcated over three centuries. The impact of those three centuries cannot be underestimated. Even our literature features fictional Christian kingdoms, notably Francisco Balagtas' epic **Florante at Laura**.

Eden-like community

As Ileto pointed out, even in revolt towards the end of the 19th century, the project felt on the grass-roots level was not for building a nation, but for creating an Eden-like community under God's aegis.[3]

Remnants of this religious mindset in fact persist today. The 1986

EDSA Revolution had a strong religious ethos, evident in the crucial role of Archbishop Jaime Cardinal Sin who called upon Filipinos to defend the military rebels against the strongman Marcos. The anti-Marcos rallyists carried Virgin Mary statuettes and rosaries as they faced the tanks. The centerpiece of the shrine constructed to commemorate the 1986 People Power Revolt is a three-storey statue of the Virgin Mary, with a Catholic chapel alongside it.

Spanish colonial policy of indirect rule, of recruiting local elites for administering the archipelago (with the Spanish and Chinese *mestizo* as its core) also served to stunt the development of a national identity.

In most of the world's strong nation-states, it was the *intelligentsia* of the elite — they had the resources after all — that was the vanguard for conceiving a nation. In 19th century Philippines though, the *mestizo* elite's agenda was for full-fledged membership in the Spanish Crown. The main project even of the *ilustrados* was not for creating a sovereign nation-state, but for reforming colonial government and the recognition of the *mestizos*, and later even *indios*, as Spanish subjects.

But who could blame them? The concept of a nation-state started to crystallize on the planet only in the 18th century. It is only in the 20th century that the nation-state has been firmly established as the prime social organization of mankind, the corporation that would determine the happiness or misery of billions of people.

Indeed, even with a Philippine Republic existing in the late-20th century, hundreds of thousands of Filipino middle and upper classes have chosen to leave the nation, to imagine themselves as members of foreign communities overseas.

Benign assimilation

American colonialism further handicapped Filipinos' ability to conceive of a national community. "Benign assimilation" wasn't just a slogan. The US conquerors attempted to mold a Filipino community that would be part, formally or informally, of a rising U.S.A., its *"little brown brother."*

That project involved the deletion of the historical memory of three and a half centuries of a people, and the decades of resistance to US colonialism. Even the language used by the revolutionists as members of the Filipino elite, Spanish, was practically eradicated in several years' time.

All over the world, accounts of a people in arms against foreign invaders had been the building blocks for imagining a national community. But the US conquerors banned such accounts of those "bandits". Not too many Filipinos in fact are aware of nationalist resistance fighters heroes such as Vicente Lukban, Miguel Malvar, and Mariano Trias who led against-all-odds resistance against US occupation.

An entire three hundred years of the existence of a people, of historical memory was practically deleted. As the scholar Benedict Anderson put it, a "virtual lobotomy has been performed" on the Filipino mind.

The vacuum left by that lobotomy was filled with an individualistic, materialistic world view as if nation-states didn't matter. After all, the quality of life in the archipelago, at least for its elite, improved vastly under the American colonial state that certainly was not the embodiment of the nation.

Liberal democracy was transplanted to replace Catholicism. But liberal democracy as an ideology evolved from the already-strong nations of France and England where the social sense of belonging to a nation had become too dominant that it was counterbalanced by liberalism's assertion of the primacy of the individual over any other social group.

But for the Philippines, with the sense of nationhood very much still embryonic, liberalism merely atomized the nation into nation-less individuals.

The Filipino *sacristan* who lived in the Church since birth was suddenly thrown out of it, into the marketplace, with no family-nation to remember, or feel attachment to.

As during the Spanish occupation, many of the Filipino elite could even conceive of the Filipino corporation only as a mere subsidiary of U.S.A. Inc. The Filipino elite forgot Spain and instead imagined America as their community. As a result, more than 4 million Filipinos have immigrated to the US, in two waves first in the 1950s and then in the 1970s.

Religious realm

The community of the Filipino Republic has not replaced that "religious realm". What substituted for it has not been the imagined community of the nation but directly felt ones, for many, solely the family and the clan.

A few even mock, and plot to smash the Philippine Republic, as the Communist Party does. The imagined community of communist chief Jose Ma. Sison is not the Filipino nation. With his dream of a Maoist revolution in the Philippines shattered in 1986, Sison's imagined community is the archipelaego's membership in some delusional Fifth Internationale of the world proletariat.

It's not hard to spot the communities Filipinos identify with and which command their loyalties. You have the corporations they belong to, especially the most prestigious ones ("My prime responsibility is to my shareholders."); churches and religious organizations such as the Iglesia ni Cristo, El Shaddai, and Opus Dei; in the 1980s for some in the military, the RAM and YOU brotherhoods; leftist and cause-oriented groups; non-governmental organizations; fraternities; big law firms, and even — for some of today's journalists, their newspapers and the television stations.

As nation-states' boundaries become more porous and with the speed of modern communications and transport, for many among our intelligentsia, the "community" has even become the world. They see themselves as cosmopolitans, international citizens with globalization as a justification for their worldview.

The nation-state is a single entity. The feebleness of Filipinos' sense of belonging to a nation has created a weak state. For the oligarchs and the elite, from the Spanish days up to now, more important than strengthening the state has been to extract wealth out of it.

The actions of a nation's state determine if millions of human beings, the members of that organization, would live in squalor or comfort. The "state" part of the nation has become the biggest organization with the largest power and resources within its territory, whose actions affect the quality of people's lives.

There has been nearly a consensus among scholars and economists — even those of contrasting political ideologies — that the crucial factor in the economic growth of Western industrial countries and of the Asian dragons and East Asian tigers, was their strong state.

Weak state

There are two conclusions most scholars agree on about the Philippines: First, it has had a weak state in much of its history; and second, the weakness of the Philippine state has been the country's overarching problem that explains its inability to develop the economy and alleviate poverty.[4]

Government corruption, which most Filipinos think has been our root problem, is only a symptom of a weak state, as the bureaucracy's resources are exploited for individuals' wealth-generation.

This consensus has been partly the result of many studies in the 1980s and '90s of the phenomenal growth of the East Asian tigers, where strong states have been the norm, in contrast to Latin American laggards (which not coincidentally were also Spanish colonies) whose weak states are manipulated by powerful dominant classes.

The state-centered analysis has not been limited to developing countries. There has been a parallel wave of analysis starting in the 1980s — "Bringing the State Back In" — that revisited and revised European economic history to focus on the prime role of the states in European countries' development.[5]

Although using various terms, many of the recent analysis of the East Asian miracle identified the strong state as a crucial factor in economic growth. For instance, a recent and authoritative review of East Asian economies noted:

"Korea, Singapore, and Taiwan, the fastest post-war industrializers, are credited with 'visionary' leadership and efficient bureaucracies. They also achieved national consensus on development goals and had a centralized political apparatus to implement their fairly interventionist strategies."[6]

The World Bank even commissioned a study, "The Role of Government in East Asian Economic Development,"[7] to investigate in detail exactly how strong states in Asia spurred growth.

The World Bank, while officially committed to the market-oriented non-interventionist development approach, nevertheless devoted one of its annual reports, for 1997, on the crucial role of the state in development.[8]

One of its major conclusions: "Development — economic, social, and sustainable — without an effective state is impossible. It is increasingly recognized that an effective state — not a minimal one — is central to economic and social development..."

A strong state does not necessarily mean an authoritarian one. In fact, most of the democratic, developed countries of the world have had strong states: France, the U.K., post-war Germany, and Japan, to a great extent because they had centuries of powerful feudal kingdoms.

There are two essential attributes of a strong state.

First, and most important, it is autonomous of dominant classes and sectors, so that it represents at every twist and turn of the nation's life the people's interest, the majority of the population, and not those of the powerful but minority groups.

Second, it has the capacity, represented mainly through a strong bureaucracy, to implement its policies.

A state is weak if dominant classes or sectors control it, or at least shape its policies, especially those dealing with the economy. Economic history worldwide show that dominant classes' myopic interests which had become state's policies have resulted in long-term economic decline.

The Philippines with its weak state has seen dominant classes or its elites controlling its economic and political policies. During the American colonial era, the economy stagnated as it was based mainly on sugar and copra exports and the consumption of finished American goods.

In the post-war period it was transformed by the elites into an oligopolistic, inefficient economy of import-substituting industries.

In the 1970s and 1980's, the Philippines became the laggard in East Asia because industrial oligopolists, who grew powerful through the import-substituting phase of the 1950s, blocked a program for an export-oriented industrialization.

* * *

In recent years there has in fact been a groundswell of sentiment that what the country needs is a strong state.

Electoral results in the past decade show a public sentiment for candidates who seemed to be capable of building a strong state. Ramos as a military man projected the image of a forthcoming strong leader. His closest rival, Miriam Defensor-Santiago's image was also one of a tough leader who would crack down on corruption, that is, make the Philippine state a capable one. Similarly, Eduardo Cojuangco's widely known image as a strongman could explain his strong performance in that election. In contrast, Ramon Mitra seemed to be the embodiment of a weak state leader, both in terms of personality traits and in terms of his being a "traditional politician," which in conceptual terms is the agent for elites' manipulation of the state.

Other than the urban middle classes, there has also emerged a major constituency for a strong state framework: the millions of Filipino workers abroad. Seeing for themselves strong states in action, in the delivery of basic services — buses and trains are precisely on time, the streets are clean of garbage, etc. — the most common comment of returning overseas contract workers and visiting migrants is in effect how inefficient, weak, the Philippine state is.

But even if there is a strong sentiment among its intelligentsia and middle class for strengthening the state, such an agenda would require strengthening the other aspect of the nation-state, i.e., the nation.

Can Filipinos build a strong nation, even if it is difficult to imagine a community without a mythical glorious past, without ancient and classic literature, without God-Emperors and their Imperial Palaces, all of which serve as powerful symbols to create a deep emotional attachment to one's nation?

We cannot ignore though that Filipinos do have their glorious past: the phenomenal heroism of Rizal, Bonifacio and our other revolutionaries. It has been the life-and-death struggles of a people that constitute the narratives for imagining a nation — the French and American revolutions, the US Civil War, the anti-colonial insurrections. Filipinos have those, and a new generation of Filipino scholars is constructing the narratives of the Philippine Revolution against Spain, of the many resistance movements against US imperialism and the anti-Japanese resistance.

Furthermore, Filipinos, as recent surveys confirm, do have a strong sense of "Filipinò-ness", a strong sense of "brotherhood", which have proven all over the world to constitute the building blocks for building a nation-state.

Our language reflects the weakness of the notion of a nation-state as the Filipinos corporation. The common term used to refer to the Philippines is *bayan*. But this originally referred only to the "town," which was built around the Spanish friars' church. The term often used to refer to the nation, *sambayanan* was an invention of the Church to refer to the congregation of the people under the Church. *Bansa,* a Malayan term derived from the Sanskrit referring to place of birth is officially (for instance, as used in government documents) the term for a nation, but is hardly used in ordinary language.

The Filipino term for "state" is the Spanish derived *"estado,"* but has been more used by the Left to connote an oppressive state, along the Leninist framework of the democratic state as the "executive committee of the ruling class." The term for government is either the Spanish-derived *"gobyerno"* or *pamahalaan*, which is derived from the root word that merely means "supervision."

Japan instructive

The history of the nation-state of Japan, one of the most nationalist and most advanced nations today though is instructive for the Philippines. Despite its centuries of state building, particularly the three centuries of the centralized, strong state of the Tokugawa Shogunate, the Japanese nation-state in the middle 19th century was practically crumbling, as it became more a collection of 200-plus practically independent domains, each ruled by powerful — and often warring — *daimyos*, or powerful feudal lords.

The imagined community (in Benedict Anderson's definition of a nation) for most Japanese in that era was not *Dai Nippon*, but membership in a feudal clan. As Tokyo University professor Kiichi Fujiwara explained, as late as the early 20th century, ordinary Japanese did not think of themselves as *Nihonjin*.

The Meiji Restoration, with its project of building the nation-state, changed all that. The modern Japanese nation-state — which made possible Japan's economic prosperity — is a construction of the 20th century. Meiji leaders were keenly conscious of their project, and swiftly adapted much of the political technology of strong European, especially German, states. They even had an association and a journal **Kokka Gakkai Zasshi** or Journal of Nation-State Studies.

The Meiji rulers very consciously made it easier for the Japanese to imagine their community by celebrating and propagating centuries-old traditions they share as a community. Some scholars claim that a few of these so-called old traditions, like *"wa"* [harmony] and *furusato* [hometown or birthplace] were Meiji-era inventions. Japanese martial arts that appear to be centuries old, such as judo and karate, were constructs of the early 20th century.[9]

One has also to keep in mind that the emergence of nation-states emerged only in the last 200 years of human civilization's 6,000-year history. People in different parts of the globe — the Japanese and

Chinese, the Germans and Israelis — built strong nation-states within just three generations.

On the other hand, there are countries today (India and Egypt, for instance) that have very ancient histories as civilizations, but which have found themselves in the 21st century still struggling to build strong nation-states.

There is a big pressure for the Philippines, as it has been for China and India, to build a strong nation-state and this is due to their huge population. From being one of the smallest in Asia at the turn of the century with a population of 4 million, the Philippines has become one of the 20 biggest "corporations" in the world with 100 million members today. Without a strong nation state, it would be nearly impossible for that huge a population to be served by the government apparatus.

Note the following descriptions by scholars:

- "Patronage-oriented political parties and free-spending corruption dominated…" "The political system consisted of a distinctive complex of a weak national administration, divided and fragmentary public authority, and non-programmatic political parties."
- The nation-state "had a weak hold on the imagination and consciousness of a people who were now forced to think of them" as one community. Most identified themselves with their province of birth, not with the nation.

Apt descriptions of the Philippines today these may be, these referred to different countries. The first described the USA in the 1930s.[10] The second described Italy in the 1920s.[11] Yet these two countries were able to build strong-nation states within a generation.

There are no compelling reasons why Filipinos can't build a strong Philippine Republic. A few million Filipinos may continue to abandon their nation-state for a better life elsewhere. But the bulk of the 100 million would still remain in this archipelago, and a third of them will live miserable lives in poverty if we fail to build a strong Republic.

We just have to persevere in building both a strong government and a strong sense of nationalism.

(October 2002)

[1] Anderson, Benedict (1983). **Imagined Communities: Reflections on the Origin and Spread of Nationalism.** London, Verso.

[2] Ileto, Reynaldo C. (1998). **Filipinos and their Revolution: Event, Discourse, and Historiography.** Quezon City, Ateneo de Manila University Press, p.81.

[3] This point is the subject of Ileto's **Pasyon and Rebolusyon: Popular Movements in the Philippines** (1979: 1840-1910 (1979). Quezon City, Ateneo de Manila University Press.

[4] Studies arguing that the Philippine state has been a weak state, or assuming that framework, include: McCoy, Alfred, "Rent-seeking Families and the State in McCoy, Alfred W. (ed.) **An Anarchy of Families: State and Family in the Philippines** (Quezon City: Ateneo de Manila University Press, 1994); Hutchcroft, Paul David **Predatory oligarchy, patrimonial state: The politics of private domestic commercial banking in the Philippines** (Yale University: Ph.D. Dissertation: 1993); and Rivera, Temario C., **Class, the state and foreign capital: The Politics of Philippine Industrialization,** 1950-1986 (University of Wisconsin-Madison: Ph.D. dissertation 1991). Rho, Byeongil's **State capability and Third World Politics: A Comparative Analysis of South Korean and Philippine Cases** (Ph.D. dissertation. State University of New York at Albany, 1992) compares the weaknesses of the Marcos state to that of the strong Korean Park state.

[5] Evans, Peter B., et al. (eds.) (1985). **Bringing the State Back In.** Cambridge, New York and Sydney, Cambridge University Press.

[6] Leipziger and Thomas in their "Overview of East Asian Experience" in Leipziger, Danny M., editor, **Lessons from East Asia.** Michigan: University of Michigan Press, 1997.

[7] Aoki, Masahiko, Kim, Hyung-Ki, and Masahiro Okuno-Fujiwara, editors. **The Role of Government in East Asian Economic Development: Comparative Institutional Analysis.** Oxford: Clarendon Press, 1996.

[8] World Bank, **The State in a Changing World** (World Development Report 1997), New York: Oxford University Press, Inc., 1997.

[9] Vlastos, Stephen (ed.) (1998). **Mirror of Modernity: Invented Traditions of Modern Japan.** Los Angeles and London, University of California Press.

[10] In Margaret Weir and Theda Skocpol, "Keynesian' Responses to the Great Depression," in Evans, Peter B., et al. (eds.) (1985). **Bringing the State Back In.** Cambridge, New York and Sydney, Cambridge University Press.

[11] In Berezin, Mabel, "Political Belonging: Emotion, Nation, and Identity in Fascist Italy," in Steinmetz, George (ed.) (1999). **State/Culture: State-Formation after the Cultural Turn.** Ithaca and London, Cornell University Press.

Media

RAPPLER SPREAD LIES TO THE WORLD

AS MARK TWAIN PUT IT, a lie can travel around the world while the truth is still putting on its shoes.

The European Union Parliament's resolution last Thursday that interfered with our justice system and condemned the government's campaign against illegal drugs read: "7,000 drug-related killings by the police and vigilantes have been reported since President Duterte took office on 30 June 2016."

That 7,000 is the same number Vice President Leni Robredo used in her message last week to the United Nations Commission on Narcotic Drugs to rant against Duterte. It is the same figure that was used in the very critical report on the country by New York-based Human Rights Watch. It is the same figure used again and again by Western media, such as CNN, BBC, Time, and even the New York Times — all citing the Philippine National Police as its source. Even Al-Jazeera and Wikipedia cite this 7,000 number.

That 7,000 figure is false, from a fake news fabricated (or stupidly calculated) by the news website Rappler (rappler.com) and repeated in Hitlerian fashion by Yellow propagandists that even Western media which normally check their figures, have assumed it to be an accurate figure released by the PNP.

Rappler has been very much an anti-Duterte news outfit, and is now mostly funded by the American firms North Base Media and Omidyar (whose owner had founded eBay).

The article by Rappler was first posted September 13 and, regularly updated, reads:

"There had been over 7,000 deaths linked to the 'war on drugs' — both from legitimate police operations and vigilante-style or unexplained killings (including deaths under investigation) from July 1, 2016 to January 31, 2017."

It gave a breakdown of its "7,080" figure, which it claimed was "based on revised PNP data at the end of that period," as follows:

HOW RAPPLER FABRICATED ITS 7,080 FIGURE	
Suspected drug personalities killed in police operations:	**2,555**
Victims in cases of "deaths under investigation or investigation concluded":	**plus 4,525**
Total of 1 and 2: "number of people killed in war on drugs since July 1, 2016":	**equals 7.080**

Deaths under investigation refer to all murders and homicides – not just drug-related cases.

The calculation is so patently wrong, I can only attribute it not to stupidity but to malice. It included 4,525 "deaths under investigation or investigation concluded" as killings related to the anti-illegal drugs war — which they aren't!

The PNP's regular reports on "victims in cases of deaths under investigation or investigation concluded" **refer to all murders and homicides,** whether it is the result of road rage, robbery, or fatal love triangles, and not just those related to the anti-illegal drug campaign.

Rappler very wrongly and perhaps maliciously classified these deaths as due to Duterte's war against illegal drugs, therefore bloating three times the number of people killed in the course of that campaign.

Western media and now even the European Union Parliament, have swallowed it hook, line and sinker, and have even disseminated it.

After Rappler's false report that its 7,080 figure referred to those killed "from legitimate police operations and vigilante-style or unexplained killings," Robredo and other yellow hacks have since used this figure, for example, in her UN message, as the number of people "killed in summary executions." This has created a very false picture of a country in which police lined up drug suspects on the wall and shot them dead.

It was only last week that a PNP spokesperson pointed out how terribly wrong that 7,000 figure which Robredo used in her message to the UN narcotics body was. He said that, according to PNP data, there were 2,582 killed in legitimate drug operations so far, not 7,000, and that "deaths under investigation" includes "all crimes happening on the streets."

Even as I, and the PNP, have pointed out its mistake to Rappler, it has not apologized for its error, nor has it deleted its fake news. Is that responsible journalism?

But do we have any means to check the PNP's figures, to find out if they are credible?

We have. To the credit of the *Philippine Daily Inquirer*, hardly a pro-Duterte newspaper, it listed, based on police blotters and the dispatches of their national network of police reporters, killings related to the anti-drug war, from July 1 to February 16, when government officially halted, temporarily, its campaign. The list was detailed, with the names of the victims if available, where they were killed in case of police operations, or if they were found dead, murdered by what the paper termed as "unidentified hit men."

Based on the PDI's raw data, we extracted the following:

- There were 2,107 killed in the campaign against illegal drugs from July 1 to February 16, which is even smaller than the PNP's figure of 2,582, even if the police's number includes drug-related deaths up to March 15.
- Out of this, 1,137, or 54 percent of the total, were killed in police "buy-bust" and Operation Tokhang* operations, as well as in the course of serving of search or arrest warrants. Some 970, or 40 percent, were found dead — "killed by unknown hit men," as the PDI described it.
- Other than the 132 killed with such notes on cardboards pinned on the corpses saying, "I am a drug lord", or a "I am a pusher," the paper however doesn't explain how it, or the police, concluded that the other 838 killed were killed as a result of the anti-drug war.
- Some 385, or 18 percent, couldn't be identified.

Some 2,107 people killed in the anti-drug war in seven and a half months of course is still deplorable, but far from the 7,000 that Rappler and Robredo claim, and certainly gives a new perspective in assessing Duterte's anti-drug war.

Furthermore, the geographical distribution of those killed in the anti-drug war is revealing: 1,131, or 55 percent, of the 2,048 cases in which their location was determined, are only in five cities, known to be havens of the illegal drug trade: Quezon City, Cebu, Manila, Pasay and Pasig.

It would make very good sense for Duterte to focus his anti-drug war on these five cities. Their mayors though should be taken to task as to why the illegal drug trade has proliferated so much in their cities: Quezon City's Herbert Bautista, Cebu City's Tomas Osmeña, Manila's Joseph Estrada, and Pasig's Robert Eusebio. As a former mayor, Duterte I'm sure, can have a heart-to-heart talk with these ineffectual mayors.

On the other hand, if Robredo and other human rights champions are really sincere about stopping the summary executions of suspected drug pushers and addicts, they should focus their limited resources on these five cities to expose and prevent human rights abuses.

Rather than just bawl and beg the UN to interfere.

(March 20, 2017)

* *"Tokhang"* is a neologism consisting of the Visayan words *toktok* (knock) and *hangyo* (beseech). Operation Tokhang supposedly involves the police knocking on the homes of suspected drug addicts and pushers to ask them to stop their criminal activities. But, the police claims, many of the suspects decided instead to fight the police, resulting in their deaths.

A CLASSIC INSTANCE OF WESTERN MEDIA SPIN

I SPILLED MY COFFEE watching CNN's 8 a.m. news, when its ticker tape flashed: "Duterte orders police to kill those resisting arrest, followed by "Duterte: Kill the idiots."

A newsreader then simply repeated those statements, adding, as it does every time there's news now about the Philippines, that Duterte's war against illegal drugs has killed "thousands".

I googled "Duterte kill the idiots," and the search results showed two dozen items showing the same headline, by news organizations such as American network ABC, the Internet-only The Daily Beast, to small local news outfits like Panay News. Credit its going "viral" to a dispatch by Reuters, whose correspondents have the knack for finding the sensational spin.

I initially thought, "Has Duterte gone mad?" As is my habit, I searched to hear exactly what he said. I managed to get quickly a video of Duterte's speech, at the National Heroes Day celebration the other day, where he purportedly made those statements.

What follows is my word-for-word transcription of Duterte's relevant statements. You judge if those news reports are really accurate or represent a classic instance of how Western media, or any media, can spin a particular quote so as to shock people:

"In the performance of their duty, tell your men that whenever their life is in danger and they are in the actual performance of their duty, your duty requires you to overcome the resistance of the person you are arresting. Not only just to shout to him to surrender because it is a [indistinct], and if he resists and it is a violent one placing in jeopardy the lives of my policemen and military, you are free to kill the idiots."

That the news story has become viral is of course partly Duterte's fault. "Kill the idiots" is such a great attention-grabbing quotable quote, on par with that classic "Kill all the lawyers."

Of course, one can insist that still, Duterte categorically said "free to kill the idiots". But do you think Duterte would have instead said: "If they resist arrest and are violent, shoot them in the legs?"

Would it be more informative if the news organizations' headline was instead: "Duterte authorizes the police to shoot-to-kill, if those resisting arrest fight back." That would be more accurate really. But would that make shocking, "viral" headlines?

And the use of idiots? That's Duterte's normal uncouth language that he is used to, but expletives certainly aren't his monopoly. I can imagine Trump similarly using "idiots" if had to refer to criminals, if he stops himself from using "motherfuckers." Should Duterte have used "cock-suckers" as a Trump aide described one of his colleagues?

Let's face it, Western media, which we think — given their reporters' high salaries and its centuries of evolution — are so professional, just aren't. Listen to CNN and Fox News, and you'll get a total contrasting picture of Trump and the US situation now.

Media herd mentality

As Philippine print media used to be, especially during the past administration (remember the anti-Corona frenzy and their idolatry of President Aquino?), US and European media occasionally are afflicted with that virus called herd mentality.

In the US case, such herd mentality even allowed President Bush to invade a sovereign nation, Iraq, destroy its cities and kill hundreds of thousands of Iraqis — on the basis of the total lie that Iraq had weapons of mass destruction.

Media herd mentality is probably one of the most dangerous social phenomena now, as it brainwashes entire peoples to believe even a total lie, so that governments could start a war that can throw the entire world into conflagration. The global scourge of terrorism now, is almost entirely due to the US invasion of Iraq that its media sold to Americans.

What is worrying — and sickening — is that herd mentality afflicts not just the most mediocre of journalists, but even the best.

Consider my former colleague Sheila Coronel who left Philippine journalism to teach rich Americans investigative journalism at Columbia University in New York, to become the director of its Stabile Center of Investigative Journalism and then academic affairs dean of the journalism school itself, considered the best in the US. (That's like a doctor trained at taxpayer-subsidized PGH and at public medical centers to become the best tuberculosis physician, only to teach tuberculosis treatment at a New York hospital catering to billionaires.)

Instead of doing investigative journalism on Trump's real wealth or connection with Russian oligarchs, or such important, but hard topics relevant to Columbia University as how American wars are responsible for US technological breakthroughs, Coronel has rushed to join the anti-Duterte mob of American journalists, and wrote several pieces in prestigious New York publications that pay unbelievably high fees painting Duterte as, to use her term, a "blood-bathed" President and Manila's streets as littered with corpses.

While Coronel writes well — in her melodramatic 1980s style using colorful heart-tugging anecdotes — I'm quite sure one of her qualifications that made editors buy her stories would be that she was a Filipino "investigative journalist." In fact, she bolsters her demonic portrayal of Duterte by referring to her coverage of him as Davao City mayor back in the 1980s, implying that he was already a killer then and she is the expert on his soul.

But Coronel wants to have her cake and eat it too, to live and work in the US, yet still pretend to be an expert on the Philippines, as most ranting anti-Duterte Fil-Ams (the most prominent being billionaire Loida Nicolas-Lewis) are fond of doing. She bases her data on what's happening in the Philippines on what other American journalists have written, and forgets the investigative skills she learned at the Philippine Center for Investigative Journalism.

In her recent article in a journal, "A Presidency Bathed in Blood," Coronel wrote: "The drug war, which Duterte officially launched on his first day in office, has claimed the lives of as many as 9,000 suspected drug dealers and users."

I asked her through Facebook's Messenger where she got that 9,000 number, a topic of considerable interest to me as I wrote three columns debunking that figure, which was based on a completely wrong article in Internet-only news site Rappler. (In my column, "How Rappler misled EU, Human Rights Watch, CNN, Time, BBC — the world," *Manila Times*, May 19, 2017)

She replied: "Numerous news reports quote that figure." She even gave me the link to her Google search results. I asked her why she "didn't bother to verify if this is fake news, used mostly by Western media."

I told her that even the Google search results she sent me had several reports specifically disproving that figure, yet she ignored those articles.

She didn't reply after that. She "unfriended" me as a Facebook friend, obviously so she won't read my posts that disturb her New York world view.

If a professor and dean of Columbia University's journalism school throws journalistic rules of verification and objectivity, and on the President of her former country, what can you expect from old and weary wire correspondents rushing to file dispatches as fast as they can to fulfill their daily quota, or from mediocre TV reporters and news readers?

(August 30, 2017)

US MEDIA ON AN ALL-OUT CAMPAIGN VS DUTERTE

IF YOU DIDN'T NOTICE, even the Liberal Party and other Yellow leaders didn't profusely congratulate the jailed Senator Leila de Lima for her inclusion by *Fortune* magazine in its 2018 list of "50 World's Greatest Leaders."

I guess even they felt that the award was so bizarre, so over the top in the magazine's attempt to paint her as the Philippine version of Myanmar's Aung San Suu Kyi, that it was embarrassing.

I don't think even Yellow leaders Benigno Aquino and Mar Roxas would say that De Lima ranks with such personalities in the 2018 list as Bill and Melinda Gates (the biggest philanthropists of all time), French President Emmanuel Macron, and tennis champion Serena Williams. Why, De Lima at the 39th slot even outranks SpaceX president Gwynne Shotwell (42nd) and Ana Botin (46th), the first female to head a world-class bank. If you still don't realize how perplexing De Lima's inclusion in the list is, past members of this super-elite list (started in 2014) were Pope Francis (for two years), Germany's Angela Merkel, and Chinese leader Xi Jinping, who is assuming the stature of the titan Mao Zedong.

C'mon, I don't think there's anybody who would even objectively put De Lima in a list of 100,000 greatest leaders of the world. She couldn't even influence her lover, her driver Ronnie Dayan, not to testify against her. Who is she leading?

Fortune's explanation on why De Lima landed in its list, is so grossly inaccurate it boggles the mind:

"President Rodrigo Duterte's hardline policies against drug dealers are polarizing globally, but in the Philippines they've faced little dissent. De Lima, who headed a committee investigating hundreds of extrajudicial killings under Duterte's leadership, has been a noble exception. Last February she was arrested and jailed for as-yet-untried crimes, but imprisonment hasn't stopped the firebrand from continuing to speak out publicly."

How could *Fortune*, a purportedly world-class media outfit, print such huge lies?

If the committee it mentioned was the Commission on Human Rights that De Lima headed during President Arroyo's administration, it did investigate the alleged "death squads" of Davao City. Its report though was inconclusive, and didn't accuse Duterte of anything. It merely asked the Justice department to further investigate the allegations.

Or maybe the magazine was referring to the Senate committee on justice that De Lima had headed? However, her colleagues in the Senate, including those on her committee, voted to remove her as its chairman. As Senator Sherwin Gatchalian very aptly explained why: She was making the committee "a hollow vehicle for the fulfillment of personal political vendettas."

That committee, when it was co-chaired by the independent senators Richard Gordon and Panfilo Lacson, concluded after six hearings that "there is no sufficient evidence to prove Duterte's administration is sponsoring summary killings" in the country.

It was De Lima who delayed the trial against her by filing a case at the Supreme Court, that she should be tried not by the regular courts but by the Sandiganbayan. That was a preposterous claim, intended to delay her trial. Any college student would know that since the charges against her were for her involvement in the illegal drug trade, it is a regular court that will try her. The Sandiganbayan is a special court that tries cases of government corruption.

The Supreme Court in October 2017 threw out De Lima's motion to move her case jurisdiction. She files another petition asking the Court to change its decision. After a thorough review, the Supreme Court last week upheld its decision that De Lima will be tried in a regular court. Yet Fortune has the temerity to claim that she is in jail without trial?

Fortune doesn't even mention that De Lima is in jail on serious illegal drug charges. One of these would be shocking to Westerners: The Bilibid prison, purportedly the country's high-security prison where the most terrible criminals are jailed, had been transformed when it was under De Lima's supervision as Justice secretary, into a command and even distribution center of drug lords who had been serving time there.

Bilibid Hilton

And the charges against her aren't just for command responsibility for this. Witnesses, which included her lover Dayan and the former head of the prison, testified that she was getting huge amounts of bribes so she would allow the national penitentiary to be a command center of drug lords. These criminals were even allowed to construct hotel-like facilities where they lived, that the prison had been dubbed the Bilibid Hilton.

The shocking details of De Lima's involvement were even televised in the hearings by the House of Representatives justice committee which heard hour upon hour of testimony from more than 30 witnesses, which even included the former head of the prison and the drug lords themselves.

I am belaboring the point: Not by any stretch of the imagination is there an iota of truth in *Fortune* magazine's portrayal of De Lima as a "prisoner of conscience," much less as among the world's greatest leaders for 2018. Even her colleagues at the Liberal Party have started to ignore her that no leader of the opposition has even visited her in the past several months.

But there is a reason for *Fortune's* madness in including her in its list of world leaders. The bizarre award, just like the Pulitzer Prize recently given to Reuters' extremely biased series on "Duterte's War," is part of the US media's heightened campaign — helped by the Yellow Cultists and especially by a New York-based Filipino-American billionaire — to bring down this President, by portraying him to the world as a mass murderer.

It is an old, overused narrative that the American media has often deployed that it is so transparent: A persecuted woman who boldly defies a strongman, as in the case of Cory Aquino or Aung San Suu Kyi, both of whom ironically turned out to be worse in terms of adherence to human rights than the dictators they brought down.

Why would US media do that? Partly because of its mindset that it is the world's champion of human rights, and after Duterte was tagged as violator, it ignores whatever proof presented that he is not. Media as anywhere in the world delights in fighting a perceived evil-doer, and they believe US journalists are infallible.

There is though a more important reason: Duterte is the first ever Philippine president to defy the US which has been the country's master for decades. He is bringing the country closer to the emerging superpower, China, which the US perceives as its biggest competitor, and even enemy in the coming decades. He is moving in his own way to weaken US hegemony in the world, and to usher in a multi-polar world.

The US Deep State just cannot allow that, especially as other nations may just follow Duterte's precedent.

(April 25, 2018)

PULITZER PRIZE-WINNING PIECE PEDDLED FAKE NEWS

I WAS STUNNED WHEN I read one of the 10 articles of the series entitled "Duterte's War," published from February to December of 2017. The series won for three Reuters reporters this week the Pulitzer Prize for international reporting.

This was the series' second article published April 18, 2017, entitled "Police describe rewards, staged crime scenes in Duterte's drug war." The lead writer is an old colleague and friend of mine, Manuel Mogato, with an American, Clare Baldwin sharing the byline. (The other nine articles in the series were bylined by Baldwin and a British reporter.)

Quite sadly, the Mogato-Baldwin article disseminated fake news, quite successfully, I must say, as its fallacies have been repeated by numerous news agencies around the world. Worse, the timing of its publication even indicates that it was, wittingly or unwittingly on the part of the writers, the media component of the plot to get the International Criminal Court (ICC) to prosecute President Duterte for the deaths in his anti-drug war.

For impact, the series was replete with gory photos of corpses and blood on the streets — obviously Photoshopped for more drama — that unequivocally, in-your-face shouts that Duterte's war against drugs have resulted in horrendous murders.

The title itself of the Mogato-Baldwin article is so misleading, it throws journalistic standards to the dustbin: "Killing Machine: Police describe kill rewards, staged crime scenes in Duterte's drug war."

For that extraordinary allegation, the article does not identify a single policeman to have made that description. In fact, the entire article's sources are just two unidentified police officials, one a retired intelligence official whose expertise had been on insurgencies, not on crime. How can we be sure that these aren't police officials loyal to the past regime, who simply want to bring Duterte down?

How can two unidentified police officials represent the "police" who "describe kill rewards, staged crime scenes in Duterte's drug war"?

The article spews fake news at its first sentences: "Almost 9,000 people, many small-time users and dealers, have been killed since Duterte took office on June 30," the article reported.

Yet the writers didn't report where they got this number.

This false information actually originated from the Internet-only news site Rappler's September 2016 article, that grossly misinterpreted police data to claim that people killed in the anti-drug war totaled 7,080 by that time. The Philippine National Police (PNP) and several of columns of mine* had debunked that figure conclusively.

However, anti-Duterte writers and politicians (particularly Senator Antonio Trillanes IV) have since used Rappler's 7,080 figure to extrapolate fake figures on the casualties of Duterte's war against illegal drugs. That is, "if it was 7,080 in September 2016, therefore there must be at least 20,000 killed today."

The Mogato-Baldwin article was published April 2017, when PNP's official figures reported at that time that the number of people killed by the police in the anti-drug war totaled only 3,100. The number rose as the anti-drug war was waged, but was only at 4,075 as of last month.

The Pulitzer-winning article claims that two-thirds, or 6,000, of the 9,000 were "killed by paid assassins operating with police backing." Where did they get this huge figure?

"From human rights monitors," it claims. But it doesn't even name these "human rights monitors." There is in fact no such "human rights monitor" that has meticulously compiled police blotters, to come up with a figure on how many were killed by vigilantes or paid assassins.

I won't be surprised if the human rights monitors were communist propagandists and most likely Trillanes, who has recently been lying to the world, alleging that Duterte's anti-drug war has killed 20,000 Filipinos.

No relatives?

The Reuters writers ignored that axiom of rationality — adopted by serious journalists — made popular by the renowned science writer Carl Sagan: "Extraordinary claims require extraordinary evidence." The claim that 6,000 Filipinos involved in the anti-drug war were killed by police-backed vigilantes is certainly an extraordinary one.

Didn't it occur in the minds of the Reuters reporters that if within less than a year, there was a program by the state to kill 6,000 people through paid assassins (practically a pogrom) this would have been big news in this country on such a scale as to bring down Duterte? That the relatives of these 6,000 people, many of whom the writers claimed were innocent, would have been able to undertake weekly massive demonstrations protesting such mass murder?

Fake news almost always is uncovered by time, and this is exactly what happened in the case of the Mogato-Baldwin piece's biggest fake claim.

What made the article sensational at the time that news outlets all over the world published it, were its claims that the police killed drug suspects because they were paid for doing so.

The article even reported: "The cash 'reward scales' for drug killings range from P20,000 ($400) for a 'street-level pusher and user,' to P50,000 for a member of a neighborhood council, P1 million for 'distributors, retailers and wholesalers,' and P5 million for 'drug lords.'" Anybody who has covered crime would laugh at those astounding prices.

Mogato-Baldwin's article is such a huge insult to our police force which, despite its many rogues, has had a professional tradition built by officers over the decades who had been trained in the Philippine Military Academy and since the 1980s by its spin-off, the Philippine National Police Academy. For Reuters' biased (or racist?) foreign journalists of course, the PNP is of the same kind as those in Somalia, Kenya, or even Burma.

Where did the Reuters staff get these reports that police did their gruesome deeds for money, and even reported a price list for different kinds of kills?

From what it thought at the time (April 2017) was an explosive 26-page paper entitled, **The State-Sponsored Extrajudicial Killings in the Philippines.** The Reuters article believed in the paper so much it called it a "document" even if the author was anonymous, whom it identified as a "retired police intelligence officer."

I know Mogato's sources since way back in the late 1990s when we both worked for the *Manila Chronicle*, and later as members of the Foreign Correspondents Club of the Philippines (of which I was once a president). I am quite confident this "retired police intelligence officer" was his — and several other journalists' — friend and regular source of information, PNP general Rodolfo "Boogie" Mendoza, who passed away only last month.

Mendoza was a brilliant intelligence officer, having captured many of the Communist Party leaders as well as foreign and local Islamic fundamentalists. Unlike nearly all intelligence operatives, Boogie developed friendships with journalists (including me) in order to develop a deeper understanding of his targets.

He retired from the service a decade ago. I don't think though that Boogie ever studied the country's illegal drug scourge nor even crime in general, because his interest — and tasking by his superiors — were focused on communists and Islamic terrorists. He was never close to the next generation of police officers in charge of Duterte's anti-drug war to be an authority on Duterte's anti-drug war.

Fake study

That the paper was by Boogie, who had been obsessed with the communist movement, is obvious in that it called the drug war a "social cleansing campaign similar to that launched in Mao Zedong's China." The Reuters article even noted that "half of the report is largely political in nature, asserting that Duterte has close ties to Communist forces in the Philippines."

The paper even claimed: "The anti-drug campaign has a mass character hinged on Marxist theory." That certainly sounds like the Boogie I know. The Reuters Pulitzer winners swallowed Boogie's musings hook, line, and sinker.

The Reuters article tried to portray Boogie's paper as credible as it was explosive. It claimed that it was shared "with leaders of the Catholic Church in the Philippines and with the government-funded Commission on Human Rights."

To portray it as credible, it asserted: "The Commission on Human Rights has reviewed the report and the accounts could open up new leads in ongoing investigations, said chairman Chito Gascon. Church officials confirmed receiving the report as well."

But if it was so credible, why is it that a year after the Reuters reporters, the anti-Duterte Church officials, and the Commission on Human Rights had acquired it, they haven't released it to the public? I'm sure CHR head Gascon would have even published it in pamphlet form and disseminated it all over the country. Contrary to his claim to Reuters, Gascon has not undertaken new investigations pointed to by Boogie's paper.

Obviously Mogato, after being given the paper by Boogie, chose to be a partisan, giving copies of it to groups and personalities he hoped would go to town over it. Mogato ceased to be a journalist and became an activist against the Duterte administration.

To this day, there is no copy made available to the public of Boogie's 26-page **The State-Sponsored Extrajudicial Killings in the Philippines.** Even the Reuters article would not post it on its website, only its first page, so it could claim it exists. I bet most readers of this column had never heard of this paper, which Mogato and Baldwin portrayed to being as much of a blockbuster as the Pentagon Papers.

"Some of the report's accusations against individuals could not be confirmed by Reuters; the news agency is therefore not publishing the full document," the article justified their stance.

But couldn't it have just "redacted" it, i.e., blocked the individuals' names? Or did Mogato and Baldwin, and perhaps their editors, realize that the paper's contents was too incredible that to publish it in full would weaken the credibility of their article which was almost entirely based on it?

The last sentence in the article reveals that Mogato and Baldwin were used, wittingly and unwittingly by the Yellow Cult, and especially by Trillanes in their plot — essentially a propaganda scheme — to get the International Criminal Court to prosecute Duterte for his anti-drug war.

That sentence read: "The [retired] intelligence officer said he hoped his report would be used as evidence at the International Criminal Court."

Indeed, about a week after the Mogato-Baldwin article was posted by Reuters, Trillanes' lawyer Jude Sabio, who claimed to represent confessed killer Edgar Matobato, filed the incredible "mass murderer" charges at the ICC. I'm sure that the Mogato-Baldwin article and the Boogie paper were among the annexes to the complaint they filed at the ICC, pretending to be proof of their charges against Duterte.

The third source of the Reuters piece was former Davao policemen and killer Arturo Lascañas, who claimed that "he was paid P3,000 to P5,000 ($60-$100) for each of the 'jobs' he performed. Lascañas was supposed to have written a journal of his killing career in Davao, which I have exposed as fake.**

The ICC prosecutor Fatou Bensouda is from Gambia, which had been a British colony. As in our case with regard to our faith in the media of our US colonizers, for Bensouda, the British-based Reuters news agency is always accurate.

But even the Pulitzer Prize awards are not infallible. In the early 1980s, a *Washington Post* article written by Janet Cooke that narrated the life of an eight-year-old heroine addict won a Pulitzer Prize. It was later discovered to be totally fabricated.

(April 20, 2018)

---

* Tiglao, Rigoberto D. "How Rappler misled EU, Human Rights Watch, CNN, Time, BBC — the world". *Manila Times*. March 20, 2017.

** Tiglao, Rigoberto D. "Trillanes, using PCIJ, taking us for fools with Lascañas' obviously fake journal." *Manila Times*. March 3, 2017.

PRESS CRUCIAL TO NATION-BUILDING

WHAT I FOUND very sad in the controversy over the website Rappler is that there really has been little outrage over its vile deed, which is indisputably as follows:

Its profit-hungry owners, influence-seeking foreigners, and its fame-lusting editor-in-chief were so willing to violate the Constitution's provision that is intended to shield media from foreigners, so as to ensure that it develop our people's consciousness as a nation.

Indeed, it is the press that is crucial to nation-building, and this is the reason the Constitution totally bans any foreign participation in media. Yet, here are people who have been spreading the fallacy that there should not even be any such restrictions.

For instance, it is so insulting to the framers of the Constitution that Fidel Ramos' former socioeconomic planning chief, Cielito Habito, in his newspaper column even dismissed the Constitution's provision banning foreign money in media as "fear of foreigners." That simply is the English translation of the "xenophobia," a pejorative term that has come to mean irrational fear and hatred of other races.

Habito, sadly, like other Rappler supporters, has been so ignorant of the most important nature of the Press.

The Press —newspapers, as well as to their digital versions and Internet-only news sites as well as broadcast media — isn't just a tool for disseminating information. It also does not just serve as a check to the powerful and the rich, even if it often has been.

The most important thing about newspapers is that they are, as the acclaimed late scholar Benedict Anderson had explained*, an embodiment of that "imagined community" we call the nation. Even in our case, the first stirrings of a nation were through a newspaper, the *La Solidaridad*, founded in 1889, even if it was published in Spain and in Spanish.

This should be clear from the obvious fact that a newspaper doesn't report everything interesting in the world, but only what happens in its particular nation, or what would interest its citizens. An American would identify, or be "in communion with" *The New York Times* (or the Washington Post) wherever he lives in the world. Even if he is in the Philippines he could never be in communion with *The Manila Times*, nor with the other three major broadsheets.

To very easily understand this: An Ateneo student would identify with The Guidon and a UP scholar with The Collegian. Even if called only "newsletters," these publications in effect are the embodiment of their schools and their ideals. (Wouldn't it be horrific if an Ateneo student financed The Collegian, at the height of their UAAP games?)

The most developed countries in the world, in fact, emerged at the turn of the century with a newspaper, or a few newspapers, developing and solidifying its citizens' consciousness as a nation: *The New York Times* (1851), *Chicago Tribune* (1847), *The Guardian* (London, 1851); the then USSR's *Pravda* (1912); and of course, China's *Renmin Ribao* (People's Daily, 1948).

The Allied Powers that won World War II knew the importance of newspapers in building a nation that they allowed the countries they destroyed to publish their newspapers soon after the war: Germany's *Süddeutsche Zeitung* (1945, the first newspaper allowed by the occupying US military) and *Frankfurter Allgemeine Zeitung* (1949), as well as Japan's *Yomiuri Shimbun* and *Asahi Shimbun*.

It isn't coincidental that the countries whose citizens are the most nationalistic have newspapers with the biggest circulations in the world: *Yomiuri Shimbun* and *Asahi Shimbun*, with readers of 9 million and 7 million, respectively. Their newspapers are able to reach most of their citizens, for them to "commune" with the nation daily, often at the breakfast table.

All countries in the world restrict or ban foreign money in their newspapers. The 20 percent foreign participation in media allowed in some countries such as the US, has been allowed only in order for these huge firms to tap the stock market, in which investors are so spread out that it is impossible for them to have any influence, let alone control, over the publication.

This is in contrast to the American North Base Media and Omidyar Network's P50 million funds in Rappler, which, concealed by the artifice called depositary receipts, represent nearly half of the outfit's capitalization.

The world's richest media mogul, Rupert Murdoch, gave up his Australian citizenship and became an American so he could be allowed to buy the biggest media conglomerate there, which owns Twentieth Century Fox and *The Wall Street Journal*.

Singapore's Lee Kuan Yew saw the media as so important to nation-building and his island-state's growth that he didn't just ban foreign ownership of media, or let Singaporean businesses operate newspapers. He, instead, set up the Singapore Press Holdings, controlled by his party, which to this day owns all of the newspapers and broadcast media in that country.

Habito, in his column so slavish to foreign capital, claimed that the Internet has torn down the nation's borders that "there's no longer any point to the nationality restriction on our mass media."

This guy is so ignorant. The top newspapers on the Internet are all still nation-bound, the majority such as cnn.com, nytimes.com and theguardian.com are simply cyber versions of their print editions, even if they have additional features, such as breaking news reportage. The sites in the Philippines that have the biggest viewers are the Internet versions of our TV networks and newspapers.

Huffingtonpost.com, the most successful website-only news outfit, is still mainly a publication devoted to the US. Its attempts to have versions for a few nations have not been successful since citizens of those countries can't relate or commune with a version of a US newsite.

Even your Facebook page is nation-bound as its algorithms will post on your timeline those made by Filipinos or in the Philippines, since your Internet service provider will be reported as Philippine-based.

The Securities and Exchange Commission was simply defending the Constitution — and its aim of developing national consciousness — by ruling that even an Internet-only news outfit falls within the definition of media.

I leave it to you, dear reader, to decide whether our Press, especially the three biggest broadsheets and the two largest TV networks, have helped build our nation and develop our national consciousness.

Or whether they have merely been tools used by the oligarchy, especially the Yellow Cult — which would explain partly why nationalism in this country has all but vanished.

(March 26, 2018)

---

* Anderson, Benedict. **Imagined Communities: Reflections on the Origin and Spread of Nationalism.** London: Verso, 1983.

WESTERN MEDIA FOOLED THE EUROPEAN PARLIAMENT

THE EUROPEAN PARLIAMENT on April 18, 2018 passed a resolution which two mainstream newspapers reported with the headline, "EU urges PH to stop extrajudicial killings of drug suspects."

The resolution was introduced and passed on the same day without debate. My sources claim this was through the efforts of the Liberal Party and its foreign supporters, the German Friedrich Naumann Foundation and the Liberal International's affiliated parties in the European Parliament.

I was also told that Vice President Leni Robredo and her Liberal Party colleagues during their trip last week to Germany sponsored by the German foundation, also met with German members of the European Parliament to urge them to have the April 18 resolution passed.

The EU resolution declared: "Since 1 July 2016, around 12,000 people, including women and children, have, reportedly, been killed in the Philippines during an ongoing campaign against drugs, internationally proclaimed as President Duterte's 'war on drugs'."

How can the EU claim such numbers killed by our police without even explaining where the hell it got that figure?

Women and children killed? I can't find any news that a single woman or child was killed in Duterte's anti-drug war. Kian de los Santos — whose death I myself believe was a clear case of police execution — was 17 years old.

Contrast the EU resolution to that of the US State Department in its recent human rights report on the country.

The US State Department paper first mentioned that "from July 2016 through October 25, 2017, law enforcement agencies reported that 3,967 'drug personalities' died in connection with anti-drug operations." (The figure was 4, 075 as of last month.)

Then it noted — very objectively — that "the reported number of alleged extrajudicial killings varied widely, as government and nongovernmental organizations (NGOs) used different definitions." Where the US State Department study quoted the number of victims based not on official sources, it pinpointed exactly where such reports were from:

"The Commission on Human Rights (CHR), an independent government agency responsible for investigating alleged human rights violations, investigated 139 complaints of alleged extrajudicial or politically motivated killings involving 174 victims as of August 2017."

"The rising death toll from the government's anti-drug campaign, compelled the CHR to separate politically motivated killings from drug-related cases in its reporting. From January to June, the CHR investigated 44 cases of drug-related extrajudicial killings involving 56 victims. The CHR suspected PNP or Philippine Drug Enforcement Agency involvement in 112 of these new complaints and AFP or paramilitary personnel in one case. The CHR attributed many of the remaining cases to insurgent/terrorist forces."

In sharp contrast to the EP resolution, the US State Department didn't repeat lies which it would have done, if it claimed that "so-and-so groups alleged that there were 12,000 EJKs."

The European Parliament resolution simply believed the lies spread by Western media, which, sadly, biased Filipino researchers and journalist have fed them.

Don't they realize that a systematic state effort to liquidate 12,000 people would by this time have generated so much outrage, that there would have been massive protests against the government, led and organized by the well-funded opposition and the Left? But there has been practically no such demonstrations, and those that have been undertaken were obviously participated in only by a few communist party activists.

If there were 12,000 EJKs, wouldn't the CHR — especially since it is headed by a Liberal Party stalwart, Chito Gascon — by now be overwhelmed by complaints? But it has received complaints of alleged EJKs of not more than 200.

For instance, investigations by human rights groups after the Chilean strongman Pinochet fell in 1990 showed that about 3,000 Chileans were killed by security forces during the dictatorship. That number was enough to have the so-called desparacidos' relatives defy the dictatorship and undertake nearly weekly demonstrations against the regime.

Don't you think that with an alleged 12,000 EJKs, with our freewheeling democracy and a well-funded Opposition, and the Communist Party so skilled in organization and agit-prop, there would have been at this time massive demonstrations over this issue.

There have been no such demonstrations, because that 12,000 figure of the European Parliament and the earlier 9,000 figure used by Reuter reporters Manuel Mogato and Clare Baldwin in their Pulitzer Prize-winning article, **were fabricated**.

THE EVOLUTION OF A COLOSSAL LIE

IN NUMBERS: The Philippines' 'war on drugs'

Rappler: "At September 2016, 7,080 EJKs."(Police calimed only 2,555 killed in anti-drug campaign.)

REUTERS

Special Report: Police describe kill rewards, staged crime scenes in Duterte's drug war

April 18, 2017: Reuters' Mogato-Baldwin article: without citing where it got it: "Almost 9,000 people, many small-time users and dealers, have been killed since Duterte took office on June 30."

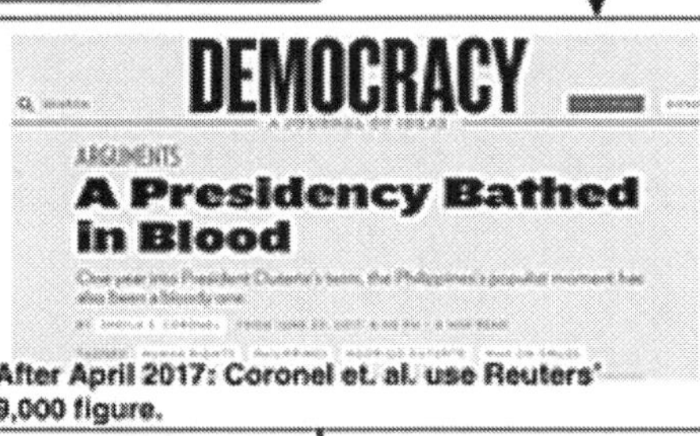

DEMOCRACY

ARGUMENTS

A Presidency Bathed in Blood

After April 2017: Coronel et. al. use Reuters' 9,000 figure.

The Sydney Morning Herald

It's unacceptable children are deemed collateral damage in Duterte's war on drugs

By Lindsay Murdoch

Bangkok: Imagine this, children as young three described as 'collateral damage'. More than 12,000 people killed in just 14 months, most of them urban slum dwellers.

If bodies continue to pile up at this rate the death toll of Philippine President Rodrigo Duterte's 'war on drugs' could top 60,000 in six years.
Where is the outrage from Australia?

August 2017: Australian Columnist invents 12,000 figure.

Philippines' 'War on Drugs'

January 2018 : Human Rights Watch adopts columnist's 12,000 invented figure.

April 2018: European Parliament uses 12,000 figure to condemn Philippines

It was the Internet-only news site Rappler.com which first bloated the number of EJKs, when a September 13, 2016 article by its researcher Michael Bueza claimed that Duterte's anti-drug campaign resulted in 7,080 killed, including those by the police or vigilantes it backed. The police, however, reported only 2,555 killed in their operations, and there is no way to determine if there were other drug suspects who were killed secretly by the police or its vigilantes.

The *Philippine Daily Inquirer's* "kill list" in 2016 and 2017 — its compilation of drug-related deaths based on police blotters — showed a smaller number, 2,107, with 40 percent of this ascribed to "unknown hit men."

Rappler didn't correct its wrong figures, and continued to post the erroneous article, even as it didn't reply at all to my and the police's debunking of its figures.

It was the Reuters' Pulitzer-winners Mogato-Baldwin piece that first reported the 9,000 figure in its April 18, 2017 article, without citing where it got it: "Almost 9,000 people, many small-time users and dealers, have been killed since Duterte took office on June 30."

After Reuters gave that false figure, Western media outlets used that figure unquestioningly.

Even such an accomplished journalist as Sheila Coronel, the head of the US-based Columbia University's Stabile Center of Investigative Journalism, in a piece in an academic journal so melodramatically entitled *"A Presidency Bathed in Blood,"* wrote: "The drug war, which Duterte officially launched on his first day in office, has claimed the lives of as many as 9,000 suspected drug dealers and users."

When I asked her where she got that 9,000 number, she replied: "Numerous news reports quote that figure." She even gave me the link to her Google search results. I asked her why she "didn't bother to verify if this figure had been conclusively debunked," she no longer replied. So much for investigative and truthful journalism.

How the 9,000 figure became the 12,000, the European Parliament claimed was the number of EJKs, is a story so absurd it beggars belief.

The New York-based Human Rights Watch in its 2018 report released last January claimed: "The epidemic of police shootings — often portrayed as 'shootouts' but repeatedly shown to be summary executions — had left more than 12,000 people killed in the roughly year and a half since Duterte took office. The vast majority of victims were young men from the slums of major cities — people who elicited little sympathy among many Filipinos." This organization mostly relies for its information and articles on our country on one Carlos Conde who started his career as a writer at the news website bulatlat.com, allegedly run by Communist Party propaganda cadres.

While the Human Rights Watch report did not explain where it got that figure, an article posted in its website had a link embedded in the "12,000 Filipinos" phrase, a practice in Internet articles to point to the source of that information.

And the source of the Human Rights Watch figure that Human Rights Watch pointed to?

An opinion column datelined Bangkok by one Lindsay Murdoch in the *Sydney Morning Herald* (August 24, 2017) entitled, "It's unacceptable children are deemed collateral damage in Duterte's war on drugs": "More than 12,000 people in the Philippines were killed in just 14 months, most of them urban slum dwellers."

He didn't mention where he got that figure, although his second sentence gives us an idea how: "If bodies continue to pile up at this rate the death toll of Philippine President Rodrigo Duterte's war on drugs could top 60,000 in six years."

He extrapolated from the Reuters figure of 9,000 killed for the 10 months since Duterte started his anti-drug campaign! The arithmetic means a rate of 900 killings per month. So Murdoch calculated: in 14 months, the figure would be 12,600.

The Australian columnist of course wasn't really interested in facts, as his opinion piece was intended to lambast Australian Foreign Minister Julie Bishop's courtesy call on Duterte in Davao City, which he claims was a "pilgrimage to a mass murderer."

The European Parliament condemns our country based on a wrong information invented by an angry Australian columnist, from false figures invented by Filipinos.

(April 23, 2018)

Harsh Realities

BORN INTO A CLASS, YOU'LL DIE IN THAT CLASS

THAT'S NOT SOME Marxist firebrand sloganeering. It's one of the many insights one can conclude from an academically rigorous book that came out earlier this year by economic historian Gregory Clarke, **The Son Also Rises: Surnames and the History of Social Mobility** (Princeton University Press: 2014).

Ingeniously using as data the prevalence of surnames in elite groups over the centuries in several countries and constructing a mathematical model involving the mass of data unearthed, Clarke demolishes a long standing myth: That modern civilization, especially under democracy and capitalism, have made it possible, for the first time in humanity's history, for a determined person to escape his social status and move to a higher economic stratum.

"The fact is that after a century of redistribution, public education and social policy seem to have done nothing to improve the social mobility rates. Social mobility is no higher in modern Sweden than in the United States or even pre-industrial England," Clarke writes.

Clarke's investigation yields the same conclusion in different nations (Sweden, USA, England, India, China, Japan, and Chile): social mobility is so slow that it takes centuries for one family's wealth to dissipate.

Quite surprisingly, Clarke concluded that even such communist political upheavals as China went through in the 20th century hadn't really overthrown the elite. After the communist takeover in 1947 and even after the Great Cultural Revolution that Mao claimed eliminated the "last vestiges of the old Chinese ruling class," it is still the descendants of the old Chinese families that had dominated the pre-communist civil service, that are now at the top echelons of power of the Communist Party.

In short, Clarke says, the social class your grandfather was born in is the predictor of what yours would be now.

Think about it in your own personal experience. Your gardener's children and grandchildren most likely will be as poor as he is, as his grandfather and great grandfather were. The children of a woman who did our laundry for decades, I recently found out, even after her heroic attempts to put them to school, remained impoverished minimum-wage laborers.

Buena familia

There is a quaint term the Filipino elite use to describe themselves, which reflects the rigidity of our class structure: *Buena familia* (good family). Even if you lose your wealth in bad business decisions or squander it on gambling, you would never lose your *buena familia* status.

A recent reunion of my Ateneo high school batchmates reminded me of this reality of the class-structured world. With, of course, a few exceptions (as there are in all phenomena of nature and society), those whose parents were capitalists are capitalists while those whose parents were professionals (especially doctors, but including teachers) and corporate executives are professionals and corporate executives. Living in an advanced capitalist society had no impact at all: Those who emigrated to Canada and the US, were in the same social class their parents and their grandparents were born into.

Out of a hundred or so in our batch, probably just a handful had moved out of the social status they were born into: one who, after failing in most jobs he took on, made his mom-and-pop roasted-chicken business into a billion-peso food conglomerate; one who was lucky to marry into a rich family and cleverly invested his in-laws' wealth in high-profit ventures; one who stumbled upon a new industry nobody knew at that time would boom in the next ten years — information technology. But these are the outliers in the bell curve, my average classmate remained in the social status they were born in.

The issue of social mobility has become a hot topic in the US, with economists' new studies after the Reagan era that the American Dream has turned out to be a myth. Thomas Piketty's unexpected bestseller, **Capital in the 21st Century** had crunched mountains of data that conclusively showed that the nature of capitalism itself has led to concentration — untenable he theorizes — of wealth in America, and that the myth of wealth democratization there and in the Western world, owed to the unique impact of World War II on the economies of the US and the rest of the world.

Nobel Prize winner and *New York Times* columnist Paul Krugman's studies have also demolished the myth that in America, anyone can be rich. He points out in a recent column his observations on US society that are also applicable to the Philippines:

"Here's what you need to know: Yes, the concentration of both income and wealth in the hands of a few people has greatly increased over the past few decades. No, the people receiving that income and owning that wealth aren't an ever-shifting group: People move fairly often from the bottom of the 1 percent to the top of the next percentile and vice versa, but both rags-to-riches and riches-to-rags stories are rare."

It is not individual greed, or lust, or selfishness that is the root of evil in this world. To borrow a term used by a Russian novelist to describe the inevitability of death, the "most general evil" in the world that no religion, no "Ten Commandments" had ever pointed out as Evil, is society's class structure that condemns billions of humans to live a life of misery — those born into the have-not social class.

Root of many evils

It is the root of many evils in the world: Wars as undertaken by ruling classes to expand the foundations of their class, and crimes against property as desperate attempts to claim upper classes' wealth.

In fact, it has been religion that had helped foster the myth of a classless society. Kings, nobles, clerics, peasants, laborers are all children of God, and each is assigned his place in life by the Deity. If you don't like your social status, just be patient and wait to enter the classless Heaven. Every Sunday is a ceremony called the Mass, in which everyone in Church is made to feel that they are all equal.

In the modern era, the emergence of states in which the people vote rulers into power has served to mask society's class structure.

The myth foisted is just as in the political realm, each citizen has one vote and therefore all citizens are equal; in the economic realm, each citizen has as much opportunity to be rich.

Masked, though, are factors that would make one rich, which the have-nots will never have access to: wealth, transferred to you by your parents or grandparents that would make up your first working capital; clan and social networks, which Filipino-Chinese businessmen have particularly relied on for capital and business connections; education, especially an expensive MBA, preferably from US universities; even your parent's predispositions, for example, a Chinese businessman hammering day in and day out on his son's or daughter's head that his or her fate can only be to "take over the business."

Feudal-age Shakespeare was wrong when he wrote in **Julius Caesar:** *"The fault, dear Brutus, is not in our stars, but in ourselves that we are underlings."* It's certainly not due to one's stars, but to one's ancestors, at least as Clarke's rigorous research shows.

If Sweden, England, and the US — after more than a hundred years of efficient bureaucracies, strong states independent of elites, and wealth redistribution policies such as high income and inheritance taxes — still have low social mobility, it's certainly a lot worse in our case. Our leaders aren't even aware of this most general evil in the world. Such a long, long journey our nation must take.

(November 21, 2014)

HOW THEY FOOL PEOPLE THROUGH POLLS

PRESIDENT AQUINO'S camp has been adept in manipulating media and polls to manufacture a counterfeit public opinion, and then claim it as "people's wisdom." Malacañang spokesmen even cavalierly justify former President Gloria Macapagal-Arroyo's anomalous arrest and the assault on the Supreme Court on grounds that "public opinion" supports these moves.

Opinion surveys are legitimate research tools. To mystify their findings though as "the voice of the people" and base our moral compass and our sense of justice and fairness on poll findings, is utter inanity or crass populism.

Such polls quantify people's current views on issues, or on consumer products. But people do not get their ideas about issues from thin air, as European scholars like Jurgen Habermas and Pierre Bourdieu have expounded.

In modern mass society, especially one where poverty bars the majority from getting accurate information and even having the intellectual tools for rational evaluation of an issue, most people get their ideas on issues almost solely from media.

If media for some reason are biased and incessantly scream allegations that a particular government official is corrupt on their front pages — with his or her rebuttals buried in a few sentences somewhere in the inside pages — people cannot but perceive that that official is corrupt.

If the press consistently reports that "X" is the case, even if it is false, the majority of respondents in an opinion poll will perceive "X" as true. How can they not, if media are their sole source of information?

The horrendous consequences of misunderstanding opinion polls have been demonstrated. Because US media was uncritical of the Bush administration's claims that Iraq had "weapons of mass destruction," 80 percent of Americans polled believed these, giving the green light to the American invasion of that oil rich country in 2003. No WMDs were found. By 2005, 60 percent opposed the Iraq war.

Case 1: "The Armed Forces of the Philippines, the Most Corrupt Institution — Pulse Asia." The AFP in opinion polls before was never perceived to be among the country's most corrupt institutions. It was usually the police, the Department of Public Works and Highways, and the Bureau of Customs. In March 2011, however, respondents in a Pulse Asia poll reported it as the most corrupt institution.

Why? The survey was taken during the Senate's televised investigations on alleged AFP corruption, which hogged the headlines for many days. Respondents naturally replied that it was the most corrupt institution, even if the allegations were about anomalies five years earlier and even if the AFP had already overhauled its system to prevent corruption.

This trick of using polls by President Aquino's propagandists involves the following steps.

First, publicize an allegation by a cooperative journalist or by an ally in Congress, ideally have investigations undertaken by Congress, and then have a subservient press run these as banner stories for days, with "outraged" opinion writers rousing people's passions.

Second, undertake a poll on the issue, when people have just been barraged in the press by the allegations. Voila! The poll findings that so and so is corrupt, the result of the press barrage in step one, are proclaimed as "public opinion."

Third, publicize the poll widely so that the bandwagon effect comes into play.

Case 2: "President Arroyo, the most corrupt president — Pulse Asia." Of course the majority in that poll picked Arroyo as the most corrupt president! The poll was made from Oct. 26 to 31, 2007, when people were barraged with front-page news every day of allegations (even today unproven) of bribes given to local officials supposedly by Arroyo amid the NBN-ZTE controversy.

But most respondents weren't even born or adults yet during the Marcos regime. Pulse Asia in effect demanded the respondents to quickly retrieve from their memory all the cases of corruption for each of the five presidents, such as Marcos' Swiss bank accounts or Estrada's P2 billion ill-gotten bank deposits. It was indisputably a loaded survey, intended for political propaganda, which no ethical, professional pollster would have undertaken.

But Pulse Asia was bankrolled and run at that time by Aquino's cousins, Antonio Cojuangco and Rapa Cojuangco Lopa. Rabid anti-Arroyo Senator Sergio Osmena Jr. financed this particular poll.

With this unscrupulous poll, anti-Arroyo politicians, unthinking journalists, and even sloppy academics would routinely state that she was the most corrupt Philippine president. (An aside on opinion polls' "truth": Surveys during Harry Truman's term made him the most unpopular US president, although historians now see him as among America's five best presidents.)

Case 3: "Ombudsman Merci Guiterrez, the most unpopular official — Pulse Asia." While the media were in a frenzy from February to March last year against the former ombudsman, Pulse Asia undertook its poll, and naturally Gutierrez came out as the most unpopular government official at that time, thereby egging on the political hyenas in Congress to gang up on her.

Case 4: "Corona the least trusted official — Pulse Asia." Aquino's operatives are now onto their old trick. As media incessantly blast Chief Justice Renato Corona, Pulse Asia undertakes its opinion survey and, naturally he comes out as "the least trusted official" — and therefore, the "people will decide" to take him out.

The Supreme Court and its Chief Justice for decades have had the highest trust ratings. That changed when a well-funded demolition job was launched against them in 2010 (starting with the plagiarism issue), initially very covertly by an associate justice lusting to be chief justice, and then by the President himself, furious over the Court's decision that will wrench Hacienda Luisita from his clan's clutches.

(January 12, 2012)

RIZAL, BONIFACIO, AND THE 'MASA' MYTH

IT WAS THE HISTORIAN Teodoro Agoncillo who popularized the myth of the masses with his biography of Andres Bonifacio, **Revolt of the Masses.** Agoncillo claimed that the Katipunan revolutionaries were the masses' representatives: "despairing spirits, the oppressed, the downtrodden," from the "lowest stratum of society."

Other writers would expand Agoncillo's thesis by contrasting the "elite" Rizal against the "proletarian" Bonifacio. Leftist activists have even been brainwashed to hate Rizal and to believe that it was the Americans who just invented him to be our national hero, since he didn't advocate armed revolution.

However, more up-to-date historians, especially those who mined the archives of the Spanish military, paint an entirely different picture of Bonifacio and the Katipuneros. *(See http://kasaysayan-kkk.info)*

British historian Jim Richardson examined the dossiers of over 200 leaders of the Katipunan, and concluded that they were not poor laborers but mostly white-collar employees and what we may call the intelligentsia, the petty bourgeoisie.

Yes, Bonifacio was a bodeguero, but this didn't refer to a downtrodden laborer carrying heavy stuff on his shoulder. Bonifacio was the employee in a German-owned company who made sure that the contents of the warehouse matched the company's books.

In that listing of 200 Katipuneros, only one was identified as a laborer.

This actually is the characteristic of the Katipunan's model itself, the French Revolution, which was a lower and middle class revolution. It was probably the pattern of all revolutions. Mao Zedong, Chou Enlai and Deng Xiaoping came from the landlord class, Pol Pot from a wealthy family who could afford to send him to Paris, and of course Jose Ma. Sison from the landlord class.

There is furthermore a distinctly elite dimension to the Katipunan, the opposite of being *masa.* The single most common characteristic among the leaders of the Katipunan was their membership in a secret elite group: Freemasonry.

Stripped of its abracadabra, Freemasonry was based on the pillars of the power of rationality and individual freedom, as against the superstition and blind obedience to the Catholic Church in the 17th to 19th centuries. The Katipunan's original core group — Bonifacio, Deodato Arellano, Valentin Diaz, Teodoro Plata, Ladislao Diwa and Jose Dizon — as well as 16 other officers were all Freemasons.

Bonifacio and Rizal were actually comrades: they were both Freemasons. This provided them with the necessary world view to defy Catholicism, which was the nearly overpowering ideological base of Spanish colonialism. Rizal was recruited to Freemasonry during his stay in Madrid starting 1882, when the society in Spain had a renaissance of sorts after many years of persecution. Bonifacio joined Freemasonry much later, in 1892, at the Taliba Lodge No. 165.

The Left's narrative has been that Rizal's Liga Filipina was the reformist group while the Katipunan was Bonifacio's armed revolutionary organization. This is false. Rizal in fact swiftly established Liga Filipina upon his return from Spain since he utilized his network of Masonic lodges. Many Katipunan leaders were also members of the Liga.

The Katipunan, an organization of Freemasons and petty-bourgeois intellectuals, led the revolution, with the masses — as always — constituting the warm bodies, and sadly the cannon fodder.

It has been mainly communist parties, especially Mao's (based on Marx's Hegelian notion of the proletariat becoming conscious of its destiny), which have propagated the notion that the masses have an intrinsic wisdom that civilization's vanguards don't have. In terms of political philosophy, the *masa* myth is the antithesis of representative democracy.

Indeed, "masses" got to be translated to *"masa"* only in the 1970s when Maoists had to translate Mao's works, which are replete with the word "masses" — with real workers even ridiculing it as meaning "dough" in Tagalog.

On the other hand, with their penchant for mythicizing, and with the very wrong notion that Jesus was a laborer, liberation theology Christians substituted the Deity for "Masses," quite obvious in that line from Atenean Eman Lacaba's poem, "The Masses are Messiah."

The myth of the masses is a very dangerous one. Academics and professionals were sent to China's hinterlands — many to die or be killed — "to learn from the masses" in the disastrous Cultural Revolution of the late 1960s which resulted in five million Chinese killed and utter political and economic chaos. College graduates were either massacred in the Khmer Rouge's killing fields, or sent to rural areas to be "re-educated by the masses."

The myth of the masses has even wormed its way into Philippine political thinking as opinion polls (which by definition is what the masses feel at a point in time) are taken to be moral imperatives to violate representative democracy. The *masa* myth nearly hijacked the spirit of the EDSA 1986 Revolution in "EDSA 3" and the several attempts at fake "people power" movements in the past several years.

It is a dangerous myth that rabble-rousers and totalitarians cultivate since it easy to claim that one speaks for the faceless masses, as New People's Army spokesmen always do. The Masses are Messiah? It was the masses that asked for Jesus' head on that fateful day.

(December 29, 2010)

THE PARTY-LIST SYSTEM: A MOCKERY OF DEMOCRACY

IF THERE'S ANY provision in our Constitution that indisputably has to be deleted, it is that which called for 20 percent of the House of Representatives seats to be given to so-called "party-list representatives," supposedly to represent the country's marginalized sector.

Unlike the usual congressmen who are elected by voters registered in a political district, party-list representatives are elected by any voter anywhere in the country, who elect not the individual but the party-list, which then designates its representatives.

Cory Aquino in 1987 pushed for such a system, partly to crush the two-party system she hated. But the system has proven to be so utterly absurd, a scandalous mockery of our democracy. And we taxpayers shoulder the party-list representatives and their staff's salaries as well as expenses in the amount of about P2 billion per year.

Instead of powerless sectors — "labor, peasant, urban poor, indigenous cultural communities, women, youth, and such other sectors" as the Constitution put it — it has only given political clout to multi-millionaires, even two billionaires, so they could defend or expand their business interests. It has also given additional seats in Congress to provincial or regional political clans, for them to increase their political clout.

Most ironically, the party-list system has put cadres of the Communist Party in the House of Representatives giving them additional resources, especially finances (raised from our taxes) to advance their agenda to violently overthrow our democracy.

The Constitution's Article VI, Section 5 (2) categorically excludes the "religious sector" from having a party-list representative. Yet "Brother" Mike Velarde who heads the huge born-again Christian group El Shaddai, set up his Buhay party-list (Buhay Hayaan Yumabong) in 2001 and since 2004 has had two to three representatives in Congress. Buhay's incumbent representatives are the preacher's son Michael Velarde, Jr. and former Manila mayor Jose "Lito" Atienza.

Scandalous

In this country steeped in religiosity, we're lucky other religious groups aren't as hungry for political clout, or as unscrupulous, or half of the party-list representatives will be from the Iglesia ni Cristo, Philippine Aglipayan Church, Eddie Villanueva's "Jesus is Lord," the Christian Restorationist church of Apollo Quiboloy, Eli Soriano's Dating Daan, and several others with followings probably bigger than El Shaddai.

Buhay's Atienza practically has been the Catholic Church's representative in Congress for its doctrinaire anti-contraception and anti-abortion stand. But a situation like that is precisely what the framers of the Constitution wanted to prevent, by banning religious sectors from having party-list representatives.

However, the perfect example of how scandalous the system has become is the fact that the purportedly richest member of the present Congress — both of the Senate and the House of Representatives, that is — is a party-list representative: Michael ("Mikee") Romero, who has reported his net worth at P7 billion.

It is astonishing that this 45-year-old businessman reports that he is richer than property magnate Manuel Villar's wife, Senator Cynthia Villar (with a net worth of P3.6 billion) and world boxing icon Senator Manny Pacquiao (P3 billion).

Who is Romero? He and another congressman represent the party "1-Pacman," a name which is as ridiculous as it is a travesty of our system of representative democracy. 1-Pacman doesn't have anything to do with our boxing hero (and now senator) Pacquiao.

The party's name is intended to fool careless, hurrying, or even ignorant voters that they are electing their hero Manny "the Pacman" Pacquiao. What the name stands for mocks our representative system. 1-Pacman purportedly is the acronym for: "One Patriotic Coalition of Marginalized Nationals."

The "1" in this outfit's name (just as a dozen other groups have done) was placed there so that it would come up first in the ballot forms, enhancing its chances of being picked by a voter.

1-Pacman doesn't even pretend to be representing any marginal group, and merely says that "among its platform is to prioritize sports development." Romero owns GlobalPort Batang Pier, a team in the commercial Philippine Basketball Association league, which even has three expensive Americans as players.

Romero's preferred sport is the "game of kings," polo, and he even owns a polo team he captains. His team competes in international polo events, which reportedly costs the billionaire at least P50 million to participate in each time because of the astronomical costs of transporting his prized stallions. He's a representative of a marginalized sector?

While the US *Forbes* magazine lists him as the country's 47th richest billionaire with a net worth of $137 million (or roughly equivalent to the P7 billion he himself claims), there is a huge doubt that he has been such a great businessman to have amassed that much.

The bulk of his claimed assets is in his holdings in Harbour Centre Port Terminals, the monopoly in break-bulk handling at the Port of Manila, which his father, construction magnate Reghis, founded in 1996. (He is also vice chairman of budget airline AirAsia Philippines, which many believe is controlled by Malaysian Anthony Francis Fernandes.)

But his father Rhegis claims that after he let the son run the company in 2012, 'Mikee' falsified papers that assigned his father's shares to him, and that he had run the company to the ground because of his mismanagement and billionaire lifestyle, which includes buying a private jet and competing in polo competitions all over the world.

Mikee in turn claims that after building up the company, his father who had become impoverished wants the company back and is demanding P1 billion from him. The case is still in the courts.

The father-son feud has become so bitter that Reghis got a court to order his son's arrest, for the alleged theft of P3.4 million in company funds last year. Mikee ran from the law and became a fugitive even after he was elected 1-Pacman representative, and surfaced only in November last year when the case was ordered dismissed by a higher court.

That is the kind of party-list representative we have.

Romero's case though would explain why somebody like him born with a silver spoon, fond of a luxurious lifestyle, who never thought of helping the "marginalized," would want to be a party-list representative.

Political clout

Being a party-list representative obviously gives him some political clout to win against his father in their billion-peso feud. His father reportedly has been so incensed with his son that he has vowed to put him in jail.

Other multi-millionaires who have become party-list representatives aren't in such deep trouble as Romero. They, or their clans, probably calculate that a seat in Congress gives them clout for their business interests.

The second richest member of the entire Congress is another party-list representative Emmeline Aglipay-Villar, who reported a net worth of P1.4 billion in her 2017 statement of assets, liabilities, and net worth (SALN). She is the nominee of the DIWA party, which stands for Democratic Independent Workers' Association.

Has the 35-year-old Aglipay-Villar ever been a leader or organizer or counsel for a union or federation?

No. She is the wife of Public Works Secretary Mark Villar, son of one of the richest real estate magnates in the country, Manuel Villar. Her P1.4 billion net worth is probably her estimated conjugal share in her husband's wealth as shareholder and executive of his father's conglomerate.

She is also the daughter of a retired police general who became Philippine National Police chief during President Gloria Arroyo's administration, Edgardo Aglipay. The latter is chairman of DIWA whose treasurer is of course Mrs. Aglipay.

How do such multi-millionaires get to be party-list representatives? Believe it or not, it is unbelievably easy, as long as one has no scruples in trampling democratic values, and of course if one sees the investment as a worthwhile one.

A party list gets a seat in Congress if it gets 2 percent of total votes, with another seat given if it gets an additional 2 percent to a maximum of three seats, with 20 percent of Congress seats required by the Constitution to be allocated to such representatives.

In the 2016 elections, 59 seats were allocated to party-list representatives. To fill up these number, 33 out of the 46 party-list winners which got less than 2 percent of the votes were given congressional seats. Thus, the party which got the lowest number of seats (Agbiag received only 240,000 votes or just 0.7 percent total votes) still managed to a seat in Congress. Agbiag, an Ilocos-based party-list, is represented by another millionaire, Michelle Antonio.

Romero's 1-Pacman party got 1.3 million votes, so it got him and another representative, multimillionaire Enrico Pineda, into Congress.

How do artificial, really fake "parties" get the votes needed to win a seat in Congress?

One, they piggy-back on the electoral campaign of a local political boss and its network — of course after a huge payment — so the party-list is "carried" in their campaign for the traditional territorial-based representatives. As will be discussed on Monday, this is the reason why many party-list representatives are in reality mere extensions of provincial and regional political clans.

Second, I was told by many sources in the past several years that most party-lists get to have their numbers by sheer manipulation of returns by corrupt Comelec officials. The going rate in the 2016 elections, I was told, was from P20 million to as high as P30 million to ensure that a party list wins.

Several years ago, I nearly fell off my seat when a Chinese-Filipino businessman mentioned over dinner that he was celebrating as his "party-list" won two seats in Congress, and he spent only P5 million.

It has been actually the easiest form of graft income in the Comelec, as the operators need not worry that a losing candidate would protest, as the party-list contest is not a one-on-one fight, with nearly every party-list aware that it is after all a bidding game.

That is how depraved the party list system has become, which had been billed by the Left and the Yellow Cult in 1987, when the Constitution was being drafted, as Cory Aquino's legacy to give political power to marginalized sectors and weaken the traditional political parties.

As with all of the Yellow Cult's noble ideals, the reality is so rotten.

(February 9, 2018)

THE THREE WORLDS OF PHILIPPINE SOCIETY

ONE OF OUR DEEPEST illusions is that we live in just a single world, a delusion that derives from the time religion was invented and portrayed society as one big happy family, presided over by the Father (the King) representing the invisible Grandfather (God), with the exploiters and the exploited all brothers and sisters simply occupying their divinely-appointed stations in life.

Centuries later, in our modern era today, there have been changes of course, but not really much. We can understand Philippine history and be more realistic about our society by realizing that there are really different worlds in our country.

The first world is the economic elite, the richest residents of the country. Forbes' magazine's list of 50 richest business people gives us a glimpse of these seeming immortals, among them the Sys, Gokongweis, Ayalas and Zobels, Tys, Consunjis, Gotianuns, Lucio Cos, Cojuangcos, Angs, Ongpins, Lopezes, and Osmeñas.

There are, however, many low-profile billionaires hardly known to the general public, many based in cities outside Metro Manila, who get to be known only when the Bureau of Internal Revenue publishes its list of top 500 taxpayers.

The income and wealth of these elites are inconceivable to us ordinary mortals. For instance, only because he complained that he wasn't included in the BIR's latest list of top taxpayers and consequently publicly disclosed his income, did we learn that Andrew Tan's net income was P540 million in 2011.

That means he earns P1.5 million a day — when 90 percent of Filipinos earn just P400 a day. Danding Cojuangco is said to have a two-storey building to park his 100 ultra-expensive cars. A banking tycoon has four mansions costing P200 million each in Forbes Park to house his mistresses, not too far from each other so it would be easier for him to move from one concubine to another.

In the rich Asian countries, the economic elites saw that their very survival as a class depended on the growth of their nation as a whole: the South Korean elite fearing a takeover by the communist-controlled North; the Japanese to rebuild a war-ravaged country; the Kuomintang to create an economic powerhouse to fend off an invasion by Mao

Zedong's mainland; and, tiny Singapore, on its own as it separated from the bigger Malay Federation.

As a consequence, Asian elites were willing to give up much of what they could earn from their control of productive assets in order to raise wage rates, go into industries that weren't immediately profitable but would develop their countries' productive forces (as in Japan and Korea), or cooperate with their competitors so the industry where they are in will be globally competitive (as in Taiwan).

Not so in our unlucky country. Most of our economic elites came from Spain, the US, and China, who mostly view the country not really as their nation but merely as a place to make money in, and then live in Spain, London, and now China. The popularity of the notion even among the young that they are global citizens is merely a reflection of the fact that our economic elite has all but discarded the sense of nationalism, of being rooted in one nation, and having the responsibility to develop it.

Little really has changed from medieval times, except the numbers. Today's economic elite were the nobility of the medieval age, who rule the country.

We can never make our nation as developed as others unless our economic elite, as occurred in the rich Asian countries, is transformed to sacrifice for the country, to view it not just as a place of business but as a nation they are responsible for. Precisely because they control the country's resources and assets, it is only the first world that normally can affect major changes in our society, with the following two other worlds only playing a secondary, supporting roles.

The we-don't-care majority

The second world, for lack of a better term, is the apathetic, we-don't-care majority. This includes the well-off, even the rich, but who aren't with the economic elite, down to the poorest who are largely unconscious of society, and don't really care about anything except their own lives.

My notion is similar to the idea of the Silent Majority, which US President Richard Nixon popularized in the late 1960s to refer to what he claimed were the vast majority of Americans who were conservatives, who just didn't get to have their views expressed publicly.

Most of your social circle, dear readers, belong to this second world, coming from different generations and socio-economic levels. He could be your boss, or the owner of the company you work for, obsessed with finally being able to buy a BMW. She could be your domestic help, living from month to month through loans from you, whose sole interest is to make sure her daughter finishes nursing school.

They hardly read newspapers, much less opinion pieces. They use their Facebook timelines mainly to post their selfies from their holidays, or their meals. They really don't care who runs the country, or where it is going — either because they are so obsessed with their own families or because they have come to believe they are powerless to change society after all.

The third world is us: readers of newspapers and columns like this; politically-aware journalists; the new "netizens" and political bloggers; and other men and women in various social gathering (like those early evening *huntahan* in front of the *sari-sari* stores) who want to talk about what's happening in the country. This world is that of the politically active minority.

These are the people who have taken seriously the modern idea of a nation, that it is a community where each and every member has a role to play in choosing who the leaders will be and how the country should be run.

The derogatory term for this notion, used in the West, is the "chattering class," which Wikipedia defines as a politically active, socially concerned and highly educated section of the "metropolitan middle class," especially those with political, media, and academic connections."

Read comments in opinion columns and posts in Facebook pages, and it is obvious that this "chattering class" is afflicted with the delusion that all their blah-blah solely will change society. They won't, unless the first world, or a part of it, says so, and the we-don't-care-majority acquiesces to such changes. Opinion columns like this aren't worth the price of the newspaper they are printed on unless it convinces a faction of the elite.

What's the use of this classification of our society into the Three Worlds of the elite, the apathetic majority, and the chattering class? The answer is that it explains much of our recent political history, and points to what likely would be its course.

EDSA 1 involved a big faction of the elite — among them, the Ayalas, the Gotianuns, and Osmeñas — and even the supranational elite, the US, moving against the Marcos dictatorship. They did so because the economic quagmire, which to a large extent was the result of the global debt crisis at the time, couldn't be resolved unless Marcos was removed.

The elite couldn't have done this "revolt" by themselves. It required the help of the anti-dictatorship chattering class that awakened a section of the silent majority to go against the dictatorship.

What is groundbreaking in the rise of President Duterte is this:

Even with only a few of the elite (mainly those based in Mindanao) behind him, and with the chattering class, represented by mainstream media, mostly against him, he was able to get the support of the silent majority by directly appealing to them.

He did this through his street-language, through his comportment as a non-elite crusader, and, most surprisingly, his tight grasp of the fact, missed by many, that what Filipinos wanted was simply personal security that had been severely eroded in the last six years by the proliferation of illegal drugs.

What is also unprecedented is that the messenger that brought Duterte's message to the silent majority was this new invention called social media, which couldn't have emerged without technology and the economies of scale that brought down cell phone prices, following the emergence of the vast China market. Social media weakened the hold of the economic elite, which controlled most of the newspapers whose views the chattering class in the past mostly followed and echoed.

The three-worlds map bodes well for Duterte. Unexpectedly, Duterte has been drawing more and more supporters from the economic elite, evidenced in part by the fact that his ratings among the ABC class, according to the latest Pulse Asia survey, jumped from 69 percent in December to 86 percent in March.

The second world of the apathetic majority has been untroubled by the intense propaganda against extrajudicial killings in mainstream media. Anecdotal reports show that more and more ordinary citizens feel safe in their neighborhoods, because of the decline in the use of illegal drugs. The issue remains the concern only of the chattering class.

Social media has been dominated by pro-Duterte netizens, and the minds even of the chattering class more and more are being molded by it. It is only a go-for-broke character like Duterte who can throw caution to the winds and go against the elite-controlled mainstream media who have been against him, principally the *Philippine Daily Inquirer*, *Philippine Star*, ABS-CBN, and GMA7.

Duterte is emerging as the President in our history that is the most independent of the economic elite. The question is whether he can undertake the reforms that the elites are adverse to, but which, as proven in the history of the rich Asian countries, were critical for their growth — such things as getting them to pay more taxes, raise workers' wages, and nationalizing the strategic telecom industries.

(April 17, 2017)

ABOUT THE AUTHOR

RIGOBERTO D. TIGLAO is a veteran political and business reporter, the only journalist to receive all four of the most prestigious awards for Philippine journalism — the Catholic Mass Media Awards for Best News Reporter in 1983, the Ten Most Outstanding Young Men for 1992 for Print Journalism, 1988 Fellowship at the Nieman Foundation for Journalism at Harvard University, and the Mitsubishi Corp.'s Best Economic Journalist for Asia 1991.

During his Nieman Fellowship in Harvard, he conceived of, and was later one of the founders of the Philippine Center for Investigative Journalism.

Tiglao was the Manila correspondent and bureau chief from 1989 to 2000 of the renowned Hong Kong-based news magazine *Far Eastern Economic Review*. From 2010 to 2012, he was a columnist at the *Philippine Daily Inquirer,* and was also the editor-in-chief and senior vice president of its website.

He was a high official in President Gloria Macapagal-Arroyo's administration from 2001 to 2010, serving as Presidential Spokesman, Press Secretary, Presidential Chief of Staff, Presidential Management Staff Head, and Philippine Ambassador to Greece and Cyprus.

Since 2013, Tiglao has been writing a thrice-weekly column for the *Manila Times*, the country's oldest and most respected broadsheet. He also has a regular column in Filipino in *Bulgar,* the country's largest circulated tabloid-newspaper.

Manufactured by Amazon.ca
Bolton, ON

25172887R00263